P9-DVV-404

READINGS IN MORAL EDUCATION

READINGS IN MORAL EDUCATION

edited by Peter Scharf

Winston Press

Library of Congress Catalog Card Number: 77-82606
ISBN: 0-03-021346-0
Printed in the United States of America

Winston Press, Inc.
430 Oak Grove
Minneapolis, MN 55403

To Doris, Adria, and Sage

Contents

READINGS IN MORAL EDUCATION

Foreword

Lawrence Kohlberg, Director of the Center for Moral Education, Graduate School of Education, Harvard University.

This reader is the second of two recent collections of articles about moral education. The first is Purpel and Ryan's *Moral Education* (1976), an expansion of a set of articles written for a special 1975 issue of *Phi Delta Kappan*. Like the Purpel and Ryan collection, this reader is compiled for those actually involved in educational practice in the schools. Unlike the Purpel and Ryan book, which is designed to provide an introduction to three different approaches to moral education (the values-clarification approach, the cognitive [or rational decision-making] approach and the cognitive-developmental approach), the present book focuses on a single approach—the cognitive-developmental. Accordingly it is able to present this approach in greater breadth and depth than the Purpel and Ryan volume. Of particular value to practitioners (and not elsewhere reprinted) are the articles by Beyer, Fenton, Wasserman, and Fraenkel taken from a special issue of *Social Education* (Fenton, 1976). Also valuable and unavailable elsewhere are the articles by Scharf, Hersh, Paolitto, and Selman from a special issue of *Contemporary Education* (Grimley, 1976).

The way to approach the articles in this collection is to view them in some historical perspective. This is my intent in this Foreword.

Let me start with the recent history of the cognitive-developmental approach. Moshe Blatt was the first graduate student of mine to actually lead me into new forms of moral education. Blatt came as a graduate student to the University of Chicago psychology department in 1965. He said that I had researched moral stage development long enough (ten years) and that it was time to do something about it educationally. He proposed a dissertation in which he would lead classroom discussions of hypothetical moral dilemmas like those I used in research interviews. He would then compare moral stage change over the year in these experimental classes with development in control classes which did not participate in moral discussion. Blatt proposed, then, an instructional method based on arousing controversy about choice and on Socratic questioning

Portions of this essay have appeared in *Contemporary Education*, Fall 1976, and *Social Education*, April 1976. Used by permission of the author.

about reasons to justify conclusions about dilemmas on which students disagreed. His research-based premise was that students would comprehend and assimilate reasoning by peers at the next stage up while discarding reasoning by peers at the stage below.

I was skeptical that Blatt's proposed verbal discussion of purely hypothetical dilemmas would lead to genuine moral stage change. But Blatt persisted in spite of my pessimism and found "the Blatt effect." The Blatt effect was the finding that one-fourth to one-half of the students in one semester of such discussion groups would move (partially or totally) to the next stage up, a change not found in control groups (Blatt and Kohlberg, 1975). Blatt's venture launched cognitive-developmental moral education in a series of projects which have consistently replicated the Blatt effect. One major replication of the effect was the Stone Foundation project, planned by Edwin Fenton (Colby, Fenton, Kohlberg, and Speicher-Dubin, 1976) and this writer. The project engaged over twenty high school social studies teachers in the Boston and Pittsburgh areas in a developmental moral discussion of hypothetical dilemmas which was incorporated into Fenton's Carnegie-Mellon Social Studies curriculum in ninth-grade civics. (Barry Beyer, author of the article in this volume on leading moral discussions, led the teacher-training team and refined the discussion techniques.) Students were pretested and post-tested on moral stage over an academic year. Change was compared to that in control classes which used the same social studies curriculum and were taught by the same teachers but took no part in moral discussions. As in the Blatt study, no upward moral change in the control classes was found in the nine-month period. There was also little change in half of the experimental classes. In the remaining experimental classes, however, the Blatt effect was found; i.e., one-quarter to one-half of the students in these classes moved significantly toward the next stage during the academic year. The fact that the Blatt effect was found in half of the social studies discussion classes indicated that it was not dependent upon any particular dilemma curriculum or upon intensive psychological and theory training and motivation such as Blatt possessed. (It is also our impression that the Blatt effect was not contingent on personality qualities of the teachers, such as being at the highest, or principled, stage themselves.)

The Stone project not only replicated the Blatt effect in twenty schools, it also demonstrated the significance of the three central elements of the Blatt approach to moral education. Any approach to education involves defining variables (1) in curriculum, (2) in student and classroom composition and characteristics, and (3) in teacher instructional behavior. The essential curriculum element of the Blatt approach was controversial moral dilemmas in areas which would arouse disagreement between students or "cognitive conflict" in choice. The central element in student or classroom composition was a mixture of students at different stages, thus exposing students to peers at the next stage above their own. The central element in teacher behavior was an open but challenging position of Socratic probing.

The Stone project indicated that each of the three elements had to be present if any change were to occur. With regard to curriculum, the Stone project demonstrated the necessity of controversial dilemmas. In the control classes without dilemmas, no change occurred. In the experimental classes with dilemmas, more change occurred in the classes which discussed twenty dilemmas than in those that discussed only ten.

With regard to student and classroom characteristics, the Stone project comparison of "change" and "no change" experimental classrooms indicated one significant difference. The "change" classes all had mixtures of students at two and usually three stages; the "no-change" classes did not.

With regard to teacher instructional behavior, the Stone project indicated one significant difference between teacher behavior in "change" and teacher behavior in "no-change" classrooms. All teachers in the classrooms in which students changed used extensive or Socratic probes of reasoning; they asked for "why's." Most of the "no-change" class teachers did not. This difference in use of Socratic probes was the only item in a 100-item observation schedule of teacher behavior which differentiated the "change" and "no-change" classes at a statistically significant level. Socratic probing, then, was central to teacher behavior in cognitive-developmental moral education.

The import of these Stone findings may be clarified by another finding from the original Blatt study (Blatt and Kohlberg, 1975). This finding represented the positive counterpart of the negative findings of Hartshorne and May (1928-1932). Hartshorne and May found that didactic instruction and preaching about honesty or services (altruism) in "character education" classes had almost no lasting or significant effect on either student moral judgment, or "knowledge," or on student moral behavior.

The positive counterpart of the finding in the Blatt study was that moral judgment did change relatively significantly and lastingly (still present in one-year follow up) without teacher preaching or lecturing. In addition to his own groups, Blatt studied groups in which students were to discuss dilemmas with one another and in which their regular teacher was present only to keep order. In a few of these groups, as much change occurred as in the Blatt-led groups.

The characteristics of the "no-change" leaderless groups were instructive. Most of these "no-change" classes were classes without stage mixture; in particular, they contained groups of students who were young (age 11-12) and at a relatively low stage. Compared to the Blatt-led classes, these classes usually suffered because (a) peers did not probe each other's reasoning as Blatt's classes did, and (b) no next-stage reasoning was presented as Blatt did if no peer would. In one case I observed, however, the class suffered not from the above but from the pressure of teacher instructional behavior. A class without such probing may be cited. The class was one of the control classes in which teachers were handed dilemmas and asked to have the students discuss them but in which the teachers were given no exposure to developmental aims and methods in dilemma discussions. In that class, the teacher presented a Blatt dilemma to a group of junior high inner-city students. The dilemma was this: Which is worse, stealing from a small store or stealing from the government? A lively discussion ensued between students who said that stealing from the government was worse because you could get in big trouble (presumably a first stage response, reasoning in terms of punishment and obedience) and other students who argued equally vehemently that stealing from a small store was worse because the storeowner didn't have that much to begin with (a second stage response, reasoning in terms of individual instrumental need). But rather than allowing the students to carry the discussion, as instructed by Blatt, the teacher remained active, though not in the Blatt manner. After briefly listening to the student discussion, the teacher turned to the board, wrote, "Stealing is wrong," underlined it, and said, "Yes, class, but the real point is that they are both *stealing* and they are both wrong." He handled the remaining dilemmas in a similar way. There was no upward stage movement in this particular "leaderless" class.

In summary, both the Blatt and the Stone students demonstrated the following assumptions of cognitive-developmental moral education:

1. Moral education is best conceived of as a natural process of dialogue among peers rather than as a process of didactic instruction or preaching.
2. The teacher and the curriculum are best conceived of as facilitators of this dialogue through presenting challenging dilemmas or situations, through probing for student reasoning and listening to reasons, and through presenting reasoning at a higher stage.
3. While no change occurs without any one of these elements in the discussion, the teacher may not be required to supply any of these conditions if the students supply them themselves.

Moshe Blatt, then, was the first gifted and courageous graduate student who led me into social education. The "Blatt effect" was the first demonstration in educational history of research confirmation of a meaningful effect of deliberate moral education on student moral development. While the Blatt effect launched recent cognitive-developmental moral education, Blatt's curriculum and instructional methods' project was "treatment condition" for experimental research rather than a philosophically defensible approach to aims, curriculum, and instructional methods in moral education. The Stone project, while developed as a part of a continuing collaboration with a sophisticated educator and curriculum-maker, Ted Fenton, should be looked at in a similar light. Like the Blatt study, it was based on what I shall call the "psychologist's fallacy" in education. The psychologist's fallacy is the fallacy that assumes that what is important for psychologists to study and know, or which is psychologically true, is also important for teachers or students to know or should be the foundation of educational programs. An example of the fallacy is behavior modification programs in education. Skinner and his colleagues have found very significant generalizations about the relations between overt behavior and rewarding consequences of these behaviors. A theory which effectively summarizes and explains these findings will be a good psychological theory, but that need not make it a good basis for developing educational practices or a good theory for teachers. Indeed, behavior modification and other approaches which commit the psychologist's fallacy often do not assume that the teacher ought to know the psychologist's theory but propose a "teacher proof" educational technology, i.e., a packaged curriculum kit and lesson plan which get the teacher to implant the theory without having to understand it.

The Stone project did not offer a teacher proof curriculum kit and lesson plan. Indeed, its results demonstrated that it was not teacher proof, that only half the teachers used Socratic probing questions as directed by the theory. But it did suffer from the psychologist's fallacy, i.e., that the educational process should be based on either transmitting a psychologist's theory to teachers or on a kit making the theory "teacher proof."

The first mistake contained in the psychologist's fallacy is the assumption that the perspective of psychological theory should dictate the perspective of educational philosophy. This assumption is evident, for instance, in Skinner's view that a psychological theorist's denial that freedom and dignity are operational variables in psychological research should dictate to the teacher that he or she ignore the philosophic conceptions of dignity and justice in designing educational programs. Even if Skinner's theory of psychology were true, it would not make his Walden II society, or a behavior modification reformatory, a philosophic paradise of justice or moral education. In this aspect, the psychologist's fallacy is the fallacy that one can derive conclusions about what human values and desires ought to be from psychological research conclusions about what human values and desires are, sliding over the distinction between what is *desired* and what is *desirable*. An example of the fallacy of sliding from desired to desirable is Skinner's statement that "good things are positive reinforcers. Behavioral science is a science of values to the extent that it concerns itself with the reinforcing effects of things."[1]

Unlike Skinner and others, my colleagues and I took some care to avoid the psychologist's fallacy in the sense of avoiding the confusion between the psychologist's and the philosopher's perspective. I realized that it was not sufficient to jump from the psychological findings of a moral stage sequence to the philosophic conclusion that attaining a higher stage should be the aim of moral education. Accordingly, I attempted to demonstrate philosophically to myself and others John Dewey's theory that development is the aim of education (Kohlberg and Mayer, 1972), and more specifically, to demonstrate (at least to myself) that a principled or higher stage method of moral reasoning was a better method of moral reasoning than were lower stage methods (Kohlberg, 1971, 1973). Indeed, the fact that cognitive-developmental moral education addresses philosophic issues in a way in which behavior modification does not is one reason that it is acceptable to teachers, parents, and students in a way that "manipulative" approaches to moral education like behavior modification are not.

There is a second related way in which cognitive-developmental theory partially avoids the psychologist's fallacy. Cognitive-developmental theory assumes that the child or adolescent is a natural philosopher. Were this assumption unfounded, the approach would have little circulation among educators. It is the interest which hypothetical moral dilemmas arouse in classrooms and in teacher workshops which primarily accounts for the popularity of the cognitive-developmental approach to moral education. The fact that our hypothetical dilemmas arouse interest is not due to the usual "psychological principles" which recommend peer heroes engaged in dilemmas, but to the fact that they set philosophic challenges before adolescents (and young children) in a concrete form.

In part, then, the Blatt approach to cognitive-developmental moral education avoided the psychologist's fallacy because its perspective was that of philosophy as well as psychology. In part, however, it did fall into the psychologist's fallacy of assuming that what was significant to the psychologist was significant to the teacher or the student. The Blatt approach rested on using hypothetical dilemmas originally developed as a method for psychological research. Our research used hypothetical dilemmas, not because our theory said that reasoning and decision making about hypothetical dilemmas was more significant than real moral decisions, but because real decisions were hard to study and were not comparable from subject to subject. The Blatt and Stone studies showed, initially, to my surprise, that the hypothetical dilemmas useful for research were also useful for stimulating stage change. The fact that they led to stage change, however, did not guarantee that we were free of the psychologist's fallacy. Hypothetical dilemmas and stage change might be significant to the psychologist (or philosopher) but might not be significant to the teacher or student. In fact, this was the conclusion I drew from some findings discovered by Stone. We earlier reported that the Stone operation was a success, for in half of the moral discussion classrooms, students demonstrated moral change. An additional finding was that though the operation was a success, the patient (or rather the experiment) died. None of the "change" classroom teachers continued doing much discussion after the one-year experiment was over. The moral discussion and stage change significant to the psychologist was not significant to the teacher, even though exposed to a workshop in the theory.

The Stone project was the culmination and the demise of the Blatt variety of cognitive-developmental moral education. The subsequent history of the approach is the history of the Danforth project, a continuing grant from the Danforth Foundation to Ted Fenton working in the Pittsburgh public schools; to Ralph Mosher and his colleagues, working in the Brookline, Massachusetts public schools; to the writer and his colleagues, working in the Cambridge public schools; and more recently to Charles Quigley, working in the Los Angeles public schools.

Central to the Danforth project has been the effort to develop social education experiences significant in students' and teachers' frame of reference, as well as in that of the psychologist or philosopher. Its outcome has been less a revision of the psychological theory, than a revision of thinking about the relation of theory to educational practice. The first obvious revision, from taking the point of view of teacher and student seriously, was to abandon the notion that moral discussion was a discrete unit in the curriculum with discrete moral education goals. Moral development should not be "a course" but a dimension of curriculum in any course, since any course raises issues of values, as well as issues of fact, in its studies. In the Danforth project, this led to integrating moral dilemma discussion with the more "academic" curriculum and objectives in English and social studies. It led to a realization that teachers need to do this integration themselves, to integrate for themselves moral discussion with other curriculum content and goals. An example is Tom Ladenberg's program described in this volume, a teacher-made integration of moral discussion with American history content and objectives.

A more fundamental revision of approach has been required to deal with the central lack of significance of the Blatt approach from the teacher and student perspective, its failure to deal with real as opposed to hypothetical dilemmas and decisions. One strand of the Danforth project, led by Ralph Mosher and his colleagues, deals with one of the problems inherent in dealing with "real" moral decisions. This is the problem: the discussion of real moral dilemmas involves serious issues of confidentiality and trust requiring a counseling orientation and ethic for teacher and other students alike. Values-clarification approaches have been criticized for using a counseling style to open up personal values dilemmas for the edification and amusement of fellow students to the embarrassment of the student "client." At least, however, the values-clarification approach is protected by the value-relative ethic which also safeguards client-centered counseling.

The cognitive-developmental approach, stressing adequacy of reasoning and ethical principles, cannot as easily let a student whose actions represent a dubious example of morality off the hook by claiming it was "right for him." Its proposed solution is outlined in the article by Mosher and Sullivan in this volume. The approach recommends discussion of real life moral decisions to be done (a) by a teacher with counseling skill and experience and (b) as part of a course or program that also teaches students "peer" counseling. Insofar as all students are counselors to one another, no one is put in the role of the embarrassed butt of the judgment of others, and all are in a position to devise and maintain an ethic of confidentiality and trust.

Both the Ladenberg and the Mosher and Sullivan outcomes of the Danforth project represent a movement away from the psychologist's fallacy toward a more democratic collaboration between psychologist-experimenter and the teacher or student. The psychologist is a consultant contributing theory and curriculum by "giving it away" for use and organization by the teacher (and student). The counseling psychologist becomes not someone in a white coat but a "peer counselor" and a teacher of peer counseling. Counselor and counselee are conceived of as equal, or reciprocal, roles.

An even more radical democratization of relations emerged from the Danforth Cambridge project of this writer, described in Elsa Wasserman's article in this volume. Its genesis may be traced to 1969, when Blatt was conducting a program of classroom dilemma discussion in a Boston area junior high school. While I was a visitor to the program, the school principal raised a familiar objection to the Blatt approach. He said, "Why is Blatt doing this science-fiction dilemma discussion when I need help with real behavior problems in the school?" What the principal wanted was a curriculum for behavior modification, not a curriculum in philosophic discussion. This same principal was guilty of the psychologist's fallacy. He wanted a theory and curriculum that would change student behavior, but not his own. In an earlier visit, he, like myself, had sat in the back of Blatt's classroom. After discussing a hypothetical dilemma, Blatt asked students if they had a real dilemma they would like to discuss. One student said, "I have a real dilemma. Last week this principal announced we all had to buy locks for our locker because there were so many rip-offs. But I don't think I should obey because I don't think it's a fair rule. If we have to have lockers, the school should buy locks for them. If we have to pay for a lock, it should be up to us whether we take the chance of being ripped-off." None of the other students presented a very convincing counter-argument, while the principal remained silent in the back of the room. The principal wanted moral discussion to effect a change in student behavior but not to affect his own behavior. Recognizing this, I replied to his request for help with behavior problems by saying, "Helping you would mean dealing with real life dilemmas, that is, school dilemmas. And dealing with behavior means not only asking what's fair or just in school dilemmas, but encouraging action to make the school more just. That means trying to promote fairness in teacher behavior and administrative behavior as well as student behavior. So if you'd like, I'd consider consulting with you and the teachers to make this school a more just community."

Luckily, the principal did not call my bluff, since I had no idea how I would do what I had proposed. It was in fact Peter Scharf, with his friend Joe Hickey, who taught me how, or at least had the courage to first try it. The first effort to set up a democratic "just community" based on cognitive-developmental theory took place not in a school but in the Niantic Connecticut Correctional Facility for Women. Scharf and Hickey entered the prison after a riot in 1971 with permission to start a cottage unit of six volunteer guards and inmates based on moral decision and participatory democracy, one person, one vote, inmate or guard. A constitution and rules were established through a series of negotiations between guards and inmates initiated by Scharf and Hickey after a theory workshop for the officers.

Encouraged by the viability of the Scharf and Hickey prison programs, and having learned a good deal from participant observation in it, I was prepared to consult on a moral education experiment in participant democracy in a high school. In 1974, the Cambridge public schools authorized an alternative school within the public high schools and asked me to consult with teachers and students planning the school. The results are described in Elsa Wasserman's article in this volume. The program reflects a fundamental shift in the relation of psychologist-theorist to students and teachers from that of the Stone project. Together with the teachers, I attempted to formulate theory in terms of the task of creating a new conception of a school community in addition to obtaining research data. Such a participant-consultant role has its perils. At a recent community meeting, a student proposed that I be demoted from participant-observer to observer and lose my vote because I had cut a number of weekly community meetings. The motion passed on a straw vote but was reversed after some sentimental tributes were made to my role in the founding of the school. At another community meeting, a student proposed a motion that "there was too much of Larry Kohlberg's moral discussion in the school and that students should be morally developed before they get into high school." She proposed beefing up the English skills curriculum so that students would be more sure of making college. The motion passed, though moral discussion goes on at this school. These, however, are a few of the perils for academic theorists if they begin to question the psychologist's fallacy in the relation of theory to educational practice and forego attempting to develop "teacher proof" or "student proof" curricula.

In spite of these perils, viable implementation of an integration of moral discussion, social studies and English curriculum, and participatory democratic self-government are going on in the Pittsburgh and Brookline, as well as the Cambridge, Danforth projects. It will take some years of experience and ongoing research to judge them.

I have reported the recent history of the cognitive-developmental approach to moral education, a history about ten years old. We need now to put the history in a larger perspective.

The cognitive-developmental approach to moral education has its origins in Socrates' Athens. Socrates believed that there was a universal conception of justice which was rational, or cognitive. Whether rational or known through philosophic intuition, justice was to be loved, lived, and died for, as Socrates demonstrated. Socrates believed that a universal conception of justice was latent in everyone (including Meno's slave), that it developed through levels, and that its development depended upon questioning, the arousal of doubt, and social dialogue. The research of my colleagues and myself has helped give the Socratic vision contemporary credibility. Our cross-cultural and longitudinal studies provide research evidence for the Socratic view of a universal conception of justice proceeding through developmental levels. The Stone Foundation project is one of the most recent confirmations of the Socratic hypothesis on the educational side.

It will be recalled that there were two features of the classrooms in which students demonstrated stage change. First, these classrooms had mixtures of students at different stages (no mixture of stages, no Socratic dialogue). Second, all the teachers in the "change" classrooms used good Socratic probes of reasoning; most of the "no-change" class teachers did not. (This was the only differentiating item on a 100-item teacher behavior observation schedule.) These findings not only reaffirmed our faith in the possibilities of moral discussions but our faith in Socratic dialogue.

The original test of the Socratic approach to moral education came by administering hemlock. Our research test of statistical significance is hardly as profound, but is easier to replicate by less committed educators. Philosophic commitment based on philosophic understanding is still required of moral educators, however. Moral education is still often considered revolutionary, as it was in Socrates' day. The only reason Socratic moral education today is less risky than in Socrates' Athens is because we can recall that our own society is grounded on a revolution oriented to moral principles. Our own society is grounded on documents (the Declaration of Independence and the Constitution) written from what we call a Stage 5 perspective, a moral and political philosophy of the social contract and of universal human rights. When Jefferson and others advocated public education, it was to prepare for citizenship in the new society, the constitutional democratic society. In our society, a person is a citizen when he or she can read the social contract, the Constitution, and sign it with informed consent. The true, American "right to read" is the right to read the Constitution.

While the American constitutional tradition provides some protection for a moral education for justice, we must still cope with Plato's conclusion from the execution of Socrates that education for justice must start with a just Republic ruled by a philosopher king. If the guardians of the society were not just, who would educate children to be virtuous or just? American radicals pose the same question and question moral education without the revolution necessary for the Utopian just society.

The cognitive-developmental approach is compatible with John Dewey's progressive answer to Plato's despair about engaging in moral education in an imperfectly just society. In *Democracy and Education* Dewey wrote the second great treatise on moral education in a just society. Dewey, even more clearly than Socrates, claimed, "the aim of education is growth or development, both intellectual and moral." Dewey claimed that developmental (or Socratic) moral education could work in a society which was democratic, even though the masses or their guardians were not yet very just. Dewey, unlike Socrates or Plato, believed that communities (schools and societies) as well as individuals could develop, and that if education in a democracy could move the individual student to a higher level of justice, it would in time lead to the development of both more just schools and a more just society. Elsa Wasserman's article on the just community school is one statement of a revival of Dewey's vision. It recognizes, like Dewey, that the moral development of a community of students is not the sum of the moral changes of each individual student. A school as a moral community can be either at a higher or lower level than the sum of the individuals in it. Our research suggests that in most schools the level of justice of the school as a social system is lower than the individual levels of students, teachers, and administrators composing it. Wasserman's article suggests that a school based on concepts of justice and participatory democracy can be a community close to the level of its highest members and continuing to progress upward.

The movement of our approach to moral education from discussion of hypothetical dilemmas to a total concept of school as just community, deciding real moral-political issues, is still new and relatively untried, but it is rooted soundly in the philosophic and psychological tradition we have described, which can be traced from Plato through Dewey to Piaget and ourselves.

Moral education, unlike other areas of education, is a field in which one cannot achieve constructive results when one starts with confused or mistaken premises. If the teaching of reading had depended upon correct psychological and philosophic assumptions to get started, people would still not be reading. While research on reading has advanced since Athens, the practice of teaching reading has not improved much as a result. One can doubt whether the teaching of reading in America today is vastly better than it was in Socrates' Athens, in spite of our much sounder and more complex psychological understanding of the reading process.

With moral education, the case is different. While this book's statement of an approach to moral education may not represent a significant advance over isolated practices like Socrates' or Dewey's laboratory school, it is a vast advance over the practice of moral education as it now goes on in American schools, just as it is over the daily practice of the schools of Athens. This we say partly because research suggests little moral development through ordinary schooling (in our control groups), partly because of the philosophic and psychological confusions involved in the assumptions of most American moral education practices. Our comments about avoiding the arrogance of the psychologist's fallacy should not imply satisfaction with "common sense" practices and thinking of teachers on this topic. I have commented elsewhere on the "common sense" approach to education, that is, teaching a "bag of virtues" through preaching and reward. This approach was shown by Hartshorne and May to be not only ineffective but based on faulty psychological assumptions, although it comes most naturally to common-sense thinking about moral education. Another version of moral education practice currently popular with teachers is "values clarification." Values clarification is indeed a first approach to Socratic or developmental moral discussions but shrinks from hard dialogue and questioning of "why's" because it has rested on the assumption that values are relative to the individual. It rests on the faulty philosophic assumption of value-relativity, that everyone should have his or her own moral bag.

The most common system of moral education in America is neither "character education," "values clarification," nor a cognitive-developmental just community approach, but no conscious system at all, the "hidden curriculum." Its limitations can be vividly seen by viewing Wiseman's film *High School* or by reading my article in this volume on the moral atmosphere of the school.

We have said that cognitive-developmental moral education is not new; it has a 2,000 year history. Why is it a "bandwagon" now? The 1970's have seen flourishing, not only cognitive-developmental moral education, but also general scholarly concern by philosophers and psychologists in the United States, Great Britain, and Canada. Why is there renewed interest in moral education, dead since the 1930's? The question receives an answer which is implicitly either conservative or liberal-progressive. Some would argue that this interest is a reaction to crime, Watergate, and the decline of traditional sexual morality, a conservative return to the social basics of moral order and discipline, like the return to traditional academic basics in curriculum. I propose instead that the current interest in moral education rises primarily from the rediscovery by liberals of the moral principles behind the liberal faith and the realization that these principles need to enter into education. Like the liberal reaction to Watergate, the liberal interest in moral education is a rediscovery in the seventies of the principles of justice behind the founding of our nation. The liberals of the sixties had lost awareness of the principles underlying liberalism, the principles of the Declaration and the Constitution. Instead of a faith in justice principles, the liberals of the sixties had faith in technology, in the social and physical sciences, and in rational political manipulation as tools of social progress.

As the liberal faith in rational instrumental social *means* has been disappointed, there has been a growing awareness of the need to have rational or moral social *ends* and principles of action and to embody these ends in education. This is fundamentally the meaning of the current interest in moral education.

Behind this interest lies the principle of justice on which our society was founded. America was the first society whose government was grounded on a conception of principles of justice. The Declaration of Independence called these principles the self-evident truths that all men are created equal with inalienable rights to life, liberty, and the pursuit of happiness. Watergate tells us that these principles have never been understood by the majority which every year votes down the Bill of Rights in the Gallup poll. The movement for moral education recognizes that in our society, all people must acquire, through education, some understanding of and acceptance of these justice principles. Watergate reminds us that justice principles cannot be maintained by force, laws, and government since the very leaders of that government failed to understand and support these principles. It reminds us of the need of an education for and through justice.

I've said that America was the first nation whose government was publicly founded on post-conventional principles of justice and the rights of human beings, rather than upon the authority central to conventional moral reasoning. This is Stage 5. At the time of our founding, our Stage 5, post-conventional or principled moral and political reasoning, was the possession of the minority, as it still is. Today, as in the time of our founding, the majority of our adults are at the conventional level, particularly the law-and-order fourth moral stage. The founders of our nation intuitively understood this without the benefit of research and designed a Constitutional government which would maintain principles of justice and the rights of all even though principled people were not in power. The machinery included checks and balances, the independent judiciary, freedom of the press. Most recently, this machinery found its use at Watergate.

The tragedy of Richard Nixon, as Harry Truman said long ago, was that he never understood the Constitution, a Stage 5 document. No public word of Nixon ever rose above Stage 4, the law-and-order stage. His last comments in the White House were of wonderment that the Republican Congress could turn on him after so many Stage 2 exchanges of favors in getting them elected. The level of reasoning in much of the White House transcripts was similar, including the discussion of laundering money. While the tragedy of Richard Nixon was that he never understood the Constitution, the triumph of America is that the Constitution understood Richard Nixon. It is not free citizens who are bound in "the chains of the Constitution" (Jefferson's phrase) but men who attain power without Stage 5 understanding or acceptance of the justice, rights, and principles enshrined in the Declaration.

The liberal reaction to Watergate has understood that Watergate is not some sign of moral decay of the nation, but rather, of the fact that understanding and action in support of justice principles is still the possession of a minority of our society, and that the moral progress of our nation has far to go. Watergate, then, reflects the slow movement of society from the conventional to the morally principled level.

The current sense of a need for moral education, then, is best conceived of as the demands which evolving standards of justice place on traditional conceptions of education and socialization. The current concern for moral education represents an awareness of a demand for a higher or post-conventional level of moral principles in our national life. Citizens are no longer to be obedient soldiers or nationalist voters but voters or soldiers whose actions are to be governed by principles.

In terms of principles of justice, Watergate and My Lai both illustrate, not the decay of morality, but the failure of conventional morality to handle civil and human rights. This is not something new in national history. What is new is the situation in which the educational system is expected to develop a majority of citizens governed by principles once assumed to be the prerogative of a moral elite. Our educational system has failed to produce a majority of citizens who think and act in terms of human rights. Rather, it has produced citizens who, like Lieutenant Calley and President Nixon, are only good at giving and taking orders.

What is specifically new to education is our expectation that high school students should be unprejudiced or non-racist. Implicitly, this is the expectation that students should go beyond the moral level of concern for upholding the norms of their group, family, and nation to the moral level of concern for universal principles of justice and respect for human dignity.

This expectation is, or should be, reflected in our current concern for desegregating the schools. Underlying the legal concern for desegregating the schools is the notion that our educational system should uphold the principle of respect for human dignity.

The Supreme Court's need to define a right to human dignity based on moral principles is involved in the enforced school busing controversy. The rationale provided by the Court for desegregation of schools has been "equal opportunity," the doctrine that schools cannot be separate but equal. This doctrine has rested on dubious statistical or social scientific evidence that educational facilities could not be separate and lead to equal educational achievement. Jencks' treatise is the last major summary indicating that school desegregation and compensatory education do little to promote equal opportunity.

If equal opportunity was a weak reason for school desegregation, it is an even weaker reason for enforced busing. Enforced busing is hardly leading to enhanced educational opportunity for either black or white students and it is clearly a restriction of liberty of whites and sometimes of blacks. The only clear rationale for enforced busing is the equal right to human dignity. It seems right to enforce desegregation not because blacks will learn better but because a school is a public facility and denial of access to a public facility to blacks is a public insult to their equal worth, just as refusing access to a bus or swimming pool is.

We have pointed to a morally principled conception of justice in education in terms of busing. Such a justification for enforced busing depends upon a conception of education for justice and not just a conception of justice in education as equalizing educational opportunity.

The educational reform movement of the last twenty years has been a movement for curriculum reform, educational technology, and educational research and development. Beneath this movement has been a vague liberal belief in justice. Through educational technology, through upgrading the curriculum and methods of instruction, our poor and disadvantaged students would learn more academically and would have a fairer chance at life's goods and opportunities. Improved curriculum and instructional methods, it was hoped, could reach those students who would be condemned to poverty without academic skills. Together with curriculum improvement, school desegregation would raise educational opportunities and later life chances for the poor and black.

The seventies finds these liberal hopes for educational technology disappointed. The Coleman Report, the Jencks Report, and many other reports indicate that curriculum innovations and desegregation do not greatly change academic achievement and that enhancing academic achievement does not greatly enhance life chances for the poor.

The fallacy of educational technology and curriculum improvement as a cure for social injustice is suggested by Ed Zigler's comment when he took over Headstart. He said Headstart had been initiated with the goal of seeing the educational achievement of the entire country clustered at the fiftieth percentile. If society's resources are distributed on a competitive normal curve, improved educational technology may raise the mean of educational achievement, but it won't change the distribution. Educational technology will not help the students to deal with problems of social injustice unless the schools help students develop a more mature and stronger sense of justice so that as a participating citizenry, they can help to fashion a more just society. The seventies require a different approach to school reform than that of the curriculum reform of the sixties—the democratizing of the schools.

In summary, the current demand for moral education is a demand that our society become more of a just community. If our society is to become a more just community based on a democracy, it needs democratic schools. This was the demand and dream of Dewey which is still as unfulfilled as Plato's. I believe that the tortured movement of our society toward justice makes Dewey's dream both more possible and more urgent in the years ahead.

Dewey and the progressives argued for democratizing the schools and had little impact. Will the generation of school reform of the 1970's get farther? I believe it may. In some part this is because the theory and experience reported in this volume represents some intellectual advance over that available in Dewey's day, an advance which may yield a more effective educational "progress." In some part, it is because we have a more effective machinery for intellectual dissemination of "progress" to the schools than was available in Dewey's day. School superintendents and principals do doctoral research and theorizing on moral education in the universities, teachers take in-service workshops, and foundations give curriculum grants. More fundamentally, however, it is because just schools were a luxury for American society in Dewey's day, and today they are a necessity. American society did not need "education for justice" in Dewey's day. The same, I believe, is true for school democracy. While there is some return of the outward signs of renewed success for "education by and for authority" rather than education by and for democracy, this success does not touch either the rebelling of the inner city high schools, nor the inner alienation of the prosperous suburban schools. American education in the next decade cannot find its moral source in arbitrary authority or cultural consensus. Rather, it must find its moral source in the ideals of democracy and moral reason. I join the editor in hoping that these articles will be of some use to those who are concerned about the education of young people. This book is neither a manual nor a final statement. Rather, it is a series of progress reports tied to an ongoing educational endeavor which began with Socrates.

Note

1. *Typically* the confusion between what the psychologist claims to find desired and what ought to be desired leads him or her to a blanket conclusion of ethical or cultural relations.

The ethical relativist seems to be saying two things. The first is that values do differ from culture to culture; some cultures value human sacrifice, some do not. The second is that, therefore, values ought to differ from culture to culture, e.g., that human sacrifice is good in the culture where it is practiced but bad in others, i.e., that there is no valid principle of moral judgment except the opinions or customs of the particular culture. Various forms of the relativist assumption seem to underlie the criticisms of moral stage theory in this volume by Samples, Sullivan, and Fraenkel. In contrast, I argue my theory holds (1) that the research facts show that in the culture studied, there is then some sequence of moral stages, and (2) that in all cultures a higher stage is a better stage in terms of rational consideration of moral principles. The higher stages in all cultures judge in terms of principles of human liberty, equality, and respect for life and personality. This may lead a higher stage person in a culture practicing human sacrifice to his death as it led Martin Luther King to his death in a culture practicing racism and segregation. But the fact that certain moral principles held at the highest stage are not usually endorsed by all people in all cultures is no proof that they are not philosophically valid. Neither is it a refutation of the facts found in cross-cultural research. Our theory is criticized as being an ethnocentric Western liberal's theory. But a criticism of our theory or any other is based on some culturally conceived principle of objectivity and non-bias. I would ask critics of the moral development theory to outline principles which are neither "Western liberation" nor "western Marxism," but which are ideally conceived.

Part I: The Philosophy and Psychology of Moral Education

It is difficult to conceive of a responsible effort in moral education which fails to develop an explicit philosophy and psychology to justify its efforts. The articles in this section seek to outline the philosophic and psychological rationales of cognitive-developmental moral education associated with the work of Lawrence Kohlberg of Harvard University and his colleagues. This approach differs markedly from other systems in use, especially from those used by indoctrinative and values-clarification educators.

The first essay overviews the philosophic and empirical foundation of developmental moral education in contrast to indoctrinative and values-clarification approaches. Lawrence Kohlberg's "The Cognitive-Developmental Approach to Moral Education" outlines both the social philosophy as well as intervention examples associated with the movement. Edwin Fenton's "Moral Education: The Research Findings" lists eleven basic claims and axioms made by the system. The three essays, as a group, offer the reader an introduction to the philosophical and psychological assumptions and developmental theory. The ideas presented are essential for an understanding of the curricula and theoretical issues discussed in the essays to follow.

Indoctrination, Values Clarification, and Developmental Moral Education as Educational Responses to Conflict and Change in Contemporary Society

Peter Scharf, Assistant Professor of Social Ecology, University of California at Irvine.

Introduction

There once was a time, according to legend, in which children could anticipate quite clearly the moral norms they would encounter as adults. The Medieval peasant lived, in a sense, in a timeless world. The Church and feudal order regulated public and private morality in a manner, which if not perfect, was ideologically harmonious and constant. There were few challenges from without. There was no rebellious press to attack the establishment, no other societies known with which to contrast one's own. The Medieval child could be raised according to tradition, one which would endure through his or her natural life.

Even my generation believed that the moral norms we were taught might remain valid for at least a generation. The children of the fifties were presented with domestic, moral, and sexual values which had at least the pretense of ordering manners and action for a life cycle. "Ozzie and Harriet" and "Father Knows Best" taught us what a good family might be. "Beaver," Lassie's friend Tommie and "Howdy Doody" told us what kids were like: rambunctious, but ultimately conforming. President Eisenhower represented political trustworthiness. Moral stereotypes presented in movies and our parents told us what was right, what was wrong, who was good, and who was bad.

Even sexuality was morally ordered. There were "nice girls" and "good girls." You sneaked into the bushes with good girls, but married nice girls. You went steady, got pinned, engaged, married, and had babies. I remember my first date with a girl named Alice, also fourteen, mostly because of the movie we saw. In it, nice girls and not nice girls were clearly portrayed. Alice got the message, and at the end of our date we did not even kiss goodnight. Alice definitely wanted to be a nice girl.

Five years later my mother informed me that Alice had died of an overdose of drugs in a section of San Francisco called Haight-Ashbury. Nobody I knew in 1964 had heard much about either drugs or Haight-Ashbury. Five years later, almost everybody knew about Haight-Ashbury as well as Woodstock, The Chicago Nine, Yippies, Hippies, LSD, draft card burners and what became known for a while as the counter-culture. This counter-culture eventually came to inform our morality. Instead of getting married at twenty and getting a mortgage, we should experiment at least until thirty and remain free to experiment our whole life through. The trustworthy Eisenhower had been replaced in the seventies by a man who, we learned, would betray the roots of any political faith which survived the Vietnamese War.

Children of the seventies face an even greater moral challenge than my generation did. They can predict the future before them even less than we could. The very affluence and security of our society is in doubt today. Few leaders inspire trust in the present order, let alone possess the moral force to lead the country into an uncertain future. While my generation was presented with at least the illusion of a moral order, today's parents often tell their children, simply, "I don't know," or "I'm not sure," when asked questions of serious moral implication.

How, we seek to ask, might schools educate the forthcoming generation to cope with the dilemmas of an uncertain society? This essay will contrast three models of moral education,* each of which attempts to grapple with the problem of teaching values to children. Each offers a radically different philosophy as well as psychology. The *indoctrination* model seeks to teach values defined by society as socially valid and correct by rewarding "good" values and punishing "bad" ones. *Values clarification,* through self-observation and analysis, seeks to help the child find values which only he or she can judge valid or invalid. *Developmental moral education* offers the hypothesis that there are stages of moral values which might be taught through moral conflict and dialogue. This latter model, we will argue, offers a unique philosophy and psychology to meet the problem of value conflict in modern society.

Moral Indoctrination as Moral Education

Moral indoctrination is one response to the moral malaise of contemporary society. Its underlying philosophy appears simple, but it should not be either accepted or rejected out of hand. Moral indoctrination defines specific values as "right" for a particular society or group. It holds that moral values may be taught directly; that is, through the repetition of moral ideas and the reinforcement of moral behaviors, children will learn to think and act morally. Children are to be exposed to the "right" values, and contact with immoral or "wrong" values is to be discouraged. To offer an example of moral indoctrination in education, we might look at an interaction I recently observed between a sixth grade boy, Tom, and his teacher in a "traditional" school in Southern California.

Teacher: Tom, did you throw that paper plane over there?
Tom: mmmmmmmmmmmmmmmm
Teacher: Tom?
Tom: Yes, Mrs. X?
Teacher: Was that disruptive behavior?
Tom: Yes.
Teacher: I don't think we can have disruptive behavior in this classroom. You know it's wrong to act disruptively. Your mother would not have you disrupt her conversations at home. Let's see a bit more of the "positive Tom."

* The positions included here reflect polar types selected for heuristic purposes. In reality there are several other coherent positions which differ in tone and orientation from the three models described here.

The teacher, as we see, defines disruptiveness as "wrong" and hopes to chastise what she sees as rude behavior. She assumes that there are "positive" moral values which should be adopted by the children in her class and that through repetition of these values her students will learn to act appropriately. Usually, the values chosen by indoctrination educators are "conventional" in that they apply to the conventions of particular societies rather than applying to all societies. Such values are often defined in terms of "virtues" or "role-defined," positive social acts. For example, Ben Franklin defined a list of virtues to help him live a moral life. Each day he would check himself to see if he had lived up to the virtues on his list, noting all errors and lapses. Here is his list:

1. Temperance—Eat not to dullness; drink not to drunkenness.
2. Silence—Speak not but what may benefit others.
3. Order—Let all your things have their places.
4. Resolution—Resolve to perform what you ought.
5. Frugality—Make only small expenses; waste nothing.
6. Industry—Lose no time; be always employed in something useful.
7. Sincerity—Use no deceit.
8. Justice—Wrong none by doing injuries.
9. Moderation—Avoid extremes.
10. Cleanliness—Tolerate no uncleanliness in body, clothes, or habits.
11. Tranquillity—Be not disturbed at trifles.
12. Chastity—Rarely use sexual pleasure but for health or offspring.
13. Humility—Imitate Jesus and Socrates.

Schools in nineteenth century America largely adopted an indoctrination approach to moral education. Horace Mann, William Harris and others encouraged the development of a school curriculum to further moral and spiritual character. The key to this effort was the selection of literature in which moral acts were rewarded and immoral ones were chastised. The *McGuffey Reader*, the basal reader for three generations of American children, provides an example of moral indoctrination in literature. A section from the *Reader* dealing with a story of a barber who honors the Sabbath in spite of his own apparent economic losses, illustrates how literature was used to teach children the moral culture of nineteenth century America.

XIII. Respect for the Sabbath Rewarded

> 1. In the city of Bath, not many years since, lived a barber who made a practice of following his ordinary occupation on the Lord's day. As he was on the way to morning's employment, he happened to look into some place of worship just as the minister was giving out his text—"Remember the Sabbath day, to keep it holy." He listened long enough to be convinced that he was constantly breaking the laws of God and man by shaving and dressing his customers on the Lord's day. He became uneasy, and went with a heavy heart to his Sabbath task.
>
> 2. At length he took courage, and opened his mind to his minister, who advised him to give up Sabbath work and worship God. He replied that

beggary would be the consequence. He had a flourishing trade, but it would almost all be lost. At length, after many a sleepless night spent in weeping and praying, he was determined to cast all his care upon God, as the more he reflected, the more his duty became apparent.

3. He discontinued his Sabbath work, went constantly and early to the public services of religion, and soon enjoyed that satisfaction of mind which is one of the rewards of our duty, and that peace which the world can neither give nor take away. The consequences he foresaw actually followed. His genteel customers left him, and he was nicknamed "Puritan" or "Methodist." He was obliged to give up his fashionable shop, and, in the course of years, became so reduced as to take a cellar under the old market house and shave the poorer people.

4. One Saturday evening, between light and dark, a stranger from one of the coaches, asking for a barber, was directed by the hostler to the cellar opposite. Coming in hastily, he requested to be shaved quickly, while they changed horses, as he did not like to violate the Sabbath. This was touching the barber on a tender chord. He burst into tears; asked the stranger to lend him a half-penny to buy a candle, as it was not light enough to shave him with safety. He did so, revolving in his mind the extreme poverty to which the poor man must be reduced.

5. When shaved, he said, "There must be something extraordinary in your history, which I have not now time to hear. Here is half a crown for you. When I return, I will call and investigate your case. What is your name?" "William Reed," said the astonished barber. "William Reed?" echoed the stranger: "William Reed, by your dialect you are from the West." "Yes, sir, from Kingston, near Taunton." "William Reed from Kingston, near Taunton? What was your father's name?" "Thomas." "Had he any brother?" "Yes, sir, one, after whom I was named; but he went to the Indies, and, as we never heard from him, we supposed him to be dead."

6. "Come along, follow me," said the stranger, "I am going to see a person who says his name is William Reed, of Kingston, near Taunton. Come and confront him. If you prove to be indeed he who you say you are, I have glorious news for you. Your uncle is dead, and has left an immense fortune, which I will put you in possession of when all legal doubts are removed."

7. They went by the coach; saw the pretended William Reed, and proved him to be an impostor. The stranger, who was a pious attorney, was soon legally satisfied of the barber's identity, and told him that he had advertised him in vain. Providence had now thrown him in his way in a most extraordinary manner, and he had great pleasure in transferring a great many thousand pounds to a worthy man, the rightful heir of the property. Thus was man's extremity God's opportunity. Had the poor barber possessed one half-penny, or even had credit for a candle, he might have remained unknown for years; but he trusted God, who never said, "Seek ye my face, in vain."[1]

Needless to say moral indoctrination as a method is not limited to the values of pioneer American society. Several observers have noted the use of indoctrinative methods in both Chinese and Russian educational systems. Herschel and Alt describe how indoctrinative methods are used to shape Russian children into the value system of Soviet comradeship:

> Beginning in the second grade children are inducted into the pioneer groups, the cub scouts, as has been said, of the Communist party. A leader from the Komsomol (Young Communist League) starts work with the children almost as soon as school opens in the fall. She tells the children that a Pioneer is a boy or girl who leads in study and behavior and who serves as an example to others. She tells them of the valorous deeds of the revolutionary pioneers and explains why Pioneers wear red ties, why the ties have three ends and are tied in a knot. She explains the Pioneer salute and teaches them the solemn promise they will give when they are nine and join the Pioneers:
>
> The Pioneer is true to the work of Lenin-Stalin
> The Pioneer loves his motherland ardently and hates her enemies
> The Pioneer considers it an honor to become a member of Lenin's Komsomol
> The Pioneer is honest and truthful. His word is firm as steel
> The Pioneer is brave as an eagle. He despises a coward
> The Pioneer has a keen eye, iron muscles, steel nerves
> The Pioneer needs knowledge as an arm in battle
> The Pioneer is not an idler, white-handed; he is industrious, work-loving
> The Pioneer is the pride of family and school
> The Pioneer is an example to all youngsters.
>
> An article in *Soviet Pedagogy* is worth quoting at length, not only for its graphic description of the induction of some youngsters in one school, but for its description of the function of such a unit. Between the lines can be seen the resistance of at least some teachers and parents to this phenomenon of Soviet social pressure:
>
> In the large Pioneer room where portraits of Lenin and Stalin were decorated with greenery, there gathered Pioneers, leaders, teachers, class instructors, director. Guests came: members of the society of old Bolsheviks who lived not far from the school, and the chairman of two neighboring collectives with which our school keeps a close friendship. The Pioneer troops lined up in squad formation. In front stood the new ones who were this day to put on red ties. Each one held in his hand a copy of the oath, handsomely executed on thick white paper.
>
> When the formations were formed and silence reigned in the room, the senior leader gave the command: "At attention! Prepare to report!" Then chairmen of the squads gave reports to the chairmen of the troops. . . .
>
> . . . . Authority of troop soviet is great in the eyes of Pioneers. The order of influence of Pioneer organization on disturbers of discipline and on Pioneers negligent in study is usually as follows with us: A Pioneer, for example, starts to study badly, does not prepare lessons, is lazy, mischievous. Conduct of Pioneer is discussed in link. If action of link proves insufficient, conduct of

> Pioneer is discussed in squad soviet. And, finally, if this does not help either, and Pioneer continues to study badly, hinder teacher during lessons, such a delinquent is called upon to appear at a meeting of troop soviet and usually after the matter is examined in the squad soviet, children "pull themselves together," begin to take their studies seriously. Yet cases happen when children must be called to troop soviet, the moral influence of which is so strong and deep that, as a rule, after this children begin to improve.
>
> We had such a case. A pupil of sixth grade, Lucy P., without knowledge of her parents began to frequent movies in the neighboring town. She returned home very late and went to bed without preparing lessons. The question of Lucy was presented at the link meeting. The girl, spoiled by her parents, only laughed at the demands of her comrades to stop her frequent movie-going which hindered preparation of lessons. The question of Lucy was discussed in squad soviet, a comradely pointing out was made to her, but this did not help. Then she was called to the troop soviet. The excited girl went up to senior leader and said timidly: "What am I to do, Ekaterina Ivanovna, I am called to the troop soviet." There were tears in Lucy's eyes. "What are you to do?" said senior leader. "You're a Pioneer yet you did not submit to squad demands. Now you must answer to the troop soviet." Chairman of the troop soviet put a question to Lucy: does she give consideration to the Pioneer organization? "Yes, of course," she answered. Pioneers, members of troop soviet, explained to Lucy how badly she had acted in not having submitted to the demands of her squad. Lucy sincerely repented of her misdeeds and gave her word to stop frequent movie-going. She kept her promise and began to study better faithfully carrying out home assignment. . . .[2]

Whether emphasizing the pioneer virtues of hard work and piety or the comradely virtues of Marxist society, indoctrinative moral education programs share three essential features:

1. They define morality in terms of the moral rules, values, and virtues of a particular society at a particular point in history. Neither the McGuffey-trained teacher nor the Russian Communist party educator would claim to be inculcating anything other than American or Marxist values. These values tend to be presented in terms of rules (e.g., "Honesty is the best policy," "Respect one's elders," etc.) rather than general, universalizable moral principles.
2. Indoctrinative educators assume that moral values can be taught directly through inculcation, modeling, repetition, and reinforcement. Following a mechanistic conception of learning defined by Locke, Watson, and later, Skinner, they assume that moral behavior may be taught through direct environmental input. Indoctrination theory accepts that children learn ideas from the moral examples provided by their parents and must be kept from experiencing harmful or negative influences. Indoctrination similarly seeks to train in "sound moral habits" and to prevent the child from developing "social vices."
3. Most indoctrinative educators assume that society's values will remain more or less constant; that values taught to a child today will have validity in the years to come; that the norms of respect and honor, lawfulness, and pride in one's country should have the moral validity in the year A.D. 2000 that they do today. While recognizing

that there are people who do not conform to these societal values, the indoctrinative approach implies that society's only hope is to bolster traditional norms even in the face of attack from conflicting values from within and without society.

Values Clarification as Moral Education

Not all moral educators have accepted the indoctrination model of moral learning. For more than a decade, what has come to be known as the values-clarification movement has consistently and forcefully attacked the assumption that societal values should and can be taught to students. A recent critique of indoctrination methods, for example, holds that the schools have, more or less uncritically, become agents of student socialization into the dominant values patterns of American society:

> Inculcation does not stop upon entering school. Many values are reinforced and actively expressed in schools by the present nature of these institutions and through the presented content matter. Among other values, schools enforce conformity, competition, and obedience. These often are not the school's goals, but through the interpretation and application of educational philosophies, they have become incorporated into the school system. Dress codes prescribe a certain dress form for students and teachers; written tests which assume only one correct answer stifle creativity; grades encourage competition, cheating, and learning for extrinsic rewards; rules and regulations control attendance and students' behavior; the teacher's authoritarian role and disciplinary power demand obedience and docility. In other words, the school promotes its own hidden curriculum. It is often not acknowledged, but evident just the same.
>
> Most of these values are reflected by the society at large, substantiating the traditional role of schools as the transmitter of culture. Although the transmittance and continuation of our culture is necessary, students have a right to learn how to discriminate between the values and the factual content of subject matter. Today, values are often presented as facts: For example, it is common for students to learn from the curriculum or teachers that democracy, our form of government, is the best government. As James Barth and Samuel Shermis have pointed out, students learn in traditional social studies classes that although capitalism was marred by exploitation, it is superior to all other economic systems. The attitude is that if students succeed in equating capitalism with democracy, no real harm is done for both ideas are good. This is a value presented as a fact, but students do not learn to discern values from facts and schools should not present values in this way.[3]

Values-clarification advocates frequently see indoctrinative moral education as not only hypocritical, but as ineffective as well. For example, Sidney Simon observes:

> What happened was the realization that all the inculcating, instilling, and fostering added up to indoctrination; and despite our best efforts at doing the indoctrinating, we've come to see that it just didn't take. Most of the people who experienced the inculcation, instillation, and fostering

> seem not the much better for it. They appear to play just as much hanky-panky with income taxes as anyone else, and concerned letters-to-the-editor are not written by them in any greater profusion. They pollute and defoliate; move to the suburbs to escape integration; buy convertibles with vinyl tops that collapse in roll-over accidents; fail to wear seat belts; and commit all kinds of sins even while they are saying the very words that have been dutifully inculcated, instilled, and fostered in them. It is discouraging.[4]

In place of indoctrination, values clarification offers a model of moral education which is open-ended in the extreme. Students will explore value problems individually and in small groups in order to become more aware of inner values and beliefs. Raths, the pioneer of the movement, suggests ten areas of value inquiry including money, friendship, love and sexual morality, character traits, leisure, politics, maturity, and work. These are to define the "content" of values-clarification exercises. Specific values are held to possess seven criteria which are insisted upon in defining what a value is and offering a working test of individual beliefs, according to Raths and Simon. In order for a "belief" to possess the status of a value it must be—

1. chosen freely
2. chosen from among alternatives
3. chosen after thoughtful consideration of consequences
4. prized and cherished
5. publicly affirmed
6. acted upon in reality
7. acted upon repeatedly

Each values-clarification exercise is designed to bring the personal values of the individual into clearer focus and to see them as possessing the criteria listed above. Through strategies which involve ranking, continuum, role-playing, and either-or choices, students are asked to weigh specific situations in terms of personal value to themselves. For example, students might be asked to choose whether they would feel worse if they were arrested or if they failed in business. Similarly, they might be asked to rank, from best to worst, three different philosophies on sex and marriage.

Even educators who are critical of the values-clarification movement are quick to concede the range of clarification activities which have proved to be successful among many students, particularly those activities which ask students to think about the meaning of everyday experiences.

Generally, most proponents of values clarification attempt to avoid what they regard as a "pressure-cooker" educational environment. "Why" questions are discouraged as are intense conflicts over issues posed during discussion. As well, students in a values-clarification class are always given the right to "pass" (i.e., to choose not to participate). Alan Lockwood, in a recent article, compares values clarification with the non-directive, client-centered therapy of Carl Rogers, noting that each assumes a learning model which emphasizes non-threatening self-exploration while rejecting conflict or direct-learning models. This parallel is evident in values-clarification's educational goals, outcomes, and strategies and in its view of the teacher-role. For example, both Rogers and Simon see the development of autonomous values as essential to leading a satisfying life. Similarly, both see the achievement of a warm, supportive, accepting approach by the treater or educator as essential to "opening up" the client or learner.

An application of a values-clarification exercise, especially interesting because of its outcome, may be found in a sex-role curriculum developed by David and Myra Sadker. In this curriculum, students are asked to engage in values voting, rank ordering, rating, and other experiences designed to help students clarify their values. One activity asks students to finish sentences, indicating their assumptions about certain sexual attitudes and values. Following their collection of value data, students then discuss the results and reflect upon their choices.

1. When I see a three-year-old boy playing with a doll, I. . . .
2. When I see a three-year-old girl playing with a doll, I. . . .
3. When I see a famous football player doing needlepoint, I. . . .
4. To me, women's liberation. . . .
5. When writing a letter to a woman, I would/would not address her as Ms. because. . . .
6. I would/would not vote for a well-qualified woman to be President because. . . .
7. Aggressive women. . . .
8. Aggressive men. . . .
9. If I had to have an operation, and the doctor scheduled to operate on me was female, I. . . .
10. To me, the phrase "the head of the house" means. . . .
11. If I could eliminate one aspect of sexism in our society, I would choose. . . .
12. The best way to reduce sexism in my school is to. . . .
13. I would/would not vote for a girl to be president of my class because. . . .
14. The treatment given to sex discrimination in the newspapers and television is. . . .
15. To me, a nonsexist book is. . . .
16. I think the women's movement and the movement for equality of other minority groups. . . .[5]

This activity and others actively elicit the subjective values of students rather than impose societal or cultural norms on them. Similarly, there is little attempt to challenge or question the student on the position he or she takes. In the view of Sadker and Sadker, if change is to take place, it emerges naturally as the child becomes uncomfortable with the beliefs he or she publicly articulates in the classroom.

When one of my graduate students tried the Sadker activity in her ninth grade classroom, she found that few students changed the positions they initially wrote down. An exception to this was a boy who, in the course of sharing some rather chauvinist values with other students, suddenly decided that "it was alright for a big football star like O.J. to do needlework as long as he got big yardage." Similarly, another student who first offered that a "man should always be head of his home," later decided that he was "wrong, because mothers now work and sometimes fathers don't like to live with the kids."

As with indoctrinative moral education, there are explicit assumptions made by values-clarification practitioners as to how values are defined as well as how the learning of values takes place:

1. Values are, to a large extent, a matter of personal opinion. No person can tell another person what is right for him or her. While values, in order to be considered as such must meet specific criteria, there exists the assumption that a particular value is neither right nor wrong. Simon has concluded workshops by saying, "You have values, I have values, we all have values." In one workshop I attended, a student asked, "What about Hitler? Does he have values?" "Yes," answered Simon. "Hitler has values, too. I don't like his values, but he might have them, too."
2. Learning, according to values-clarification theorists, is largely a matter of increasing awareness of the self. Values clarification sees the child as developing his or her own values apart from social others rather than accepting society's values.
3. In values clarification, there is the implicit assumption that the moral norms of society have largely broken down, and further, that the moral pluralism of today's society forces individuals to define their own value commitments.

Developmental Learning as Moral Education

Many teachers find the choice between indoctrination and values clarification to be an impossible one to make. Uncomfortable with the method of indoctrination and unwilling to accept the moral relativity (i.e., that an individual's freely-chosen values are right for him or her) of values clarification, the teacher is caught in a pedagogical and moral "no man's land."

It is hoped that developmental moral education, as represented by the authors in this volume, offers an alternative which avoids both the philosophic and psychological problems left unresolved in other systems of moral education. It differs in both philosophy and psychology from indoctrinative and values-clarification models of moral education in two basic ways:

1. It suggests that the teacher should be philosophically guided by universal ethical principles rather than by either societal values or the student's personal values.
2. It suggests that a child's moral learning takes place through the changing of his or her ideas of right and wrong in a series of six moral stages, rather than through the internalization of societal behavior norms or by an increased awareness of his or her own inner values.

Developmental psychology has perhaps been most closely identified with the work of Jean Piaget and his associates. Piaget's research with children postulates that the child's conception of the physical and social world evolves through a sequence of invariant stages (or serial philosophies) of thought. Piaget assumes a radically different metaphor of the development of human knowing (called *epistemology* by philosophers) than would an indoctrination or values-clarification theorist. According to Piaget, knowledge changes through an interactional dialogue between the child and his or her world. Rather than a passive recipient of societal input or an acquirer of self-awareness, the child is conceived of as an active philosopher in the search of a more complete comprehension of his or her physical and social universe. (See Appendix for a synopsis of Piaget's theory.)

Lawrence Kohlberg's theory of moral judgment parallels Piaget's work on logical development. Kohlberg has sought to document an invariant progression of six stages of moral judgment. The stage progression makes three fundamental claims: First, the stages form a universal invariant sequence. That is, the stages progress in the same order. Thus, Stage 3 must follow Stage 2 (4 follows 3, etc.) in any society, subculture, or historical age (Kohlberg, 1977). Also, each stage must possess the characteristic that Piaget calls a "psychological whole." That is, each stage provides a comprehensive theory of moral relationships and claims as well as a complete model of society. Finally, each stage must be defined as more philosophically adequate than are antecedent stages. That is, each higher stage defines a more coherent and rational way of resolving moral conflict. Thus, a higher stage must represent a more moral, adequate means to resolve moral conflicts than do earlier or less mature stages of thinking. The following table provides a synopsis of Kohlberg's six-stage developmental theory.

In the preconventional stages (1 and 2), individuals have a physical conception of morality. At Stage 1, the physical consequences of human action determine right and wrong. What is right is that which is demanded by obedience to superior power. At Stage 2, right action becomes that which satisfies one's own needs. Human relationships are viewed in terms of the market place; reciprocity becomes, "You scratch my back and I'll scratch yours."

The conventional level (Stages 3 and 4) becomes dominant in late preadolescence. Justifying and maintaining the expectations, rules, and standards of the family group, peer group, or nation become important at this level. At Stage 3, individuals have what is called the "good-boy/good-girl" orientation. "Good" behavior is that which helps others and is approved by them. One gains approval by being "nice" or exhibiting behavior which will be approved by others. At Stage 4, there is a shift toward fixed definitions of social duty, concern with firm social rules, and a respect for formal authority. The individual recognizes that laws and other social institutions have clear social utility and are justified in terms of their order-maintaining function.

The post-conventional, or principled, level (Stages 5 and 6), first appears in adolescence and is characterized by a major thrust toward autonomous moral principles. These principles have validity apart from the authority of the group or concrete individuals. The principled thinker is able to evaluate, through tests of more general justice principles, the moral validity of concrete social rules and norms. At Stage 5, individuals have a legalistic-contract orientation, generally with utilitarian overtones. Law has a basis in consent and the welfare of citizens rather than simply, as at Stage 4, in respect for authority. Laws which are not constitutional, which violate human rights, or which are not in the general interest are judged to be invalid. At Stage 6, Kohlberg suggests, there is a basis for rational agreement to moral principles. There is an orientation toward ethical principles appealing to logical consistency, comprehensiveness, and universality.

Basis of Moral Judgments	Levels	Stages of Development	Typical Responses
I	Moral value resides in external, quasi-physical happening, in bad acts, or in quasi-physical needs rather than in persons and standards.	*Stage 1:* Obedience and punishment orientation. Egocentric deference to superior power or prestige or to a trouble-avoiding set. Objective responsibility.	"I'll do it 'cause I don't want to do more time." "I do it 'cause I want to keep out of trouble."
		Stage 2: Naively egoistic orientation. Right action is that which instrumentally satisfies the self's needs and occasionally others' needs. Awareness of relativism of value to each actor's needs and perspectives. Naive egalitarianism and orientation to exchange and reciprocity.	"I'm number one. I look after me. If you help me out, maybe I'll help you sometime."
II	Moral value resides in performing good or right roles, in maintaining the conventional order and the expectancies of others.	*Stage 3:* "Good-boy" orientation to approval and to pleasing and helping others. Conformity to stereotypical images of majority or natural role behavior, and judgment by intentions.	"Sure I'd help another guy out. I'd be thinking about how he'd be feeling. Any decent person would help him."
		Stage 4: Authority and social-order maintenance orientation. Orientation to "doing duty" and to showing respect for authority and maintaining the given social order for its own sake. Regard for earned expectations of others.	"Look, you're supposed to help others. It's like a rule. Without people doing their jobs, society couldn't function."
III	Moral value resides in conformity by the self to shared or shareable standards, rights, or duties.	*Stage 5:* Contractual, legalistic orientation. Recognition of an arbitrary element or starting point in rules or expectations for the sake of agreement. Duty defined in terms of contract, general avoidance of violation of the will or rights of others, and majority will and welfare.	"It's a law that the people consented to. We all have an obligation to work through the agreed structure to get laws which appear wrong changed. When an injustice is committed, it is best to work through the system to end it."
		Stage 6: Conscience or principle orientation. Orientation not only to actually ordained social rules but to principles of choice involving appeal to logical universality and consistency. Orientation to conscience as a directing agent and to mutual respect and trust.	"The law should be subordinate to higher principles of justice. One should act in accordance with these superordinate principles rather than maintain simple conformity to the law."

The principles are abstract rather than concrete. These principles—of justice and ideal reciprocity, the equality of human rights, and the respect for the dignity of human beings as individual persons—are universal.

Kohlberg and his research colleagues suggested that achievement of particular moral stages require specific, logical capacities as described by Piaget (in Appendix). For each moral stage, there exists a necessary, but not sufficient, logical capacity. That is, attainment of a specific logical stage does not ensure attainment of a moral stage. Many individuals who are capable of abstract or formal operational thought (Piaget's highest stage) are morally primitive. The case of the German nuclear physicists who almost created the atom bomb for Hitler provides a frightening example of such gaps between logical and moral thought. That a person has sufficient intelligence to create an atomic weapon does *not* mean that he or she possesses the moral wisdom to decide the context in which it might be used. An educational system which has divided technical from moral education has, perhaps, created an unnecessary gap in the thinking of many citizens who operate with scientific logic in technical areas while still thinking in a morally immature manner.

The evidence for Kohlberg's theory rests primarily on a longitudinal study of fifty-six male subjects interviewed once every three years over twenty-four years. Kohlberg suggests that these interviews document the stepwise interpretation of the development of moral thought. Each of the subjects in his study was found to mature towards higher-stage thinking in each of the sequential interviews. While most of his subjects tended to stabilize, in terms of moral thought, in their mid-twenties, a few continued to mature through their third decade of life.

Kohlberg claims that while the content of thinking may fluctuate (for example, one young man in the study was politically conservative at eighteen and a radical activist at twenty-five), change in the structure of thought follows a step-wise progression. Here, Kohlberg describes the shifts in one individual, given the code name "Richard." Richard is responding to a dilemma wherein a terminally ill woman, suffering great pain, asks to die.

> At age 13, Richard said about mercy killing, "If she requests it, it's really up to her. She is in such terrible pain, just the same as people are always putting animals out of their pain." In general, his response showed a mixture of Stage 2 and Stage 3 concepts concerning the value of life. At 16, he said, "It's not a right or privilege of man to decide who shall live and who should die. God put life into everybody on earth and you're taking away something from that person that came directly from God, . . . it's almost destroying a part of God when you kill a person." Richard displayed a Stage 4 concept of life as sacred in terms of its place in a categorical moral or religious order. The value of human life is universal but it is not an autonomous human value—it is still dependent upon something else, upon request for God and God's authority. At this stage, moral value is defined by a conventional order that is maintained by fixed rules, laws, and authority.
>
> While Richard confused the value of life with authority at Stage 4, he

> began to make these distinctions as he aged, which can be seen in his responses when he was 20.
>
> "It's her own choice. I think there are certain rights and privileges that go along with being a human being. I am a human being and have certain desires for life and I think everybody else does too. You have a world of which you are the center, and everybody else does too and in that sense we're all equal."
>
> Richard's response is clearly Stage 5, in that the value of life is defined in terms of equal and universal human rights in a context of relativity ("You have a world of which you are the center and in that sense we're all equal."), as well as a concern for utility or welfare consequences. At 24, Richard reached Stage 6. He answered the question as follows:
>
> "A human life takes precedence over any other moral or legal value, whoever it is. A human life has inherent value whether or not it is valued by a particular individual. The worth of an individual human being is central. . . ."[6]

Similarly, cross-sectional analysis indicates that in a variety of cultures development occurs through the same sequence. In contrast, both the rate of growth and eventual adult stage differ markedly. In both Western and Eastern urban societies, large numbers of adolescents reach at least the conventional stages of moral thought. In rural, extremely isolated villages, however, even adults rarely achieve Stage 3 moral thought.

These differences in rates of development are explained by the interactional effect of the environment upon moral development. While moral thinking cannot be taught directly, certain environmental conditions determine the speed of development and the eventual stage attained. Generally, environments encouraging moral dialogue and interchanges are associated with rapid moral development. These would presumably be absent in an isolated village society. Similarly, environments perceived as just or legitimate are associated with rapid positive moral change as are environments encouraging interpersonal role-taking and empathy.

As illustrated in detail in Part Two of this volume, there have been numerous documented experiments designed to apply this theoretical system to the problem of moral education. The first clinical experiment in developmental moral education was conducted by Moshe Blatt, at that time a doctoral student at the University of Chicago as well as a Sunday Hebrew School teacher. Blatt suggested to Kohlberg that it might be possible to change the reasoning of his students by exposing them to dilemma situations and discussions. Using a pre and post test design, Blatt found that his students had changed nearly one-third of a moral stage over a period of several months. Later studies replicated these results with a variety of students of different ages, sexes, ethnic backgrounds, and family experiences. Subsequent follow-ups indicated that students who "changed" in the discussion groups maintained their new reasoning for several years after the intervention. This indicated that the discussion groups had effected more than the "language" of the students involved.

To briefly illustrate the approach used by Blatt and to give the reader the "flavor" of developmental moral education, let me offer an example from a discussion group led by Blatt which deals with an issue of whether a person has the moral obligation to inconvenience oneself to help a person in need. In this dilemma a man decides not to give his car to another man whose son (Mike) has been seriously hurt in a car accident, because by lending the car, he will miss an important job interview.

Mr. Blatt: What is the problem? Was the man legally wrong for refusing to drive Mr. Jones and Mike to the hospital?
Student A: It's his car, he doesn't have to drive.
Mr. B: Well, Mike was hurt. You said no, he's not legally responsible, because, why not?
Student A: Because it's his car.
Mr. B: It's his car. It's his property, and he has the right of property and he can legally . . .
Student B: But a life is at stake.
Mr. B: Okay. It's not so easy. Like, here is property . . . but here is life, so the conflict here is between life—Mike's life—or that man's car.
Student B: But if Mike died, then that guy could be charged with murder, because, you know. . . .
Student C: No, he couldn't. (argument over whether he could or could not be charged with murder)
Mr. B: But do people think this man has a right, a legal right, to refuse to give Mr. Jones the car?
Student D: Does that man have children? He probably has to support a family, he's got a family, he can't just. . . .
Student E: So? He can always find a job. . . .
Mr. B: The question is, do you think that the man who had the job, wouldn't he understand if you came up to him and said, "Look, I was here, I wanted to be on time, but I saw this boy bleeding, and I wanted to help him out." Don't you think he would understand? (chorus of "yes" and "no")
Student F: No, because if you're supposed to go on the job . . .
Student G: You could make him show some proof.
Student F: Bring the kid there when he's well.
Mr. B: All right. This man, who refused to give the car was not legally wrong. You couldn't take him to court. But do you think he was wrong in any way? (chorus of "yes")
Student B: He was just all wrong because if that kid died, I don't know what he'd be charged with, but he'd be charged with something. There's something, I don't know what it is, but there's something they could charge him with.

Dr. Blatt in these discussions seeks to actively challenge the thinking of the students. He Socratically questions his students' initial assumptions about the man's responsibilities to the hurt boy, seeking to get them to actively consider Mike's right to life as well as the man's right to his car ("Do you think this man has a right to refuse his car?").

His educational strategy differs in several ways from that which might be employed by a moral educator trained in either indoctrination or values-clarification methods:

1. There is an assumption that there is a "right" answer to the dilemma, but that this "answer" reflects a universalizable ethical principle of fairness, rather than being a product of a social norm or a purely individual decision. A developmental moral educator would reject the notion that "what the law says" defines necessarily what is right, as he or she would reject the idea that the man's decision is simply a matter of his "personal feelings or choice."
2. Dr. Blatt seeks to create a certain amount of intellectual conflict in order to challenge his students towards more mature resolutions of the dilemma. Instead of "showing them" the "right" answer (as society might see it) or allowing the students to feel comfortable with their first arguments, the developmental educator follows the Socratic strategy of finding truth through questions.
3. The method assumes, that while society changes and mores and customs relate to particular periods, the ultimate values of humanity, as well as the principles defining what is right, remain constant. To illustrate, the fact that a society has a totalitarian leader does not change what *should* be our moral obligation to our fellow human beings.

Conclusion: Cautions to "Consumers" of Moral Education Theory

According to John Dewey, to make education a reflective science, the educator must seek to resolve three questions:

1. What should be taught? (philosophy)
2. How do children learn? (psychology)
3. What type of society do we live in and wish to live in? (sociology)

Dewey's dictum seems especially appropriate to those educators brave enough to face the intellectual perils implicit in serious efforts at moral education. To be a wise and effective educator one must be at once a philosopher, psychologist, and social theorist. To reject these roles is to deny the teacher's mandate to set educational ends and to be responsible for confronting the philosophical, psychological, and social questions implied in moral education. To deny the importance of philosophy is to accept the direction of "the system" or perhaps of personal whim. To reject psychology as a tool of teaching is to fall back on unverifiable and unreproduceable "teacher tricks." To fail to define educational goals in terms of a sense of history is to accept society as it is and not to point towards what it could be.

The three "systems" of moral education discussed in this chapter make rather different assumptions about what is right, about how children learn, and about the status quo. These differences are summarized on page 34.

	Indoctrination	Values Clarification	Developmental Moral Education
What is right?	Determined by societal and cultural norms	Determined by individual through reflection on alternative value premises	Determined by philosophic rightness. Ethic principles should be universally valid
How children learn or change moral ideas	Through repetition, association, modeling, reward, and example	Through self-analysis and awareness of implications of value choices	Through conflict, dialogue, role-taking, and moral interchange
State of society	Under threat, but capable to return to traditional values	In state of more or less continual value flux	While societal norms and mores are subject to change, moral principles are eternal

A decision to adopt any one of these models of moral education (or for that matter any system of moral education) assumes an intellectual confrontation with its essential premises and assumptions. While the creation of a social philosophy is beyond the abilities of most professional philosophers, let alone teachers faced with twenty-five or more class periods a week, nevertheless most teachers feel they have an obligation to question the assumptions underlying any curriculum they use.

Needless to say, the choice of a curriculum model in the field of moral education reflects critical assumptions of value and fact. This volume represents an effort to present and to critically evaluate developmental moral education as a reflection of a unique set of philosophic, psychological, and social propositions. It seeks to present developmental moral education as an alternative to existing forms of moral education. We would be disappointed, however, if readers accepted the propositions argued here too readily. Similarly, we would be disappointed if they were rejected without serious intellectual consideration. Developmental education is at this point based on an evolving, positive, but by no means complete, paradigm. In order for the field to develop, we require ongoing intellectual dialogue and reflection. With that in mind, the following chapters are aimed at accomplishing these goals: to present a succinct explanation of developmental moral education theory and research; to provide educators with a methodology for curriculum use; to include some of the most responsible integrations with other methods; and to give reasoned and perceptive criticisms of the developmental approach to moral education. We hope they will be read in the spirit of active inquiry, rather than as a dogma to be uncritically applied.

Notes

1. *McGuffey's Fifth Eclectic Reader* (New York: American Book, 1879): 69–71.

2. Herschel Alt and Edith Alt, *Russia's Children* (New York: Bookman's Associates, 1959): 87–88.

3. *Values Concepts and Techniques*, ed. Felton (Washington, D.C.: National Education Association, 1976): 135–36.

4. Ibid., p. 36.

5. Ibid., p. 197.

6. Lawrence Kohlberg, *Psychology and the Process of Schooling in the Next Decade*, ed. M. Reynolds (Minneapolis: University of Minnesota Department of Audio-Visual Extension, 1972).

The Cognitive-Developmental Approach to Moral Education

Lawrence Kohlberg, Director of the Center for Moral Education, Graduate School of Education, Harvard University.

In this article, I present an overview of the cognitive-developmental approach to moral education and its research foundations, compare it with other approaches, and report the experimental work my colleagues and I are doing to apply the approach.

I. Moral Stages

The cognitive-developmental approach was fully stated for the first time by John Dewey. The approach is called *cognitive* because it recognizes that moral education, like intellectual education, has its basis in stimulating the *active thinking* of the child about moral issues and decisions. It is called *developmental* because it sees the aims of moral education as movement through moral stages. According to Dewey:

> The aim of education is growth or *development*, both intellectual and moral. Ethical and psychological principles can aid the school in the *greatest of all constructions—the building of a free and powerful character*. Only knowledge of the *order and connection of the stages in psychological development can insure this*. Education is the work of *supplying the conditions* which will enable the psychological functions to mature in the freest and fullest manner.[1]

Dewey postulated three levels of moral development: 1) the *pre-moral* or *preconventional* level "of behavior motivated by biological and social impulses with results for morals," 2) the *conventional* level of behavior "in which the individual accepts with little critical reflection the standards of his group," and 3) the *autonomous* level of behavior in which "conduct is guided by the individual thinking and judging for himself whether a purpose is good, and does not accept the standard of his group without reflection."*

* These levels correspond roughly to our three major levels: the preconventional, the conventional, and the principled. Similar levels were propounded by William McDougall, Leonard Hobhouse, and James Mark Baldwin.

Dewey's thinking about moral stages was theoretical. Building upon his prior studies of cognitive stages, Jean Piaget made the first effort to define stages of moral reasoning in children through actual interviews and through observations of children (in games with rules).[2] Using this interview material, Piaget defined the pre-moral, the conventional, and the autonomous levels as follows: 1) the *pre-moral stage*, where there was no sense of obligation to rules; 2) the *heteronomous stage*, where the right was literal obedience to rules and an equation of obligation with submission to power and punishment (roughly ages 4–8); and 3) the *autonomous stage*, where the purpose and consequences of following rules are considered and obligation is based on reciprocity and exchange (roughly ages 8–12).*

In 1955 I started to redefine and validate (through longitudinal and cross-cultural study) the Dewey-Piaget levels and stages. The resulting stages are presented in Table 1. (See page 50-51.)

We claim to have validated the stages defined in Table 1. The notion that stages can be *validated* by longitudinal study implies that stages have definite empirical characteristics.[3] The concept of stages (as used by Piaget and myself) implies the following characteristics:

1. Stages are "structured wholes," or organized systems of thought. Individuals are *consistent* in level of moral judgment.
2. Stages form an *invariant sequence*. Under all conditions except extreme trauma, movement is always forward, never backward. Individuals never skip stages; movement is always to the next stage up.
3. Stages are "hierarchical integrations." Thinking at a higher stage includes or comprehends within it lower-stage thinking. There is a tendency to function at or prefer the highest stage available.

Each of these characteristics has been demonstrated for moral stages. Stages are defined by responses to a set of verbal moral dilemmas classified according to an elaborate scoring scheme. Validating studies include:

- a twenty-year study of fifty Chicago-area boys, middle- and working-class. Initially interviewed at ages 10–16, they have been reinterviewed at three-year intervals thereafter
- a small, six-year longitudinal study of Turkish village and city boys of the same age
- a variety of other cross-sectional studies in Canada, Britain, Israel, Taiwan, Yucatan, Honduras, and India.

With regard to the structured whole or consistency criterion, we have found that more than 50 percent of an individual's thinking is always at one stage, with the remainder at the next adjacent stage (which he is leaving or which he is moving into).

With regard to invariant sequence, our longitudinal results have been presented in the *American Journal of Orthopsychiatry* (see footnote 8) and indicate that on every retest

*Piaget's stages correspond to our first three stages: Stage 0 (pre-moral), Stage 1 (heteronomous), and Stage 2 (instrumental reciprocity).

individuals were either at the same stage as three years earlier or had moved up. This was true in Turkey as well as in the United States.

With regard to the hierarchical integration criterion, it has been demonstrated that adolescents exposed to written statements at each of the six stages comprehend or correctly put in their own words all statements at or below their own stage but fail to comprehend any statements more than one stage above their own.[4] Some individuals comprehend the next stage above their own; some do not. Adolescents prefer (or rank as best) the highest stage they can comprehend.

To understand moral stages, it is important to clarify their relations to stage of logic or intelligence, on the one hand, and to moral behavior on the other. Maturity of moral judgment is not highly correlated with IQ or verbal intelligence (correlations are only in the thirties, accounting for 10 percent of the variance). Cognitive development, in the stage sense, however, is more important for moral development than such correlations suggest. Piaget has found that after the child learns to speak there are three major stages of reasoning: the intuitive, the concrete operational, and the formal operational. At around age seven, the child enters the stage of concrete logical thought. He can make logical inferences, classify, and handle quantitative relations about concrete things. In adolescence individuals usually enter the stage of formal operations. At this stage they can reason abstractly, i.e., consider all possibilities, form hypotheses, deduce implications from hypotheses, and test them against reality.*

Since moral reasoning clearly is reasoning, advanced moral reasoning depends upon advanced logical reasoning; a person's logical stage puts a certain ceiling on the moral stage he can attain. A person whose logical stage is only concrete operational is limited to the preconventional moral stages (Stages 1 and 2). A person whose logical stage is only partially formal operational is limited to the conventional moral stages (Stages 3 and 4). While logical development is necessary for moral development and sets limits to it, most individuals are higher in logical stage than they are in moral stage. As an example, over 50 percent of late adolescents and adults are capable of full formal reasoning, but only 10 percent of these adults (all formal operational) display principled (Stages 5 and 6) moral reasoning.

The moral stages are *structures of moral judgment* or *moral reasoning. Structures* of moral judgment must be distinguished from the *content* of moral judgment. As an example, we cite responses to a dilemma used in our various studies to identify moral stage. The dilemma raises the issue of stealing a drug to save a dying woman. The inventor of the drug is selling it for ten times what it costs him to make it. The woman's husband cannot raise the money, and the seller refuses to lower the price or wait for payment. What should the husband do?

The choice endorsed by a subject (steal, don't steal) is called the *content* of his moral judgment in the situation. His reasoning about the choice defines the structure of

*Many adolescents and adults only partially attain the stage of formal operations. They do consider all the actual relations of one thing to another at the same time, but they do not consider all possibilities and form abstract hypotheses. A few do not advance this far, remaining "concrete operational."

his moral judgment. This reasoning centers on the following 10 universal moral values or issues of concern to persons in these moral dilemmas:

1. Punishment
2. Property
3. Roles and concerns of affection
4. Roles and concerns of authority
5. Law
6. Life
7. Liberty
8. Distributive justice
9. Truth
10. Sex

A moral choice involves choosing between two (or more) of these values as they *conflict* in concrete situations of choice.

The stage or structure of a person's moral judgment defines: 1) *what* he finds valuable in each of these moral issues (life, law), i.e., how he defines the value, and 2) *why* he finds it valuable, i.e., the reasons he gives for valuing it. As an example, at Stage 1 life is valued in terms of the power or possessions of the person involved; at Stage 2, for its usefulness in satisfying the needs of the individual in question or others; at Stage 3, in terms of the individual's relations with others and their valuation of him; at Stage 4, in terms of social or religious law. Only at Stages 5 and 6 is each life seen as inherently worthwhile, aside from other considerations.

Moral Judgment vs. Moral Action

Having clarified the nature of stages of moral *judgment*, we must consider the relation of moral judgment to moral *action*. If logical reasoning is a necessary but not sufficient condition for mature moral judgment, mature moral judgment is a necessary but not sufficient condition for mature moral action. One cannot follow moral principles if one does not understand (or believe in) moral principles. However, one can reason in terms of principles and not live up to these principles. As an example, Richard Krebs and I found that only 15 percent of students showing some principled thinking cheated as compared to 55 percent of conventional subjects and 70 percent of preconventional subjects.[5] Nevertheless, 15 percent of the principled subjects did cheat, suggesting that factors additional to moral judgment are necessary for principled moral reasoning to be translated into "moral action." Partly, these factors include the situation and its pressures. Partly, what happens depends upon the individual's motives and emotions. Partly, what the individual does depends upon a general sense of will, purpose, or "ego strength." As an example of the role of will or ego strength in moral behavior, we may cite the study by Krebs: Slightly more than half of his conventional subjects cheated. These subjects were also divided by a measure of attention/will. Only 26 percent of the "strong-willed" conventional subjects cheated; however, 74 percent of the "weak-willed" subjects cheated.

If maturity of moral reasoning is only one factor in moral behavior, why does the cognitive-developmental approach to moral education focus so heavily upon moral reasoning? For the following reasons:

1. Moral judgment, while only one factor in moral behavior, is the single most important or influential factor yet discovered in moral behavior.
2. While other factors influence moral behavior, moral judgment is the only distinctively *moral* factor in moral behavior. To illustrate, we noted that the Krebs study indicated that "strong-willed" conventional stage subjects resisted cheating more than "weak-willed" subjects. For those at a preconventional level of moral reasoning, however, "will" had an opposite effect. "Strong-willed" Stages 1 and 2 subjects cheated more, not less, than "weak-willed" subjects, i.e., they had the "courage of their (amoral) convictions" that it was worthwhile to cheat. "Will," then, is an important factor in moral behavior, but it is not distinctively moral; it becomes moral only when informed by mature moral judgment.
3. Moral judgment change is long-range or irreversible; a higher stage is never lost. Moral behavior as such is largely situational and reversible or "losable" in new situations.

II. Aims of Moral and Civic Education

Moral psychology describes what moral development is, as studied empirically. Moral education must also consider moral philosophy, which strives to tell us what moral development ideally *ought to be*. Psychology finds an invariant sequence of moral stages; moral philosophy must be invoked to answer whether a later stage is a better stage. The "stage" of senescence and death follows the "stage" of adulthood, but that does not mean that senescence and death are better. Our claim that the latest or principled stages of moral reasoning are morally better stages, then, must rest on considerations of moral philosophy.

The tradition of moral philosophy to which we appeal is the liberal or rational tradition, in particular the "formalistic" or "deontological" tradition running from Immanuel Kant to John Rawls.[6] Central to this tradition is the claim that an adequate morality is *principled*, i.e., that it makes judgments in terms of *universal* principles applicable to all mankind. *Principles* are to be distinguished from *rules*. Conventional morality is grounded on rules, primarily "thou shalt nots" such as are represented by the Ten Commandments, prescriptions of kinds of actions. Principles are, rather, universal guides to making a moral decision. An example is Kant's "categorical imperative," formulated in two ways. The first is the maxim of respect for human personality, "Act always toward the other as an end, not as a means." The second is the maxim of universalization, "Choose only as you would be willing to have everyone choose in your situation." Principles like that of Kant's state the formal conditions of a moral choice or action. In the dilemma in which a woman is dying because a druggist refuses to release his drug for less than the stated price, the druggist is not acting morally, though he is not violating the ordinary moral rules (he is not actually stealing or murdering). But he is violating principles: He is treating the woman simply as a means to his ends of profit, and he is not choosing as he would wish anyone to choose (if the druggist were in the dying woman's place, he would not want a druggist to choose as he is choosing). Under most circumstances, choice in terms of conventional moral rules and choice in terms of principles coincide. Ordinarily, principles dictate not stealing (avoiding stealing is implied by acting in terms of a regard for others as ends and in terms of what one would want everyone to do). In a situation where stealing is the only means to save a life, however, principles contradict the ordinary rules and would dictate stealing. Unlike rules which are supported by social authority, principles are freely chosen by the individual because of their intrinsic moral validity.*

The conception that a moral choice is a choice made in terms of moral principles is related to the claim of liberal moral philosophy that moral principles are ultimately principles of justice. In essence, moral conflicts are conflicts between the claims of persons, and principles for resolving these claims are principles of justice, "for giving each his due." Central to justice are the demands of *liberty*, *equality*, and *reciprocity*. At every moral stage, there is a concern for justice. The most damning statement a school child can make about a teacher is that "he's not fair." At each higher stage, however, the conception of justice is reorganized. At Stage 1, justice is punishing the bad in terms of "an eye for an eye and a tooth for a tooth." At Stage 2, it is exchanging favors and goods in an equal manner. At Stages 3 and 4, it is treating people as they desire in terms of the conventional rules. At Stage 5, it is recognized that all rules and laws flow from justice, from a social contract between the governors and the governed designed to protect the equal rights of all. At Stage 6, personally chosen moral principles are also principles of justice, the principles any member of a society would choose for that society if he did not know what his position was to be in the society and in which he might be the least advantaged.[7] Principles chosen from this point of view are, first, the maximum liberty compatible with the like liberty of others and, second, no inequalities of goods and respect which are not to the benefit of all, including the least advantaged.

As an example of stage progression in the orientation to justice, we may take judgments about capital punishment.[8] Capital punishment is only firmly rejected at the two principled stages, when the notion of justice as vengeance or retribution is abandoned. At the sixth stage, capital punishment is not condoned even if it may have some useful deterrent effect in promoting law and order. This is because it is not a punishment we would choose for a society if we assumed we had as much chance of being born into the position of a criminal or murderer as being born into the position of a law abider.

Why are decisions based on universal principles of justice better decisions? Because they are decisions on which all moral men could agree. When decisions are based on conventional moral rules, men will disagree, since they adhere to conflicting systems of rules dependent on culture and social position. Throughout history men have killed one another in the name of conflicting moral rules and values, most recently in Vietnam and the Middle East. Truly moral or just resolutions of conflicts require principles which are, or can be, universalizable.

Alternative Approaches

We have given a philosophic rationale for stage advance as the aim of moral education. Given this rationale, the developmental approach to moral education can avoid the

*Not all freely chosen values or rules are principles, however. Hitler chose the "rule," "exterminate the enemies of the Aryan race," but such a rule is not a universalizable principle.

problems inherent in the other two major approaches to moral education. The first alternative approach is that of indoctrinative moral education, the preaching and imposition of the rules and values of the teacher and his culture on the child. In America, when this indoctrinative approach has been developed in a systematic manner, it has usually been termed "character education."

Moral values, in the character education approach, are preached or taught in terms of what may be called the "bag of virtues." In the classic studies of character by Hugh Hartshorne and Mark May, the virtues chosen were honesty, service, and self-control.[9] It is easy to get superficial consensus on such a bag of virtues—until one examines in detail the list of virtues involved and the details of their definition. Is the Hartshorne and May bag more adequate than the Boy Scout bag (a Scout should be honest, loyal, reverent, clean, brave, etc.)? When one turns to the details of defining each virtue, one finds equal uncertainty or difficulty in reaching consensus. Does honesty mean one should not steal to save a life? Does it mean that a student should not help another student with his homework?

Character education and other forms of indoctrinative moral education have aimed at teaching universal values (it is assumed that honesty or service are desirable traits for all men in all societies), but the detailed definitions used are relative; they are defined by the opinions of the teacher and the conventional culture and rest on the authority of the teacher for their justification. In this sense character education is close to the unreflective valuings by teachers which constitute the hidden curriculum of the school.* Because of the current unpopularity of indoctrinative approaches to moral education, a family of approaches called "values clarification" has become appealing to teachers. Values clarification takes the first step implied by a rational approach to moral education: the eliciting of the child's own judgment or opinion about issues or situations in which values conflict, rather than imposing the teacher's opinion on him. Values clarification, however, does not attempt to go further than eliciting awareness of values; it is assumed that becoming more self-aware about one's values is an end in itself. Fundamentally, the definition of the end of values education as self-awareness derives from a belief in ethical relativity held by many value-clarifiers. As stated by Peter Engel, "One must contrast value clarification and value inculcation. Value clarification implies the principle that in the consideration of values there is no single correct answer." Within these premises of "no correct answer," children are to discuss moral dilemmas in such a way as to reveal different values and discuss their value differences with each other. The teacher is to stress that "our values are different," not that one value is more adequate than others. If this program is systematically followed, students will themselves become relativists, believing there is no "right" moral answer. For instance, a student caught cheating might argue that he did nothing wrong, since his own hierarchy of values, which may be different from that of the teacher, made it right for him to cheat.

Like values clarification, the cognitive-developmental approach to moral education stresses open or Socratic peer discussion of value dilemmas. Such discussion, however, has an aim: stimulation of movement to the next stage of moral reasoning. Like

*As an example of the "hidden curriculum," we may cite a second-grade classroom. My son came home from this classroom one day saying he did not want to be "one of the bad boys." Asked "Who are the bad boys?" he replied, "The ones who don't put their books back and get yelled at."

values clarification, the developmental approach opposes indoctrination. Stimulation of movement to the next stage of reasoning is not indoctrinative, for the following reasons:

1. Change is in the way of reasoning rather than in the particular beliefs involved.
2. Students in a class are at different stages; the aim is to aid movement of each to the next stage, not convergence on a common pattern.
3. The teacher's own opinion is neither stressed nor invoked as authoritative. It enters in only as one of many opinions, hopefully one of those at a next higher stage.
4. The notion that some judgments are more adequate than others is communicated. Fundamentally, however, this means that the student is encouraged to articulate a position which seems most adequate to him and to judge the adequacy of the reasoning of others.

In addition to having more definite aims than values clarification, the moral development approach restricts value education to that which is moral or, more specifically, to justice. This is for two reasons. First, it is not clear that the whole realm of personal, political, and religious values is a realm which is nonrelative, i.e., in which there are universals and a direction of development. Second, it is not clear that the public school has a right or mandate to develop values in general.* In our view, value education in the public schools should be restricted to that which the school has the right and mandate to develop: an awareness of justice, or of the rights of others in our Constitutional system. While the Bill of Rights prohibits the teaching of religious beliefs, or of specific value systems, it does not prohibit the teaching of the awareness of rights and principles of justice fundamental to the Constitution itself.

When moral education is recognized as centered in justice and differentiated from value education or affective education, it becomes apparent that moral and civic education are much the same thing. This equation, taken for granted by the classic philosophers of education from Plato and Aristotle to Dewey, is basic to our claim that a concern for moral education is central to the educational objectives of social studies.

The term *civic education* is used to refer to social studies as more than the study of the facts and concepts of social science, history, and civics. It is education for the analytic understanding, value principles, and motivation necessary for a citizen in a democracy if democracy is to be an effective process. It is political education. Civic or political education means the stimulation of development of more advanced patterns of reasoning about political and social decisions and their implementation in action. These patterns are patterns of moral reasoning. Our studies show that reasoning and decision making about political decisions are directly derivative of broader patterns of moral reasoning and decision making. We have interviewed high school and college students about concrete political situations involving laws to govern open housing, civil disobedience

*Restriction of deliberate value education to the moral may be clarified by our example of the second-grade teacher who made tidying up of books a matter of moral indoctrination. Tidiness is a value, but it is not a moral value. Cheating is a moral issue, intrinsically one of fairness. It involves issues of violation of trust and taking advantage. Failing to tidy the room may under certain conditions be an issue of fairness, when it puts an undue burden on others. If it is handled by the teacher as a matter of cooperation among the group in this sense, it is a legitimate focus of deliberate moral education. If it is not, it simply represents the arbitrary imposition of the teacher's values on the child.

for peace in Vietnam, free press rights to publish what might disturb national order, and distribution of income through taxation. We find that reasoning on these political decisions can be classified according to moral stage and that an individual's stage on political dilemmas is at the same level as on nonpolitical moral dilemmas (euthanasia, violating authority to maintain trust in a family, stealing a drug to save one's dying wife). Turning from reasoning to action, similar findings are obtained. In 1968 a study was made of those who sat in at the University of California, Berkeley, administration building and those who did not in the Free Speech Movement crisis. Of those at Stage 6, 80 percent sat in, believing that principles of free speech were being compromised, and that all efforts to compromise and negotiate with the administration had failed. In contrast, only 15 percent of the conventional (Stage 3 or Stage 4) subjects sat in. (Stage 5 subjects were in between.)

From a psychological side, then, political development is part of moral development. The same is true from the philosophic side. In the *Republic,* Plato sees political education as part of a broader education for moral justice and finds a rationale for such education in terms of universal philosophic principles rather than the demands of a particular society. More recently, Dewey claims the same.

In historical perspective, America was the first nation whose government was publicly founded on postconventional principles of justice, rather than upon the authority central to conventional moral reasoning. At the time of our founding, postconventional or principled moral and political reasoning was the possession of the minority, as it still is. Today, as in the time of our founding, the majority of our adults are at the conventional level, particularly the "law and order" (fourth) moral stage. (Every few years the Gallup Poll circulates the Bill of Rights unidentified, and every year it is turned down.) The Founding Fathers intuitively understood this without benefit of our elaborate social science research; they constructed a document designing a government which would maintain principles of justice and the rights of man even though principled men were not the men in power. The machinery included checks and balances, the independent judiciary, and freedom of the press. Most recently, this machinery found its use at Watergate. The tragedy of Richard Nixon, as Harry Truman said long ago, was that he never understood the Constitution (a Stage 5 document), but the Constitution understood Richard Nixon.*

Watergate, then, is not some sign of moral decay of the nation, but rather of the fact that understanding and action in support of justice principles are still the possession of a minority of our society. Insofar as there is moral decay, it represents the weakening of conventional morality in the face of social and value conflict today. This can lead the less fortunate adolescent to fixation at the preconventional level, the more fortunate to movement to principles. We find a larger proportion of youths at the principled level today than was the case in their fathers' day, but also a larger proportion at the preconventional level.

Given this state, moral and civic education in the schools becomes a more urgent

*No public or private word or deed of Nixon ever rose above Stage 4, the "law and order" stage. His last comments in the White House were of wonderment that the Republican Congress could turn on him after so many Stage 2 exchanges of favors in getting them elected.

task. In the high school today, one often hears both preconventional adolescents and those beginning to move beyond convention sounding the same note of disaffection for the school. While our political institutions are in principle Stage 5 (i.e., vehicles for maintaining universal rights through the democratic process), our schools have traditionally been Stage 4 institutions of convention and authority. Today more than ever, democratic schools systematically engaged in civic education are required.

Our approach to moral and civic education relates the study of law and government to the actual creation of a democratic school in which moral dilemmas are discussed and resolved in a manner which will stimulate moral development.

Planned Moral Education

For many years, moral development was held by psychologists to be primarily a result of family upbringing and family conditions. In particular, conditions of affection and authority in the home were believed to be critical, some balance of warmth and firmness being optimal for moral development. This view arises if morality is conceived as an internalization of the arbitrary rules of parents and culture, since such acceptance must be based on affection and respect for parents as authorities rather than on the rational nature of the rules involved.

Studies of family correlates of moral stage development do not support this internalization view of the conditions for moral development. Instead, they suggest that the conditions for moral development in homes and schools are similar and that the conditions are consistent with cognitive-developmental theory. In the cognitive-developmental view, morality is a natural product of a universal human tendency toward empathy or role taking, toward putting oneself in the shoes of other conscious beings. It is also a product of a universal human concern for justice, for reciprocity or equality in the relation of one person to another. As an example, when my son was 4, he became a morally principled vegetarian and refused to eat meat, resisting all parental persuasion to increase his protein intake. His reason was, "It's bad to kill animals." His moral commitment to vegetarianism was not taught or acquired from parental authority; it was the result of the universal tendency of the young self to project its consciousness and values into other living things, other selves. My son's vegetarianism also involved a sense of justice, revealed when I read him a book about Eskimos in which a real hunting expedition was described. His response was to say, "Daddy, there is one kind of meat I would eat—Eskimo meat. It's all right to eat Eskimos because they eat animals." This natural sense of justice or reciprocity was Stage 1—an eye for an eye, a tooth for a tooth. My son's sense of the value of life was also Stage 1 and involved no differentiation between human personality and physical life. His morality, though Stage 1, was, however, natural and internal. Moral development past Stage 1, then, is not an internalization but the reconstruction of role taking and conceptions of justice toward greater adequacy. These reconstructions occur in order to achieve a better match between the child's own moral structures and the structures of the social and moral situations he confronts. We divide these conditions of match into two kinds: those dealing with moral discussions and communication and those dealing with the total moral environment or atmosphere in which the child lives.

In terms of moral discussion, the important conditions appear to be:

1. exposure to the next higher stage of reasoning;
2. exposure to situations posing problems and contradictions for the child's current moral structure, leading to dissatisfaction with his current level;
3. an atmosphere of interchange and dialogue combining the first two conditions, in which conflicting moral views are compared in an open manner.

Studies of families in India and America suggest that morally advanced children have parents at higher stages. Parents expose children to the next higher stage, raising moral issues and engaging in open dialogue or interchange about such issues.[10]

Drawing on this notion of the discussion conditions stimulating advance, Moshe Blatt conducted classroom discussions of conflict-laden hypothetical moral dilemmas with four classes of junior high and high school students for a semester.[11] In each of these classes, students were to be found at three stages. Since the children were not all responding at the same stage, the arguments they used with each other were at different levels. In the course of these discussions among the students, the teacher first supported and clarified those arguments that were one stage above the lowest stage among the children; for example, the teacher supported Stage 3 rather than Stage 2. When it seemed that these arguments were understood by the students, the teacher then challenged that stage, using new situations, and clarified the arguments one stage above the previous one: Stage 4 rather than Stage 3. At the end of the semester, all the students were retested; they showed significant upward change when compared to the controls, and they maintained the change one year later. In the experimental classrooms, from one-fourth to one-half of the students moved up a stage, while there was essentially no change during the course of the experiment in the control group.

Given the Blatt studies showing that moral discussion could raise moral stage, we undertook the next step: to see if teachers could conduct moral discussions in the course of teaching high school social studies with the same results. This step we took in cooperation with Edwin Fenton, who introduced moral dilemmas in his ninth- and eleventh-grade social studies texts. Twenty-four teachers in the Boston and Pittsburgh areas were given some instruction in conducting moral discussions around the dilemmas in the text. About half of the teachers stimulated significant developmental change in their classrooms—upward stage movement of one-quarter to one-half a stage. In control classes using the text but no moral dilemma discussions, the same teachers failed to stimulate any moral change in the students. Moral discussion, then, can be a usable and effective part of the curriculum at any grade level. Working with filmstrip dilemmas produced in cooperation with Guidance Associates, second-grade teachers conducted moral discussions yielding a similar amount of moral stage movement.

Moral discussion and curriculum, however, constitute only one portion of the conditions stimulating moral growth. When we turn to analyzing the broader life environment, we turn to a consideration of the *moral atmosphere* of the home, the school, and the broader society. The first basic dimension of social atmosphere is the role-taking opportunities it provides, the extent to which it encourages the child to take the point of view of others. Role taking is related to the amount of social interaction and social communication in which the child engages, as well as to his sense of efficacy in influencing attitudes of others. The second dimension of social atmosphere, more strictly moral, is the level of justice of the environment or institution. The justice structure of an institution refers to the perceived rules or principles for distributing rewards, punishments, responsibilities, and privileges among institutional members. This structure may exist or be perceived at any of our moral stages. As an example, a study of a traditional prison revealed that inmates perceived it as Stage 1, regardless of their own level.[12] Obedience to arbitrary command by power figures and punishment for disobedience were seen as the governing justice norms of the prison. A behavior-modification prison using point rewards for conformity was perceived as a Stage 2 system of instrumental exchange. Inmates at Stage 3 or 4 perceived this institution as more fair than the traditional prison, but not as fair in their own terms.

These and other studies suggest that a higher level of institutional justice is a condition for individual development of a higher sense of justice. Working on these premises, Joseph Hickey, Peter Scharf, and I worked with guards and inmates in a women's prison to create a more just community.[13] A social contract was set up in which guards and inmates each had a vote of one and in which rules were made and conflicts resolved through discussions of fairness and a democratic vote in a community meeting. The program has been operating four years and has stimulated moral stage advance in inmates, though it is still too early to draw conclusions as to its overall long-range effectiveness for rehabilitation.

One year ago, Fenton, Ralph Mosher, and I received a grant from the Danforth Foundation (with additional support from the Kennedy Foundation) to make moral education a living matter in two high schools in the Boston area (Cambridge and Brookline) and two in Pittsburgh. The plan had two components. The first was training counselors and social studies and English teachers in conducting moral discussions and making moral discussion an integral part of the curriculum. The second was establishing a just community school within a public high school.

We have stated the theory of the just community high school, postulating that discussing real-life moral situations and actions as issues of fairness and as matters for democratic decision would stimulate advance in both moral reasoning and moral action. A participatory democracy provides more extensive opportunities for role taking and a higher level of perceived institutional justice than does any other social arrangement. Most alternative schools strive to establish a democratic governance, but none we have observed has achieved a vital or viable participatory democracy. Our theory suggested reasons why we might succeed where others failed. First, we felt that democracy had to be a central commitment of a school, rather than a humanitarian frill. Democracy as moral education provides that commitment. Second, democracy in alternative schools often fails because it bores the students. Students prefer to let teachers make decisions about staff, courses, and schedules, rather than to attend lengthy, complicated meetings. Our theory said that the issues a democracy should focus on are issues of morality and fairness. Real issues concerning drugs, stealing, disruptions, and grading are never boring if handled as issues of fairness. Third, our theory told us that if large, democratic community meetings were preceded by small-group moral discussion, higher-stage thinking by students would win out in later decisions, avoiding the disasters of mob rule.*

Currently, we can report that the school based on our theory makes democracy work or function where other schools have failed. It is too early to make any claims for its effectiveness in causing moral development, however.

Our Cambridge just community school within the public high school was started after a small summer planning session of volunteer teachers, students, and parents. At the time the school opened in the fall, only a commitment to democracy and a skeleton program of English and social studies had been decided on. The school started with six teachers from the regular school and sixty students, twenty from academic professional homes and twenty from working-class homes. The other twenty were dropouts and troublemakers or petty delinquents in terms of previous record. The usual mistakes and usual chaos of a beginning alternative school ensued. Within a few weeks, however, a successful democratic community process had been established. Rules were made around pressing issues: disturbances, drugs, hooking. A student discipline committee or jury was formed. The resulting rules and enforcement have been relatively effective and reasonable. We do not see reasonable rules as ends in themselves, however, but as vehicles for moral discussion and an emerging sense of community. This sense of community and a resulting morale are perhaps the most immediate signs of success. This sense of community seems to lead to behavior change of a positive sort. An example is a fifteen-year-old student who started as one of the greatest combinations of humor, aggression, light-fingeredness, and hyperactivity I have ever known. From being the principal disturber of all community meetings, he has become an excellent community meeting participant and occasional chairman. He is still more ready to enforce rules for others than to observe them himself, yet his commitment to the school has led to a steady decrease in exotic behavior. In addition, he has become more involved in classes and projects and has begun to listen and ask questions in order to pursue a line of interest.

We attribute such behavior change not only to peer pressure and moral discussion but to the sense of community which has emerged from the democratic process in which angry conflicts are resolved through fairness and community decision. This sense of community is reflected in statements of the students to us that there are no cliques—that the blacks and the whites, the professors' sons and the project students, are friends. These statements are supported by observation. Such a sense of community is needed where students in a given classroom range in reading level from fifth-grade to college.

Fenton, Mosher, the Cambridge and Brookline teachers, and I are now planning a four-year curriculum in English and social studies centering on moral discussion, on role taking and communication, and on relating the government, laws, and justice system of

*An example of the need for small-group discussion comes from an alternative school community meeting called because a pair of the students had stolen the school's video-recorder. The resulting majority decision was that the school should buy back the recorder from the culprits through a fence. The teachers could not accept this decision and returned to a more authoritative approach. I believe if the moral reasoning of students urging this solution had been confronted by students at a higher stage, a different decision would have emerged.

the school to that of the American society and other world societies. This will integrate an intellectual curriculum for a higher level of understanding of society with the experiential components of school democracy and moral decision.

There is very little new in this—or in anything else we are doing. Dewey wanted democratic experimental schools for moral and intellectual development 70 years ago. Perhaps Dewey's time has come.

Notes

1. John Dewey, "What Psychology Can Do for the Teacher," in *John Dewey on Education: Selected Writings*, ed. Reginald Archambault (New York: Random House, 1964).

2. Jean Piaget, *The Moral Judgment of the Child*, 2d ed. (Glencoe, Ill.: Free Press, 1948).

3. Lawrence Kohlberg, "Moral Stages and Moralization: The Cognitive-Developmental Approach," in *Man, Morality, and Society*, ed. T. Lickona (New York: Holt, Rinehart & Winston, 1976).

4. James Rest, "Comprehension, Preference, and Spontaneous Usage in Moral Judgment," in *Recent Research in Moral Development*, ed. L. Kohlberg (New York: Holt, Rinehart & Winston, 1973).

James Rest, Elliot Turiel, and Lawrence Kohlberg, "Relations between Level of Moral Judgment and Preference and Comprehension of the Moral Judgment of Others," *Journal of Personality* 37 (1969): 225–52.

5. Richard Krebs and Lawrence Kohlberg, "Moral Judgment and Ego Controls as Determinants of Resistance to Cheating," in *Recent Research*, ed. L. Kohlberg.

6. John Rawls, *A Theory of Justice* (Cambridge: Harvard University Press, 1971).

7. Ibid.

8. Lawrence Kohlberg and Donald Elfenbein, "Development of Moral Reasoning and Attitudes Toward Capital Punishment," *American Journal of Orthopsychiatry*, Summer 1975.

9. Hugh Hartshorne and Marcus May, *Studies in Deceit*, *Studies in Service and Self-Control*, and *Studies in Organization of Character*, Studies in the Nature of Character, vols. 1–3 (New York: Macmillan, 1928–30).

10. Bindu Parilch, "A Cross-Cultural Study of Parent-Child Moral Judgment" (Ph.D. dissertation, Harvard University, 1975).

11. Moshe Blatt and Lawrence Kohlberg, "Effects of Classroom Discussions upon Children's Level of Moral Judgment," in *Recent Research*, ed. L. Kohlberg.

12. Lawrence Kohlberg, Peter Scharf, and Joseph Hickey, "The Justice Structure of the Prison: A Theory and an Intervention," *The Prison Journal*, Autumn–Winter 1972.

13. Lawrence Kohlberg, Kelsey Kauffman, Peter Scharf, and Joseph Hickey, *The Just Community Approach to Corrections: A Manual, Part I* (Cambridge, Mass.: Education Research Foundation, 1973).

Table 1. Definition of Moral Stages

I. Preconventional level

At this level, the child is responsive to cultural rules and labels of good and bad, right or wrong, but interprets these labels either in terms of the physical or the hedonistic consequences of action (punishment, reward, exchange of favors) or in terms of the physical power of those who enunciate the rules and labels. The level is divided into the following two stages:

Stage 1: *The punishment-and-obedience orientation.* The physical consequences of action determine its goodness or badness, regardless of the human meaning or value of these consequences. Avoidance of punishment and unquestioning deference to power are valued in their own right, not in terms of respect for an underlying moral order supported by punishment and authority (the latter being Stage 4).

Stage 2: *The instrumental-relativist orientation.* Right action consists of that which instrumentally satisfies one's own needs and occasionally the needs of others. Human relations are viewed in terms like those of the marketplace. Elements of fairness, of reciprocity, and of equal sharing are present, but they are always interpreted in a physical, pragmatic way. Reciprocity is a matter of "you scratch my back and I'll scratch yours," not of loyalty, gratitude, or justice.

II. Conventional level

At this level, maintaining the expectations of the individual's family, group, or nation is perceived as valuable in its own right, regardless of immediate and obvious consequences. The attitude is not only one of *conformity* to personal expectations and social order, but of loyalty to it, of actively *maintaining*, supporting, and justifying the order, and of identifying with the persons or group involved in it. At this level, there are the following two stages:

Stage 3: *The interpersonal concordance or "good boy—nice girl" orientation.* Good behavior is that which pleases or helps others and is approved by them. There is much conformity to stereotypical images of what is majority or "natural" behavior. Behavior is frequently judged by intention—"he means well" becomes important for the first time. One earns approval by being "nice."

Stage 4: *The "law and order" orientation.* There is orientation toward authority, fixed rules, and the maintenance of the social order. Right behavior consists of doing one's duty, showing respect for authority, and maintaining the given social order for its own sake.

III. Postconventional, autonomous, or principled level

At this level, there is a clear effort to define moral values and principles that have validity and application apart from the authority of the groups or persons holding these principles and apart from the individual's own identification with these groups. This level also has two stages:

Stage 5: *The social-contract, legalistic orientation,* generally with utilitarian overtones. Right action tends to be defined in terms of general individual rights and standards which have been critically examined and agreed upon by the whole society. There is a clear awareness of the relativism of personal values and opinions and a corresponding emphasis upon procedural rules for reaching consensus. Aside from what is constitutionally and democratically agreed upon, the right is a matter of personal "values" and "opinion." The result is an emphasis upon the "legal point of view," but with an emphasis upon the possibility of changing law in terms of rational considerations of social utility (rather than freezing it in terms of Stage 4 "law and order"). Outside the legal realm, free agreement and contract is the binding element of obligation. This is the "official" morality of the American government and constitution.

Stage 6: *The universal-ethical-principle orientation*. Right is defined by the decision of conscience in accord with self-chosen *ethical principles* appealing to logical comprehensiveness, universality, and consistency. These principles are abstract and ethical (the Golden Rule, the categorical imperative); they are not concrete moral rules like the Ten Commandments. At heart, these are universal principles of *justice*, of the *reciprocity* and *equality* of human *rights*, and of respect for the dignity of human beings as *individual persons* ("From Is to Ought," pp. 164, 165).

Moral Education: The Research Findings

Edwin Fenton, Professor of History, Carnegie-Mellon University.

During the last twenty years, Lawrence Kohlberg, his colleagues, and their graduate students have been carving out a new field of psychological, philosophical, and educational research. Three words—cognitive moral development—capture the essence of their work. Cognitive stresses organized thought processes. Moral involves decision making in situations where unusual values, such as the sanctity of life and the need for authority, come in conflict. And development suggests that patterns of thinking about moral issues improve qualitatively over time.

Within the past few years, Kohlberg and his colleagues have begun to investigate the educational implications of their research. They have intervened in correctional institutions to determine whether or not deliberate programs of cognitive moral development would affect the lives of inmates. They have also intervened in educational institutions, particularly public schools, in order to facilitate cognitive moral development. These efforts, still in their beginning phases, have attracted widespread attention.

This article presents eleven generalizations which have grown out of the research into cognitive moral development of the Kohlberg group. The generalizations have been selected in an attempt to explain to social studies teachers the major research findings from this field which impinge upon their discipline.

I. People think about moral issues in six qualitatively different stages arranged in three levels of two stages each. Kohlberg has labeled these levels preconventional, conventional, and principled moral thought. [See Appendix for a delineation of these levels and stages.]

II. The most reliable way to determine a stage of moral thought is through a moral interview. A trained interviewer presents a subject with three dilemmas, each of which sets forth a situation for which the culture lends some conventional support for a number of actions which the protagonists could take. Here is one such dilemma from one of the interview forms.

Joe is a fourteen-year-old boy who wanted to go to camp very much. His father promised him he could go if he saved up the money for it himself. So Joe worked hard at his paper route and saved up the forty dollars it cost to go to camp and a little more besides. But just before camp was going to start, his father changed his mind. Some of his friends decided to go on a special fishing trip, and Joe's father was short of the money it would cost. So he told Joe to give him the money he had saved from the paper route. Joe didn't want to give up going to camp, so he thought of refusing to give his father the money.

After presenting the dilemma, the interviewer asks the following questions:

1. Should Joe refuse to give his father the money? Why?
2. Is there any way in which the father has a right to tell the son to give him the money? Why?
3. What is the most important thing a good father should recognize in his relation to his son? Why that?
4. What is the most important thing a good son should recognize in his relation to his father? Why that?
5. Why should a promise be kept?
6. What makes a person feel bad if a promise is broken?
7. Why is it important to keep a promise to someone you don't know well or are not close to?

Over a period of twenty years, Kohlberg and his colleagues have identified typical answers to the questions on the moral interview at each of the six stages of moral thought. Scorers compare the responses given by the subject to these typical questions in order to determine moral stage. Trained scorers show 90 percent agreement in identifying stage despite the difficult and sophisticated scoring techniques involved in scoring qualitative, open-ended data.

This scoring system provides a context for the following two statements. First, you cannot tell accurately the stage at which a person typically thinks from listening to a chance comment or two. But once a person knows Kohlberg's stages well, he or she can identify a typical pattern of thought with tolerable accuracy. Which leads to the second point: people should not fall prey to the temptation to label others by stage—"What do you expect me to do with that Stage 2 kid?" As the moral interview implies, a stage is neither a type of person nor a type of behavior; it is a way of thinking. Two people who think mainly at Stage 2 can be radically different from each other, one bright and the other dull, one humorless and the other delightful, one friendly and the other hostile. All people deserve respect simply because they are human. A person should not be denigrated because he or she thinks at a preconventional or conventional level.

III. A stage is an organized system of thought. Presented with several moral dilemmas, a person who reasons predominately at Stage 3 will consistently give Stage 3 answers, although the content of the dilemmas may vary widely. For example, Stage 3 thinkers will argue that they should do what pleases or helps others whether the issue involves obeying the law, affection between friends, or reasons to punish people.

Three responses at one stage to a single moral problem may further illuminate the nature of a psychological stage. Suppose that Jill steals a sweater from a store and the security officer tells her companion, Sharon, who is also Jill's best friend, that she (Sharon) will get in trouble unless she reveals her friend's name. Here are three responses to this dilemma, all at Stage 2:

Sharon ought to tell. After all, Jill walked out and left Sharon to take the rap. Sharon should give as good as she got. That's fair. Why should she get in trouble for Jill when Jill walked out on her?

Sharon shouldn't tell. The store probably charges enough to cover a few rip-offs. All the stores do that. It's just for Jill to get back something that she and all the rest of us have paid for anyway.

Sharon shouldn't tell. Neither the storeowner nor the security guard ever did anything for her. So it wouldn't be right for her to help them out by giving Jill's name.

These three responses differ in the act they recommend since two say that Sharon should not give Jill's name and the third says that she should. They also define what is fair or just or right in different terms. But the underlying structure of thought is the same. Each response invokes an element of fairness based on reciprocity, on mutual back scratching. This common element in the thought is its structure.

IV. An individual reasons predominately at one stage of thought and uses contiguous stages as a secondary thinking pattern. For example, a young teenager might respond to moral dilemmas in Stage 3 terms 70 percent of the time and employ Stage 2 thought the remaining 30 percent. This person is finishing the transition from Stage 2 thought to Stage 3 thought. Another person who responds at Stage 3 seventy percent of the time and at Stage 4 thirty percent probably stands at the beginning of the transition to Stage 4 thought.

V. These stages are natural steps in ethical development, not something artificial or invented. To find them, Kohlberg gave moral interviews to people of different ages—10, 13, 16, 20—and then classified answers into groups, each of which exhibited a similar reasoning process. Subsequently he conducted a longitudinal study, interviewing the same fifty subjects every three years. The longitudinal data helped him to revise and clarify his statements of the stages.

Kohlberg's research was conducted originally in the United States. Parallel cross-sectional research, however, has been conducted in a number of additional places including Turkey, Mexico, Taiwan, Israel, Yucatan, Canada, and India. In each of these places, researchers have found the same stages of moral thought as Kohlberg discovered in the United States except that principled stages (Stages 5 and 6) do not appear among respondents interviewed in traditional societies.

VI. All people move through these stages in invariant sequence, although any individual may stop at a particular stage. Everyone reasons as a young child at Stage 1. Most people then move to Stage 2. As early as age nine, but usually later, most Americans enter Stage 3, and some of them then pass into Stage 4 in middle or late adolescence. The transition to Stage 5 takes place, if at all, when people are in their late teens or early twenties, or even later in life. Very few people attain Stage 6, and those who do are usually older than thirty. So far as we know, no one ever skips a stage, and once someone has attained a particular stage, he or she never retrogresses to earlier ones. But people can have their development arrested at any stage. Most adult Americans think at the conventional level, Stages 4 or 3, and only a small minority—perhaps 5 or 10 percent—attain full Stage 5 thought. Few, if any, high school students reason mainly at Stage 5.

But if people develop naturally through the stages, why try to facilitate development in schools or community organizations? Because many people reason morally at stages well below those which they could reach under better conditions. Two major factors limit the development of higher stages of moral thought. The first is limited cognitive capacity, a limited ability to use formal, abstract thought. Beginning formal operational thought on the Piagetian scale is a necessary but not sufficient condition for Stage 3 moral thought, and more complete formal operational thought is a similar prerequisite for Stage 4 and 5 thought on the Kohlberg scale. However, many people who think at the early formal operational level still reason at Stages 1 or 2 morally, while most people who are fully formal operational do not reason at Kohlberg's Stage 5. They fail to develop mainly because they have not had experiences which set up the cognitive conflict leading to stage change. [See Appendix for the Piaget scale.]

Children who come from families and who associate with friends who use Stage 1 and 2 arguments almost exclusively have little opportunity to advance up the moral scale. Society deprives them of a full opportunity for ethical development unless some societal institution, such as the school or the church, intervenes. Society should intervene. Educational intervention to stimulate universal stages of moral development is constitutional; it is not indoctrination, and it violates no constitutional or civil right. It is philosophically justified; moral philosophers throughout history—such people as Plato, Kant, and John Rawls—have articulated an ethic which corresponds to Stages 5 and 6. It is socially useful; persons who think at a higher moral level reason better and act in accordance with their judgment more frequently than less developed thinkers. We have every reason to intervene educationally; we have no reason not to do so.

VII. People can understand moral arguments at their own stage, at all stages beneath their own, and usually at one stage higher than their own. Suppose that moral interviews have identified a group of people who think primarily at Stage 3. A researcher presents these people with a moral dilemma and with answers at all six stages. The subjects successfully paraphrase the answers at Stages 3, 2, and 1, and most of them successfully paraphrase the Stage 4 answer. But they will express the Stage 5 response in Stage 3 terms, a result which indicates that they have not understood the arguments two stages higher than their own. Think of the implications of this conclusion for civic education.

The Constitution is based on a Stage 5 morality. It posits the existence of basic rights—life, liberty, and the dignity of the individual—which antedate the society. The society comes into existence to protect people in the use of these rights. The Declaration of Independence, another Stage 5 document, puts the case in this way:

> We hold these truths to be self-evident, that all men are created equal, that they are endowed by their Creator with certain unalienable rights, that among these are life, liberty, and the pursuit of happiness. That to secure these rights, governments are instituted among men, deriving their just powers from the consent of the governed. That whenever any form of government becomes destructive of these ends, it is the right of the people to alter or to abolish it, and to institute new government, laying its foundation on such principles and organizing its powers in such forms, as to them shall seem most likely to effect their safety and happiness.

As a minimal goal of civic education, we should aim to raise the level of moral thinking of all children to the stage that will enable them to understand the principles behind the Declaration of Independence and the Constitution. That is the societal maintenance stage, Stage 4. Getting most high school seniors to Stage 4 thought will be no easy task. To reach this goal, family, community, and school must work together to establish societies based on principles of justice, the principles involved in Stage 5 and 6 thought.

VIII. Higher moral stages are better than lower ones. Two arguments, chosen for purposes of illustration from a larger number which could be used, can illustrate this conclusion. Problems can be solved at higher stages better than at lower ones. Take Stages 3 and 4 and a conflict between two ethnic communities, for example. At Stage 3, members of each community define what is good by what the majority of people in their group approve of and how they behave. Therefore, if the members of the two communities approve of different ways of life, they may come into conflict when a specific issue, such as busing to achieve integration of the schools, arises. But at Stage 4, thought in both groups would orient toward maintaining the social order through obeying authorities and conforming to the law of the land. This thought pattern would be more likely to suggest a solution which could be fair and could avoid conflict if people embrace it. Stage 4 thought is better than Stage 3 thought in this case because it could solve a problem which cannot be solved successfully at the lower stage.

Higher stages are better than lower ones for a second reason: they are more differentiated, more integrated, and more universal. More differentiated means that at higher stages, people draw a distinction between such different things as the value of life and the value of property. At Stage 1, people do not make this differentiation. More integrated means that at higher stages, people place such things as life and property in a hierarchy and integrate them with other items in that hierarchy, such as law or justice. More universal means that higher stages appeal to more universal principles such as the social contract or fundamental principles of justice, while lower stages stress narrow principles such as avoiding punishment for oneself or gaining a reward. Hence, higher stage thought is more consistent than lower stage thought.

IX. Stage transition takes place primarily because encountering real life or hypothetical moral dilemmas sets up cognitive conflict in a person's mind and makes the person uncomfortable. Let's take Mary, who customarily reasons at Stage 2. Mary thinks in terms of reciprocity—"I'll help her because I want her to help me next time." Then she hears another argument—"People will like you more if you help them. They will approve of you because good people help each other, and that's a good thing to do for its own sake." This higher level reasoning makes Mary uncomfortable because it challenges her customary belief, and it appeals to her because people prefer the highest stage of moral thought that they can comprehend, and Mary can comprehend one stage of reasoning higher than her own. She sees the difference in the two arguments and prefers the one on a higher stage.

Stage change takes place slowly. Typical elementary school students stay in Stage 2 for several years. But most of them encounter Stage 3 arguments all the time. Their lives in the community revolve increasingly around their peer groups whose members expect them to be faithful to friends, to behave in ways of which other teenagers will approve, and to help others whenever they can. Their parents often raise similar arguments—particularly if they know Kohlberg's works. And so, over a period of several years and on one moral issue after another, Mary is won over to a new organized system of thought, a new stage. But what if Mary lives in a peer group where she hears only Stage 2 arguments, and what if her family talks to her in Stage 1 terms: "Do it because I tell you to. If you don't, you'll be punished and then you'll know how wrong you are"?

X. Deliberate attempts to facilitate stage change in schools through educational programs have been successful. Within the last decade, more than a score of investigators has attempted to facilitate stage change by leading moral discussions. Some of the discussion techniques they have used are described in the article by Barry Beyer which appears later in this volume. They have worked in elementary schools, junior and senior high schools, and on the college level. Although results vary in detail, one generalization about this research stands out: Compared to the students in control groups, students in experimental groups who participate in moral discussions show significant increases in the stage of moral thought they commonly use.

In these programs, Kohlberg and his colleagues use hypothetical moral dilemmas to trigger moral discussions particularly in social studies and English classes. The dilemmas present situations for which the culture lends some conventional support for a number of actions which the protagonists could take. Teachers present dilemmas in a variety of forms: orally; written; by recordings, sound tapes, film, or videotape; or as skits or role-playing exercises. The discussion leader then attempts to get students to confront the arguments one stage above their own. This confrontation takes place either when students who think at contiguous moral stages discuss reasoning or when the teacher poses a higher level argument through a probe question or a comment.

Beginning in 1974, the Harvard group began to intervene in a new way by setting up what Kohlberg calls a Just Community School. About seventy students and their teachers compose this school within a school which is located within Cambridge High and Latin School just a few blocks from Harvard. A description of the school and the theory behind it follows in the article by Elsa Wasserman. Staff and students together draw up a constitution, and they make decisions through community meetings in which each person has one vote. Processing real life moral dilemmas in community meetings should lead to change on the Kohlberg scale, but the staff will not have data which bear on this hypothesis until the end of the 1977–78 academic year.

XI. Moral judgment is a necessary but not sufficient condition for moral action. On the surface, this statement seems simple enough. It implies that one must understand and believe in moral principles before one can follow them; it also implies that a person can reason in terms of moral principles and not act upon them. Beneath the surface, however, the relationship of moral thought to action is not as simple as it appears for four major reasons.

First, at preconventional and conventional moral levels it is possible to recommend either of two possible courses of action in a moral dilemma and to support these recommendations by reasoning at a single stage. Here, for example, are two Stage 4 responses to the shop-lifting dilemma involving Sharon and Jill and described earlier in this article:

Sharon ought to tell for everyone's sake. She ought to help enforce the laws against stealing and help Jill to learn what her responsibilities to a society as a citizen are. How could society hold together if everyone went around ignoring laws when it pleased them?

Sharon shouldn't tell. Society is built upon the principle of trust. If you couldn't rely on people, then no business, school, or even family would be able to work.

As these responses imply, merely knowing a person's stage of moral thought or raising thought from one stage to the next one will not usually enable anyone to predict what action a person will take in response to a particular dilemma.

At the principled level (Stages 5 and 6), however, it becomes very difficult to construct equally forceful yes and no responses to a dilemma. One of Kohlberg's classic dilemmas raises the issue of whether a man is justified to steal a drug to save his dying wife. A local druggist had developed the drug and charges ten times what it costs to produce. He refuses to reduce the price, grant credit, or make any concessions, and the man exhausted every means to raise the money. The overwhelming majority of Stage 5 thinkers argue that he should steal the drug, and they find a Stage 5 argument that he should not steal it unpersuasive. Here is such an argument:

It would be wrong for the man to steal the drug. Although the druggist's position seems unreasonable, he is entitled to the drug since he did not violate anyone's rights when he discovered and produced it. I agree that no one has the right to take or seriously interfere with another person's life. But this is different from saying that anyone who gets sick has a right to force others to help him if the others are unwilling to do so freely, or that it is all right to steal.

The argument that he should steal the drug strikes most Stage 5 thinkers as far more reasonable since it is more firmly grounded in basic, presocietal rights:

Yes, he should steal it. A human life is infinitely valuable, while any material object—in this case the drug—is not. The woman's right to live exceeds the druggist's right to make a profit.

Stage 6 thinkers, given agreement on the facts and circumstances of the dilemma, will arrive at the same decision about action—that the man should steal the drug. At Stages 5 and 6, then, the structure of thought will be likely to recommend a single action in a dilemma, a statement which is not true of thought at either the preconventional or the conventional levels.

Second, and despite the above disclaimer, at least two experimenters have found a high correlation between moral thought and action in experimental situations. In one of them, the experimenter asked subjects to fill out and return a questionnaire. She provided a stamped, addressed envelope, paid the subjects in advance, and told them that failure to send the questionnaires back on time would cause her to fail her research course. There were no Stage 1 or Stage 6 subjects. Of Stage 2 and 3 subjects, only about 30 percent did the moral thing; that is, they mailed the questionnaire on time. But more than 70 percent of the Stage 4 subjects did so, and 100 percent of the Stage 5 thinkers faithfully filled out and mailed the questionnaire. The second experiment determined whether or not students would cheat when they were relatively sure they would not be caught. About 70 percent of the preconventional students cheated; about 55 percent of conventional subjects also cheated; but only about 15 percent of the subjects showing some principled thinking on a moral interview cheated. But note three aspects of these experiments: neither placed the subjects in situations involving much emotional or situational stress; in each case people acted as individual moral agents without being able to diffuse responsibility for moral decisions and without observing the examples of others; and the situations were simple ones so that the moral issue was clear and the facts of the case unambiguous.

Third, at least three factors in addition to moral thought influence moral action: situational stress, diffused responsibility, and the complexity of the moral issues involved. My Lai offers an example of all of these factors. Soldiers there faced severe emotional and situational stress since many of their buddies had been killed and they believed that any Vietnamese person from the village might well be an armed enemy. Rather than being solely responsible for making a moral decision, the soldiers could diffuse responsibility to all the officers and men at My Lai; one man's shot could act as a releaser to others. And the moral issue was extremely complicated and unclear: officers' orders, every person a potential guerilla, loyalty to buddies who had died, the sanctity of life, and the very nature of war itself. Would the men who shot under these circumstances fire at American civilians in peace time, no matter what their moral stage? Or do particular circumstances help to explain their actions?

Fourth, the development of Just Community Schools has brought a new perspective to the matter of moral action. Observers report that these schools influence the behavior patterns of many of their students. They attend class more regularly. They take greater responsibility for their own behavior and for the behavior of others. They show greater respect for students in the school who come from different racial, religious, ethnic, or social backgrounds. These changed behaviors are probably not the result of changes in the moral stages of the students involved, but they are the indirect result of developing a school based firmly on the findings of research in cognitive moral development. In the long run, these changes in action may hold great significance for American education.

These eleven generalizations provide an introduction to the research findings on which intervention techniques designed to facilitate cognitive moral development have been based.

Part II: Classroom Moral Education

The first documented attempt to raise the level of student moral thinking was that of Moshe Blatt in 1967 who demonstrated for the first time that moral thinking might be raised through intensive dilemma discussions. Blatt, working with four groups of Chicago junior high students, found that the students in his groups changed an average of nearly one-third of a moral stage over a three-month period. Subsequent efforts by more than two-dozen clinical and educational researchers have demonstrated that similar results might be attained using a variety of approaches with a wide range of students.

Since Blatt's pilot project, researchers have developed a range of techniques and strategies which have been shown to have a developmental impact upon student moral thinking. Mosher and Sprinthall demonstrated that a curriculum in peer counseling produced developmental changes quite similar to those reported by Blatt. Boyd, working with classes of high school students, found that students who were forced to think systematically about political and moral choices changed dramatically in terms of moral thinking. Similarly, Joseph Hickey, working with delinquents, Lois Erickson with female adolescents, and Robert Selman with disturbed children have developed imaginative strategies and techniques appropriate to special populations of students.

Moral education has "infiltrated" nearly every subject area and age level in the school curriculum. Fenton, Tom Ladenberg, and Alan Lockwood have developed social studies curricula in which high school students are exposed to moral dilemmas presented in the context of the study of history. Swanger, Forbes, Scharf, and others have demonstrated how moral dilemmas might be analyzed through the study of literature. The Biological Curriculum Study's "Human Sciences" program has developed dilemmas related to students investigating biological and social problems. Similarly, the "Bio Med" curriculum has utilized dilemmas in the study of medical professions. Other curricula have been developed and implemented in physical education, work study, and physics which utilize developmental moral education techniques in discussing moral problems which emerge from the systematic study of social and natural phenomena. At this point, there has been pilot developmental moral education experiments at every age level from elementary school through the college years.

This section presents some exemplary curricula in the field of moral education. Ralph Mosher and Paul Sullivan offer a practical, holistic program to facilitate moral and psychological growth of adolescents. They describe a six-phase curriculum in which students engage in moral discussions, counsel other students, and teach moral education techniques to others. This program offers a model for schools which wish to assign a place in the curriculum for intentional moral education, conducted from a developmental perspective. Tom Ladenberg's article on social studies education indicates how moral education techniques might be utilized in traditional academic subject areas. Selman and Jaquette's article on a curriculum for disturbed children and Lois Erickson's piece on developmental curricula show how developmental techniques might be adapted to special categories of students. Barry Beyer offers some extremely useful suggestions on how to structure successful moral discussions in the classroom, and my piece on "Creating Dilemmas for the Classroom" gives some recommendations to teachers who wish to find or create dilemmas for classroom use.

Conducting Moral Discussions in the Classroom

Barry K. Beyer, Associate Professor of History, Carnegie-Mellon University.

Research by Lawrence Kohlberg and his associates suggests that individuals at any given stage of moral development exhibit three characteristics which have important implications for education. First, most individuals can comprehend reasoning about moral issues at the next higher stage of reasoning above their present stage, but at no stage higher than that. Thus, for example, a person reasoning predominately at Stage 2 probably comprehends Stage 3 reasoning, but not reasoning at Stages 4, 5, or 6. Second, individuals prefer reasoning at the highest stage they can comprehend, because higher stage reasoning offers a way to resolve moral issues which cannot be resolved as satisfactorily at a lower stage. Finally, when individuals examine reasoning about moral issues repeatedly, they tend to move up to the next higher stage.

If these findings are accurate, then it is reasonable to assume that educators can devise classroom activities to help their students move from one stage of moral reasoning to the next.[1] Recent classroom experimentation supports this assumption, for moral discussions in classrooms have facilitated cognitive moral development.[2]

A moral discussion consists of a purposeful conversation about moral issues. Most moral discussions are triggered by moral dilemmas which present situations for which the culture supplies some support for a number of actions which the protagonists could take. Discussions of these situations focus on the moral issues involved in a dilemma and the reasoning used to justify recommended actions.

Perhaps the best way to illustrate the nature of a moral discussion is to examine a transcript of a portion of such a discussion. In the dialogue that follows, junior high school students discuss Sharon's dilemma. This dilemma involves the following situation:

> Sharon and Jill were best friends. One day they went shopping together. Jill tried on a sweater and then, to Sharon's surprise, walked out of the

store wearing the sweater under her coat. A moment later, the store's security officer stopped Sharon and demanded that she tell him the name of the girl who had walked out. He told the storeowner that he had seen the two girls together and that he was sure that the one who left had been shoplifting. The storeowner told Sharon that she could really get in trouble if she didn't give her friend's name.[3]

The students are discussing whether or not Sharon should give Jill's name to the security officer. The excerpt begins mid-way in the class discussion.

George: Jill could say "I don't even know her. I just walked in the store off the street, and I don't even know where she lives. I just met her."

Teacher: So what she ought to do is lie for a friend, right?

George: Yah.

Teacher: What is going to happen to all of us if everyone lies whenever they feel like it, whenever it suits their convenience? What kind of life are you going to have? Peter.

Peter: If everyone goes around shoplifting, if someone goes and steals a whole bunch of things from somebody's store, then you go back to your store and see everything from your store missing, do you know what kind of life that would be? Everybody would just be walking around stealing everybody else's stuff.

Teacher: Mary Lu, do you want to comment about what he said?

Mary Lu: Yah, but everybody doesn't steal and everybody wouldn't, and the thing is that the storeowner probably has a large enough margin of profit anyway to cover some few ripoffs he might have.

George: But the store can't exist if everybody is stealing, there are so many people, and it is getting worse and worse every day. It said in the story, they can't afford to stay.

Mary Lu: I'm not sure I believe the storeowner.

Roland: I am saying so what? It is like stealing from the rich and giving to the poor. It just doesn't work, you know.

Teacher: Why doesn't it work, Roland?

Roland: Because it is exactly what Dan said. Mary Lu can say everybody does not do it, but the only thing that holds it together is the government, and you don't have government if everybody does not follow the rules. Well, we'll have government, but we won't follow the rules. . . .

(After more discussion, the teacher utilized reports from small groups which had developed reasons why Sharon should or should not tell and had written them on the chalkboard.)

Teacher: Let's look over on the board for a minute where the chairpersons from the small groups wrote the best reasons the groups could think of for giving Jill's name and for not giving it. The first reason the "should nots" gave was friendship. Will you explain what you mean by friendship?

Irene: The thing is, friendship is like a person matters more than a rule and that you have someone's friendship. The rules are upstanding when you need them; they are there. But the thing is you are going to go by them most of the time. But you've got a friend, and I at least would value a lot higher a friend and somebody who I could talk to, a lot higher than a sweater, than something material. There is absolutely no comparison between emotions and material things.

Teacher: I think you have explained what you mean by friendship very well. Let's get the other group to explain "Thou shalt not steal." Perry?

Perry: Well, you shouldn't steal. I said it once before; it is just not fair if everybody steals; you can't live if everybody is stealing.

Teacher: Perry, what about the whole matter of these two reasons. "Thou shalt not steal" is one reason, but your friendship is another. Which is more important to you?

Perry: I say that if you steal and you don't tell on your friend, you will probably keep your crummy friend who left you in the store and is really a liar and all that, but even if you lose your friend and you tell, somewhere along the line you will get some other friends, because I am sure that one or two people in this world are straight.

Four characteristics of this discussion should be noted. First, the students evidently feel free to air their opinions; they do not seem to think that they will be censured or embarrassed for what they say. Second, the discussion centers on moral reasoning—on why Sharon should or should not tell—not on what action she should take. Third, most of the conversation takes place among students who comment on and challenge each other's reasoning. Finally, the teacher facilitates discussions of reasoning at contiguous stages of the Kohlberg scale by involving students who reason at adjacent stages, using questions which stimulate one-stage-higher reasoning, and focusing discussion on arguments at different stages. The following analysis of goals, materials, strategies, and teacher competencies will clarify the use of moral discussions such as this one as a vehicle for facilitating cognitive moral development.

The goals of moral discussions should not be defined too narrowly. By becoming an integral part of a course, these discussions can contribute to the realization of existing overall course objectives as well as bring new objectives to the learning situation. Among the general educational goals which can be reached by using a program of moral discussions are the following:

1. Improving learning skills. Moral discussions can help students to develop listening skills, skills of oral communication, and the ability to participate constructively in group discussions.
2. Improving self-esteem. Properly conducted, moral discussions can improve a student's self-esteem if teachers and students focus classroom dialogue on the substance of student remarks, accept statements and points of view as given, and treat each other and each other's ideas with respect.
3. Improving attitudes toward school. Most students find moral discussions fascinating

and look forward to these discussions in class. Hence, school can seem a more interesting and relevant place to them.

4. Improving knowledge of key concepts. Moral discussions often involve key concepts which students understand in stage-related terms. For example, definitions of justice relate to stages of moral reasoning as follows: Stage 1: Justice is getting rewarded for something I do. Stage 2: Justice means that you will do something for me later if I help you now. Stage 3: Justice means doing what all the people in the group approve of. Stage 4: Justice comes about when everyone follows the rules on which we have agreed. Stage 5: Justice means that people get their basic rights for which government was originally founded. By reasoning at increasingly higher moral stages, individuals can develop a more sophisticated understanding of basic concepts that underlie the structure of the society in which they live.
5. Facilitating stage change. Stage change takes place slowly, as the article about research findings points out. Hence, a realistic goal in this area might be stated in the following terms: As a result of several years of moral discussions as an integral part of social studies classes, the typical high school student who began as a freshman thinking in a mixture of Stage 2 and 3 terms will think predominately at Stage 4.

Students will be more likely to achieve objectives derived from these five sets of goals when teachers establish a non-judgmental classroom climate that reflects trust, informality, and tolerance. To help create such an atmosphere, students can sit in a large circle so that everyone can face and clearly hear each other. By joining this circle, a teacher can take a role as a discussant and leader or mediator rather than as an authority figure who has established a separate teacher space. This type of class arrangement helps teachers to listen to what students say and to guide the discussion in response to their cues. The resulting classroom atmosphere encourages exchange and interaction, two keys to effective moral discussions.

Moral discussions can be best initiated by considering a moral problem or dilemma. Dilemmas are stories which present a central character in a problematic situation for which there are several possible responses and in which a number of moral issues come in conflict. To be most useful, a moral dilemma should meet four criteria. First, it should be as simple as possible. The dilemma should involve only a few characters in a relatively uncomplicated situation which students can grasp readily. Complicated dilemmas confuse students who are then forced to spend time clarifying facts and circumstances rather than discussing reasons for suggested actions. Second, a moral dilemma should be open-ended. It should present a problematic situation to which there is no single obvious right answer. Third, a dilemma should involve two or more issues that have moral implications. Among the key issues Kohlberg has identified are punishment, affectional relations, authority, contract, property, life, civil liberties, and personal conscience. In Sharon's dilemma, for example, Sharon's affectional relationship with Jill conflicts with both authority and property. Sharon faces the prospect of being punished herself if she fails to give Jill's name or of bringing punishment on Jill if she does tell her name. At the same time Sharon faces the possibility of losing Jill's friendship if she tells or of losing the affection of her own family if she becomes a party to the shoplifting. Finally, an effective dilemma must offer a choice of actions and pose the question "What should the central character do?" Note the use of the word *should*. This word focuses thinking on moral reasoning, for it asks students to decide what is the right or correct or good thing to do. "Would" questions, on the other hand, are predictive and do not necessarily generate moral reasoning.

Dilemmas may be derived from three main sources. Life in our society abounds with moral dilemmas. Should a terminally ill patient be allowed to die or be kept alive by a life support system? Should police officials use force to capture criminals who are holding hostages? The life experiences of students also offer sources of dilemmas. Should a student let another student copy examination answers? Should a child tell parents that a brother or sister did something he or she had been told not to do? Such dilemmas may be used as they are found or recast as hypothetical incidents involving fictional characters, such as in Sharon's dilemma. Course content can also serve as a major source of moral dilemmas, especially in social studies classes. Such dilemmas may be based on actual incidents (Should Thoreau have gone to jail rather than pay taxes to support a war of which he disapproved?) or on imaginary incidents or characters which are true in general to historic fact (Should Private Black follow orders to shoot the Indian women and children in the cavalry attack on Sand Creek?). Dilemmas that fit naturally into a course enable teachers to engage students in moral reasoning while at the same time they add to student knowledge of and feeling for the subject under discussion. Literature, history, and the problems of modern society provide many dilemmas that can trigger moral discussions.

Dilemmas may be presented to students in many ways—for example, in the form of short readings, or via a film, filmstrip, recording, or sound filmstrip. Dilemmas may also be presented orally by the teacher or as a role play or simulation. Regardless of the media used to present the dilemma, however, it is the way in which a dilemma is used that makes the ensuing classroom activity an effective moral discussion.

To facilitate cognitive moral development most effectively, a moral discussion must be carefully organized. One tested approach for conducting moral discussions requires that the teacher help students engage in sequence in five distinct activities: (1) to confront a dilemma; (2) to recommend tentative courses of action to resolve the dilemma and to justify these recommendations; (3) to discuss their reasoning in small groups; (4) to examine as a class their reasoning and the reasoning others use as they justify recommended solutions to the dilemma; and (5) to reflect on this reasoning as they bring temporary closure to their discussion.[4] A brief analysis of teaching techniques useful in conducting each of these types of activities follows.

Presenting the Dilemma. To launch a moral discussion, teachers or students present a dilemma to a class. It is sometimes useful to precede presentation of the dilemma with comments or questions designed to prepare the students for the kind of situation or character described in the dilemma. For example, before introducing Sharon's dilemma to a class, a teacher might point out that crimes involving property are a major type of teenage crime today and that shoplifting losses represent a significant portion of the price paid for retail items in stores. The teacher might also ask if students have ever heard of anyone actually stealing something from a store or if they have known of someone who once had to decide whether or not to tell on a friend. After students hear or see the dilemma, the teacher should ask questions in order to help students to clarify the circumstances involved in the dilemma, define terms, identify the characteristics of the central character, and state the exact nature of the dilemma and the action choice open to the central character. Little more than five minutes need be devoted to this part of the strategy.

Dividing on Action. Once students have stated the dilemma, each individual should take a tentative position about what action he or she thinks the central character should take. This can be done by asking students to reflect briefly on the situation facing the central character and then to state tentatively whether the character should or should not take a certain action, usually answered in terms of a written "Yes" or "No" response to an action alternative. This phase of the lesson usually requires about four or five minutes.

Organizing Small Group Discussion. From this point on, the students can engage in small group and large group discussions about the reasoning used to justify the actions they recommend. However, in order to conduct a meaningful discussion, the teacher must first find out what action positions were taken by the students. A good dilemma usually generates a division within the class on the action that the central character should take. A significant number of students should favor one course of action, while others should favor another. A fairly even division over action generates the kind of confrontation that motivates a critical evaluation of moral reasoning. In order to know how to proceed, therefore, the teacher must determine whether there has been a split about action and, if so, what proportion of students has selected each alternative action. Students can indicate by a show of hands how many support each position. When students divide on action on at least a 75–25 basis, discussion can begin.

The teacher must next focus the discussion on the moral issues of the dilemma. Teachers sometimes ask for several volunteers to state reasons for the positions they have taken. This opportunity usually stimulates a number of students to state their reasons or to criticize reasons they have just heard. Teachers can use the interest thus generated to embark on the discussions that should follow.

The most productive moral discussion involves small group discussions followed by a discussion involving the entire class. Approximately a third of a regular class period ought to be devoted to each of these two activities. Small group discussions maximize student-to-student interaction, generate thinking about a variety of reasons for supporting a particular position, create a supportive feeling within each group, and set up the larger class discussion that follows. Students feel comfortable in small group situations because all members of a single group have often made the same action decision. Students also tend to feel comfortable because such groups maximize the opportunity for them to contribute to the group discussion with relatively little apparent risk of failure.

Any of several different grouping strategies may be used. Where the class division on action is uneven, groups of from four to six students can be created in which all members of each group hold the same position. The students in a group can list all the reasons they have for their position, choose the best of these reasons, and then state why this reason is the best one. With a fairly even class division about action, the teacher can organize groups in which an equal number of students represent opposing positions. The group members can discuss their positions and reasons in order to make a list of the two best reasons for each position represented. Students should feel free to switch from one group to another if, in the midst of a group discussion, they decide to change their position on action. When these group tasks have been completed, students can then convene as an entire class to continue their discussion.

While students meet in small groups, the teacher should move from one group to another, helping students to focus on the assigned tasks, to clarify their reasoning, to avoid arguing about the facts of the dilemma, and to list questions to ask of those who took an opposing position. But when the class reconvenes, the teacher assumes a quite different role.

Conducting a Class Discussion. A discussion with the full class gives students a chance to report the reasoning which supports their positions and to hear reasons given for other positions or different reasons given for the positions they have taken, to challenge these reasons, and to hear their own reasoning challenged. This process of examining moral reasoning critically lies at the heart of an effective moral discussion. The process of stating, challenging, being challenged, defending, explaining, criticizing, and comparing highlights the existence of a gap between one's own stage of reasoning and the reasoning at the next higher stage. In time, students become conscious of this gap and move to close it.

Class discussions may follow various formats. Recorders from each group can report the positions and reasons given in their groups while other students challenge what they hear. Or various groups can pose questions to those who took an opposing view and attempt to persuade them of the validity of their own positions and reasoning. Students can list reasons on the chalkboard, and members of the class can then choose the best reason for each position. As students discuss the merit of one reason over another, they engage in the type of thinking that facilitates cognitive moral development.

In a class discussion, teachers have two main tasks—to promote student-to-student interaction and to keep the discussion a moral discussion. Student interaction can be promoted by the way student seating is arranged, by the classroom climate, and by using questions or comments to draw students into the discussion. For example, silent students can be asked to paraphrase a comment, react to a statement, summarize points already made, or take a stand regarding a particular statement.

Teachers can use three techniques to keep the discussion focused on moral issues. First, they should short-circuit substantive diversions—arguments or comments about the facts and circumstances of a dilemma. Instead of permitting speculation about facts and circumstances, teachers can simply state what the facts are and return the discussion to reasoning. Second, they should (at least ideally) encourage discussion between students who argue at contiguous stages of the Kohlberg scale, perhaps by calling on a person who has made a comment representing Stage 3 reasoning to respond to a Stage 2 comment. Alternatively, inviting comments on reasons at contiguous stages from lists on the chalkboard will accomplish the same goal. Finally, the teacher should use probe questions to help students examine issues they had ignored or to think about reasoning at a higher stage.

Any of five types of probe questions can be used.[5] A clarifying probe calls on students to define terms they have used or to explain a comment which does not convey reasoning. For example, if a student says "I think that stealing is immoral," the teacher might respond with a clarifying probe, "What do you mean by immoral?" An issue-specific probe encourages students to examine their thoughts about one of the ten major issues which Kohlberg argues provide a focus for moral reasoning. In discussing Sharon's dilemma, an example of such a probe question might be "What obligations do you owe to a friend?" This question gets at the specific issue of affectional relations. An inter-issue probe encourages students to think about what to do when a conflict occurs between two separate issues: "Which is more important, loyalty to a friend or the obligation to obey the law? Why?" A role-switch probe puts the students in the position of someone else involved in the dilemma in order to get them to see another side of the problem. Such a question might be "From the point of view of Jill's parents, should Sharon tell?" Finally, a universal-consequence probe asks students to consider what might happen if such a position or such reasoning were applied to everyone. For example, "Is it ever right to tell on a friend?"

Probe questions play a crucial role in guiding a moral discussion. These questions require students to do a number of things which seem to facilitate movement from the lower to the higher stages of moral reasoning—(1) to think increasingly in more generalizable terms, (2) to develop an increasingly broad societal perspective, (3) to develop an ability to see and empathize with more than one side of an issue, and (4) to focus increasingly on the larger moral issues implicit in a moral dilemma. Without specific efforts to help students develop these abilities, discussions are unlikely to facilitate cognitive moral development.

Closing the Discussion. The final activity involved in a moral discussion consists of helping students bring the discussion to a close. This task usually occupies the final few minutes of a class. Students can be asked to summarize all the reasons given for the positions being considered and then choose individually the reason they now find most persuasive. Public declaration of the results is neither necessary nor desirable, for doing so might imply that there is a correct answer, an assumption antithetical to this entire strategy. Alternatively, a teacher may choose to extend the lesson beyond the class period. Students can be asked to write an essay about their solution to a dilemma. They could describe a similar dilemma and its resolution or question their peers or parents about how they would respond to the dilemma discussed in class. Students can also be assigned to find dilemmas in newspapers, television shows, textbooks, or other sources involving issues similar to the class dilemma. Finally, in succeeding weeks students can discuss other dilemmas that involve similar issues and compare their reasoning across all these dilemmas.

Figure 1 on page 70 illustrates the basic elements of the strategy described here. The five activities listed down the center of the diagram in boxes represent what the teacher does. The activities listed at either side represent what students do as they engage in the core activities.

The strategy described here aims to point up the gap between an individual's stage of reasoning about moral problems and reasoning at the next higher stage. It

Figure 1
A Strategy for Guiding Moral Discussions

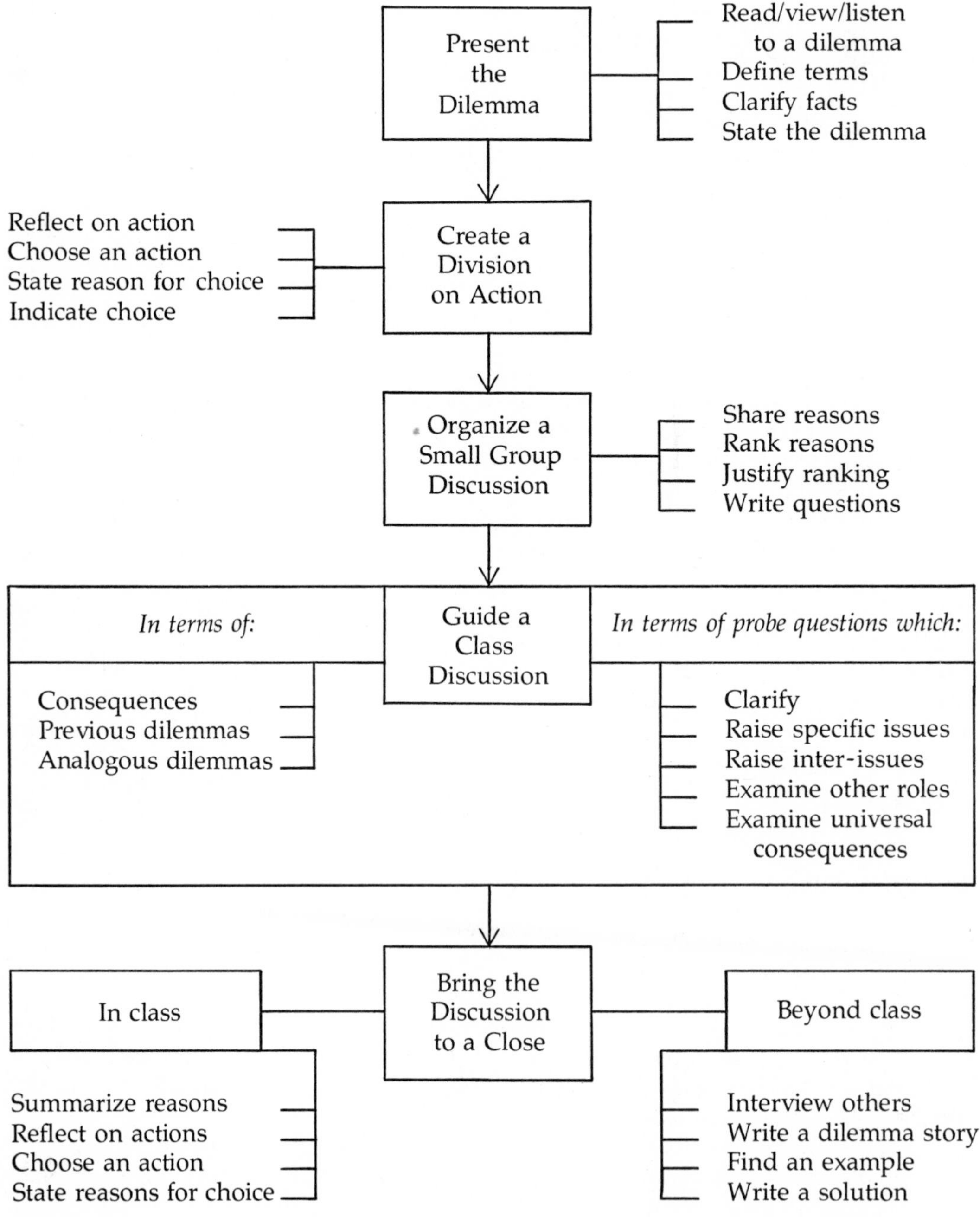

attempts to force individuals to confront consciously the inadequacies of their present stages of reasoning so that they will become dissatisfied with them, recall other reasons that suggest more adequate solutions, and move toward the next higher stage of reasoning. In short, the approach creates cognitive dissonance and uses that dissonance to generate cognitive development.

Many variations of this basic strategy can be employed. For example, instead of asking students to identify a single course of action that should be taken, students can be asked to brainstorm courses of action that the central character could take. The class can then attempt to identify the possible consequences for each course of action. When these consequences have been listed and examined, students can choose the course of action they think should be taken, state their reasons for their choice, and launch a class discussion.

Regardless of the specific techniques used in conducting a moral discussion, however, the processes of confronting a dilemma, taking a tentative position, and examining and reflecting on the reasoning behind various positions remain essential activities. Crucial, too, are the student-to-student interaction, the constant focus on moral issues and reasoning, and the emphasis on a supportive, trusting, informal classroom atmosphere. The extent to which the teacher can direct the entire process without assuming an expository or authoritarian role largely determines the success of a moral discussion.

Chances of success in using this strategy may be even further enhanced by being alert to some of its many nuances. For example, teachers need not devote an entire class period to every moral discussion. Students often tire of a discussion technique when it is used to excess. Varying the amount of time devoted to discussions can provide variety and heighten interest. Sometimes moral discussions arise spontaneously as part of a lesson in which the major goals are acquisition of knowledge or the development of skills. In such cases moral dilemmas embedded in the content of a course can serve as take-off points for discussions of perhaps ten or fifteen minutes duration. A lesson about the underground railroad, for example, can lend itself to discussing the morality of breaking a law in order to help slaves. A teacher can introduce the issue orally and without elaborate preparation: "Do you think people were justified to break the law in order to help slaves escape?" The class as a whole can then discuss this issue without dividing into small groups, hearing reports, or carefully identifying best reasons.

Three developments may impede a discussion at the point where students are called upon to make a decision upon action in a dilemma. Sometimes all or most members of a class take the same position on a choice of action. When they do so, the teacher can pose an alternative to the original dilemma—a twist to the story that alters some of the circumstances without changing the characters involved or the central issues. For example, if an entire class agreed, in responding to Sharon's dilemma, that Sharon should not tell on Jill, the teacher could suggest this twist to the original story: "Suppose that earlier Jill had told their teacher that Sharon had cheated on an examination. What should Sharon do in this case?" Such alternatives prepared in advance for just this type of situation often generate an appropriate class division.

Three other options may also be used when a class fails to divide on an action. First, the class can be divided into groups with half the students being assigned to defend their original positions and the other half to defend the opposite position as they imagine those who might take such a position would argue. After each group picks its best reasons, the class can reconvene and proceed, using one of the class discussion formats outlined above. Or, without any disagreement about action, students can be divided into groups. Each group can then share and rank the reasons given for its position. These reasons can be listed on the board so that the class can discuss the top two or three reasons. Finally, if no division occurs it may be that the students fail to perceive a dilemma in the story. In this case, students can be asked "Why isn't this a dilemma? What would have to exist to make it a dilemma?" Most students are eager to respond to such questions and are quite frank in their replies and suggestions. Once students have responded, the teacher can note their suggestions for later use in revising the dilemma and suggest that the conditions introduced by the students be assumed to exist in this case. The class can then proceed to a division and subsequent discussion.

A second obstacle to continuing a moral discussion sometimes arises when students refuse to take a position on a dilemma until they have more facts about it. For example, in discussing Sharon's dilemma, they may want to know how much the sweater which Jill stole was worth. Many students want to weigh the cost of the item stolen against the possible consequences of stealing it. Attempting to determine the value of the sweater, however, will divert attention from moral issues. To avoid this development, the teacher can ask students why they need this information. Why is stealing a valuable article worse than stealing one which costs little? In this way, a request for more data can be used to refocus a discussion on moral issues.

A third obstacle to a discussion sometimes appears when some students cannot make up their minds about an appropriate action in a dilemma. The teacher can group such undecided students together and give them an active role in the discussion. They can be asked to list the major reasons why they are undecided, and the subsequent class discussion can then be focused for a time on their report of these reasons. Undecided students can also serve as an audience for a debate between the pro and con groups who try to win them over to one set of reasons or another. Or undecided students can be encouraged to question individuals who have taken positions about the reasons they give to justify their actions.

Two final points remain. Guiding moral discussions successfully requires special efforts to avoid "putting students down." There is often the temptation to interview students—that is, to interrogate a single student with a rapid-fire series of questions. This tendency should be avoided, for it tends to intimidate students and it gets in the way of student-to-student interaction. A second potentially threatening situation can occur when a teacher wishes to have certain students attend to stage-higher remarks. Here attention must be called to a particular statement without threatening the speaker. The extent to which a teacher can support a student in this situation will go far toward turning an exchange into a valuable learning experience.

Teachers need not be able to identify the stages of reasoning their students use in order to be able to lead moral discussions. Unless a class is extraordinarily homogeneous, it will usually contain students who think at two and often three stages. For example, most eleventh-grade students probably use Stage 3 thought predominately, but many will reason mainly at Stage 2 or Stage 4. Teachers who learn to encourage students to respond to each other can usually engage them in arguments at contiguous stages. With experience and with re-reading reports of Kohlberg's research, teachers eventually can become more skilled at identifying the stages at which their students reason. They can then use probe questions more skillfully and encourage student-to-student interaction with a higher probability of success.

The teaching plan which follows illustrates how the five basic activities comprising this strategy can be used to guide a moral discussion of Sharon's dilemma. Teachers can devise similar plans for any moral dilemma which they create.

Teaching Plan for Sharon's Dilemma

Part I—Presenting the Dilemma Distribute the handout which describes Sharon's dilemma. Make sure that the students understand any difficult terms or phrases in the dilemma. Have the students clarify the facts of the situation. Have a volunteer state and explain the nature of the moral dilemma Sharon faces.

Part II—Dividing on Action Ask the students to think for a moment about what they think Sharon should do. They should then write their recommendation and reason for their recommendation on a sheet of paper. Determine by a show of hands or in some other way how many students think Sharon should or should not tell her friend's name to the security officer. Have a volunteer representing each position explain the reasons for their positions.

If the class fails to divide satisfactorily, use these alternatives as appropriate:

If the members of the class agree that Sharon *should* tell:

1. Suppose Sharon knows that Jill is on parole and will be sent back to a reformatory if she is caught stealing. What should she do in that case?
2. Suppose that Jill has done Sharon many favors and that Sharon knows that she will lose many of her friends if she tells on Jill. What should she do in that case?

If the members of the class agree that Sharon *should not* tell:

1. Suppose that on a previous occasion, Jill had told their teacher that Sharon had cheated on an examination. What should Sharon do in that case?
2. Suppose that instead of being a friend, Jill was only an acquaintance whom Sharon knew casually. What should Sharon do in that case?

If the alternative dilemmas fail to provoke a division, have students role play different sides of the dilemma or have them revise the dilemma and then take positions. Then have a volunteer representing each position explain the reasons for their positions.

Part III—Small Group Discussions When the class divides with no less than one-quarter of the students on each side of the issue, organize a small group discussion in which students can share their reasons, choose those reasons they think are best for the position recommended, and decide why these reasons are their "best" reasons.

Part IV—Class Discussion Reconvene the class in a large group. Have students from each small group report the group decisions or list their decisions on the board. Encourage students to discuss the merits of the reasons given by each group. Use some of the following probe questions where appropriate to focus the discussion:

1. What is a "best friend"?
2. Does Sharon have an obligation to Jill? the storeowner? the law? herself? Why or why not?
3. Which set of obligations, to Jill, to the storeowner, or to the law, are most important? Why?
4. From the point of view of Jill (of the storeowner, of Sharon's parents) should Sharon tell? Why or why not?
5. Is it ever right to tell on a friend? Why or why not?

Part V—Closing the Discussion Have the students who feel that Sharon should tell summarize all the reasons given by those who argued that Sharon should not tell. Have the students who said Sharon should not tell summarize the reasons given by those who argued Sharon should tell. Then have the students think about what they have heard, choose again what they think Sharon should do, and write their choice and a reason for their choice on a piece of paper. Do *not* collect the papers.

In order to lead moral discussions, a teacher should be able to use the following curricular skills:

- identify suitable places in a course to conduct moral discussions
- locate appropriate, already-prepared moral dilemmas
- prepare new moral dilemmas
- use prepared lesson plans or write new plans for moral discussions

A teacher should also be able to employ the following teaching skills:

- establish and maintain a supportive classroom atmosphere
- involve students in moral discussions
- ask questions which do not threaten students
- encourage student-to-student interaction
- identify and cope with substantive diversions

Many teachers lack some of these competencies. In order to acquire them, they need knowledge of Kohlberg's research findings and supervised practice in conducting moral discussions. Teachers can embark on a self-directed study of the research findings by consulting the relevant literature.[6] Programs of self-study will be doubly effective if several colleagues embark on them simultaneously and hold periodic discussions. Teachers can also begin to lead moral discussions using the techniques outlined in this article. Working with colleagues who agree to critique classes will increase the effectiveness of this learning process.

Notes

1. Kohlberg's research findings are not without their critics. See, for example, William Kurtines and Esther B. Greif, "The Development of Moral Thought: Review and Evaluation of Kohlberg's Approach," *Psychological Bulletin* 81, no. 8 (August 1974): 453–70; Elizabeth L. Simpson, "Moral Development Research: A Case Study of Scientific Cultural Bias," *Human Development* 17 (1974): 81–106; D. C. Phillips and Mavis E. Kelly, "Hierarchical Theories of Development in Education and Psychology," *Harvard Educational Review* 45, no. 3 (August 1975): 351–75; and James Rest, "The Cognitive Developmental Approach to Morality: The State of the Art," *Counseling and Values* 18, no. 2 (Winter 1964): 64–78.
2. Moshe Blatt and Lawrence Kohlberg, "The Effects of Classroom Moral Discussion Upon Children's Level of Moral Judgment," *Journal of Moral Education* 4 (1975): 129–61 and Marcus Lieberman, "Evaluation of a Social Studies Curriculum Based on an Inquiry Method and a Cognitive Developmental Approach to Moral Education," paper presented to AERA Annual Meeting, April 1975.
3. This dilemma situation is based on a story created by Dr. Frank Alessi, a member of the staff of the Carnegie-Mellon/Harvard Values Education Project. He is now Social Studies Chairperson of the Cortland (New York) City Schools.
4. An earlier version of this strategy has been presented in detail in Ronald E. Galbraith and Thomas M. Jones, "Teaching Strategies for Moral Dilemmas," *Social Education* 39, no 1 (January 1975): 16–22. Ronald Galbraith is currently Director of the Division of Teacher Education/Curriculum Development of the American Institute for Character Education in San Antonio, Texas; Thomas Jones is a member of the social studies faculty of the West Irondequoit High School in Rochester, New York.
5. For a detailed analysis of probe questions as used in this strategy see Edwin Fenton, Anne Colby and Betsy Speicher-Dubin, "Developing Moral Dilemmas for Social Studies Classes," unpublished paper available from Moral Education and Research Foundation, Harvard University.
6. See the annotated bibliography by Linda Rosenzweig in *Social Education*, April 1976.

Creating Moral Dilemmas for the Classroom

Peter Scharf, Assistant Professor of Social Ecology,
University of California at Irvine.

Introduction

A moral dilemma, or a situation involving conflict in moral claims, is the basic curriculum tool in classroom developmental moral education. Teachers who know and use Kohlberg's developmental moral education theory discover that it is relatively easy to find, adapt, or create moral dilemmas for use in their classrooms. Successful dilemmas have certain common qualities, though their form and content may differ dramatically. In general:

1. Effective dilemmas have conflicting claims, both or all of which on the surface appear to be plausible and reasonable. For example, a dilemma dealing with a conflict between human life and law is powerful because most people believe in both the importance of life and the individual's responsibility to the law. Similarly, a dilemma involving a conflict between telling the truth and hurting someone's feelings is powerful because most people neither like to lie nor to hurt someone else.
2. Effective dilemmas focus at a particular stage level. For example, a good dilemma for Stage 2 and 3 children might focus on issues of concern for others versus an individual's self interest (Should you stop to help a friend who has had a bike accident if you are late getting home for your birthday party?). Similarly, a good dilemma for Stage 3 and 4 adolescents might involve a conflict between the law and group allegiance (Should you turn in a good friend who you know has committed a crime?). Finally, most successful dilemmas for older principled students (Stage 5 or above) involve some conflict between the law or other social convention and a higher moral principle (Should one steal a drug to save a human life? or, Is it ever right to take a human life?).
3. Effective dilemmas involve some life experience that is real to the participants' situations. For example, most exciting dilemmas for elementary school children involve problems with peers or parents (Should you lie to your parents so that you can go to a movie with your friends?). Often, interesting dilemmas for teenagers involve the

issues of sex, grades, drugs, as well as those of peers and the family (Susy and Bill are alone studying together. They have been "going together" for a long time. . .). Successful dilemmas for adults often deal with issues of politics, work, or the economy (Should welfare families have as much money as low-income workers?).

4. Effective dilemmas involve a moral issue in which the facts are clearly defined and limited so that the primary focus becomes the ethical issue rather than the scientific or historical issue. For example, if a teacher were to go to a class and say, "What do you think of the Watergate problem?" she would soon be deluged by observations, opinions, and facts not necessarily relevant to the ethical issues implied. Successful dilemmas often involve real historical or scientific cases but are focused so that the facts and probable consequences, as well as the moral issue of the case, are clearly defined.
5. Effective dilemmas include questions which force students to think more deeply about the moral issues implied in a particular case. These questions should not be too abstract, nor too rhetorical. Typically, they will move from a clarification of the facts, to a general question of the ethical issue, to more complex inquiries. For example, in a dilemma dealing with euthanasia, a possible order of questioning might include:
   a) What is the law in your state on mercy killing?
   b) If you were the doctor in this case, what would you do?
   c) If you were the son of the dying woman, what would you think if the doctor gave her an injection to make her die?
   d) Write a law dealing with mercy killing which would protect the terminally ill from unnecessary suffering as well as protect the sick from possible abuse by doctors and relatives.

Matching Students and Dilemmas

One of the most difficult tasks is matching students to particular dilemmas. As we noted previously, a good match between a dilemma and a group of students includes an assessment of the students' moral stage and the types of issues which genuinely interest and excite them. The following dilemmas, written by William McCoy of Laguna Beach Unified School District, reflect an effort to find dilemma situations for a class of sixth graders. They primarily involve conflicts that deal with Stage 2 and Stage 3 issues which involve sixth graders most intimately (relationships with parents, peers, and pets).

The following dilemma raises the Stage 3 consideration of others' feelings and the Stage 2 consideration of one's own pleasure.

Stacy wanted to go to a movie that she knew her parents wouldn't want her to see. She knew it would be wrong to lie to her parents but she really wanted to see the movie. Stacy told them she would be at her friend Jenny's house, but her parents discovered the truth. The girls had gone to the movie.

Stacy felt that what she had done was wrong, but she didn't think the punishment was right either: no movies for three months.

1. Do you agree with Stacy that what she did was wrong? Why?
2. Should she be punished for what she did? Why?
3. Do you agree with Stacy that the punishment was too much? Why?
4. Do you think that punishments are useful? What are they good for?

5. How can you decide whether or not a punishment is too severe?
6. Do children have a right to help decide what a punishment should be?
7. Should parents be allowed to spank, paddle, or in any other way hit their children as a punishment?

The following dilemma raises the Stage 1 or 2 consideration of protecting oneself from possible harm and the Stage 3 consideration of preventing people from hurting one another.

Chad and two of his friends, Mary and Phil, were spending Saturday afternoon playing in the park. They came upon two boys, about their age, who were fighting.

Phil suggested that they break up the fight. He felt people shouldn't fight because there are better ways to settle problems. Chad disagreed. He thought they should stay out of the fight, that it was none of their business.

As the one boy finally started to get the better of the other and started to kick him, Mary sided with Phil and said that they should break up the fight. She said that someone might get hurt if they didn't.

Chad still maintained that they should mind their own business and he managed to convince his two friends. They left the two fighters to themselves and walked off to another part of the park.

1. Was Chad right? Did he and his two friends do the right thing by not stopping the fight? Why?
2. Explain Chad's argument that they should "mind their own business." Is this a good rule to follow?
3. Who had the best reason for thinking it was wrong to let the boys go on fighting—Phil, who felt fighting was wrong because there are better ways for people to settle problems, or Mary, who felt that someone might get hurt in the fight?
4. Would it make a difference if someone was obviously being badly hurt in the fight? Why?

The next dilemma involves a Stage 4 concern for property rights and a Stage 3 concern for animals.

Denise's great love for animals has usually brought her a great deal of satisfaction and enjoyment. She had a dog, two cats, a turtle, and a mouse. They were a lot of fun for her and it felt good to care for them well.

But this same love and concern brought her trouble and worry when she found out about her neighbor. He was an older man who had a dog he mistreated. He kept the dog tied up all the time, did not feed it properly, and never kept it clean. Often Denise could hear the man beating the dog when he was angry.

When she put her eye up close to the backyard fence, Denise could see the dog and each time it looked more miserable. Denise worried that the poor dog was suffering and might die from the bad treatment.

Finally she decided that she must do something for the dog. One evening when her neighbor was gone Denise went into his yard and untied the dog, hoping it would leave. She was very glad to see that it did. The dog never came back, and for a long time afterwards the old man complained bitterly about the "sneak" who stole his dog.

1. Was what Denise did right or wrong? Why?
2. Should Denise have done anything else?
3. Is it right for people to own animals? Did Denise steal the dog?
4. Can a person do anything he or she wishes to do with his or her animal?

It is possible to organize dilemmas around particular types of moral issues. For example, the following dilemma sequence written for the *Human Sciences Program* of the Biological Science Curriculum Study of Boulder, Colorado, was intended to provide three related dilemmas dealing with conflicts of loyalty and obligation comprehensible to sixth graders.

The day started well. The boys played hide-and-seek in the sports department and made faces at the customers in "ladies wear." They bought popcorn and cokes for lunch and were having a good time. Early in the afternoon, one boy, named Freddy, suggested that they steal some baseball gloves. Baseball season had just started, and all the boys had old, beaten-up gloves. Freddy said his brother had shown him how to shoplift by sneaking stuff under his shirt and walking out the door with it.

None of the other boys wanted to shoplift with Freddy. Some said they were afraid; others said that stealing was wrong.

Freddy said he would do it, even if the other kids had "no guts." He grabbed a first baseman's mitt, a Hank Aaron Special Fielder's Glove, and a "regulation" major league baseball and tucked them under his shirt. They made him look very lumpy. As all the boys headed to the door, Freddy turned to his friend Tony and said, "Why don't you carry this first baseman's mitt out for me? If you do, I'll give you the baseball." Tony tucked the mitt under his shirt.

As they reached the door, a store detective stopped them and said, "Boys, you better come with me." Tony and Freddy sat nervously in the store detective's office. The detective asked, "Which of you boys is responsible for this? Whoever it is, is in big trouble." Tony sat thinking about what to do. He didn't want Freddy to get in even bigger trouble if he told the detective that it was Freddy's idea. But he didn't want to be in trouble either. On the other hand, if Freddy told the other kids that Tony had reported him, they all would think Tony was a "rat fink."

What should Tony do?

During the war, a woman married a man from a foreign country. She had known him only a short time and did not know much about his past. During the war, her husband worked as a scientist in a factory testing new kinds of atomic weapons. Now he was working as a clerk in the same factory.

After a few months, the woman noticed that several strange men were visiting her husband and that her husband was out until late several nights a week. Something strange was going on!

One day at home she found a blueprint of one of the atomic weapons her husband was working on in the factory. He had told her many times that everything he worked on was "Top Secret" and that he could not bring anything home.

She confronted him with what she had found, and he admitted to selling information to some secret agents. Although he was getting some money for the blueprints, the main reason he was stealing them was because the agents had threatened to kill his parents and brothers and sisters who still lived overseas.

The woman thought about it. She was afraid that if the enemy got the secrets to the weapons, they would win a war. On the other hand, she loved her husband and did not want to see his family harmed.

What should the woman do?

Penny, who was thirteen, had a sixteen-year-old brother named Robert. They shared ideas and talked about almost everything, including boyfriends and girlfriends. When school started in September, Robert began hanging around with some new kids. He started to lose weight, and his personality began to change. He had always been a happy-go-lucky person, but now he was always nervous and fearful. His parents were very worried about him. At dinner they would ask him what was wrong, but he would always tell them that they were just being nosy and that there was nothing wrong.

Late one night Penny and Robert were talking. Robert began to cry and said that he had started taking drugs. The other kids he hung around with were doing it, and as a result, he got involved. He also said that he had shoplifted in order to pay for the drugs, which were very expensive. He said that the drugs made him feel very good, but that he felt sick when he couldn't get any. He made Penny promise not to tell anyone what he said—especially their parents. He promised to stop taking the drugs as soon as he could.

The next day Penny's mother came to her and asked her if she knew what was wrong with Robert. She knew Penny and Robert talked about everything, and she expected Penny to tell the truth.

What should Penny do?

Dilemmas for Special Students and Situations

Some students in some situations require special dilemma cases. For example, Joseph Hickey and I ran an experimental class in a maximum security prison in the state of Connecticut. The following are among the dilemmas developed for inmates. We found them to be especially successful because they focused primarily on Stage 2 and Stage 3 moral issues and dealt particularly with the unique problems of prison life.

A prison has a segregation unit. The prison rules state that every inmate is to have a mattress and a blanket every night while in this unit. Some guards like to deny these to the inmates. An inmate works in this unit. One of his jobs is to distribute the mattresses and blankets every evening. One day the officer in charge tells him not to distribute mattresses to certain noisy inmates. This is against the rules, but the inmate does what he is told. From then on he does similar illegal acts for the officer who rewards him with extra food, showers, clean clothes.

1. Did the guard have the right to break the rule?
2. Was the inmate justified in breaking the rule? Why did he do it?
3. Would it have been better for all concerned if he had refused to break the rule in the first place?

Let's suppose you are living at home and you start getting into a lot of trouble, stealing cars, staying out late, etc. Your parents are very worried, but they can't seem to get you to stop. One night you are caught breaking and entering and are shot at by the police. You are almost killed, but you get away. Your parents find out.

What should your parents do?

Writing Your Own Dilemmas

Here are some suggestions for teachers who are willing to engage in dilemma writing:

1. Know your students. Decide:
   a) What moral issues are of concern to them? (A sixth-grade class might be especially concerned about moral issues involving peer conformity and lying but may be uninterested in issues involving the law.)
   b) What topics seem especially pressing? (For example, a class in biology might be especially concerned about questions involving euthanasia or eugenics.)
2. Reread the newspaper and the textbook for dilemma situations.
   a) In most newspapers there are literally dozens of dilemmas waiting to be adapted for dilemma discussion purposes.
   b) Similarly, in most units, even in conventional textbooks, there are dozens of dilemmas waiting to be adapted for use by an imaginative teacher.

Teachers who choose to write their own dilemmas will find that even while undergoing frustration, they will learn more about their students as well as the learning process. When a dilemma "misses" the student audience, one is forced to confront the differences in moral perspective between adults and children. For example, one of my students tried to write a dilemma for her junior high school classroom. She was initially quite surprised that her dilemma "What to decide at Nuremberg" (raising Stage 5 and 6 issues of international law) failed to interest her Stage 2 and 3 students. Once she realized this, she began writing successful dilemmas more appropriate to her students and found the discussion process both exciting and useful.

To conclude, including ethical dilemmas in the curriculum provides a means to bring the ethical issues of life into clearer focus for discussion with students. Dilemmas can be used either as a separate activity or welded into nearly any content area in the curriculum. Dilemmas are a core vehicle of classroom developmental moral education.

A Curriculum in Moral Education for Adolescents

Ralph Mosher, Professor of Counselor Education, Boston University.

Paul Sullivan, Project Director, Values Education Project, Tacoma Public Schools.

Introduction

In this chapter we will describe a course in moral education which is being developed for high school students. Its basic purpose is to stimulate moral reasoning, i.e., the way in which adolescents think about, or analyze, complex social and personal moral dilemmas. The course does not teach a new catechism or set of "right" answers or behaviors; it does involve the adolescent in hard thinking about the ideological, valuing, or ethical issues which so preoccupy this age group. The aim is to stimulate the development of more differentiated, integrated, and comprehensive ways of thinking about values or morality. The supposition is that more mature thinking will be related to positive moral action.

Development as the Aim of Education

Two general assumptions underlie the course. One has to do with the purpose of education; the second involves our views of adolescent psychology. A premise of the course is that the essential purpose of education is the stimulation of individual development. The education of adolescents must stimulate cognitive or intellectual growth, moral sensibilities and reasoning, social skills, vocational competencies, aesthetic development, and physical maturation. The basic notion is that education should discern and provide those systematic experiences or stimuli which give the individual optimal opportunity to develop or grow in interaction with his or her environment.

This conception of education is as old or as "progressive" as John Dewey:

> Only knowledge of the order and connection of the stages in the development of the psychical functions can insure the full maturing of the psychical powers. Education is the work of supplying the conditions which will

Portions of this paper first appeared in *Administration and the Valuing Process*, edited by Alvin Myhre et al and published by the Council on School Administration of the Alberta Teachers' Association in 1975. Used by permission of Gordon McIntosh, director.

> enable the psychical functions, as they successively arise, to mature and pass into higher functions in the freest and fullest manner.

It has recently been re-stated by Lawrence Kohlberg:

> The stream of educational ideology which is still best termed "progressive" following Dewey . . . holds that education should nourish the child's natural interaction with a developing society or environment . . . development [is] a progression through invariant, ordered, sequential stages. The educational goal is the eventual attainment of a higher level or stage of development in adulthood, not merely the healthy functioning of the child at a present level. . . . This aim requires an educational environment that actively stimulates development through the presentation of resolvable but genuine problems or conflicts. For progressives, the organizing and developing force in the child's experience is the child's active thinking, and thinking is stimulated by the problematic, by cognitive conflict. Educational experience makes the child think—think in ways which organize both cognition and emotion. . . . The acquisition of "knowledge" is an active change in patterns of thinking brought about by experiential problem-solving situations. Similarly . . . the progressive sees the acquisition of morality as an active change in patterns of response to problematic social situations rather than the learning of culturally accepted rules.

The general point is that we see the purpose of this course as the support and stimulation of a major aspect in the adolescent's development (i.e., morality). It is further an example of educational programs designed to stimulate overall ego development in adolescence (Mosher and Sprinthall, 1971).

Coming of Age in America

This brings us to some general assumptions about adolescents. Adolescence is a distinct stage in the process of human growth. While psychologists disagree as to a definitive theory of adolescence, they generally agree that a number of things happen in the teenager's development that have a significant influence on what he or she is interested in learning. We will mention several aspects of adolescent interest and development which have special relevance to our program in moral education.

A first point is that most adolescents are capable of adult thought. Many have achieved what Piaget calls "formal operations." In essence, these adolescents think in ways which are qualitatively different from the thinking patterns of children. They can conceive of probabilities; they can think abstractly and hypothetically; their sense of time perspective changes; and they can see issues and themselves in a variety of ways both present and future. Further, they enjoy using this capacity. W. Rohwer has argued, that as a result, adolescence is the prime time for intellectual or cognitive stimulation and education.

Adolescents are concerned, however, with more than intellectual development. They actively seek individuals and ideals with which to identify. Most people who write about adolescents refer to the idealism of this age group. Adolescents have to make difficult personal decisions of right and wrong. Their moral concern and sensibility may be easily subverted into rigid political ideology, into new and exotic moralities or religions, or into despair. Even so, adolescents are concerned with making moral and ethical sense of their world. Kohlberg's finding that people progress through stages of moral reasoning is very helpful in understanding this aspect of adolescence.

Adolescence is usually portrayed as a time when peers become the most influential arbiters or sources of reference for the individual. Adolescents are tribal people. Even if society did not segregate them, they probably would choose to be with one another much of the time. There are several reasons for this interpersonal impetus. Adolescents supposedly are concerned with issues of their own sexual identity and sexual relationships. But more is at stake for them than simply "making out." The much subtler issue of intimate interpersonal relationships with people of the same sex and especially of the opposite sex is a central preoccupation. They are beginning to struggle with human intimacy, the process of how to live with, relate to, and love others. So adolescents want to be together, to do things together, to socialize, to reach out and communicate with one another. It is a time of chums, of friends and gangs, of important beginning steps away from the family to new social relationships.

Depending in important degree on social class, the world of work also affects adolescents. Work may be nothing more than a part-time job at MacDonald's as a way to achieve some financial independence of the family. For some students, like those entering the armed services or an apprenticeship at the end of high school, work can be an imminent issue. For many adolescents, those who are college bound, the issue is more *what college* than *what job*. For them, career decisions are deferred until the end of college or perhaps longer. But work, as one more attribute of what it is to be adult, impinges on the adolescent.

It is almost a cliché in discussions of adolescence to talk about this period in terms of "identity formation." Erikson has stated that the central problem the teenager faces is to define oneself—to create a sense of one's own identity. This argument will not be elaborated here. Essentially, adolescents are struggling to form more comprehensive answers to the question, Who am I? Their new intellectual capabilities are applied to that task. Our position is that because Who am I? is a central question, developmentally, it must also be a basic focus of education. The fact that identity is an elusive, derivative, and evolving quality makes the educator's problem in this regard not unlike that of lawyers who, in Senator Baker's characterization, spend their professional lives "shoveling smoke."

What is often not said about adolescents is that they can be remarkably competent people. Some adolescents can learn to teach or counsel other people as effectively as graduate students or practicing professionals. They can carry out sophisticated programs of social research and action. They learn to fly military aircraft and to use complicated weaponry in the armed services. They can produce musicals, conduct complicated scientific experiments, and write subtle poetry. Extensive opportunities to do these things are essential if adolescents are to develop into competent adults. Significant evidence in the literature of psychology and education supports this. Adolescents need opportunities to take active social roles, to have significant and systematic responsibility for analysis and action on real problems, and to be held accountable.

In summary, physical development is completed in adolescence. Sexual maturity is achieved. Adult intellectual capacity is being reached. Idealism is strong. Family influence wanes and is supplanted by that of contemporaries. Economic independence is possible. So, too, are many adult competencies. The rites of passage (a driver's license, a diploma, the right to vote, legal permission to use alcohol) are available or within view. Obviously no longer a child, the adolescent is not quite an adult. Education best serves adolescents if it actively supports them in making the critical developmental transition from youth to adult.

Moral Development

Our curriculum work in moral education draws heavily on Kohlberg's empirical and theoretical study of moral development. Because of Kohlberg's major theoretical contributions, we have a relatively clear blueprint for the moral aspect of adolescent development. That is, we know the characteristics of adolescent moral thinking, its progression, and some, at least, of the experiences critical to its stimulation. While, in our view, the major educational and curricular *applications* of Kohlberg's theory remain to be done, we believe that the theoretical understanding of moral development now available allows that practical work to go forward with dispatch and promise.

A major part of this chapter will describe what the writers have learned about moral education with high school adolescents. But we will first review Kohlberg's moral development theory. We do so for several reasons. The first we have already noted: Our curriculum and teaching is an extension and application of this particular theory. Our view is, further, that a reasonably sophisticated understanding of the theory permits the teacher to comprehend better the flow of adolescent argument about moral dilemmas, to categorize it (i.e., to differentiate stages and subtleties in moral discussion), and to make appropriate responses (e.g., clarifying questions, probes, counter-arguments at a "higher" stage). Finally, the theory suggests educational experiences beyond the analysis or discussion of moral issues (e.g., the importance of role-taking) which may have important developmental consequences.

Kohlberg's Cognitive-Developmental Theory of Moral Growth

In Kohlberg's conceptualization, "moral" refers basically to thought processes, i.e., to judgment, reasoning, or decision making in situations wherein the person has conflicting responsibilities. Moral principles are principles of choice for resolving conflicts of obligation. These principles reflect the strong cognitive and philosophic elements in the theory. "Moral" is not simply a tag to be attached to actions we approve of. Morality is an overall mental "structure," a means for deciding what one should or should not do in situations involving competing moral values. Each stage of moral development has a characteristic way of resolving such conflicts. Furthermore, these stages of moral development are empirically derived. Kohlberg has found that these characteristic ways of thinking about moral choice exist across class and culture; they are universal and developmental.

The principles one uses in making decisions develop from the egocentric, limited, and externally derived canons usually characteristic of younger children to the autonomous, universal, and inclusive principles which characterize the highest levels of moral reasoning. Moral thinking becomes increasingly differentiated and integrated in the course of development. Each successive stage produces more complex, more cognitively and philosophically satisfactory principles. At the highest level, principles such as justice provide a universal mode of choosing, one which we would want all people to adopt in all situations.

The basic concept of justice is present in all the stages of moral development, but only at the highest level does it become a universal principle. The process of moral development involves a restructuring, i.e., a reorganization in more comprehensive, differentiated, and integrated terms of the concept of justice as well as these related moral categories: respect for authority, society, or persons; prudence or self-interest; and concern for the welfare of others. Justice takes into account all of these other categories at the highest stage and provides a set of principles for deciding between competing claims of individuals. [Refer to Appendix for a description of the stages of moral development.]

Apart from the six stages described in an appendix of this volume, there is another quasi-stage or transition phase which is of considerable significance to our work with high school students: "Stage 4½." This transitional phase occurs in some people who are moving from Stage 4 to 5. One of the necessary but not sufficient conditions for attaining postconventional moral reasoning is formal operational thought in Piaget's terms (i.e., the capacity for abstract thinking which includes, of course, the ability to think about justification and values per se). This capacity for abstract thinking allows the individual to see any given system of thought or action as only one of many possibilities. Thus the individual at Stage 4½ sees morality as being a Stage 4-type system of arbitrarily maintained laws or rules and then questions the validity of this particular form of morality. It is merely one of many possible moralities to the individual who reasons at this transitional phase. Superficially, Stage 4½ reasoning seems much like Stage 2—very relativistic and egocentric. But there are fundamental differences. Stage 4½ relativists do not make simplistic judgments of right as being whatever the individual wishes. Instead they deny the absolute validity of any other standard of right. Individuals clearly recognize that there is a socially accepted morality (laws, rules, etc.) which is the "official" morality. But they reject this point of view as the basis for determining right and wrong. This metaethical stance is not present at Stage 2.

The following excerpt from *Little Murders* by Jules Feiffer exemplifies the extreme relativist position. In this scene Alfred and Patsy are being married by Reverend Dupas of the First Existentialist Church. Here is the Reverend Dupas' wedding speech:

> You all know why we're here. Alfred has certain beliefs which I assume you all know. He is an atheist, which is perfectly all right. Really it is. . . . First let me state frankly to you, Alfred, and to you, Patricia, that of the 200 marriages I've performed, all but 7 have failed. So the odds are not good. . . . Why does one decide to marry? Social pressure? Boredom? Loneliness? Sexual appeasement? Love? Each in its own way is adequate. Each is all right. . . .
>
> Marriage is a small single step. If it works—fine! If it fails—fine! Look elsewhere for satisfaction. Perhaps to more marriages—fine! As many as one likes—fine! To homosexuality—fine! To drug addiction—I won't put it down. Each of these is an answer—for somebody. . . .

Stage 4½ typically occurs in late adolescence and early adulthood and therefore is of particular significance in moral education programs in high school. It is a transition for many people to Stage 5 moral reasoning wherein the problems of relativity and competing moralities are partially resolved by the social contract. Only at Stage 6 can these problems be fully resolved. Of course, not all of those who enter this transitional phase achieve postconventional thought. Some remain as confirmed relativists; some revert to Stage 4 moral reasoning. This points up the necessity to provide experiences which encourage development to Stage 5 reasoning.

Stimulation of Moral Development

Kohlberg's cross-cultural studies show that the vast majority of people in a culture (approximately 80 percent) never develop autonomous moral principles. That this is true of United States citizens is especially ironic since the United States Constitution is primarily a Stage 5, utilitarian, social contract document. We must conclude that the majority of citizens are unable to comprehend fully the moral principles which underlie their own Constitution. These findings underscore the importance of promoting moral growth.

Apparently, transitions between the three levels of moral development are most easily accomplished during particular age periods. The first "open" period occurs from ages ten to thirteen when the transition from preconventional to conventional moral reasoning is most likely to occur. Longitudinal studies show that children who do not achieve conventional moral thinking by age thirteen probably will not achieve postconventional thinking in adulthood. The second period of transition occurs from fifteen to nineteen years of age. Those people who do not begin to use some (at least 20 percent) postconventional or principled thinking in this period are also unlikely to achieve postconventional moral reasoning in adulthood.

In light of these transition or "open" periods, the key function of a course in moral and ethical reasoning is to stimulate *overall* moral development and to attempt to insure that these transitions occur. Individuals who remain at a particular stage for long periods of time tend to become fixated at that stage. Our educational objective is to stimulate normal development and prevent any such fixation.

Kohlberg contends that the central stimulus and precondition for moral development is "role-taking." Role-taking is (*a*) an awareness by the individual that there are other people who are like himself or herself but who have different feelings, desires, and ways of seeing the world, and (*b*) the tendency to look at one's own behavior from these others' points of view and interests. Moral conflict could not occur if individuals were unable to take the role of others, for they would not see any conflict.

To put oneself in the place of others implies recognition of an equality and mutual interdependence between the self and others. Such empathy is the central component of justice. Role-taking becomes more complex at each stage of moral reasoning. At the same time, the principle of justice—with its admonition to take account equally of everyone's perspective in moral conflict—is also elaborated. Justice and idealized role-taking become essentially one and the same at the highest stages of moral development. Thus the stimulation of role-taking capacities is a powerful means for promoting a more complex sense of justice.

The primary opportunity for role-taking by individuals is their participation in a social group or institution, e.g., family, peer group, government, the law, and possibly work. Interaction and communication within the group provide the role-taking opportunities. To communicate effectively, individuals must be able to imagine how other people see them and what they have to say. If an individual is responsible for decisions in the group, he or she must increasingly take the role of others in order to judge the implications of those decisions for others. The more responsibility the individual has in the group and the more democratic the group structure, the more role-taking will occur.

As the individual interacts in these social groups and especially if he or she is part of the decision-making process, that individual experiences (moral) conflict between various others in the groups. This conflict is a result of the person's capacity for role-taking and is an essential step in restructuring moral reasoning. Once the conflict is perceived, the individual reasons about how to resolve the conflict. If a person places himself or herself in the positions of each of the participants in the conflict (i.e., cognitively takes the role of the others) that person may begin to see that his or her reasoning does not provide an adequate or fair resolution. *Cognitive dissonance*, the realization that one's "answers" or ways of reasoning about a conflict are inadequate, may result. This realization can stimulate the individual to change the way he or she reasons to a more complex, differentiated form of thinking which resolves the conflict in a more equitable and just way. Thus role-taking can act in a number of ways to stimulate moral development.

Another closely related and effective means of stimulating development is the discussion of moral dilemmas. Essentially the same process occurs as that which was outlined in the preceding description of role-taking. One major difference is that the individual is dealing with an abstract and vicarious conflict rather than one in which he or she is directly involved. While discussing a moral dilemma, individuals may come to see certain inadequacies in their reasoning as a result of interacting with more complex arguments made by other people. Or individuals may be asked to place themselves in the roles of the various parties in the dilemma and to examine their own reasoning from these several perspectives. They may then see that their thinking does not adequately resolve the dilemma. Cognitive dissonance may result and the intellectual process previously described may be engaged. Discussions of moral dilemmas provide a good opportunity for individuals to interact with other forms of reasoning and to examine their own reasoning in a deliberate and systematic manner.

The work of Turiel (1966), Rest (1969), and Blatt (1973) is relevant to this manner of promoting moral development. The Rest and Turiel studies indicate that the most effective arguments in bringing about change in a person's level of moral reasoning are those at the next higher stage than that which the person characteristically uses. Individuals consistently prefer the reasoning used at stages higher than their own but also tend to translate or "corrupt" that reasoning to their own level. They also reject lower levels of reasoning as inadequate. The next higher stage argument is effective in stimulating dissonance because it is the most easily understood and assimilated form of more complex reasoning. As outlined previously, conflict induced by hearing these more adequate arguments may be resolved by a restructuring of the individual's moral reasoning to the more complex level. Genuine growth is not simply learning new arguments, however.

Rather, it involves qualitative changes in the way in which the individual thinks, analyzes, or reasons about moral issues.

From this discussion there follow some broad teaching implications. Those persons who lead moral discussions must help the adolescent to focus on the moral conflict issues in a dilemma and to examine his or her reasoning about the issues. Then the inconsistencies in the teenager's reasoning should be clarified, highlighting the cognitive conflict. Finally, an attempt should be made to find some resolution for his or her inconsistencies. The resolution may be to reason at the next "higher" stage of moral development.

Upward stage change may come about as a result of an individual's hearing of more adequate arguments by other students or the teacher. But individuals do not change their structure of reasoning immediately. Rather, they go through a gradual process of seeing intellectual inadequacy, formulating new reasoning to resolve it, trying the new reasoning out, and then reformulating it again if necessary.

Moral Education for Adolescents

Introduction

The course we will describe is intended primarily for juniors and seniors in high school. The course presently is taken for credit as a social studies elective. It could, with equal logic, be offered in a guidance, human development, psychology, or philosophy curriculum. The course can be taught both within a regular four period per week schedule or as an after-school course for three hours once per week. It is designed to be taught for one semester or for a full year.

The course is introduced to the students in a relatively simple and straightforward way. They are told that they will be taking a course in ethical and moral reasoning and that the fundamental purpose of the experience is to have them think deeply and at length about a variety of complex social and personal moral dilemmas or issues. We suggest certain general synonyms for the term *moral*, e.g., that we will be talking about questions of "right" and "wrong"; value issues—both social and personal; questions of the individual's rights; a person's obligations to others and to family, etc. We emphasize that our purpose is not to teach a set of right and wrong answers. We also emphasize that attendance and participation in discussions are the two essential requirements of the course. Ordinarily this introduction takes ten to fifteen minutes of the first class. We use the remainder of that class period to administer the Kohlberg moral dilemmas scale as a pre-test. We do this because it is a relatively well-validated criterion measure for moral development and because our work involves curriculum development and a careful assessment of the effects of the course materials on adolescent moral thinking. This is not to suggest that every high school teacher experimenting with moral discussion in the classroom needs to use this instrument on a pre- and post-basis. However, it is now available in a relatively short and standardized form and can be applied by the teacher interested in "objective" data regarding the effect of his or her teaching. Further, the scoring of students' moral reasoning is an effective way to focus on the general characteristics as well as the nuances in the Kohlberg stages.

Units in the Course

In order to describe distinctive and sequential stages in the course, we will refer to its "phases." However, the educational experiences characteristic of these several phases need not be offered in the order we used in introducing them to the students. They are best seen as units or components in an overall course which involves high school students in systematic intellectual analysis of moral dilemmas and in a variety of role-taking experiences, e.g., "ethical" counseling with other adolescents or acting as moral educators with peers or younger children. The basic learning paradigm is to involve the adolescents' ways of thinking about moral questions and issues with the perspectives and thought of other adolescents and the teacher. The student is then put in "real" situations or experiences where he or she must apply moral thought to the ethical problems or dilemmas of other people and see such dilemmas and their resolution as others would choose that resolution.

Phase 1: Personal introductions. In this phase students introduce themselves, and if they choose, talk about some recent experience which involved special significance or learning for them. Some students make extended introductions in which they talk about adverse experiences with drugs, learning to fly, Outward Bound "solo" experiences, disciplinary problems with housemasters at school or with parents, problems with boyfriends or girlfriends, etc. Other students (those less verbal, less secure in a new group) introduce themselves briefly and with some embarrassment. The teacher supports a student in this introduction and often, in a subtle way, focuses on the personal moral issues mentioned by the student. Adolescents are unaware that they are introducing ethical dilemmas in the formal Kohlberg sense. (A student's understanding of Kohlberg's theory is not a concern of this phase.) Here is an example of the kind of moral dilemma we hear in these introductions.

A student talked about the very difficult problem of pleasing her friends. Friends were very important to her; she wanted to be seen as a source of counsel and support to them. This desire to nurture or parent others was very real. In many ways her thinking seemed to be classically Stage 3 in Kohlberg's terms—wanting to be a good friend. One of the problems for someone at Stage 3 is that one cannot please all of one's friends all of the time. Friends make contradictory demands. This girl was increasingly finding this to be the case. As a sophomore she had been relatively successful in satisfying a large circle of friends. Now, as a junior, it was not easy. Specifically, expectations relative to sex and drugs were very troublesome to her. Not that she was prudish or "square." Yet there was an emerging sense of her own standards. In the final analysis, however, she could not bring herself to hurt her friends (i.e., deny them what they asked of her). There were elements in her introduction of very genuine concern and compassion for friends, a belief that she really could help others through their personal difficulties and crises.

Other students argued that she had rights of her own that her friends should respect, that they were not "true" friends if they did not respect her wishes and decisions. They further noted that she was not helping her friends by, in every case, giving in to them, doing what they wanted, or letting them manipulate her. The exploration of these questions took much of one class period. Students returned to these issues during the remainder of the course.

Another girl talked at length about a disciplinary conference with her housemaster, her father, and her guidance counselor which was pending the following day at school. She, like many other students, recounted an experience of what she perceived as the arbitrary and unfair use of teacher sanctions and adult authority against her. The case involved issues of truancy and incomplete academic work—a scenario which will be familiar to most people who know schools. Her mood was one of angry defiance of authority. Issues of this kind, which involve the adolescent directly with the authority structure of the parents, the family, or the school, offer entry or exposure to Stage 4 reasoning. A number of students sympathized with her position or offered analogous "atrocity stories" of their own, relative to the arbitrariness of teachers and school personnel. Even at that early point in the course, however, several students justified school rules in general and argued that the system offered means for the redress of grievances. Fundamentally, they were arguing the case for rules and conformity to them but also that the student had not exhausted the opportunities for fair treatment or justice within the existing system. In a sense, they were making prototypical Stage 4 arguments. Heated discussions of rules systems within school and family groups occurred repeatedly during the course. The terms the argument took varied, of course, from situation to situation and from person to person. But adolescents obviously struggle to understand and find some system of rights as well as obligations within the general rule structure of the school and the family. The dilemmas which arise as a result are "real" ones; they elicit reasoning, feelings, and choices which are real. In short, they represent "natural" moral issues (or moral curriculum) for adolescents.

Teachers ask us how we elicit personal material in student introductions. We find that if we let students talk, these kinds of issues will emerge. Ethical issues are part of adolescents' lives. The fact that both of us have had training in counseling *may* be somewhat contributory, however, for our training and experience help us to wait and listen—to permit the person to talk about himself or herself. When we intervene as teachers at this stage in the course, we hope to clarify the elements in the dilemma the students raise rather than to confront or quiz them about their attitudes. It is very important to let other students in the class respond to an individual's dilemma. They will do so rather directly, and in that way the several stages of moral reasoning which are represented in any cross section of adolescents are brought into conflict with one another. Ordinarily, another adolescent will eventually present a higher stage argument to the student. If that does not happen, we raise, with the student, an alternative way of looking at or analyzing the dilemma. However, we make it clear that the dilemma is a personal one and that our purpose simply is to help the student see it and act on it in more comprehensive and personally satisfying ways. One further point may be pertinent. When students do not initially introduce material of this kind, our experience suggests that one does not push heavily for it. It will come as individuals feel more trust in the other students and in the teacher. Sometimes teachers can break the ice and establish a "model" by introducing themselves early in the process.

We discourage overly long introductions in order to avoid undue anxiety for any student, excessive egocentrism, or an autobiographical competition. Teachers, too, should introduce themselves at some point in this initial phase. The first six to nine hours of the course is probably an adequate time schedule for personal introductions.

Phase 2: Discussion and analysis of moral dilemmas through the case study method. We use two kinds of case study materials. One is films, either full length or edited segments of feature films which depict ethical dilemmas; the other is written case study material presenting moral dilemmas.

In the spring semester course in 1973, several films from the Learning Corporation of America series, *Searching for Values*, were used. This series is made up of edited versions of fourteen feature length films. They are edited in terms of length to focus on a salient moral dilemma. We discuss dilemmas from full length feature films as well. For example, Michael Corleone, the young Don in *The Godfather*, is a very compelling figure for adolescents—one with whom they can and do identify.

The reader may recall that one first meets Michael Corleone at the family wedding. He is pictured as the decorated war hero, the college graduate, as someone who has transcended the criminal intrigue, violence, and "business" of the family. *Yet that image is subverted*. Following an unsuccessful assassination attempt on the life of the Godfather, Michael, incensed by the treachery of this attack, agrees to avenge his father by murdering a rival gang leader and a corrupt New York city police captain.

Despite this premeditated, cold-blooded killing, high school students see Michael as an attractive and compelling figure. Many students argue that Michael killed out of love and loyalty for his father; that his country had decorated him for killing in defense of his country; that they, too, would kill to save the lives of members of their family. At that point we raise the issue of whether Michael is justified in taking the law into his own hands and we suggest more appropriate alternative actions which Michael might have taken, posing higher stage arguments to counter student arguments.

We are not suggesting that higher stage arguments will immediately be persuasive with adolescents. But they can be made in the context of highly animated analysis and discussion which the power of the film evokes for the students.

Phase 3: Teaching counseling skills to students. Some years ago we used the Kohlberg moral development scale as one *developmental* measure to assess the effect of teaching counseling to high school students. We selected the instrument because it was designed to measure growth-developmental change and not because of any postulated relationship between learning to counsel and moral development. What we found, to our surprise, was that students studying counseling for a semester developed, on the average, about a half stage in terms of measured moral reasoning. This was a change roughly equivalent to that achieved by Moshe Blatt in courses designed specifically and directly to analyze and discuss moral dilemmas and, thereby, to effect moral development.

On reflection, it became apparent to us that adolescents, in learning to counsel, at first (and quite typically) responded to personal dilemmas in the lives of people they were attempting to help by either judging behavior as appropriate or inappropriate, "good" or "bad," or by writing the other person a prescription, i.e., by telling him or her what to do. However, the cumulative effect of the experience of counseling under supervision was that the adolescent came to see that human problems are very complex and different and that judging another person's behavior or prescribing what to do is not really very useful. In short, we were training adolescents to understand a person's ideas, feelings, and dilemmas in more complex, comprehensive, and subtle ways and to respond to them on their own terms and with more options.

There are, we now see, further theoretical reasons to assume that training in counseling may contribute to moral reasoning. Kohlberg suggests that at least two central things are happening in the process of moral development. One of these is that the individual's capacity for empathy develops; the other has to do with the emergence of a more comprehensive understanding of the principle of justice in human relationships and human social units. Clearly, in teaching adolescents to counsel, we are offering them *systematic* theoretical and, especially, *applied* training in empathy. We are teaching them to accurately identify and sensitively respond to the feelings and ideas of another person. Thus, a method of training once unique to counselors or therapists (i.e., the offering of an empathic relationship to another human being) was found to have an impact on the development of greater moral awareness.

A brief overview of the procedures we employ when we teach counseling may be useful. A unit on counseling probably should not take less than six weeks of the course time (i.e., eighteen to twenty hours) and could be expanded to occupy a large part of one semester. Recall that during the students' personal introductions teachers tend to "model" some counseling responses. They listen and respond to the central feelings, personal concerns, or ethical issues raised by the students in a supportive and, at that point, non-confronting way. We first involve students in exercises adapted from Carkhuff in which they are asked as helpers to respond to brief role plays of "client" personal problems done by other students. They are taught to rate their responses for degree of empathy, specificity, and related counseling behavior, argued by Rogers, Carkhuff and others as essential to effectiveness. We then ask them to prepare a longer case-problem or ethical issue to be discussed with a counselor, and we divide the students into pairs and have them alternate in the roles of helper, or counselor, and client. These discussions are taped. One or more of them is analyzed and discussed before the group as a whole. The supervision is quite specific and intensive. The teacher reacts to the tapes with the two students present, and the feedback of the student who has been the "client" is used as the final evaluation of the perceptiveness and sensitivity of the counselor/helper. Students make a number of these tapes in both helper and helpee roles.

Real life dilemmas often emerge from these counseling sessions. One girl talked about the problem of a friend—the oldest child in a family of six in which the parents were divorced. Late one evening the friend had picked up an extension phone to hear her mother planning an assignation with the husband of one of her mother's best friends. The obvious question is what the daughter does with that kind of information. This is a dramatic illustration of the kinds of personal ethical issues which are raised in counseling. It raises another question relative to a course in moral reasoning. Put rhetorically, the question is this: Should the teacher deal with the ethical issues and their analysis in somewhat abstract terms or should the teacher deal directly (e.g., counsel or give advice) with the very real moral dilemma that the adolescent is experiencing? We believe a teacher should attempt to both probe the student's analysis of the dilemma and to assist the student to arrive at a reasonable resolution. It is a delicate matter for the teacher in such a situation to avoid either being wishy-washy or trying directly (or subtly) to persuade an adolescent of the "rightness" of a particular course of action. But a thorough examination or analysis of the problem, the courses of action open to the individual and their consequences, plus support for the individual's reasoned decision about the dilemma seems to us to be the responsible and defensible path for the teacher.

Phase 4: Teaching moral psychology and philosophy. Initially, in teaching the course, we deliberately waited until almost the end of the semester to introduce the Kohlberg theory, for two reasons. First, we were worried that the students might become overly concerned or self-conscious about the level or stage of their own reasoning. Second, we thought students might use stage theory as a way to determine a person's worth. Higher stage reasoning is more adequate intellectually and philosophically, but there can be no assumption that individuals who use higher stage reasoning are "better" people. In fact, the principles which constitute higher stage thinking philosophically exclude any such assumptions. Each person is of equal worth regardless of his or her level of moral reasoning.

We found that we were overly concerned in this regard. The students accepted the explanation of the theory with interest and saw in it justification for some of the things in the course. But they were not unduly concerned about their own stage, nor did they use the stage categories to pigeonhole other people and their way of thinking to any measurable degree. (This may prove to be more a problem with teachers than with adolescents.)

In teaching Kohlberg's theory of moral development, we try to provide a simple description of each stage along with examples of typical stage reasoning from moral judgment interviews. We have the students read a section on the Kohlberg theory in *Moral Reasoning: The Value of Life*. This includes brief stage descriptions and examples of stage reasoning on two issues, the value of human life and reasons for engaging in moral action. We elaborate these brief descriptions and deal with some material not covered, e.g., the strongly relativistic transition phase—Stage 4½.

We then talk briefly about why and how changes in style of moral reasoning occur. We explain the function of role-taking, moral discussions, etc., in promoting moral development. Finally, we discuss why and in what ways higher stages are more adequate.* Here we deal directly with the issue of labeling people by stage or deciding a person's worth by his or her stage of moral reasoning. Forthrightly addressing these questions seems to allay fears of inadequacy and to make the students less likely to use stage theory as a new way to rank-order people. At the same time, this discussion provides an opportunity for the students to examine our assumptions and theoretical orientation and to question it.

There are several other justifications for teaching moral philosophy and moral development theory. The first is a practical one. It establishes a basis for Phase 5 of the

*Higher stages of moral reasoning are "better" only because they are more differentiated and integrated than lower stages. In developmental terms, this creates a more stable form of reasoning able to deal with more situations. Moral reasoning and ethical responsiveness is present in all stages but only at the higher ones is this reasoning fully elaborated. Higher stage thinking produces judgments which are more universal, consistent, and based on objective, impersonal criteria. None of these aspects of moral reasoning, however, tell us the ultimate aims of humankind, what the good life is, or who to praise or blame. Moral reasoning is the process for deciding what to do in a situation in which a person has conflicting obligations. Higher stage judgments simply better fulfill the decision-making criteria of universality, objectivity, etc. So by saying a person uses higher stage reasoning, we are not assigning more intrinsic value to that individual.

course which has students working as "moral educators" with younger children or peers. A working knowledge of Kohlberg's theory and of moral philosophy should help them to be effective teachers. Hopefully, they will be able eventually to discriminate between moral and non-moral issues and between stages of moral reasoning and be able to make or phrase specific stage arguments, lead moral discussions, etc. Learning the Kohlberg theory and studying topics in moral philosophy is an initial step in this process.

Another justification is developmental. As noted earlier, many adolescents are achieving "formal operations," or the capacity for abstract thought. Adolescents make assumptions, create hypotheses, theorize about many things. They are very conscious of their own thinking, examining and judging it. They seek to create systematic ways of looking at themselves and the world. The area of morality and ethics is no exception. The adolescent "naturally" begins to construct his or her own ethical theories and principles. By looking at the much more elaborate theories of philosophers and psychologists, the adolescent can compare his or her ethical reasoning with theirs. In some cases this material helps adolescents reorganize their own thinking so that they can more adequately deal with moral dilemmas or issues.

Phases 5 and 6. We turn now to two phases of the course which are extensions of the methods used in the earlier phases.

The first involves training some of the students who take the course in moral reasoning to be moral educators of younger children or peers. These are students who will have experienced Phases 1 through 4 of the course. This teaching experience seeks to give students systematic practice in role-taking. We want to put them in real roles—as teachers—wherein they can apply or use, under supervision, what they have learned about moral development and moral reasoning. Our experience in related courses, in which high school students have taught in elementary schools or counseled on community "hot lines" or worked in peer counseling programs at the high school level, suggests to us that these kinds of role-taking experiences are growth producing. Our supposition is, that by being involved in teaching moral reasoning to younger children or peers, the adolescent's own moral development will be stimulated. One learns by doing. (Parenthetically, the writers' *own* understanding of moral development theory and ethical analysis has become much more comprehensive under the stimulus of creating this curriculum and teaching it to adolescents. We expect that this will be true for most teachers and not simply for the adolescents who teach.)

This Phase 5 of the course will consist of a weekly seminar and a practicum for the adolescents lasting most of a semester. The practicum opportunities we are exploring include "home room" discussions of moral dilemmas at the high school level, teaching in religious school (where adolescents typically act as student aides), and teaching in regular elementary classrooms. The curriculum materials for high school will be based largely on the film and written case material noted in Phase 2. Guidance Associates now have available analogous filmstrip case material for use in the elementary classroom which is especially adapted to the concerns and attention span of younger children.

An important aspect of this phase is the on-going seminar and the supervision of the adolescents. They need support, and they need a forum to examine the experience they are having. We will help the students prepare for the moral discussions and then allow them to analyze what has occurred. On-the-spot supervision of the actual teaching will be provided as often as possible; classroom discussions will be tape-recorded. Taping affords the possibility of referring back to situations and statements during the seminar. Our plan is to have the adolescent co-teach with at least one other teenager, thereby creating mutual support.

We might hypothesize that the structure of the seminar itself may be growth inducing. Every effort is made to create a democratically structured, cooperative educational venture. Each individual participates in decisions and has responsibility for carrying them out. A collegiality among the adolescents and the teachers, based on mutual respect and a common task, hopefully will be established.

Still at the initial stage is Phase 6, a more ambitious program in moral education. It involves working with a small number of high school students (circa 50 to 100), teachers, counselors, administrators, and parents in the creation of an alternative high school. One of the basic purposes of this high school is to give students systematic experience in rule-making, in writing a social contract for the governance of all members of the school. Students and faculty create rules for the operation of the school, a procedure for making and changing such rules (i.e., a system of governance—perhaps patterned on the model of the New England town meeting), a disciplinary system, and an adjudication and grievance procedure. In short, the students have a genuine role in making the rules and regulations (and in administering those regulations justly) relative to issues of fairness in their school. (The school is described more fully on pages 164–172.)

Conclusion

We have presented a model for including a curriculum in the deliberate moral education of adolescents in the public schools. This model is currently being implemented in both the Brookline, Massachusetts and Tacoma, Washington public school systems. The model is supported by the National Endowment for the Humanities and the Danforth Foundation. We hope soon to report on the efficacy of the program upon the moral development of youth and to describe the strategies used in training teachers to implement similar programs.

Bibliography

Beck, Clive. *Ethics*. Toronto: McGraw-Hill-Ryerson, 1972.

Blatt, Moshe, and Kohlberg, Lawrence. "Effects of Classroom Discussion upon Children's Level of Moral Judgment." In *Recent Research in Moral Development*, edited by L. Kohlberg and E. Turiel. New York: Holt, Rinehart & Winston, 1973.

Dewey, John, and McLellan, J. "The Psychology of Numbers." In *John Dewey on Education: Selected Writings*, edited by R. Archambault. New York: Random House, 1964.

Dulit, E. "Adolescent Thinking à la Piaget: The Formal Stage." *Journal of Youth and Adolescence* 1 (1972):281–301.

Kohlberg, Lawrence. *Collected Papers on Moral Development and Moral Education*. Cambridge: Harvard University Center for Moral Education, Laboratory of Human Development, Spring 1973.

Kohlberg, Lawrence. "Continuities in Childhood and Adult Moral Development Revisited." In *Collected Papers on Moral Development and Moral Education*, edited by L. Kohlberg. Cambridge: Harvard University Center for Moral Education, Laboratory of Human Development, Spring 1973.

Kohlberg, Lawrence, and Mayer, Rochelle. "Development as the Aim of Education." *Harvard Educational Review* 42 (November 1972):449–96.

Kohlberg, Lawrence; Scharf, Peter; and Hickey, Joseph. "The Justice Structure of the Prison: A Theory and an Intervention." *The Prison Journal* 51 (Autumn/Winter 1972):3–14.

Lockwood, Alan. *Moral Reasoning: The Value of Life*. Harvard Project Social Studies. Middletown, Conn.: American Education Publications, 1972.

Mosher, Ralph L., and Sprinthall, Norman A. "Psychological Education: A Means to Promote Personal Development during Adolescence." *The Counseling Psychologist* 2 (1971):3–81.

Rawls, John. *A Theory of Justice*. Cambridge: Harvard University Press, 1971.

Rest, James; Turiel, Elliot; and Kohlberg, Lawrence. "Relations between Level of Moral Judgment and Preference and Comprehension of Moral Judgment of Others." *Journal of Personality*, 1969.

Rohwer, William J. "Prime Time for Education: Early Childhood or Adolescence?" *Harvard Educational Review* 41 (1971):316–41.

Sullivan, Paul. "A Program in Moral Education for Adolescents." Ed.D. dissertation, Boston University School of Education, 1974.

Turiel, Elliot. "An Experimental Analysis of Developmental Stages in the Child's Moral Judgment." *Journal of Personality and Social Psychology*, 1966.

Cognitive Development and the Teaching of Social Studies

Thomas J. Ladenberg, History Teacher, Brookline High School, Brookline, Massachusetts.

The idea that development should be the aim of education was first stated by John Dewey in 1855:

> The aim of education is growth or development both intellectual and moral. . . . Only knowledge of the order and connection of the stages in psychological development can insure the maturing of psychic powers. Education is the work of supplying the conditions which will enable the psychological functions to mature and pass into higher functions in the freest and fullest manner.[1]

While Dewey envisioned the development of intellectual capacities as a goal, he did not have the "knowledge of the order and connection of the stages" or the tools to measure them. This work was done by Jean Piaget and his colleagues in the 1930s. Through their precise, longitudinal studies, they learned to distinguish between the qualitatively different types of mental capacities which they defined as cognitive operations, from reasoning about concrete data to the ability to think about thought or formal operations. This orderly and sequential progression, Piaget informed us, is a universal hallmark of human development. Building on Piaget's discoveries, Professor Lawrence Kohlberg identified six distinct stages of reasoning about moral issues and verified his conclusions with longitudinal and cross-cultural studies. [See Appendixes for complete information.] He differentiated these modes of thought by the increasing complexity and inclusiveness of each stage. They move from a primitive obedience to authority and the avoidance of pain to the egocentric realization of reciprocal exchange; from the recognition of the need for loyalty to family and peers to the incorporation of a societal perspective and finally to the recognition of global or universal principles of human dignity and equality.

Professor Kohlberg's great contribution to developmental psychology is his discovery that these stages of reasoning are developmental in the sense that each involves the incorporation of previous stages; that they are invariant in that it is impossible to omit a stage; and that they are universal in the sense that these modes of reasoning and their progressive development are not bound by cultural mores. Kohlberg's great contribution to developmental education was his and his colleagues' (Moshe Blatt, Ralph Mosher, and Norman Sprinthall) revolutionary discovery that educational interventions could stimulate the development of moral reasoning from lower to higher, more complete and holistic stages. This knowledge, verified in numerous experiments, has made it possible to realize Dewey's dictum that the "aim of education is growth or development both intellectual and moral" and has provided the impetus for the growing field of developmental education.

Courses designed to stimulate the development of the ability to reason about moral issues typically include two components. First, they involve students in resolving moral dilemmas, generally short, hypothetical case studies which pose important moral choices between somewhat equally compelling alternatives. Students are usually prodded with "probe" questions designed to elicit full explanations of the reasons supporting their resolutions of these dilemmas. Then they are exposed to solutions reasoned at slightly higher and therefore more attractive stages. Second, these courses involve an affective component, with students learning the skills to either lead moral dilemma discussions with younger children or participate in peer counseling. In one academic year, the combination of these rich ingredients has often stimulated students to reason a full stage up from their beginning level while control groups show little or no growth.

While this work has served as the cutting edge of a new curriculum movement, it has failed to gain widespread acceptance in schools throughout the country. If we are to define "intellectual" as mastering traditional subject matter, and "developmental" as stimulating increased affective or cognitive capacities, the schools generally see their roles more in terms of intellectual than developmental education. However, there is no need to continue maintaining these artificial distinctions. Since Kohlberg and his colleagues have provided the tools and data which enable us to actuate the full potentials of Dewey's insights, developmental education can and should be integrated into the traditional curriculum in general and into the teaching of history and social studies in particular.

Fortunately, this work has already begun. Several school systems—Tacoma, Washington, Brookline and Cambridge, Massachusetts, Pittsburgh, Pennsylvania and Minneapolis, Minnesota—are in the process of producing and distributing experimental materials designed to stimulate development. Moshe Blatt and others have published a collection of hypothetical dilemmas for classroom use, and Edwin Fenton has produced a series of filmstrips for Guidance Associates. Thomas Jones and Ronald Galbraith and Barry Beyer have written carefully constructed guides to help teachers lead discussions of moral issues.

Up to this point, however, the work produced and made available by the social studies educators has not been as rich in its conception and as varied in its execution as the course materials produced by developmental educators. In general, the social studies materials have been modeled after the dilemmas used by Dr. Kohlberg to test and validate his theory of moral reasoning—they typically involve individuals in hypothetical, a-historic dilemmas. The individuals are left to choose between two courses of action involving a contrived moral conflict. Writing in *Social Education*, Barry Beyer gives the rationale for this design. He cautions that the dilemma "should be as simple as possible" involving "only a few characters in a relatively uncomplicated situation."[2]

Jack Fraenkel, in the same issue of *Social Education*, criticizes this approach. If students "are to find out about the nature of the world in which they live," he argues, "they must be exposed to a wide variety of different kinds of issues and dilemmas."[3] I heartily concur with Professor Fraenkel. Social studies educators must build on the techniques espoused by Jones, Galbraith, and Beyer by constructing vastly more complex dilemmas encompassing a variety of historic issues. Otherwise they run the danger of reducing the study of history and its persuasive, recurrent moral themes to simplistic, hypothetical case studies, devoid of the complexity of the discipline and incapable of helping students bridge the gap between fictional accounts and historic realities.

In addition to the hypothetical dilemmas produced to date, the history curriculum can and should include dilemmas as rich and varied as those faced by the founding fathers in writing the Constitution, by Congress in ratifying the Jay Treaty, and by Franklin Roosevelt in proposing the social security system. Dilemmas of this dimension have the power to become the central building blocks of a new "new social studies" that achieves the cognitive and affective goals of the developmentalists without sacrificing the traditional intellectual objectives of the schools.

The central purpose of this article is to begin developing a rationale and model that will help teachers and curriculum writers accomplish this necessary task. In order for history teachers to reach this ambitious goal, it is essential—

1 that the high school teacher be provided with an acceptable definition of subject area which also embraces developmental goals;
2 that this definition be translated into a model for teaching history and developing social studies curricula that combines subject matter with developmental education and allows cognitive development and moral reasoning to be used as a means of teaching the discipline as well as to be ends in themselves;
3. that the concept of a moral dilemma be broadened to include a continuum of teaching strategies ranging from simple, hypothetical dilemmas on one end to complex, moral-development units on the other;
4. that specific examples of units that bridge the gap between teaching subject matter and stimulating growth be provided as examples, enabling teachers to apply principles inherent in the model to their own curriculum.

A Definition of History That Embraces Developmental Goals

In his book, *The Aims of Education*, Alfred North Whitehead defines education as "the art of the utilization of knowledge" and reminds us that "ideas which are not utilized are positively harmful."[4] It seems that unless they become more concerned with the reasons certain decisions are made than with the decisions themselves, history teachers are particularly open to the accusation of imparting information which is no longer usable. Fortunately, the new social studies has placed more emphasis on process and discovery than on isolated facts. But even here history does not come alive for students unless they are somehow involved in the process of making or re-thinking historic decisions. Indeed, it is this very idea of process that forms the link between the past and present. History is saved from the garbage heap of inert ideas because it can, in the very way it unfolds, bridge the gap between the past and the present. As the past gives meaning to the present, the present helps us determine what we must know about what has been.

By taking part in the process of making and evaluating decisions, students become participants in a continual drama. Through simulations, discussions, and debates, they learn to use facts and concepts in order to buttress an argument, support a point, or reason to a new conclusion. These interchanges may be called dialogues with the past; the knowledge gleaned from history is applied to current problems or to analogous cases. When students thus become conversant in history, they incorporate new ideas and facts into their thought processes; if the subject matter is carefully chosen, they become participants in the historic-political culture which has shaped our past and now defines our present.

People operate within a time frame or context. They perceive problems and make decisions from alternatives open to them. At some future moment they can look back and more clearly analyze the reasons for their decisions. This model of human beings as the decision-makers within the context of time—people standing apart from the decisions, but reflecting back on them—also helps us to understand the many and diverse activities of the historian, the nature of the discipline, and the four basically different types of questions which historians attempt to answer:

1. What was the particular and unique situation within which the decision was made?
2. What sequence of events actually took place?
3. What was the morally correct decision to make at that particular time?
4. Why was that decision made at that time?

In posing the first question, historians are guided by their interest in the past as a unique and singular example of humankind as a universal entity. Their search into specific kinds of history—the social, economic, political and intellectual—give rise to specialties in these areas. In seeking answers to the second question, historians probe into events with the skill of trained detectives and attempt to learn exactly what transpired. Whether consciously or not, historians pass judgments on events, sometimes using standards which even they cannot or do not define, and thus—in the role of moral philosophers—answer the third question, on ethics. Finally, historians seek answers to the question of why it happened. Here they uncover the motives of men and women, wrestle with the problem of inevitability, and uncover causes in social, economic, and/or political-ideological circumstances.

A Model for Teaching That Combines Subject Matter with Developmental Goals

The academic historian can afford to specialize in one aspect of history or in one period of time. The high school history teacher does not have this luxury. He or she must deal with each of the four basic questions outlining different areas of concern. In posing these questions and involving students in the search for their answers, the teacher can impart a small but representative sampling of the total import of the discipline which he or she teaches. But the teacher also now has a model which allows the subject area to help him or her attain one of the developmentalist's central goals, i.e., to encourage cognitive growth by stimulating the students' ability to reason at higher and more complex stages. This is possible because the questions posed in the classroom are both sequential and consequential; students learn about the general context of any period; this information allows them to understand the events; they then resolve the decision maker's dilemma by participating in a reconstruction of the decision-making process; and they reflect back on their own deliberations as they analyze why the decision was made. At each stage, the students seek answers which they can understand only at their particular level of reasoning. Each set of conclusions is therefore tailor-made to a student's intellectual ability. As students progress from one stage of questioning to the next, their levels of understanding will grow and deepen, and their abilities to master facts or comprehend concepts are similarly expanded.

It is easy to see how this four-stage model applies to a unit on the American Revolution. First, the teacher explores the first question by asking what the climate of the times was and leads students through an examination of the social, economic, political, and ideological background of the Revolution. Youngsters study the class structure of colonial America, the mercantile policies of England, the relationship between colonial governments and British Parliament, and the colonists' conceptions of "liberty" and "power."

Secondly, classes inquire into the events which actually took place at the time, occasionally using the historian's inquiry tools to sift through conflicting source materials. Here they learn of the French and Indian war, the problems of ruling an Empire, the Stamp Act and the protest which it aroused, the Boston Massacre, the Tea Party, the Battle of Lexington, and the Declaration of Independence. This is traditional fare.

But interlaced with descriptions of these events as products of economic and social conditions, students are involved in the third level of questioning. They make moral judgments about decisions that were reached and were about to be made. They may be asked whether the Stamp Act riots were justified, whether British soldiers had the right to fire at colonists on King Street, and whether the British were justified in imposing the Intolerable Acts as punishment for the Tea Party.

Finally, and only after completing the earlier stages of questioning, students are required to reflect on the series of events they have studied and are asked what caused the Revolution, or, more simply, why disagreements were not resolved peacefully. Here students are forced to seek adequate explanations for events they studied within the context of the historical period and which they have measured against their own structures of moral reasoning.

This model—requiring sequential development of four different types of questions—can and should form the blueprint governing the construction of most history courses. The planning involved, of course, is extremely complex, and the ideal may not always be attained. But the payoff in terms of developmental and traditional intellectual education can hardly be exaggerated. Every question prepares the way for the next, and the final exercise allows the dilemmas built into the unit to provide evidence for the analysis required at the end.

A Broadened Definition of Moral Dilemmas

Besides linking the "what" and the "why" questions, moral dilemmas also have the unique quality of turning students on. The query, What should so and so do? or, Was so and so justified? or, Who was right?, whether asked in the context of the Stamp Act, the Tea Party, or the Battle of Lexington, is always, in my experience, the question that excites most interest, discussion, and/or debate. The reasons for its power to elicit a response are partially a matter of speculation, but they seem closely connected to Piagetian and Kohlbergian conceptions. Every student has formulated a mental construct, uniquely his or her own, concerning issues of justice, fairness, or right and wrong. An opposing opinion, or one argued at a higher stage, jarring this construct, attacks the structure of the student's reasoning and remains opposed as long as there are intellectually valid reasons to combat it. In defending their views against alien ideas, students are forced to dig deeply into their own resources and ultimately to modify their own structure of moral thought. Facts become weapons that are used to reinforce their ideas or to eventually batter down their citadels. As the mind is exposed to reasoning which it recognizes as more complex or complete, it alters or modifies its views, incorporating these newer and more adequate concepts. Thus dilemma discussions are the means by which we encourage students to deal with new ideas and to modify their patterns of thought. Moral dilemmas have more power to accomplish this change than abstract discussions of causality because they more immediately address distinctions of right and wrong which are always with us and which press uniquely on adolescents.

Since moral dilemmas necessarily play so central a role in cognitive development and moral reasoning, it is important to distinguish between several kinds of dilemmas which may be used. At one end of the scale are the cases involving hypothetical dilemmas. They deal with universal principles of right and wrong, devoid of considerations of either time or place. The classic in the Kohlberg literature is the case of Heinz, whose wife will die of a rare disease because he cannot afford to pay the druggist's exorbitant price for the necessary medicine. Should Heinz steal the medicine? the subject is asked. This dilemma was a central one used by Dr. Kohlberg to discover and validate the character of the six stages of moral reasoning. The value of this and similar dilemmas involving fictionalized case studies is limited from the standpoint of the history teacher, because the ethical questions they raise are lacking an historical context. Heinz's dilemma is equally perplexing whether he is seen to live in Europe at the turn of the century or in America in the 1970s. The dilemma reveals nothing about the nature of any particular point in time, nor does it force students to come to a deeper understanding of any historical period.

The historical dilemma is more complex than the a-historical dilemma. Like the former it deals with a person caught in an ethical problem, but this time the situation contains another dimension—consideration of the nature of the time period within which the decision must be made. An example of the historical dilemma is the case of Helga who is asked by her friend Rachel to hide her from the Nazis, or the case involving a man who must decide whether he will hide a run-away slave and violate the fugitive slave law.

In an article appearing in *Social Education*, Ronald Galbraith and Thomas Jones clearly elucidate a strategy to teach this type of historical dilemma.[5] It involves reviewing the facts of the case, clarifying alternatives for the decision maker, and eliciting reasons for each opposing course of action. Discussions are to focus on the reasoning employed. If the class does not divide naturally into opposing camps, the terms of the dilemma are changed somewhat by the teacher. What if Rachel were only an acquaintance instead of a good friend? What if the punishment for hiding Jews were imprisonment in a concentration camp? Once a clear division is found in the class, opposing arguments are presented and student discussion is focused on reasons rather than solutions.

While these strategies meet the needs of the developmental psychologists in their research, it is doubtful whether they are equally useful in teaching history. If dilemmas are to serve as a means for teaching subject matter as well as developing moral reasoning, other and more complex dilemmas need to be used. And with the wealth that historical events afford, there is ample reason to require that the dilemma be real rather than hypothetical. The case of the slave mother who kills her child rather than permit the master to sell the child, as he has the other three, is one example. So, too, is the case of Johnathan Harrington, who must choose between his loyalty to family and his allegiance to friends and the Revolution when he decides whether or not to stand with the Lexington militia in the face of superior British forces. Both of these dilemmas are real and reveal something of the nature of the conditions surrounding them.

Even more complex historical dilemmas might involve the cases of real decision-makers making crucial decisions. Several examples easily come to mind: Abraham Lincoln, agonizing over the Emancipation Proclamation; Harry Truman, debating over whether to drop the atomic bomb on Hiroshima; a juror, deliberating at the trial of the soldiers involved in the Boston Massacre. The reasoning needed to engage in these dilemmas must of necessity be interlaced with a consideration of the historical factors which played a role in the decision.

A single historical dilemma can easily be made the basis for a two- or three-day activity and involve many of the thinking and reasoning skills necessary to the learning of history. For example, students can be given the information to stage a mock trial of the British soldiers accused of murder in the Boston Massacre. During the trial, youngsters may act out the parts of witnesses, defendants, lawyers, judges, or jurors. In the process, students will learn a great deal about our advocacy system of justice and will be required to think through some complex legal issues.

The enterprising teacher can build this lesson on the Boston Massacre into a dilemma mini-unit, the third kind of moral dilemma useful to the history teacher. He or she could follow the mock trial with a reading on the Kent State incident and ask who were the people more clearly to blame, the British soldiers at the Boston Massacre or the National Guardsmen at Kent State. This discussion may be continued, using the Battle of Lexington as another case study, and students could add the militia's stand on the Green, the shot from an unknown source, and the subsequent killings of New England farmers as a parallel case to follow the Boston Massacre and Kent State discussions. These three lessons could form the basis of the mini-unit and would undoubtedly evoke controversy, hard thinking, and the search for some general principles regarding dissent and protest. By this time, students should be sufficiently immersed in history as process, making decisions that they will later stand away from and try to analyze.

Historical mini-units can be built around a number of other events. One which works very well examines the issue of how to deal with a great wrong such as slavery. Rather than involve students in a hypothetical case of the runaway slave, teachers can have youngsters recreate the Lincoln-Douglas debate over how the nation should resolve the question of slavery in the territories, followed by a discussion of John Brown's dramatic raid on Harper's Ferry, and ending with an analysis of Lincoln's decision to put priority on saving the Union rather than ending slavery.

Units That Bridge the Gap between Subject and Developmental Goals

It is hoped that teachers will not stop with the dilemma mini-units. The next step can be to construct entire units (designed to stimulate cognitive development and moral reasoning) and history courses, using moral issues to promote the desired development. The basic pattern for such units has already been described. It revolves around posing the four questions which historians attempt to answer. A sample of such a unit, on the writing of the United States Constitution, was developed by this author and refined as part of the Brookline, Massachusetts Moral Development Project. It has been taught to over 350 students and meets most of the established criteria for a moral development unit. The unit is described here in the hopes that it will encourage other teachers to try similar enterprises.

The heart of the unit is a simulation requiring that youngsters assume the roles of the Founding Fathers and resolve five major issues before the Constitutional Convention. Each student delegate is prepared for his or her role by analyzing the Articles of Confederation, debating the justification of Shay's rebellion, and reading excerpts from Madison's Federalist #10. With this exposure to the social, economic and political-ideological background to the Convention, the student delegate is given an explanation of the issues to be resolved and a political biography of the delegates which includes their views on the issues.

The mock convention opens with the delegates attempting to resolve the conflict between the large and small states over representation. Students spend roughly equal amounts of time hearing prepared speeches, debating the issues as a "committee of the whole," jawboning with students during "caucuses," and analyzing or voting on conflicting resolutions. On succeeding days, the mock convention considers how power should be divided between the national and state governments, what powers should be given the President, the Congress, and the people, what should be done about slavery and the slave trade, and whether to write a Bill of Rights.

After each of these issues is resolved through simulation, students read the Constitution and learn how these same questions were resolved in 1789. Now, aware that the solutions of 1789 were not necessarily perfect, they debate ratification and read several historians' interpretations of the Founders' motives. Thus prepared, they reflect back over the historical context of the times, the problems faced by the founders, their solutions as embodied in the Constitution, and the experience of the simulation itself in an attempt to determine why the Constitution was written as it was.

On the surface, discussions focusing on such issues as dividing power between the national and state governments may not appear to involve moral dilemmas. Certainly, they involve questions far more complex than those raised in the Heinz or Rachel cases. But, behind all political decisions lies the fundamental question of justice, which is central to the resolution of all moral dilemmas and at the very heart of the political process. It is impossible to separate moral questions from political issues, and indeed, any attempt to do so would be to deny the latter their essential character.

The exercise of writing a Constitution, whether by our Founding Fathers or by a group of students, is really an experience in arriving at a Stage 5 social contract. The writers must consider more than simple obedience to the law; they must decide what the fundamental arrangements governing our political institutions should be. However, in arriving at this Stage 5 concept of social contract, many lower stage arguments are used. The following dialogue was recorded during the mock convention and illustrates distinct stages of reasoning used by students in discussing the issue of dividing power between the national and state governments:

Luther Martin:	The purpose of these United States was because we needed to protect the state government from bigger powers. Before they were the United States they had to be protected from the British power and now you want to just impose the power of the national government on each state. The state of Massachusetts should have the right to take care of any law itself. . . .
Gouverneur Morris:	Do you realize what might have happened if Shay's rebellion had occurred in another state? It might have been taken care of in a completely different way. They might all have been executed—maybe they would have been tarred and feathered. We don't know. We can't have that type of disorder going around. We have to have a unified type of law that will affect everyone in every state; that they will get the same punishment no matter what state the rebellion took place in.
John Lansing:	I really disagree with that statement. That is saying that each person's feelings and each person's ideas are the same throughout the whole country, and people in New Hampshire, say, are going to have different issues and are going to feel differently about things than people in Georgia, which is about nine hundred miles away—so you can't say that in one country each person is going to feel the same way and going to want to react the same way; so you can't have one law govern all those people.
Charles Pinckney:	What has been stated as an idea is that all men are equal. If all men are equal they deserve to have the same rights, the same laws governing them. . . .
John Lansing:	You are saying that all men are robots—that's what you are saying.
Charles Pinckney:	I'm not saying that; I'm saying they deserve to have equal rights; they deserve to be treated equally; which means they must have equal laws.

Assumed in this author's definition of history is the premise that students must be involved in the process of making historic decisions and that there is no fundamental conflict between teaching subject matter conceived as decision making and stimulating cognitive development or moral reasoning. By playing the roles assigned them in the convention, students not only partake in their nation's political-historical culture, they gain practice in perspective taking, the ability to see a situation from another point of view, which is an essential factor in cognitive development. Perceiving problems from a responsible adult perspective also provides the adolescent with conditions that promote the confidence, self-esteem, and sense of mastery so important to psychological development. Thus, the young man who argues against the national government on the basis that its power may be excessive learns something for himself about the relationship between authority and freedom. And the young woman (Gouverneur Morris) who tells the convention that because of Shay's rebellion "we obviously need a stronger federal government" examines the same relationship from the perspective of exerting controls rather than experiencing them.

As Madison and Wilson could cite their Aristotle, Sidney, Locke, or Hobbes and make references to Greek city-states and European constitutional monarchies, so the veterans of the mock convention are able to refer to Federalist #10, the theory behind England's unwritten constitution, the ineffectiveness of the Articles of Confederation, and Hobbes' concept of the state of nature. In becoming conversant with the problems confronting the Constitution-makers, students begin to incorporate into their own thought processes the political science concepts and factual information necessary to understand the complexities of framing the Constitution. They are prepared, not only to discuss the Constitution intelligently, but to participate in discussions of analogous problems confronting the nation today. Thus, the convention fulfills Whitehead's definition of education as the "utilization of knowledge."

It is possible to design an entire history course which continues the dialogue begun at the convention and uses many of the same techniques. The Federalist era, for instance, can be seen as the working out, through concrete policy decisions, the broad and general conceptions of government discussed at the convention. Debates over funding the national debt, establishing the Bank, suppressing the Whiskey rebellion, supporting the Alien and Sedition Acts and the Virginia and Kentucky Resolutions, after all, raise issues and problems very similar to those decided at the convention. The issues raised by the Tariff of Abominations, the Bank veto, the Compromises, the Dred Scott decision and secession continue the dialogue, involving students in reasoning through the underlying dilemmas posed by our conceptions of majority rule and minority rights.

Resolving the problem of justice for Black Americans may start with debates over the extension of slavery and continue in arguments over balancing the need to preserve the Union against the moral necessity of ending slavery. Related issues can be raised in a unit on Reconstruction, debating the relative merits of Lincoln's and Steven's plans for dealing with the South, simulating the trial of Andrew Johnson, examining the opposing arguments in the Plessy decision, and considering current manifestations such as the cases for and against compensatory treatment and busing.

The Rise of Industrial America raises other perplexing dilemmas, pitting the freedom of business against the needs of consumers, the rights of workers against the prerogatives of employers, and the plight of immigrants against the obligations of society. Foreign policy is similarly laced with fundamental moral concerns regarding the true national interests and obligations, the moral restraints on pursuing those interests, and the necessity of foreign involvements. Finally, the Twenties and the Depression raise issues concerning the obligation of the national government to the plight of the unemployed and disabled within the context of considering fiscal and monetary policies geared toward encouraging economic expansion or combatting inflation.

In all of the units briefly outlined above, it is possible and desirable to continue involving students in the dialogue initiated at the convention, to teach the economic and sociological concepts that make the present understandable, and finally to involve students in the process of making decisions as well as requiring them to analyze the reasons they were made. Knowledge thus given will never be inert but will create citizens competent to take part in the political process which is the outgrowth of our historical experience. Students thus equipped will undoubtedly reason at higher moral and cognitive levels and will, in Dewey's words, "mature and pass into higher functions in the freest and fullest manner."

Involving low-ability students in discussing moral issues is more difficult than working with honors students. Nevertheless, the same principles that govern the successful use of hypothetical dilemmas, historical dilemmas, mini and full dilemma units for the intellectually talented will work in teaching the less intellectually talented. Students who are not motivated are less likely to respond to traditional methods, and dilemmas often induce discussion where other methods fail. The challenge is to develop or find material at the correct reading and conceptual level.

The Constitution unit described here has also been written for low ability students, and a sample version has worked with fifth graders. Since youngsters cannot discuss ideas they do not understand, it is important to translate problems into familiar terms. The fifth-grade class discussed the issues of secession rather than the question of power between national and state governments. One student translated the issue into his own words: "If you join a club, you can't quit and take the clubhouse with you."

Other units described here also worked well with less able students; however, the reasoning employed was at lower stages. The mock trial of the soldiers involved in the Massacre was a great success. In arguing over analogies to the Kent State incident, several youngsters allowed that the dead students deserved their fate because they would not have been shot if they had not done something wrong. Several viewed the situation from the guardsman's point of view, claiming they were shooting in self defense; some adopted the victim's perspective and asked, "How would you like to be shot (like Sandy Sheur) for looking for a lost dog?" Taking a more philosophical outlook, others argued, "It all depends on who you were."

Although the level of discussion seldom reaches Stage 4, teachers should avoid despair. Instead, they should realize that the best way to raise the level of reasoning is through continued exposure to arguments at higher levels that will eventually cause the more complete and developed sentiments to become incorporated into the youngster's reasoning structure, thus advancing his or her capacity for logical, structured thought. The field studies by Kohlberg, Mosher, and their students have clearly demonstrated that point.

In general, units used with low-ability students seem to work well in proportion to how much the material presented is about *people* rather than *things*. A unit on slavery can be particularly successful because cases like that of the woman who killed her child, the girl who was beaten severely for avoiding work, and Frederick Douglass beating his master were real dilemmas, illustrative of the society which systematically repressed human rights and dignity. Other successful units revolve around the plight of Native Americans and immigrants, areas equally rich in human-interest stories illustrative of fundamental issues involving the conflict between individuals and society.

This is not to say that moral dilemmas which pose significant political problems cannot be raised within the context of an American history course designed for the non-academic student. A unit on the limits of war is generally successful. It employs the Luisitania case, Hiroshima, and the My Lai massacre. Similarly, the New Deal raises important political and economic issues in an ethical context, and students of all ability levels can and should be involved in discussions of post-war foreign policy questions such as the Truman-McArthur debate, the Cuban missile crisis, the Berlin blockade, and the Marshall Plan. Nor should the curriculum avoid discussions of civil rights, feminism, the counter culture, etc.

Teachers should not be discouraged if some youngsters are not facile with sophisticated concepts. Too many of us have tried and failed to teach the distinction between the protective and revenue tariff, learning the lesson that we cannot teach what the student is unwilling or intellectually unable to absorb. Rather than be defeated by this experience, teachers should concentrate on understandable concepts and design historical materials and mini-units that involve their classes in the process of confronting the dilemmas of history. One must rely on the reasoning processes revealed in the classroom to stimulate cognitive and moral growth. History can be taught in significant ways to students of all ability groups. The limiting factors are not the youngsters themselves but the time and the imagination of the teacher and the availability of materials.

The time has arrived for social studies educators to apply the developmental educator's knowledge, insights, and techniques to their own disciplines. Unfortunately, the work done to date, although a necessary beginning, has been too simplistic to encompass or exploit the rich and varied cloth of historic experience. Social studies people must develop moral dilemma units which follow the model of the person as decision-maker operating within a context of time. Students can then experience historical dilemmas by participating in the decision-making process and then analyzing the reasons these decisions were made. Only after this difficult but necessary challenge to create a new "new social studies" is accepted can the social studies teacher claim his or her rightful and central role in stimulating both cognitive development and moral reasoning.

Notes

1. Lawrence Kohlberg, "Moral Development and the New Social Studies," in *Collected Papers on Moral Development and Moral Education*, vol. 1, ed. L. Kohlberg (Cambridge: Harvard University Center for Moral Education, Spring 1973).

2. Barry K. Beyer, "Conducting Moral Discussions in the Classroom," *Social Education* 40 (April 1976): 196.

3. Jack R. Fraenkel, "The Kohlberg Bandwagon: Some Reservations," *Social Education* 40 (April 1976): 221.

4. Alfred North Whitehead, *The Aims of Education* (New York: Mentor Books, 1956): 15–16.

5. Ronald E. Galbraith and Thomas M. Jones, "Teaching Strategies for Moral Dilemmas: An Application of Kohlberg's Theory to the Social Studies Classroom," *Social Education* 39 (January 1975): 16–22.

The Development of Women: An Issue of Justice

V. Lois Erickson, Assistant Professor of Education, University of Minnesota.

During this renaissance in the women's movement, one key justice issue is that of equality in the pursuit of one's maturity. It is the purpose of this paper to examine the psychological maturation process of women from a cognitive-developmental perspective of theory, research, and practice.

In this paper I will briefly:

—present some cognitive-developmental assumptions on the acquisition of sex-role concepts and attitudes;
—discuss issues of equality in education in terms of developmental maturity;
—argue the need for curricula to facilitate the development of women;
—highlight an experimental curriculum for women in terms of its content and process;
—summarize its impact on the pre, post, and longitudinal measures of ego and moral maturity; and
—present the implications of curricula for women's growth in the broader context of human development—such that the mutuality and the integration of sexual roles become a deliberate focus.

The Acquisition of Sex-Role Concepts and Attitudes

Kohlberg (1966) has developed a theoretical framework for describing how sex-typed attitudes and behaviors are acquired. His theory is based on cognitive organization and development and on competency motivation. He believes that early sex-role labeling with the words "girl" and "boy" results in a self-categorization which initiates sex-typing in a young child.

Kohlberg believes that a sense of efficacy leads a child to reorganize his or her sexual self-concept.

Portions of this essay have appeared in *Counseling and Values*, Winter 1974, *Counselor Education and Supervision*, June 1975, and *The Counseling Psychologist* 6, no. 4, 1977. Used by permission.

A stable gender identity, feminine values, and also a cognitive sense of similarity leads to preferential attachment of the girl to her mother. Kohlberg (1969) stresses that a cognitive perception of similar identity often precedes dependency and attachment. Similarly, by ages 3–5, children perceive the skills and virtues of an individual by that individual's physical size and strength. And by the early school years, the child acknowledges psychological and sex-typed attributions in others.

Kohlberg writes that in the years from 4–7, girls develop a perception that feminine competence and status are based on being attractive and nice rather than on being powerful, aggressive, and fearless. This conception of appropriate role behavior leads to the channeling of a female's motivation into specific directions. Girls learn early that their abilities are most appropriately channeled into traditional female roles. In a study by Looft (1971), when children (aged 6–8) were asked what they wanted to be when they grew up, 75 percent of the girls' responses were in two categories—teacher or nurse. Only 10 percent of the boys selected the two most popular categories for boys—football player and fireman. Eight potential occupations were listed by the girls; eighteen were listed by the boys.

Kohlberg's studies (1969) indicated that children of both sexes, by age 4–5, perceive fathers as bigger, stronger, and more aggressive than mothers. And by ages 6–7, they see fathers as both more powerful and prestigious than mothers. Kohlberg indicates that this is related to the valuing of the economic function in families with a traditional sexual division of labor. By ages 6–8, the child, using concrete operational thinking, recognizes for the first time the need and importance of the work role for its cash value. Thus, in families with a traditional division of labor, children cognitively perceive the father's economic role as of higher value than the mother's child-care role because of the concrete results of the father's income. Kohlberg (1969) found that the trend for both girls and boys was for them to designate greater authority to the father-role. This pattern parallels a developmental increase in modeling older males from ages 4–7. He indicates that for girls this modeling is not a part of a global desire to be like the father but exists on the belief that "he is smarter and knows the right way to do things better than mother does."

Girls and boys therefore often have beliefs that males are more valued than females—for their size and strength and later for their earning power. This learning is likely not a cultural learning of the male dominant values of the American culture but a development based on concrete levels of cognition. Sex-typed cognitions are formed early in life on concrete levels of thinking. Role assignments and social reinforcement to maintain the roles then perpetuate these understandings.

This process, however, is not without conflict. Girls do grow and mature and learn. Physically, many girls surpass boys of the same age during the preadolescent period, and some continue to grow to be taller than their male peers. However, instead of experiencing pride and delight in their strength and size, girls cognitively process their physical ability as "sex-role inappropriate" and a shaky self concept is often the result. Academically, too, many girls master their studies in ways that clearly equal or surpass their male schoolmates, yet the "will to fail" (Horner, 1968) persists, and bright girls "choose" to fail when experiencing the dissonance of this sex-inappropriate role.

Differential socialization of children in the public schools has been documented in studies by Saario, Jacklin, and Tittle (1973). They indicate that textbooks, testing, and curriculum patterns portray males and females in rigid, idealized, and non-overlapping roles. Yet it appears as if the channeling toward sex-appropriate competency motivation does not take hold until adolescence. Often there are few male-female differences in achievement, career aspirations, self-concept, and moral development during the primary school years. The premature stabilization of competency and personal growth in these areas for females does not seem to become readily evident until the adolescent years. By middle-age few women are confident of their intellectual competencies outside of the "sex-appropriate" areas.

Perhaps the experience of female adolescents is not unlike a specific developmental regression seen in Malaysian Atayal children (Kohlberg, 1969). The Atayal elders perpetuate a belief system that dreams are real. This contrasts with most other societies in which younger children believe dreams are real (e.g., "A lion was in my room last night.") while adults believe dreams to be subjective, psychological experiences. By age eleven the Atayal children develop the subjective conception of dreams. By late adolescence, however, they have regressed towards the more primitive notion that dreams are real.

Analogously, pre-adolescent girls in our society experience a level of early physical and mental competence and exuberance which is directed into areas not too unlike that of boys. But the belief systems of "the village elders" descend upon them in their adolescent years, and soon the adolescent girl regresses into an earlier, and more primitive, childish "conventionality."

Sadly, the pressure on an adolescent girl to play the feminine game—to "functionally regress"—is imposed from females as well as male peers, from mothers as well as fathers. The desire to be competent in the new heterosexual role, in the socially defined way, necessitates for the female adolescent an ironic compromise.

The Smallest Piece of the Educational Pie

At this point in the history of the women's movement, one might conclude that it is no longer necessary to define and redefine "the problem." The legal arguments for educational equality between women and men have been well made, and some humble progress toward that goal has been accomplished. However, the issue is a much broader and deeper one than the issue of legal equality. John Dewey stated that *true* education *is* development, development along the hierarchical stages of growth. In this perspective, women are still getting the smallest piece of the educational pie. Recent studies indicate that a smaller percentage of women than men reach the highest stages of developmental maturity (reviewed in Erickson, 1973, 1974). Viewed from the perspective of various measures of human growth, it appears that young girls and boys show no significant differences in such areas as academic achievement, career aspirations, self-concept, and moral judgment. Yet, by adolescence, developmental scores for females appear to prematurely plateau.

This phenomenon is demonstrated in several areas of social development. Reports from Project TALENT (Flanagan, 1973), using nationally representative samples, indicate that girls performed as well as, or slightly better than, boys when tested on measures of abstract reasoning, arithmetic reasoning, reading comprehension, and creativity near the end of the ninth grade. However, when a sample was retested near the end of the twelfth grade, it was found that on all the measures, the boys had gained more than the girls. The author concludes that the boys' gains were notably larger than those of the girls on tests of arithmetic reasoning and creativity and that most of the girls forgot more than they learned with respect to both mathematics and science during their high school years. Of parallel concern are the recent findings on the decline of SAT scores of high school students (*Newsweek*, 1976). Perhaps the most significant revelation in the data is that the sharpest overall drop in the achievement test scores has been among females. Even on the verbal SAT's, on which women have consistently scored above men since they were first administered in 1948, the women's scores now fall below the men's. Keeping in mind the difficulty of assessing statistics in education, the problems of professional achievement for women are clearly before us. Even today, only 7 percent of the lawyers in the United States are women, only 9 percent of physicians are women, only 18 women served in the 94th Congress, and as yet no women serve as priests in the Roman Catholic church (*Time*, 1976).

Perhaps research in the areas of career aspirations can further enlarge the perspective just presented. Matthews and Tiedeman's study on vocational orientation (1964), using a sample of 1,237 girls and women aged 11–25, indicates that a definite change in girls' vocational orientation occurred between junior high and high school. The shift was from a strong vocational orientation in the seventh grade to a strong marriage orientation in the twelfth grade. A theme emerging at every level was the common perception that men view women's use of their intelligence negatively. This conflict, between being bright and competent, and being desirable to the opposite sex, is now being recognized as a double-bind that has contributed heavily to the "lid" that has been placed on women's growth in our society. Let us examine the effects of this in relation to self-esteem. Maccoby and Jacklin (1974) suggest that on most measures of self-esteem girls and women show at least as much satisfaction with themselves as do boys and men. However, during the college years, sex differentiation emerges—women have less confidence than men in their ability to perform well on a variety of tasks assigned to them; they have less sense of being able to control the events that affect them; and they do tend to define themselves more frequently in "social" terms than do men. Of importance, it is during this age period that many young adults marry or form some kind of committed sexual liaison. Perhaps it is this period more than any other, when individuals are defining themselves in terms of their "masculinity" and "femininity," that a solidifying of "sex-appropriate" roles takes hold and a critical branching becomes most evident between the focus on agency (one's own competence) in the lives of males and the focus on communion (concern for others) in the lives of females (Block, 1973). Block, in an excellent research article on cross-cultural and longitudinal perspectives of sex-roles, presents a developmental sex-role acquisition model derived from the work of Loevinger (1966), Loevinger and Wessler (1970), and Bakan (1966). Block suggests that during the impulse-ridden and self-protective stages of ego growth both sexes are concerned with self-assertion, self-expression, and self-extension—the characteristics Bakan describes as "unmitigated agency."

Block hypothesizes that it is at the conformity level of ego development (Loevinger's ego-stage 3) that the critical branching is evident and both sexes develop a sound set of sex-role stereotypes conforming to the cultural definitions of appropriate girl or boy roles. In our society this role assignment means an exaggerated focus on communion for females and an agency-oriented focus for males.

The cognitive-developmental position presented by Lawrence Kohlberg would not posit structural sex differences in moral orientation. (See Appendix for description of moral stages.) A structural view of moral development implies that the same stages appear in the thinking process of both girls and boys. However, studies using the Kohlberg moral judgment scales show that males and females make parallel gains in moral development through childhood, while in adolescence males begin to advance more rapidly than females. This trend is evident in a study by Turiel (Kohlberg and Turiel, 1974). Turiel concluded that while boys and girls pass through the same stages of moral reasoning, there appears to be differences in the rate of development through the stages. In his study of 104 boys and 106 girls, on the average, at ages 10 and 13, the girls are more advanced than the boys. By age 16, the boys are more advanced than the girls. The age by sex interaction is statistically significant, indicating that sex role and stage of development, when taken together, are powerful predictors of developmental adaptation.

In samples of college students, Haan (1968) found that more men than women attain moral judgment Stages 4, 5, and 6, while twice as many college women as men stay at moral judgment Stage 3, the stage of social conformity. Holstein (1973), from a sample of upper-middle class parents, found four times as many women at Stage 3 as men. Moral judgment Stage 3 appears to be a stable adult stage of development for most women. More men than women are likely to attain Stages 4, 5, and 6. We can hypothesize that this apparent discrepancy between men and women on moral judgment scores is due to the limitations imposed on women's growth in our society. Men fill roles requiring more social participation and responsibility, which stimulates their maturity. However, when these factors are equalized between the sexes, so are the indices of moral growth. In support of this position, the results of the Turiel study cited above can be examined by types of school ("progressive," "traditional," "parochial"). It becomes evident that environmental differences in treatment and expectations for males and females may be important variables for determining rate of stage attainment. Overall, female subjects in this study from the progressive school were more advanced in moral judgment than those from the traditional school, who in turn were more advanced than those in the parochial school. Turiel asserts that in environments in which males and females have experiences of similar nature, as in the progressive school, no sex differences in moral judgment are apparent. In addition, a study by Weisbroth (1970) concludes that professional women or those attending graduate school attain the higher moral stages with the same frequency as men with similar backgrounds, lending some further evidence that the "problem" isn't in the genes. However, the development of women toward achieving their own potentials has barely begun.

President Abraham Lincoln wrote, during the darker days of the Civil War, "If we could first know where we are, and whither we are tending, we could better judge what we do, and do it better." Perhaps the directions and the tasks we are tending during this period of human history are still unclear, but in the movement for equality today we do have some handles on where we might go and how we might do it better. Erik Erikson, in his book *Dimensions of a New Identity*, differentiates between liberty and liberation—between the revolutionary actions which secure the first and the inner emancipation that frees the second. Ultimately, women will find true liberation only through their own emancipation, their own personal development. Block (1973) indicates that it is not until the conscientious stage of ego development that one's own values can be weighed against those set forth by society. Kohlberg (1975) claims that this conscientious stage of development presents a critical period for educational intervention. It is at this stage that the balancing of agency with communion can begin, a process associated with developmental growth. If true personal integration of agency and communion is to occur, it in all probability requires different considerations for men and women. Block states that for men such an integration would require that:

> . . . self-assertion, self-interest, and self-extension be tempered by considerations of mutuality, interdependence, and joint welfare. For women, integration of communion with agency requires that the concern for harmonious functioning of the group, the submersion of self, and the importance of consensus characteristics of communion be amended to include aspects of agentic self-assertion and self-expression—aspects that are essential for personal integration and self-actualization (p. 515).

Personal maturity was found to be empirically associated with greater integration of the sense agency (individuality) and communion (attachment). It is our hope that this personal development *can* be deliberately promoted through education—such development can be the aim of education (Kohlberg and Mayer, 1972).

Francoise Giroud, State Secretary for la Condition Feminine, has the job assignment of "overseeing the integration of women into contemporary French society." She sees the dimensions of women's growth clearly. What really counts, she says, is to be able to point with pride not to "ten bright, visible women, but to the average level of women in the country. . ." (*Time*, 1974). How do we intervene to raise the stage of development for the average woman in a country? How do we prevent the erosion of competency in half of the human race? A major injustice is before us. Women are being denied an equal opportunity to develop their human potentials. What do we propose as educational programs for the great silent majority of women?

Psychological Growth for Women:
A Curriculum Model

David Riesman, in a response to a query about women seeking equality of choices, replied: "Yes, when you're as far along as men" (Riesman, 1974). Dr. Riesman may be correct; however women will not automatically develop toward higher stages of growth without a new form of education. Surely, sexual injustice calls for action. The following curriculum, developed under a joint sponsorship of the Minneapolis Public School System (Southeast Alternatives Project) and the University of Minnesota, is a beginning approach to such a deliberate intervention.[1] It represents an attempt to promote psychological growth in young women through the mainstream of the school—the school curriculum.

The experimental course described in this section was taught to a group of twenty-three sophomore women who registered for a one-quarter class, "A Study of Women through Literature," at a Minneapolis public high school in the spring of 1973. The follow-up data reported in this paper was collected one year later on 21 of the 23 students. Five year follow-up data on the development of these young women is now being scored and analyzed (Erickson, in press). (For a more comprehensive review of the sample, rationale, curriculum, and instructional model, see Erickson, 1974.)

The general format of the women's growth class followed a deliberate psychological education model for learning psychology by doing psychology. Field interviewing of girls and women across the life span provided the responsible role-taking experience for viewing the process of women's development through different ages, stages, and tasks. This practicum was coupled with reflection seminars to further examine and integrate the experience on a personal level. The initial practicum units involved the structured learning of communication and interviewing skills. The young women practiced listening and responding skills until they could give accurate content and feeling responses on an empathy scale. In-class role-play interviews and then pairing off for actual interviewing sessions with classmates followed. Through this process the women students learned the skills of asking Piagetian-type questions; they learned to identify important content areas that would give information on the nature of women's development at different stages; and they began to develop a sense of genuine communion with each other.

Field interviews with girls and women across the life cycle were then carried out by the students. Interview formats included general value questions and social role questions related to vocational, educational, intellectual, and marital roles of women. The student interviewers attempted to understand the inner motivations and values of their female interviewees and learned to discern moral stage differences in them.

Thus, in the practicum sessions the young women had first-hand experience in identifying many of the major social issues related to the renaissance of the women's movement. The focus in the seminar sessions was on examining their interviewee's responses for complexity of thinking, expression of feelings, social-perspective taking, identification of psychological causes of behavior, and perceptions of choices in life situations. These themes were used to sort the interview data into a framework for examining stages of human development. Taken together, the field interviewing experience and the coordinated seminar seemed to provide the stretching and searching process that promotes growth. The seminars were also used to study current articles on sexual stereotypes, inequality expressed through language, the equal rights amendment, and selected roles of women portrayed in literary works. A framework for an historical as well as a developmental perspective of women's rights and roles was provided. Play readings and short stories were selected to get a developmental view of stages of ego and moral maturity. Katherine in *The Taming of the Shrew*, Laura in *The Glass Menagerie*, Elisa in John Steinbeck's *The Chrysanthemum*, Nora in *A Doll's House*, and the sixteen-year-old Greek princess, Sophocles' Antigone, were examined by the students through their perspective of developmental stage theory. The dilemmas of each of the women characters were presented to the students with a focus on possible feelings the students themselves might experience in the dilemma situation, their own feelings of empathy for the characters in the selections, multiple perspectives for understanding the behavior of the literary characters, the level of complexity of the reasoning of each character, the possible choices the students perceived in the situation, and how they themselves would make decisions given the alternatives. In the class sessions they also examined the process and content similarities between the selected literature and the field data. Most importantly, throughout this exercise the pupils continually examined their own emerging choices in their own life situations. In this way, there was a continuous, three-way connection between field interview data, works of literature, and an examination of "the self."

Research

The design chosen for this curriculum study seeks to facilitate the development of new curriculum directions within the school setting. A series of intervention-evaluation cycles are examined to identify the specific inputs that promote psychological growth in the pupils. Continual modifications of the curriculum materials and procedures are made in the process. Multiple assessments for this women's course included psychological growth measures as developed by Kohlberg (1969) and Loevinger and Wessler (1970), attitudes toward women as measured by Spence (1973), and clinical measure of personal growth as recorded in journals, questionnaires, class climate checks, student interviews, tapes of classes, and attendance. Comparison group data was available for interpretation of the results.

Results and Discussion: From Iphigenia to Antigone

The pre to post scores on the Kohlberg moral maturity measure (see Table 1.1) for the experimental women's class indicates a change of one-third of a stage during the one quarter intervention. This change was typically from Stage 3 (other-directed conformity as a basis for moral judgment) toward Stage 4 (judgment based on general rules, rights, and duties).

Table 1.1 Selected Statistics on the Kohlberg Moral Maturity Scores of the Women's Class

	N*	Mean Score	Standard Deviation	t Value	p Value (1-tailed)	d.f.
PRE	21	304.24	68.72			
				2.07	<.026	20
POST	21	346.00	75.91			
				3.59	<.001	20
One Year Follow-up	21	382.71	69.22			

*21 of the 23 students in the original intervention study completed follow-up testing.

It should be noted that movement from Stage 3 to Stage 4 is a major developmental shift that almost half the adolescent population never accomplishes. Blatt and Kohlberg report that in high school control samples no significant change in mean moral judgment scores occurred during the intervention periods (Kohlberg and Turiel, 1974). Control groups of regular high school classes have been tested in deliberate psychological education research at Newton, Massachusetts (Mosher and Sprinthall, 1971), and no change in the level of moral reasoning was measured. However, the experimental classes in the above studies and in a similar study by Rustad and Rogers (1975) show moral maturity gains during the deliberate interventions. In longitudinal studies on both experimental and control groups, Blatt and Kohlberg report that all of the groups increased about one-third of a stage during a one year follow-up period. Thus, the 42 point increase over the one quarter women's curriculum intervention is within range of the one-third stage movement trends reported in similar intervention studies. The 37 point change during the one year follow-up phase is likewise in line with other follow-up data on moral education.

The pre to post changes on the Loevinger-Wessler ego maturity instrument, using a 10 point scale[2] are summarized in Table 1.2. A significant shift from Stage 3 (conformist) and Stage 3/4 (transition from conformist to conscientious) toward Stage 4 (conscientious) and Stage 4/5 (transition from conscientious to autonomous) occurred during the one quarter curriculum intervention.

Table 1.2 Selected Statistics on the Loevinger Scores of the Experimental Class (Using a 10 Point Scale)

	N*	Mean Score	Standard Deviation	t Value	p Value (1-tailed)	d.f.
PRE	21	6.29	0.78			
				1.79	<.05	20
POST	21	6.67	1.07			
				4.56	<.001	20
One Year Follow-up	21	7.38	0.97			

*21 of the 23 students in the original intervention study completed the follow-up testing.

A person at Loevinger's Stage 4 ego level not only displays complex thinking but also perceives complexity. Absolute standards and rules are often replaced at this stage with ones in comparative and contingent form. The Stage 4 person sees life as presenting choices. She is not a pawn of fate but holds the origin of her own destiny. The achievement motivation is at its height at this stage, as is a strong sense of responsibility, a conception of privileges, rights, justice, and fairness. Self-evaluated standards, differentiated feelings, and concerns for communication are all manifested in the Stage 4 ego level. The Stage 4/5 person evidences greater complexity in conception of interpersonal interaction, in psychological causality, and in the concept of individuality.

Conclusions and Implications: "Disturbers of 'Mankind's' Sleep"?

Erik Erikson (1974) reports that Freud compared his own ideas with those of Copernicus and Darwin as "disturbers of mankind's sleep." Erikson indicates he would add to this illustrious list Einstein's concepts on relativity in the physical world and would include in Freud's concepts of the unconscious the discovery of a class unconscious. The author would also specifically include the discovery of unconscious sexism. Surely, the new awareness of women as people in their own right is a disturbing extension of human consciousness in our time.

Erikson points out that such new facts in the consciousness seem to shatter what we continue to think must be real. They "create a lag between what we know and what we can 'realize'—a dangerous situation, indeed" (Erikson, 1974, p. 104). But as Erikson indicates, this dangerous situation in the collective consciousness should be valued—as creating a state of disequilibrium which is a necessary state for cognitive restructuring to occur in the process of ego development. Perhaps now, more than ever before, the new collective consciousness with regard to justice issues between men and women has reached a prime height—a peak at which deliberate interventions for human growth toward mutuality can occur. Surely, the current struggle for growth by the women of the world is creating a disequilibrium in which a restructuring of our concept of humanness is more possible.

This curriculum model provides the beginning evidence that it is possible for educators to promote psychological growth deliberately through the school curriculum, linking instructional and counseling models to a given theoretical position. Of major importance, this curriculum research lends some additional evidence that women are not destined to be Iphigenias, whose lives are to be sacrificed to the prevailing belief systems. They can become Antigones—young women who perceive choices and who make decisions which determine the directions of their own lives. Finally, the research suggests that only if we continue to promote growth through the conscientious and autonomous stages can we examine true mutuality in a world view, based on the highest principles of human justice.

Notes

1. Acknowledgements are extended to Mary Mozey, an English teacher, and to Charlotte Rogers, a high school counselor, who teamed with the author in the curriculum project. Funding was from the USOE Experimental Schools Program and the University of Minnesota.

2. The Loevinger stage scores were transformed into a 10 point scale. This assumes that developmental scores represent interval data, an assumption usually followed in the Kohlberg scales.

Bibliography

Bakan, David. *The Duality of Human Existence*. Chicago: Rand McNally, 1966.

Block, James H. "Conceptions of Sex Role: Some Cross-Cultural and Longitudinal Perspectives." *American Psychologist*, June 1973, pp. 512–26.

Broverman, Donald M.; Clarkson, Frank E.; Rosenkrantz, Paul S.; and Vogel, Susan R. "Sex-Role Stereotypes and Clinical Judgments of Mental Health." *Journal of Consulting Psychology* 34 (1970):1–7.

Dewey, John. *Experience and Education*. 1938. New York: Collier, 1963.

Erickson, V. Lois. "Beyond Cinderella: Ego Maturity and Attitudes towards the Rights and Roles of Women." In press.

Erickson, V. Lois. "Deliberate Psychological Education for Women: From Iphigenia to Antigone." *Counselor Education and Supervision*, June 1975, pp. 297–309.

Erickson, V. Lois. "Deliberate Psychological Education for Women: A Curriculum Follow-up Study." *The Counseling Psychologist* 6/4 (1977):25–29.

Erickson, V. Lois. "Psychological Growth for Women: A Cognitive-Developmental Curriculum Intervention." Ph.D. dissertation, University of Minnesota, 1973. Also in *Counseling and Values* 18 (Winter 1974):102–16.

Erikson, Erik H. *Dimensions of a New Identity*. New York: Norton, 1974.

Flanagan, John C. "Education: How and for What." *American Psychologist*, July 1973, pp. 551–56.

Haan, N.; Smith, M. B.; and Bock, J. "Political, Family, and Personality Correlates of Adolescent Moral Judgment." *Journal of Personality and Social Psychology*, 1968.

Horner, M. "Women's Will to Fail." *Psychology Today* 3/6 (1968):36–38.

Holstein, Constance B. "Moral Judgment in Early Adolescence and Middle Ages: A Longitudinal Study." Paper presented at the biennial meeting of the Society for Research in Child Development, 29 March–1 April 1973, Philadelphia, Pennsylvania.

Kohlberg, Lawrence. "A Cognitive-Developmental Analysis of Children's Sex-Role Concepts and Attitudes." In *The Development of Sex Differences*, edited by E. E. Maccoby. Stanford: Stanford University Press, 1966.

Kohlberg, Lawrence. "Counseling and Counselor Education: A Developmental Approach." *Counselor Education and Supervision* 14 (June 1975):250–56.

Kohlberg, Lawrence. "Stage and Sequence: The Cognitive-Developmental Approach to

Socialization." In *Handbook of Socialization Theory and Research*, edited by D. A. Goslin. Chicago: Rand McNally, 1969.

Kohlberg, Lawrence, and Gilligan, Carol. "The Adolescent as a Philosopher: The Discovery of the Self in a Post-Conventional World." *Daedalus*, Journal of the American Academy of Arts and Sciences, 1971.

Kohlberg, Lawrence, and Mayer, Rochelle. "Development as the Aim of Education." *Harvard Educational Review* 42 (November 1972):449–96.

Kohlberg, Lawrence, and Turiel, Elliot. *Moralization: The Cognitive-Developmental Approach*. New York: Holt, Rinehart & Winston, 1974.

Kohlberg, Lawrence, and Zigler, Ed. "The Impact of Cognitive Maturity on Sex-Role Attitudes in the Years Four to Eight." *Genetic Psychology Monograph* 75 (1967):89–165.

Loevinger, Jane. "The Meaning and Measurement of Ego Development." *American Psychologist* 21 (1966):195–206.

Loevinger, Jane, and Wessler, Ruth. *Measuring Ego Development*. 2 vols. San Francisco: Jossey-Bass, 1970.

Looft, William R. "Sex Differences in the Expression of Vocational Aspirations by Elementary School Children." *Developmental Psychology* 5 (1971):366.

Maccoby, Eleanor E., and Jacklin, Carol N. *The Psychology of Sex Differences*. Stanford: Stanford University Press, 1974.

Matthews, E., and Tiedeman, D. "Attitudes toward Careers and Marriage and the Development of Life-Style in Young Women." *Journal of Counseling Psychology* 11 (1964):375–84.

Mosher, Ralph L., and Sprinthall, Norman A. "Deliberate Psychological Education." *The Counseling Psychologist* 2/4 (1971):3–82.

Newsweek, 8 March 1976, p. 58.

Riesman, D. "Dilemmas for Women in Higher Education." *Harvard Today*, Summer 1974.

Rustad, Ken, and Rogers, Charlotte. "Promoting Psychological Growth in a High School Class." *Counselor Education and Supervision* 14 (June 1975):277–85.

Saario, Terry N.; Tittle, Carol K.; and Jacklin, Carol N. "Sex-Role Stereotyping in the Public Schools." *Harvard Educational Review* 43 (1973):386–416.

Spence, J., and Helmreich, R. *The Attitudes toward the Rights and Roles of Women in Contemporary Society*. Washington, D.C.: Journal Supplement Abstract Service, American Psychological Association, 1973.

Sprinthall, Norman A. "A Curriculum for Secondary Schools: Counselors as Teachers for Psychological Growth." *The School Counselor* 20 (1973):361–69.

Sprinthall, Norman A. "Fantasy and Reality in Research: How to Move beyond the Unproductive Paradox." *Counselor Education and Supervision* 14 (June 1975):310–22.

Sprinthall, Norman A., and Erickson, V. Lois. "Learning Psychology by Doing Psychology: Guidance through the Curriculum." *The Personnel and Guidance Journal* 52 (February 1974):399–411.

Time 104/3 (1974):33.

Time, 5 January 1976, p. 6–16.

Weisbroth, Stephanie P. "Moral Judgment, Sex, and Parental Identification in Adults." *Developmental Psychology* 2 (1970):396–402.

White, Charles B. "Moral Development in Bahamian School Children: A Cross-Cultural Examination of Kohlberg's Stages of Moral Reasoning." *Developmental Psychology* 11 (1975):535–36.

White, R. W. "Motivation Reconsidered: The Concept of Competence." *Psychological Review* 66 (1959):297–333.

To Understand and To Help: Implications of Developmental Research for the Education of Children with Interpersonal Problems

Robert L. Selman, Assistant Professor of Human Development, Harvard Graduate School of Education.

Dan Jaquette, Research Associate, Judge Baker Guidance Center, Boston, Massachusetts.

In a recent critical review of a tract on development education, one of us wrote: "If we psychologists are going to see ourselves as educators, we must do more than consult for school systems or develop curriculum. We must recognize the same constraints and responsibilities for the education of children as those to whom we direct or advise"(Selman, 1975). In September 1975, that author was given the opportunity to put these beliefs into practice, to leave the relatively tranquil abode of basic research to become director of the Manville School within the Judge Baker Guidance Center, a school for children experiencing learning problems and interpersonal adjustment difficulties. The previous year Selman and his colleagues had begun a basic longitudinal study* comparing the development of logical and interpersonal thinking in the children at the Manville School with a matched sample of reportedly well adjusted peers in the public schools.‡ Children between the ages of seven and thirteen attending the Manville School were ascertained and matched with a peer of the same sex, race, socioeconomic status, psychometric intelligence scores, and chronological age from the public school system. A battery of interview measures assessed each child's level of logical thinking, his ability to conceptualize the relation of other individuals' perspective to his own, the nature of interpersonal relationships, and the maturity of his reasoning about issues of justice. This paper describes how this basic developmental research informs and guides the effort to construct an educational model for children with special educational and emotional needs.

Developmental Studies of Conceptions of Interpersonal Relations

Whereas the clinician's basic concern is to treat dysfunction in children and to facilitate

*This four-year project, the Harvard-Judge Baker Social Reasoning Project, is funded by The Spencer Foundation.

‡Subjects in the clinic sample actually came from two schools with similar enrollments, the Manville and Gifford Schools. For sake of simplicity throughout this paper we will refer to subjects from both schools as the Manville sample.

From *Contemporary Education*, Fall 1976. Used by permission.

healthy development, the social-developmental researcher seeks to understand sequential developmental patterns universal to all children so that one can evaluate the progress of the individual child along a universal developmental continuum. Both the therapist and the social-developmental psychologist share, however, an interest in the child as a social being with friends, peer groups, [and] parents and [an interest in] internal psychological structures and processes which help to shape interpersonal functioning. Our study of developing conceptions of self and others is expected to provide an index for the clinician or educator of the maturity of an individual child's social-cognitive development. The study of the child's view of the interpersonal world has two major goals: (1) the elaboration of the knowledge base about the development of interpersonal functioning in all children, and (2) the development of a more precise diagnostic framework to inform understanding of the individual child's functioning and to guide intervention.

Following a basic structural-developmental model, we expect to find a relative coherence of thinking for a child across the various interpersonal relations (friends, peer-group, parent-child, etc.), such that higher stages are more adequate and complete representations of interpersonal reality than the pattern of reasoning at lower stages, and an invariant sequence of development of thinking in a child as he develops. We have begun a descriptive analysis of the sequence of interpersonal relations concepts (Selman, 1976) and are undertaking longitudinal research to test the validity of the descriptions in accordance with developmental criteria.

In addition, our research seeks to elucidate the relation of interpersonal or social cognition to cognition about physical and logical reality. The interconnectedness of social-emotional and intellectual development is increasingly recognized by researchers in developmental psychology (Kohlberg, 1969; Damon, 1975), by students of childhood psychopathology (Prentice and Sperry, 1965), and by educators (Furth and Wachs, 1974). Piaget (1926) demonstrates how characteristics of primitive logical thinking such as radical egocentrism are intrinsically opposed to social cooperation and meaningful social interaction. Werner and Kaplan (1963) pointed out that when primitive thinking endures beyond its normal phase, it acquires a host of pathological characteristics.

Recent research has demonstrated that social-cognitive processes mediate fundamental cognitive structures and social behavior. Social developmental research then provides both a theoretical and a practical interface between basic research in cognitive development and clinical and educational application (Shantz, 1976). The research presented here, reflecting the influences of Mead (1934), Piaget (1950), and Kohlberg (1969), has investigated developmental stages in children's interpersonal concepts, their relation to other indices of social and cognitive development and to social behavior (Selman, 1976). The research design reflects the authors' attention to issues concerning practice and intervention in an educational and child mental health setting.

Basic Background: Developmental Stages in Children's Conception of Friendship

We have used several procedures in our developmental analysis of categories of children's interpersonal experience—discussions of both real and hypothetical interpersonal dilemmas, drawings and their interpretation, and responses to projective measures. Yet we have found the richest and most reliable method to be the open-ended clinical interview. Following the clinical method of Piaget, we have asked a wide age range (ages four to forty) of both sexes a series of semi-structured questions designed to tap various aspects of each of the four interpersonal relations (friendship, peer group, parent-child, and intrapsychic). For example, in the area of intrapsychic awareness we explore the elements of personal subjectivity, self-reflection, personality traits, and personality transformation, while in peer groups we look for the child's awareness of various group dynamics such as conformity, group solidarity, or comradeship. Our interest is in the individual as a naive but insightful psychologist whose own theory of interpersonal and psychological relations helps to shape his orientation to himself and his social world.

Aspects of Friendship Relations

Because of their significance in understanding childhood interpersonal disturbance, we have been particularly interested in conceptions of friendship and the more complex organizational issues of peer group relations such as how those relations are seen to be formed or a new member included (Inclusion-Formation Phase), how they are maintained through various interpersonal issues (Maintenance Phase), and the causes of their termination or a member's exclusion (Exclusion-Termination Phase).

For example, we have found six interpersonal issues of importance to children in the maintenance of dyadic friendships. To study the child's conception of the *continuity* of friendships we ask questions such as "Is how long two friends know each other important for a friendship? Why?" *Affectional* issues are touched upon by questions such as "What makes two friends really close? What do they talk about or know about each other? Why?" Issues of *similarity-complementarity* are explored through questions which probe children's beliefs in how necessary it is and what it means for friends to be alike or different from one another. *Reciprocity* deals with the child's concern over what kind of things friends do for each other and the meaning of trust between friends. The child's orientation to *intimacy versus generality* in friendships is explored by questions pertaining to the relative merits of single best friends versus multiple friendships of a more superficial nature. Finally, issues of *conflict-resolution* assess the child's understanding of ways to settle disputes between friends as they arise.

We find that at different ages, children have qualitatively different conceptions of each of these issues. Our interest is in finding an underlying pattern (or structure) which seems to influence a child's response across all these issues. Being interested in both the reasoning behind and the content of developing beliefs, we ask children and adults to clarify or justify their beliefs, to respond to questions about why they hold a particular belief or why they believe a certain issue is important.

Methods for Studying Friendship Relations

One specific clinical method we have used in our research is to ask the child to resolve hypothetical interpersonal dilemmas. For each of the four relations under study we have produced a commonplace and familiar dilemma depicted by preadolescent actors on audio-visual filmstrips of six to eight minutes duration. This film is followed by a standard but open-ended interview designed to elicit the subject's interpersonal reasoning as applied to the resolution of the dilemma.

For example, to study dyadic friendship concepts, we present a dilemma in which a young girl, Kathy, has been asked by a new girl in town, Jeanette, to go to the ice show with her the next afternoon. Unfortunately, this conflicts with a long-standing date with a longtime close friend, Becky. To complicate matters, in the filmstrip it is made quite clear that Becky, the old friend, does not like Jeanette, the new girl in town. Following the presentation of the dilemma, we ask questions to which the child, in responding, applies his or her level of friendship concepts. Although these procedures assess the performance of the child on the task and do not necessarily assess the child's "best" level of thinking, we do have evidence that reasoning elicited by this hypothetical procedure corresponds fairly well to the interpersonal reasoning obtained through more intensive clinical interviewing about the way a child reasons about real-life relations. For example, although in real-life situations a child might decide to go to the ice show, and on the hypothetical dilemma say he or she would stay with the old friend, we find that the structure of reasoning behind these choices is usually at the same stage.

Stage Conceptions of Friendship Relations

In the domain of friendship, for example, we find the following stages (briefly described) and give an example of how they apply to peer friendship formation:

Stage 0 (ages 2.6 to five). Non-psychological relations.* The child at Stage 0 is aware of certain purely overt or surface characteristics of friendship; however, he does not differentiate others' mental experience from his own. Consequently, friendships are seen as formed on the basis of physical (non-psychological) determinants such as proximity, gender, size, etc. The ease with which friendships are made is judged through non-psychological circumstances ("I can't make friends with him because he is playing with someone else."). The qualities of someone who makes a good friend are descriptions of simple physical traits ("Americans" or "boys make good friends") without reference to covert properties of persons.

Stage 1 (ages four to eight). One-way relations. At Stage 1, the child can begin to differentiate between his subjective perspective on interpersonal issues and that of his peer. However, he does not yet understand the reciprocal relationship between these viewpoints. That is, he is unable to see that the other has a perspective on his viewpoint and that his own viewpoint is in part determined by how others see him. Hence friendships are viewed as one-way: one member's subjective reaction (e.g., happy, sad, mad) to the other's overt actions; or overt acts toward friends as motivated by one's subjective predispositions (e.g., want, like). This basic chaining of overt acts with simple, unreciprocated feelings pervades the child's thinking about friendships at this stage. Making friends is seen as important simply because one member's actions serve the subjective desires of the other ("You want to have someone to play with.").

Stage 2 (ages five to fourteen). Context-specific reciprocal relations. With the development of an ability to see relations as the reciprocity of subjective viewpoints, the child's conceptions of friendships move to a plane of interlocking subjective relations. Each participant must take into account the other's perspective on the self. However, this reciprocal relation is yet to be mutual; the child sees friendships either from the viewpoint of other or from the viewpoint of self but not as a common psychological relationship. The resulting conception of friendship can be characterized as one of détente

*Age ranges in parentheses are approximations which we have found in pilot interviewing with random samples of lower- and middle-class children.

where the actions of each party are influenced by the other's expectations concerning the self without recognition of mutual understandings held at the next stage. The making of friendships becomes more a psychological concern for how the self is viewed in the eyes of potential friends ("The other guy is all nervous and sort of thinks that the other guy doesn't like him, so he doesn't go over.").

Stage 3 (twelve to adulthood). Mutual relations. Perhaps the most striking changes in the individual's views of friendship emerge in the transition from the subjective context-specific exchanges of Stage 2 to the mutual and ongoing relationships of Stage 3. The individual is able to stand outside the friendship and view it as a system. There is a shift (in H.S. Sullivan's terms) from friendship as cooperation with other in the self's interest to collaboration for mutual and common interests (Sullivan, 1953). Simultaneously there is a developing awareness of the self and other as persons, each with a system of traits, or "personalities." Making friends becomes more clearly a "step-by-step" process whereby one comes to "know" the other person in the sense described above ("I don't just go up and say hello, how are you—you are my friend. I show them I am a good sportsman and I look for someone who is a good sportsman.").

Stage 4 (ages sixteen to adulthood). Interdependent relations. The highest level we have so far clearly identified empirically is Stage 4 where the subject organizes relations along multidimensional and qualitatively distinct levels. At Stage 3 both personalities and relationships, while seen as ongoing systems, are simplistic. The commonality is the overlap of simple personality traits, which is not so much an active process as it is merely the spontaneous matching of common personal interests. At Stage 4, the subject distinguishes several psychological domains to each person (needs, ambitions, fears, etc.), and friendship is seen as an active accommodation of each member to a common viewpoint or an underlying meaning which "unites" complex personalities into an interdependent system. The formation of friendship is seen as originating in each individual's primary need for "belonging," a need to find meaning for the self in relationship to another through psychological interdependence. ("By having a common focal point about which they are both concerned in the same way, they have a unity, they have a oneness with each other.").

The range of ages within which we typically find a stage of reasoning increases as we proceed from the lower to the higher stages; e.g., we find a greater range of stages of reasoning across a sample of fourteen-year-olds than across a sample of four-year-olds. This wider variation in stage usage for older subjects indicates that experience plays an important part in the rate of progressive stage movement. One hypothesis that can be drawn is that children who have experienced inconsistent or disruptive interpersonal experiences and who manifest difficulties in their own peer relations might not develop through this particular domain of reasoning as steadily as children with more reciprocal relationships.

Using the various methods described above, we have completed the first phase of an ongoing longitudinal study comparing the reasoning performance of children at the Manville School on a range of logical (Piaget and Inhelder, 1958) and interpersonal reasoning tasks with that of a group of better adjusted children matched on chronological age, sex, race, social class, and psychometric intelligence scores.

Our statistical analysis of the performance levels for each area of reasoning suggests that children at Manville, as a group, do no less adequately on Piagetian-type tasks of logico-physical cognition than do their public school peers. However, the clinic children, as a group, do significantly less well on measures of inter-personal cognition. These results are interesting for a number of reasons. First of all, remember that the children referred to Judge Baker's Manville school have both learning and interpersonal-emotional disabilities. Their learning problems are evidenced in traditional school subjects, reading and math, and in attitudes and motivation toward learning; descriptions such as "anxious," "bored," "distractable" are not uncommon adjectives for these children. Our results give some indication of an area of relative strength in these children—although they have difficulty learning (specific facts and skills of acquisition), they do not have much more difficulty "thinking" than do children functioning adequately in school, at least when given interesting scientific or logical problems which are evaluated on the basis of the process of reasoning rather than scored as a right or wrong answer.

However, on tasks assessing reasoning about the resolution of hypothetical personal problems, the matched sample performs significantly better than the clinic sample. It appears that for normal children, as a group, logical and interpersonal development are synchronous; e.g., if a child is at Stage 3 on a logical task he is likely to be at the same stage or lag slightly behind on a social reasoning task. For the Manville school children as a group, there is greater discordance across domains. For eighteen of the twenty-four Manville children, interpersonal reasoning was two levels below logico-physical reasoning. Only six of the control children had this discrepant pattern.

Although we have generally found poorer performance in interpersonal concept development in the Manville sample as a group, it is important to emphasize that this is not true for each child. Some children referred to clinic schools because of interpersonal difficulties do quite well on the battery of interpersonal concept measures. If we are to draw more specific clinical inferences from our research, we must move from the analysis of similarities and differences across samples to the analysis of patterns within individual cases.

For example, a closer comparison of the logical and social cognitive patterns within individual children in the Manville sample leads to some interesting but still speculative conclusions. Patterns of reasoning within individual children in the Manville sample can be roughly divided into three types: (1) those who do well on both logico-physical and interpersonal cognitive measures; (2) those who do well on the logical measure but poorly on the social cognition task; and (3) those who do poorly on both. (A fourth category—low logico-physical cognition-high social cognition—is also theoretically possible but empirically nonevident in our data.)

We are currently examining the behavioral and learning correlates of each of these "types." Observed trends which are to be systematically investigated are the tendency of the high-high child to exhibit more neurotic learning disability symptoms. The child with mature cognitive but immature social reasoning is more likely to be an impulsive, aggressive, and hyperactive child. The child who is low in both measures tends to be more "retarded" in a general cognitive sense, regardless of his or her manifest behavior. While such descriptions are incomplete and somewhat speculative, the basic research may eventually lead to a more complete and precise diagnostic taxonomy.*

*For a more complete discussion of diagnostic implications of social-developmental approaches see Robert Selman, "Toward a Structural Analysis of Developing Interpersonal Relations Concepts."

Educationally, the most interesting finding is the discrepancy between performance on logico-physical tasks and reasoning about social relations among the disturbed sample. In those skill areas thought to be necessary for successful functioning in the social world, in knowing how to make friends and in knowing what trust is in a friendship, for example, the Manville children fall far behind their public school age peers.

In attempting to draw educational implications from this research, three basic behavior patterns which are consistently observed by therapists and teachers of Manville pupils have influenced the direction of the inferences drawn. First, despite staff encouragement and reassurance, Manville children tend to be overly anxious about getting right answers, or they defend against feelings of intellectual inadequacy by rejecting any evaluation of their work by either themselves or teachers. Second, a family context where verbal and sometimes physical abuse is frequently directed toward the child leads to a generalized expectation of criticism where children are sometimes afraid to express their points of view for fear of severe derogation. Finally, many of the children's difficulties are associated with an egocentric or over-reactive concern with the self, in low self-esteem, fear of bodily injury, or undue concern about the acquisition of personal goods. These three prevalent features of the children referred to Manville School, (1) fear of failure, (2) the expectation of critical and often hostile feedback based upon past experience, and (3) concerns with egocentric rather than social values, appear fundamentally to underlie their failure academically and interpersonally. A program in educational schools for disturbed children must address itself to remediating these fundamental attitudes in order to liberate the children for the process of learning. As the research results suggest, the problems of these children have less to do with cognitive deficiencies than with social and emotional realities.

Implications for a Program of Developmental Education at the Manville School

This paper began by assuming that cognitive and social development are interrelated and synchronous in competent functioning children. With the assumption of interrelatedness in mind, and in collaboration with colleagues W. Damon and A. McCaffrey, an educational program for elementary-age emotionally disturbed children with serious learning problems is being developed and evaluated. Three central curricula are oriented toward a developmental approach to learning. Each of the curricula focuses on a skill necessary for the education and socialization of the emotionally disturbed child. The skills are taught through the interaction of the child with his/her peers and with a teacher trained in developmental group-process techniques.

More specifically, the three central curricula are, respectively, (1) logical skills, (2) perspective taking and interpersonal and communication skills, and (3) fairness and social reciprocity skills. The logical curriculum will primarily train mathematical and physical conceptions such as number, classification, proportionality, weight, speed, density, and balance. Perspective taking and interpersonal and communication skills training will focus on adapting verbal, written, and nonverbal exchange to the social perspectives of others and to the unique demands of social situations. The fairness and social reciprocity curriculum is directed towards improving children's knowledge of and actual behavior related to social-moral concerns such as sharing, fighting, leadership, and authority.

This approach is being developed to correspond to three basic principles of education derived from developmental theory which can be juxtaposed against the three basic difficulties shared by many of the children at the Manville School as cited above.

First, developmental theory and training focuses on the level of adequacy of reasoning rather than on right or wrong answers. This is a particularly important educational reorientation for children, such as those at Manville, who have experienced repeated failure when judged by the standard of "correct answers" or by standards of reading and math achievement alone.

Second, educational procedures which provide direct and consistent nonhostile feedback for each child's thoughts and ideas are emphasized. Feedback may involve reaction to actions or materials or direct feedback by peers on group social and intellectual problem solving. This provides children with an alternative model for influencing and interacting with others which is nonpunitive and effective. They learn that they can venture thoughts or feelings without risking physical or psychological hurt.

Third, common to developmental theory and training is the progression from processes of thought which focus on self (egocentric) to processes of thought which can take into account multiple aspects of perspectives, including oneself. Training to develop the ability to decenter, to become aware of points of view other than his or her own as a process of intellectual and social consensual validation (see Sullivan, 1953, for a similar orientation to healthy interpersonal relations), is fundamental to the development of mature social relationships and is also thought to enable the integration of other perspectives and aspects of reality which is fundamental to learning.

These three developmental principles are thought to underlie and facilitate growth in both social-affective and intellectual-educational areas. Adequacy of reasoning, positive feedback, and the development of decentered thought may be best facilitated through a program which makes use of peer-group learning procedures. A child-child orientation complements and balances the usual child-teacher relation and allows each child to be exposed to the reasoning of his peer and his peer's evaluation of his reasoning. Small group problem solving of intellectual, scientific, and social problems can be teacher-guided, but the content of the discussion is generated by the children rather than by the teacher.

A discussion of two developmental curricula will provide concrete examples of the application of these principles. The first, based on the authors' own descriptive research, has been used successfully in the public schools; the second, a communication skills project, is currently being evaluated at Manville.

The assumption underlying these curricula is that more mature reasoning about persons and relationships is related to better social problem solving, greater interpersonal awareness, better communication and persuasion skills, and more mature moral thought and behavior. With the first curriculum, filmstrips and recordings, presenting interpersonal dilemmas, are used to stimulate discussion which is expected to enhance the child's ability to perceive and understand perspectives other than his own. Although filmstrips differ in specific content, each presents a dramatic story involving children of primary school age in conflict over two or more ideas. Each story emphasizes taking another person's perspective as part of the resolution of the dilemma. Rather than presenting a resolution to the dilemma, each story provides arguments both for and against several suggested resolutions. Arguments are presented at various levels of social development in order to stimulate children to advance into more complex stages of social reasoning. For example, one dilemma, focusing on interpersonal awareness, depicts two boys who are trying to figure out what to get a friend for his birthday:

Greg has already bought some checkers for Mike, but Tom can't decide whether to get Mike a football or a little toy truck. The boys see Mike across the street and decide to hint around to see what he'd like for his birthday. Greg and Tom ask Mike about trucks and football, but nothing seems to interest him. He's very sad because his dog, Pepper, has been lost for two weeks. When Greg suggests that Mike could get a new dog, Mike says he doesn't even like to look at other dogs because they make him miss Pepper so much. He runs off home, nearly crying. Greg and Tom are left with the dilemma of what to get Mike. On their way to the toy store, they pass a store with a sign in the window—"Puppies for Sale." There are only two dogs left. Tom has to make up his mind whether to get Mike a puppy before the last two are sold.

After the presentation of the filmstrip the teacher asks the children to discuss in small groups what should be done to resolve the dilemma, to give reasons for each choice, and to debate about whether some reasons are more adequate than others. Role playing and class debates are also used. Teachers are encouraged to use these discussions as models for dealing with real-life dilemmas that arise in class.

Pilot testing of the social dilemmas indicates that children often disagree how the conflicts should be resolved and have difficulty making up their minds on the best resolution. It is precisely this kind of conflict and peer group discussion which should help children develop more advanced forms of social reasoning. As one second grader said, "After the movie you might want to know other people's good reasons, good reasons from other people. Because you might just think 'well, he shouldn't do that' and then you can change your mind."

Education is basically an empirical discipline; no matter how logical a program sounds, it must be tested to see if it works. Interestingly, the social development program described above, which appears to be quite successful in the public schools, has failed to generate cohesive peer discussion when it has been implemented in classes for disturbed children at Manville. One possible explanation for this difficulty is that the interpersonal and affective content is too threatening for the children. (The children do enjoy watching the films but do not readily enter into dialogue with one another.) A second explanation is that the Manville children lack some of the basic communication skills which would naturally facilitate functioning under the relatively unstructured conditions of the discussion group. Observations of Manville children indicate that the latter hypothesis is at least a partial explanation. To test this hypothesis, a program in basic communication skills based upon the same developmental principles of (1) active peer group interaction, (2) opportunities to use materials and procedures at a range of appropriate levels, and (3) reflection and feedback on experience (but less laden with affective overtones) is being adapted and evaluated.

The communication skills curriculum, developed by McCaffrey (1975), is particularly appropriate for children in the Manville School, for it facilitates the use of basic perceptual, cognitive, linguistic, and social skills. For example, one procedure has children in pairs or small groups play games which require one child (the encoder) to describe an array of blocks to another (the decoder) whose view of the encoder's array is blocked by an opaque screen. The decoder duplicates the array on the other side of the screen with a second set of identical blocks. The teacher's role is to encourage reciprocal communication between encoder and decoder so that they are able to match arrays. This curriculum specifically encourages learning and emotionally disabled children to be able to (1) use language to communicate, (2) relay information efficiently and precisely, and (3) process and interpret other perspectives. The children appear to enjoy the activities and the teachers use them effectively. Curricula developing basic skills and attitudes are fundamental to the implementation of a more sophisticated developmental curriculum, but they are not sufficient to ensure that children will acquire the full range of developmental skills necessary for learning. Several questions must be addressed in order to establish the educational validity of this approach.

1. Which types of tasks are appropriate for which children and at which level? Building flexibility of procedures into a particular paradigm is basic to the concept of levels of adequacy in a developmental approach. For example, on the prototype communication skills task described above, children find it less difficult to describe an already constructed array than to describe the array as they build it, a procedure which involves cognitive and psycholinguistic processing simultaneously with the process of construction.
2. What effect do developmental skills such as those used in the development of communication effectiveness have on traditional school skills such as reading and math? It is still an untested assumption that developmental curricula facilitate academic skill acquisition. Evaluative research will assess the effectiveness of these procedures to stimulate increased academic and social competence.
3. To what extent can developmental education be integrated, both practically and philosophically, with "traditional education"? Although much of this paper has been concerned with "content areas," the hidden curriculum focuses on teaching methods which stimulate cognitive processes thought necessary for learning across a wide range of content areas. The view of this paper is that the role of the teacher is to integrate the process of coming to know or understand with the content of knowledge.

For emotionally disabled children, more broadly defined educational goals are needed. Educators must include, at times, untraditional techniques for addressing aspects of development not customarily considered part of an educational curriculum, including techniques of psychotherapy and/or behavioral management. A developmental analytic framework can be used to evaluate whether educational or psychotherapeutic interventions meet developmental criteria. For example, one-to-one psychotherapy uses a strong feedback system in which the therapist (rather than a peer) provides the child with a means for the child to reflect upon the meaning of his or her behavior. A developmental analysis would examine the extent to which this approach, or other approaches to social or cognitive development—be it behavior modification, individual psychotherapy, or developmental education, stimulates a reorganization of behavior to a higher level of functioning. This allows greater confidence that a given curriculum or intervention will generate the fundamental developmental growth essential to educational effectiveness with learning and emotionally disabled children.

Bibliography

Damon, William. "Early Conceptions of Positive Justice as Related to the Development of Logical Operations." *Child Development* 46 (June 1975):301–13.

Furth, Hans G., and Wachs, Harry. *Thinking Goes to School: Piaget's Theory in Practice*. New York: Oxford University Press, 1974.

Kohlberg, Lawrence. "Stage and Sequence: The Cognitive-Developmental Approach to Socialization." In *Handbook of Socialization Theory and Research*, edited by D. A. Goslin. New York: Rand McNally, 1969.

McCaffrey, A. "Communicative Competence: How It Can Be Measured and How It Can Be Fostered in Young Children." Paper presented to the Third International Symposium on Child Language, September 1975, University of London.

Mead, George H. *Mind, Self, and Society*. Chicago: University of Chicago Press, 1934.

Piaget, Jean. *The Language and Thought of the Child*. 1926. Cleveland, Ohio: World, 1955.

Piaget, Jean. *The Psychology of Intelligence*. London: Routledge & Kegan Paul, 1950.

Piaget, Jean, and Inhelder, Barbel. *The Growth of Logical Thinking: From Childhood to Adolescence*. New York: Basic Books, 1958.

Prentice, N., and Sperry, B. "Therapeutically Oriented Tutoring of Children with Primary Neurotic Learning Inhibitions." *American Journal of Orthopsychiatry* 30 (1965):521–30.

Selman, Robert. "Review of Thinking Goes to School." *Harvard Education Review* 45 (1975):127–34.

Selman, Robert. "Toward a Structural Analysis of Developing Interpersonal Relations Concepts: Research with Normal and Disturbed Preadolescent Boys." In *X Annual Minnesota Symposium on Child Psychology*, edited by A. Pick. Minneapolis: University of Minnesota Press, 1976.

Shantz, C. "The Development of Social Cognition." In *Review of Child Development Research*, vol. 5, edited by M. Heatherington. Chicago: University of Chicago Press, 1976.

Sullivan, Harry S. *The Interpersonal Theory of Psychiatry*. New York: Norton, 1953.

Werner, Heinz, and Kaplan, Bernard. *Symbol Formation*. New York: Wiley, 1963.

Part III: Teacher as Moral Educator and School as Social Curriculum

The teacher is obviously the critical element in determining the success of any program in moral education. While there are many aspects of teacher effectiveness, as yet unexplored, we are beginning to understand how teaching style impacts student moral stage change in a classroom committed to promote moral development. Kohlberg reports that teachers who effectively probe student opinions tend to stimulate sizable moral change in their students, while unsuccessful teachers fail to engage students through active questioning. My own research in prisons, using moral education techniques, indicates similarly that line correctional officers who both actively listen to inmate ideas as well as challenge inmate reasoning, tend to be more successful in running "small discussion groups" than do officers who assume a more judgmental stand towards the inmates.

These results might be illustrated in comparing briefly two excerpts from discussions using the same dilemma in the same junior high school. Both classes were presented with the familiar "Lifeboat Dilemma" in which the boat will sink unless several people jump overboard. Mrs. B, a teacher in one of the classes, seemed to instinctively accept her students' ideas, yet found ways to challenge them towards more mature thought:

Mrs. B: Well, what should the captain in the lifeboat do?

Alice: I think he should throw the old lady out. She had lived a long time. Younger people should live.

Tom: Yeah, it's only right. If one person has twenty years to live and another has only two, it's only right to have the old person go.

Mrs. B: That sounds good, especially if you're only thirteen (class giggles). What about if you were old, would you still think that was fair?

Tom: Well, my grandma is eighty and she moves around faster than most kids here.

A second teacher, Mr. X, seemed more intent on having his students accept his ideas and be impressed with his experiences than on allowing them to develop their own ideas as to what would be the right thing to do in the situation:

Mr. X: Well, that captain has a responsibility to get as many people back as possible. What should he do?

Cathy: I think that it's wrong for him to say who should live or die. He doesn't really have the right. Just because he's captain.

Al: Yeah, they should have a rebellion or something. It's not his job.

Mr. X: I can see you kids don't know about the army. When I was in World War II, I saw this kind of thing happen all the time. The captain is responsible. He has the authority. The law says he is in charge. If someone would try and interfere that would be a capital offense. . . .

I observed similar patterns in comparing the effectiveness of teachers using moral discussion techniques in a large urban school system. Two teachers whose major technique was to pontificate their own viewpoints actually produced an apparent moral regression in their classes during a three-month period. Three other teachers in the same school who had great rapport, respect, and tact with their students, yet probed the logic underlying their ideas, produced sizable gains in moral maturity. These preliminary results indicate the importance of teacher style in effectively implementing any program in moral education.

It goes without saying that any discussion of the teacher role in moral education must transcend the area of educational technique and strategy. If the school is to be successful in implementing a program in moral education, it is the teacher who must convince both parents and community of its legitimacy. Similarly, the organization of the school as it reflects a conscious effort to be just toward students, faculty, and community, depends upon the commitment of the teachers to be both fair and to insist on an environment of fairness.

Speaking to this point, Richard Hersh and Diana Paolitto look at the importance of the teacher's educational philosophy in successful programs in moral education. Other articles in this section explore both the impact and possible educational use of the structure of the school itself in moral education curricula. Social educators have long understood that the way rules are enforced and roles allocated has a powerful impact upon a student's values. Dreeben, Jackson, and Friedenberg, among others, have systematically observed the obvious link between school authority and culture and the student's values. Dreeben sees the traditional school day, divided by periods, "bells," and examinations as related to the values of an industrial, bureaucratized society. Similarly, both Jackson and Friedenberg see the school as dominated by an implicit, hidden, unexamined curriculum which covertly shapes the behavior and values of both students and teachers.

Research conducted from a developmental vantage point has indicated that social institutions have a powerful impact upon the moral reasoning of children. Institutions which provide opportunities for social role-taking, which allow for moral dialogue, and which are perceived as just, tend to encourage rapid moral development. For example,

Thrower found that orphans tend to be markedly fixated in terms of moral thinking, while Kohlberg and Bar Yam report that children raised in Israeli kibbutzim, which encourage democratic peer participation, tend to be more advanced in terms of moral maturity than are similarly gifted children in even the most advanced American suburbs. One's social role seems to affect moral development. Developmental theory suggests that adolescents who assume authority roles tend to be more advanced than youths who remain followers. Thus, juvenile gang leaders as well as school leaders were found to be more morally mature than were youths who remained in non-leadership positions.

Developmental theory might suggest that the typical comprehensive American school provides a rather poor environment for rapid moral development. There is little effort to involve students in decisions, nor is there any attempt to explain the moral rationale for particular rules. The scene in Wiseman's documentary film, *High School*, where the "Dean of Discipline" tells a boy, "Look, we're here to teach you how to obey orders," seems all too typical of American schooling. Schools too often conceive of themselves as educational factories, dedicated to credentialing students and maintaining order with little thought given to the impact of either the goals of education or the school's social structure upon student social development.

Because of the obvious impact of the school upon moral values, developmental educators since John Dewey have been concerned with the creation of a school structure which encourages the development of mature moral thinking. John Dewey reported favorably on the Gary schools, which made the maintenance of the school itself a part of the core educational curriculum. More recently, Kohlberg, Scharf, Fenton, Mosher, and others have attempted to develop mini-school and whole school programs which, through the encouragement of democratic participation, seek to facilitate the creation of a just community involving both teachers and students and to encourage more mature moral thinking. In this section Tom Lickona and Elsa Wasserman explore this "Just School" idea. My own paper on school democracy seeks to outline some endemic tensions implicit in democratizing large bureaucratic schools. Lawrence Kohlberg's "The Moral Atmosphere of the School" analyzes some of the implicit ideological assumptions adopted by both collective and "romantic" educators. These assumptions, he suggests, tend to lead to justice decisions which are neither substantively just, nor adequately understood, by those who adopt them.

Moral Development: Implications for Pedagogy

Richard H. Hersh, Associate Dean of Education, University of Oregon.

Diana Pritchard Paolitto, Assistant Professor of Counselor Education, Boston College.

The concern for values and moral education has taken on greater urgency during the past several years in light of such issues as war, racial conflict, political corruption, and drug abuse. Teachers need and search for ways to approach the values education issue. Perhaps the most pervasive attempt to recognize the legitimacy of the study of values in schools is the values clarification approach. Proponents of values clarification acknowledge that values are not absolute. In addition, they are concerned with the descriptive "is," rather than the prescriptive "ought." "What *do* you do?" demands a different type of explanation than "What *ought* you to do?" The absence of prescriptive (should/ought) questions in values clarification is related to a failure to distinguish between moral and non-moral issues. What this educational approach lacks is the substance to help students confront questions of ethics, issues "of basic principles, criteria, or standards by which we are to determine what we morally ought to do, what is morally right or wrong, and what our moral rights are."[1]

Lawrence Kohlberg's work in moral development . . . offers an approach which confronts these limitations. His work in moral development, however, requires reconsideration of the role of teacher. Teaching within a cognitive developmental framework demands a philosophical, psychological, and educational perspective that is significantly different from that provided by traditional teacher training or in-service education. Such a reformulation of the teacher's role does not mean that what teachers presently know or do is ineffective or unnecessary. Rather, an understanding of moral development may provide an explanation of the complexity of the interaction between teacher and student which may help more adequately to reform teacher behavior.

From *Contemporary Education*, Fall 1976. Used by permission.The reader may wish to refer to "Pedagogical Implications for Stimulating Moral Development in the Classroom," in *Reflections on Values Education*, edited by John Meyer, Wilfred Laurier University Press, Waterloo, Ontario, 1976, from which major portions of this article have been taken.

A major goal of the teacher who embraces cognitive developmental psychology is not simply to help students accumulate knowledge but to help them develop more complex ways of reasoning. In essence, the teacher wants to facilitate intellectual or cognitive development. Moral judgment is defined as that aspect of intellectual functioning which focuses on a person's ability to reason about moral questions. The purpose of moral education from a cognitive developmental framework therefore becomes the stimulation of the student's capacity for moral judgment. The developmental conception of cognition assumes that mental processes are structures—internally organized wholes or systems which relate one idea to another. These systems or structures function according to logical "rules" for processing information or connecting events. The cognitive structures consist of active processes which depend on experience to produce change or development in the way the individual makes sense of the world. Cognitive development therefore results from the dialogue between the child's structures and the complexity presented by environment. This interactionist definition of moral development demands an environment which will facilitate dialogue between the self and others. The process of moral development involves both stimulation of reasoning to higher levels and an expansion of reasoning to new areas of thought. The more people encounter situations of moral conflict that are not adequately resolved by their present reasoning structure, the more likely they are to develop more complex ways of thinking about and resolving such conflicts.

The Teacher as Developmental Educator

The stimulation of moral development requires that the teacher create the conditions for specific modes of classroom interaction. Such interaction requires that students go beyond the mere sharing of information; they must reveal thoughts which concern their basic beliefs. The theory of moral development demands self-reflection stimulated by dialogue. The teacher within this framework must be concerned with four types of interactions: (1) student dialogue with self, (2) student dialogue with other students, (3) student dialogue with teacher, and (4) teacher dialogue with self. Ultimately the interaction-dialogue process is intended to stimulate student reflection upon one's own thinking process. It is the student's dialogue with self that creates internal cognitive conflict. The need to resolve such conflict eventually results in development.

The teacher initiates those conditions necessary to all subsequent interaction that develops at the teacher-student, student-student, and student-with-self levels. This prerequisite does not imply that the teacher is the center and controlling force of the moral education classroom. Rather, the teacher enters the moral education classroom with deliberate and systematic pedagogical skills and acts as a catalyst whereby interaction leading to development may take place. These interactions expose students to stages of thinking above their own and thus stimulate them to move beyond their present stage of thinking. Such a process may also result in the teacher's dialogue with self, since the teacher can also grow in such a process. Research has been conducted in classrooms at each level of schooling to determine a variety of means by which teachers may facilitate moral development. Following is a brief review of the more salient studies bearing on the pedagogy of moral education.

Moshe Blatt indicated that moral discussions could serve as a vehicle for moral development. By utilizing hypothetical moral dilemmas, encouraging interaction among students at different stages of development, probing student responses, and presenting arguments by the teacher one stage above a student's level, Blatt demonstrated that moral development could be promoted by systematic pedagogy. Joseph Hickey extended the use of moral dilemmas in a discussion group by encouraging members to raise personal moral dilemmas which they would then discuss in the group. This format also resulted in significant developmental change.

Several researchers moved beyond conducting moral discussions as merely heuristic by integrating this approach with Ralph Mosher and Norm Sprinthall's concept of "deliberate psychological education." Dowell (1971) found significant developmental change in adolescents who participated in a peer-counseling course. Mackie (1974) found a similar effect on the moral reasoning of a group of "disadvantaged" high school students who participated in peer counseling. Lorish (1974) also found a significant effect on the moral reasoning of male prison inmates who were taught to counsel. These studies revealed that the development of empathy and more complex social competencies were important to stimulating moral development, at least in late adolescence. The assumption of real and responsible roles by students was indicated to be a significant factor in the promotion of moral development. Atkins (1972) extended the opportunity to assume such roles to the experience of tutoring younger children. Cross-age teaching also resulted in significant developmental change for the high school adolescents in his program.

Building on the findings of these studies as well as on the work of Beck, Sullivan, and Taylor (1972), who taught an ethics and philosophy course to adolescents, Sullivan (1975) constructed a one-year psychology course for high school students. Sullivan's students (a) engaged in moral discussions using such feature length movies as *Serpico, On the Waterfront, The Godfather*, (b) participated in peer counseling, (c) led moral discussions with elementary students, and (d) learned about different theories of moral philosophy. In addition, the students in this course organized a school-wide board of appeals to promote increased justice in their school. The significant results achieved by Sullivan pointed to the cumulative effects of a variety of learning experiences.

Related intervention has been conducted at the elementary and junior high school levels. Grimes (1974), recognizing the influence of the family in the moral education of the elementary school child, measured the effect of a ten-week course in moral reasoning taught to middle-class fifth and sixth graders and their mothers. Those children whose mothers also participated in the course changed more than children whose mothers had not participated, whereas the control group not exposed to moral discussions showed no change.

Paolitto taught a one-semester course for eighth graders from working-class and lower-class families. Paolitto's curriculum included the discussion of both hypothetical and "personal" moral dilemmas through the use of small group discussions, films, journal writing, and role play. In addition, the students engaged in intensive role-taking opportunities by first interviewing each other and various school personnel based on their own written dilemmas and later conducting interviews with community members invited to class to share the moral dilemmas in their own lives. These people included a nun, waitress, pediatrician, juvenile lawyer, and fireman. This curriculum also resulted in significant stage change in the group.

A more recent approach to stimulate moral development has integrated the discussion of moral dilemmas into existing curricula, rather than through the development of separate psychology or social studies courses. Currently, curricula in English, social studies, and guidance are being created in the Boston area (Brookline, Cambridge, Hyde Park); Pittsburgh; Tacoma, Washington; and Toronto Public Schools to add the Kohlbergian approach to already existing goals and learning methods. Kohlberg and Edwin Fenton conducted an initial pilot study in American history classes in the Boston and Pittsburgh areas. After a one-week teacher education workshop to introduce the theory and pedagogy of moral education to teachers in the study, each teacher participant led moral discussions in the context of their history curriculum over the course of twenty weeks. In a pre-test, post-test design with an equal number of comparison groups from the same school districts, the results indicated a significant increase in the students' stages of moral reasoning in the experimental classes. A significant finding of this study was the fact that probing questions by teachers was a critical behavioral factor in promoting stage change.

This review of literature suggests various developmental strategies for teachers to stimulate moral development: role playing, peer counseling, learning ethical philosophy, tutoring, interviewing, and moral discussions. However, the persons who engaged in these intervention strategies had a sophisticated philosophical, psychological, and methodological conception of the "function" or role of the teacher as a moral educator. Teachers who wish to engage in the activities described above must understand the complexity of the teacher role implicit in the research literature. For example, miscommunication between teachers and students about values often occurs not because the values of teacher and student differ but because the level of explanation is not appropriate to the student's level of moral development.

By virtue of the teacher's own developmental difference as an adult, he or she may have a different social perspective, personal and emotional perspective, and probably a moral reasoning level different from that of the students. The teacher brings interpersonal and pedagogical skills into the classroom which hopefully reflect this more complex developmental pattern. Recognition of this difference is fundamental to all other areas of creating a climate within which student development can take place, since the teacher needs to be able to comprehend the perspectives of the students and thereby stimulate their thinking to more complex levels. The reverse of this process is not likely to be true, however; that is, the students may not have the ability to take the more complicated cognitive perspective of the adult.

Given that the goal of a moral education classroom is to enhance students' development, an atmosphere of mutual trust and respect is essential. There is an interaction between the level of structural development and a student's ability to conceive of a particular concept like "trust." A seventh-grade youngster who reasons primarily at Stage 2 in moral judgment, for example, has a limited ability to take the perspective of others within a hedonistic framework of bargaining. That person might conceive of trust as "doing what you can get away with" or not being open with anyone "until you can prove they'll be honest with you, too." A person with a Stage 3 conception of trust, on the other hand, has the ability to take into account what others believe to be "good" behavior; that individual can then reason out his or her own behavior and that of others according to the standard of another person or group. At Stage 3 trust is perceived as helping to maintain relationships. [See Appendix for a synopsis of the six stages of moral reasoning.]

It takes time for mutual trust and respect to evolve in the moral education classroom, especially among students who are at the pre-conventional level of moral reasoning. That is to say that development takes time. Certain activities like role plays and interviews require the group to cooperate in order to organize themselves effectively in deciding what to do and what is fair to expect of each other in accomplishing a task. For students to learn to evaluate their own discussions and role plays means that critical self-reflection and evaluation of others are encouraged in relation to developmental goals.

The teacher's respect for individual autonomy is a related and important aspect of a trusting learning environment which fosters development. Initially the teacher needs to channel any focus on personal disagreements into setting a contract involving what is fair to expect of another in the group. Before students know each other, the teacher can also refocus personality clashes into an examination of disagreement about issues. Later, as trust develops, personal conflicts in the group can be presented as "real" moral dilemmas to be worked out by the group.

Part of the respect for autonomy involves the capacity for empathy. Understanding what the students in the class are experiencing from their point of view is a critical aspect of a developmental classroom environment. Cognitive developmental theory defines the structural aspect of empathy as social role taking, or the ability to put oneself in the place of another and see the world through the other person's eyes. Taking the perspective of others is a necessary pre-condition for moral development. Robert Selman notes that the link between intellectual development and moral development may be found in the ability of a person to take an increasingly differentiated view of the interaction between oneself and others. This process involves helping students to perceive others as similar to themselves but different in respect to their specific thoughts, feelings, and ways of viewing the world.

The teacher in a moral education class is the primary role taker in the group. The ability of the teacher to take the perspective of each student is a vital "skill." It is all too frequent that during a teacher-student dialogue, the teacher is unaware of how the student perceives a given situation. This failure often leads to a belief on the part of both student and teacher that each is not hearing the other. In one sense this problem is a case of not communicating. Within a cognitive developmental framework this lack can be further identified as an instance of not understanding or not accepting the particular complexity of perspective-taking. The onus of failure in this regard, however, must be placed on the teacher, since the teacher will most often be in a better position to take the perspective of the students rather than the reverse. At the same time the teacher will need to create conditions in which student-to-student dialogue helps to develop an increasingly more differentiated and integrated social role-taking perspective. Questions like "What do you think so-and-so is thinking about this situation?" or "How would so-and-so think you would resolve this question?" are as important to the development of social role taking as the question "What do you think about the problem?"

Teachers, like their students, are moral philosophers. Teachers, too, must ask questions concerning what is right and what is good before entering the classroom as well as during actual classroom interaction. The classroom itself confronts teachers and students with a myriad of potential moral dilemmas surrounding issues like cheating, stealing, truth-telling, and keeping promises. The teacher must also be a developmentalist, with a knowledge of the psychology of moral development and the pedagogy of moral discussions. At best, aspects of these roles have always been a part of sound teaching practice. The developmental perspective as a rationale for education demands that teachers become competent not only in knowledge and skills in their content area, but also in the ability to create the conditions for social interaction conducive to developmental change. To realize the teacher's function as developmental educator, one must be able to take the social perspective of each of the stages reflected in the reasoning of one's students and to create an environment in which students are brought into contact with those differing perspectives.

The teacher who engages in a cognitive developmental approach to moral education is not only a moral discussion leader. The essence of moral education is that the teacher create the opportunity for students to organize their own experiences in more complex ways. The moral educator is actually teaching the students a cognitive developmental approach for pursuing their own education after the formal educational process has ended.

Note

1. William K. Frankena, *Ethics*, p. 47.

Bibliography

Atkins, Victor S. "High School Students Who Teach: An Approach to Personal Learning." Ph.D. dissertation, Harvard University School of Education, 1972.

Beck, Clive; Sullivan, Edmund V.; and Taylor, Nancy. "Stimulating Transition to Post-Conventional Morality: The Pickering High School Study." *Interchange* 3 (1972): 28–37.

Beyer, Barry K. "Conducting Moral Discussions in the Classroom." *Social Education*, April 1976.

Blatt, Moshe. "Studies on the Effects of Classroom Discussions upon Children's Moral Development." Ph.D. dissertation, University of Chicago, 1970.

Byrne, Diane F. "The Development of Role-Taking in Adolescence." Ph.D. dissertation, Harvard University, 1973.

Colby, Anne. "Values Clarification: Book Review." *Harvard Educational Review* 42 (1975):134–43.

DiStefano, A. "Teaching Moral Reasoning about Sexual and Interpersonal Dilemmas." Ph.D. dissertation, Boston University, 1976.

Frankena, William K. *Ethics*. Englewood Cliffs, N.J.: Prentice-Hall, 1963.

Grimes, Patricia M. "Teaching Moral Reasoning to Eleven Year Olds and Their Mothers: A Means of Promoting Moral Development." Ph.D. dissertation, Boston University, 1974.

Hickey, Joseph. "The Effects of Guided Moral Discussion upon Youthful Offenders' Level of Moral Judgment." Ph.D. dissertation, Boston University, 1972.

Holstein, Constance B. "Parental Determinants of the Development of Moral Judgment." Ph.D. dissertation, University of California at Berkeley, 1969.

Hunt, Maurice P., and Metcalf, Lawrence E. *Teaching High School Social Studies*. New York: Harper & Row, 1968.

Jackson, Philip W. *Life in Classrooms*. New York: Holt, Rinehart & Winston, 1968.

Kohlberg, Lawrence. "Education for Justice: A Modern Statement of the Platonic View." In *Moral Education*, edited by T. Sizer. Cambridge: Harvard University Press, 1970.

Kohlberg, Lawrence. "Stage and Sequence: The Cognitive-Developmental Approach to Socialization." In *Handbook of Socialization Theory and Research*, edited by D. A. Goslin. New York: Rand McNally, 1969.

Kohlberg, Lawrence. "Stage of Moral Development as a Basis for Moral Education." In *Moral Education*, edited by C. Beck and E. Sullivan. Toronto: University of Toronto Press, 1970.

Lorish, R. "Teaching Counseling to Disadvantaged Young Adults." Ed.D. dissertation, Boston University School of Education, 1974.

Mackie, Peter A. "Teaching Counseling Skills to Low Achieving High School Students." Ed.D. dissertation, Boston University School of Education, 1974.

Meyer, John, ed. "Pedagogical Implications for Stimulating Moral Development in the Classroom." *Reflections on Values Education*. Waterloo, Ontario: Wilfred Laurier University Press, 1976.

The Moral Atmosphere of the School

Lawrence Kohlberg, Director of the Center for Moral Education, Graduate School of Education, Harvard University.

I have to start by saying that Philip Jackson* is responsible for my paper, by which I mean he is "to blame."

First, he is responsible because he invented the term "hidden" or "unstudied curriculum" to refer to 90 percent of what goes on in classrooms. Second, he is responsible because he induced me to speak about the unstudied curriculum when my only qualification to do so is that I have never studied it. While I have done plenty of observing of children in and out of classrooms, such observation has always been with reference to developing personality and behavior and not in terms of the nature of classroom life and its influence on children. Third, he is to blame because he wrote a book defining the hidden curriculum on which I based this paper, and then he prepared a document, defining the unstudied curriculum in a completely different way, leaving me holding the bag.

The Hidden Curriculum and Moral Education

Anyhow, I am going to revenge myself on Dr. Jackson for putting me in this awkward spot by claiming that I am the only person who is really an intellectual expert on this problem of the hidden curriculum. I say this because it will be my claim that the only integrated way of thinking about the hidden curriculum is to think of it as moral education, a topic about which few other academicians besides myself are currently concerned. To make educational sense out of the insights of Jackson, Robert Dreeben, Edgar Friedenberg, and Rosenthal, I shall claim, you must put them in the framework of the ideas and concerns in *moral* education propounded by such writers as Emile Durkheim, John Dewey, and Jean Piaget.

*Dr. Philip Jackson, Chairman, ASCD Elementary Education Council.

From "The Unstudied Curriculum," N. Overly, editor. Monograph for the Association for Supervision in Curriculum Development, Washington, D. C., 1970. Used by permission of the author.

To make my point, I shall start with the central question most of us have about the hidden curriculum, that of whether it educates, miseducates, or does neither. I shall claim that the answer to this question depends upon a viable conception of moral development. The question itself, that of whether the hidden curriculum educates, is posed by the very phrase, "hidden curriculum." The phrase indicates that children are learning much in school that is not formal curriculum, and the phrase also asks whether such learning is truly educative.

In *Life in Classrooms*, Philip Jackson summarizes three central characteristics of school life: the crowds, the praise, and the power. Learning to live in the classroom means, first, learning to live and to be treated as a member of a crowd of same-age, same-status others.

Second, learning to live in the classroom means learning to live in a world in which there is impersonal authority, in which a relative stranger gives orders and wields power. Robert Dreeben emphasizes similar characteristics, first and foremost learning to live with authority. Both Jackson and Dreeben stress the fact that the hidden curriculum provides a way station between the personal relations of the family and the impersonal achievement and authority-oriented roles of adult occupational and sociopolitical life.

The perspectives of Jackson and Dreeben derive from a long and great tradition of educational sociology founded by Emile Durkheim in France at the end of the nineteenth century. According to Durkheim:

> There is a great distance between the state in which the child finds himself as he leaves the family and the one toward which he must strive. Intermediaries are necessary, the school environment the most desirable. It is more extensive than the family or the group of friends. It results neither from blood nor free choice but from a meeting among subjects of similar age and condition. In that sense, it resembles political society. On the other hand it is limited enough so that personal relations can crystallize. It is groups of young persons more or less like those of the social system of the school which have enabled the formation of societies larger than the family. Even in simple societies without schools, the elders would assemble the group at a given age and initiate them collectively into the moral and intellectual patrimony of the group. Induction into the moral patrimony of the group has never been conducted entirely within the family.[1]

What this sociological tradition of Durkheim and Dreeben is telling us is that you cannot get rid of authority in the classroom, because you need people who can live with it in the bigger society. Edgar Friedenberg starts out with the same Durkheim perspective before turning it on its ear. I hesitate to restate Dr. Friedenberg. I am tempted to say that he is the only person in the world who can state a message in many syllables and make it come across with one-syllable impact. In *Coming of Age in America* Friedenberg says,

> After the family the school is the first social institution an individual must deal with, the place in which he learns to handle himself with strangers. Free societies depend upon their members to learn early and thoroughly that public authority is not like that of the family, but must rely basically on the impersonal application of general formulae.[2]

However, Friedenberg's observations of the hidden curriculum suggest that it is less a vehicle of socialization into a free society than that caricature of socialization we call a jail. Says Friedenberg:

> Between classes at Milgrim High, no student may walk down the corridor without a form signed by a teacher, telling where he is coming from, where he is going, and the time to the minute at which the pass is valid. There is no physical freedom whatever in Milgrim, there is no time or place in which a student may simply go about his business. Privacy is strictly forbidden. Toilets are locked. There are more different washrooms than there must have been in the Confederate Navy.[3]

Friedenberg's style of observation of the hidden curriculum is colored by his view that its function of socialization into large-scale society means socialization into a mass middle-class society of mediocrity, banality, and conformity. From this point of view, the hidden curriculum consists of "the ways in which education subverts the highest function of education, which is to help people understand the meaning of their lives and those of others."

I have summarized utterances by our other speakers to indicate how the perceived nature of the hidden curriculum rests on a prior perspective which is both a social theory and a mode of valuing. The fact that this must necessarily be the case in social inquiry, I learned in an illuminating course by Friedenberg on social science method. The observation and study of a reading curriculum rest on assumptions of both what reading is and what reading as a desirable skill ought to be. The same is true of the hidden curriculum.

Educational Consequences of Moral Education

As the educational philosopher R. S. Peters points out, "the concept 'education' has built into it the criterion that something worthwhile should be achieved. It implies something worthwhile is being transmitted in a morally acceptable manner."[4] To discuss the educational consequences of the hidden curriculum is to discuss whether it does or can lead to the transmission of something worthwhile in a morally acceptable manner. While Friedenberg assumes this, Dreeben claims a value-neutral stance. Dreeben concludes an earlier article by saying,

> The argument of this paper presents a formulation of how schooling contributes to the emergence of certain psychological outcomes, not to provide an apology or justification for these outcomes on ideological grounds. From the viewpoint of ideological justification, the process of schooling is problematic in that outcomes morally desirable from one perspective are undesirable from another.[5]

It is hard to understand what conclusions to draw from Dreeben's analysis if it is really value-neutral. The analysis points out that authority is necessary in adult society, so it is necessary to have a hidden curriculum by which it is learned in the school.

Nature of School Discipline

If Dreeben's analysis has real educational force, however, it is contained in the implicit value-perspective of functional sociology, the perspective that the invisible hand of societal survival guides the shaping of human institutions and gives them a value or wisdom not apparent at first glance. Durkheim, the founder of functional sociology, understood that functional sociology was not a value-free position, but essentially represented a moral point of view. Durkheim articulately and explicitly argued that the sociologist's definition of the invisible hand of the social system was also the definition of rational or scientific morality. So Durkheim goes further than saying that acceptance of authority is one of the key elements of the child's moral development.

Durkheim argues that the crowds, the praise, and the power which look so wasteful from the point of view of intellectual development are the necessary conditions for the moral development of the child. According to Durkheim,

> Morality is respect for rule and is altruistic attachment to the social group. . . . although family education is an excellent preparation for the moral life, its usefulness is restricted, above all with respect to the spirit of discipline. That which is essential to the spirit of discipline, respect for the rule, can scarcely develop in the familial setting, which is not subject to general impersonal immutable regulation, and should have an air of freedom. But the child must learn respect for the rule; he must learn to do his duty because it is his duty, even though the task may not seem an easy one.
>
> Such an apprenticeship must devolve upon the school. Too often, it is true, people conceive of school discipline so as to preclude endowing it with such an important moral function. Some see in it a simple way of guaranteeing superficial peace and order in the class. Under such conditions, one can quite reasonably come to view these imperative requirements as barbarous, as a tyranny of complicated rules. In reality, however, school discipline is not a simple device for securing superficial peace in the classroom; it is the morality of the classroom as a small society.[6]

Durkheim's System

I shall not go into Durkheim's system of moral education in detail in this paper except to say it is, in my opinion, the most philosophically and scientifically comprehensive, clear, and workable approach to moral education extant. Its workability has been demonstrated not in France but in Soviet Russia, where it has been elaborated from the point of view of Marxist rather than Durkheimian sociology. Like Durkheim, the Russians hold that altruistic concern or sacrifice, like the sense of duty, is always basically directed toward the group rather than to another individual or to an abstract principle. Durkheim reasons that altruism is always sacrificing the self for something greater than the self, and another self can never be greater than the self except as it stands for the group or for society. Accordingly, a central part of moral education is the sense of belonging to, and sacrificing for, a group. Says Durkheim,

> In order to commit ourselves to collective ends, we must have above all a feeling and affection for the collectivity. We have seen that such feelings cannot arise in the family where solidarity is based on blood and intimate relationship since the bonds uniting the citizens of a country have nothing to do with such relationships. The only way to instill the inclination to collective life is to get hold of the child when he leaves his family and enters

school. We will succeed the more easily because in certain respects he is more amenable to this joining of minds in a common consciousness than is the adult. To achieve this tonic effect on the child, the class must really share in a collective life. Such phrases as "the class," "the spirit of the class," and "the honor of the class" must become something more than abstract expressions in the student's mind. A means to awaken the feeling of solidarity is the discreet and deliberate use of collective punishments and rewards. Collective sanctions play a very important part in the life of the classroom. The most powerful means to instill in children the feeling of solidarity is to feel that the value of each is a function of the worth of all.[7]

A Russian Example

One of the logical but to us rather horrifying innovations in the hidden curriculum Durkheim suggests on this basis is the use of collective responsibility, collective punishment and reward. Here is how a Russian moral education manual (quoted by Urie Bronfenbrenner) tells us this and other aspects of moral education are to be done in a third-grade classroom:

Class 3-B is just an ordinary class; it's not especially well disciplined.

The teacher has led this class now for three years, and she has earned affection, respect, and acceptance as an authority from her pupils. Her word is law for them.

The bell has rung, but the teacher has not yet arrived. She has delayed deliberately in order to check how the class will conduct itself.

In the class all is quiet. After the noisy class break, it isn't so easy to mobilize yourself and to quell the restlessness within you! Two monitors at the desk silently observe the class. On their faces is reflected the full importance and seriousness of the job they are performing. But there is no need for them to make any reprimands; the youngsters with pleasure and pride maintain scrupulous discipline; they are proud of the fact that their class conducts itself in a manner that merits the confidence of the teacher. And when the teacher enters and quietly says be seated, all understand that she deliberately refrains from praising them for the quiet and order, since in their class it could not be otherwise.

During the lesson, the teacher gives an exceptional amount of attention to collective competition between "links." (The links are the smallest unit of the Communist youth organization at this age level.) Throughout the entire lesson the youngsters are constantly hearing which link has best prepared its lesson, which link has done the best at numbers, which is the most disciplined, which has turned in the best work.

The best link not only gets a verbal positive evaluation but receives the right to leave the classroom first during the break and to have its notebooks checked before the others. As a result the links receive the benefit of collective education, common responsibility, and mutual aid.

"What are you fooling around for? You're holding up the whole link," whispers Kolya to his neighbor during the preparation period for the lesson. And during the break he teaches her how better to organize her books and pads in her knapsack.

"Count more carefully," says Olya to her girl friend. "See, on account of you our link got behind today. You come to me and we'll count together at home."[8]

I do not need to say any more to indicate that Durkheim and the Russians know how to make the hidden curriculum explicit and how to make it work. Furthermore, it is clear that Durkheim has simply taken to its logical conclusion a justification of the hidden curriculum which many teachers vaguely assume, the justification that the discipline of group life directly promotes moral character. We see, however, that when this line of thinking is carried to its logical conclusion, it leads to a definition of moral education as the promotion of collective national discipline which most of us feel is neither rational ethics nor the American constitutional tradition.

Valuing the Hidden Curriculum

What I am arguing is that the trouble with Durkheim's approach to the hidden curriculum is not that of starting from a conception of moral development, but of starting from a wrong conception of moral development. Before having the arrogance to present the right conception of moral development, I want to indicate briefly how analyses of the hidden curriculum which do not articulate an explicit conception of the moral fail to provide a framework an educator can really get hold of. We have pointed out that Dreeben sees the hidden curriculum as shaped by the invisible hand of the social system without being willing to say whether what serves the social system is good or bad. In contrast, Friedenberg seems to see the hidden curriculum as shaped by pretty much the same invisible hand of society or lower-middle class society, but to see this invisible hand as bad, as destroying the hearts and minds of the poor, the aristocrats, and the non-middle class in general. The core difficulty of Friedenberg's analysis is his willingness to call things good or bad without systematic criteria of morality behind his judgments. This is reflected in the question, "If you don't like the values which dominate education, what set of values should dominate education?"

The core badness of the hidden curriculum, in Friedenberg's view, is its injustice, its violation of the rights and dignity of adolescents who do not meet the mass image. One might, therefore, expect Friedenberg to hold that the optimal moral consequence of a good curriculum would be the cultivation of just men, of the sense of justice. Instead he comes out for a bag of aristocratic virtues which are as arbitrary as the middle-class virtues he rejects. Put in different terms, he says, "Leave kids alone. Respect their freedom!" without asking whether an education that leaves them alone will educate them to respect the freedom of others.

The School—Transmitter of Values

If lack of explicitness in moral framework creates confusion in Friedenberg's analysis, Dreeben's and Jackson's moral neutrality presents worse puzzles in interpreting their cogent observations. For instance, Dreeben points out that the school arbitrarily demands independent performance on tasks while cooperation in tasks is considered a good thing under other circumstances. In school tests and assignments, cooperation is cheating, while it is legitimate on other occasions. Jackson makes a similar point.

> Another course of action engaged in by most students at least some of the time is to disguise the failure to comply, that is, to cheat. Learning to make it in school involves, in part, learning how to falsify our behavior.[9]

It is not quite correct to say, as Jackson does, that the hidden curriculum of the school teaches children to cheat. More accurately, the school teaches children about cheating and leads to the development of styles of approach to the issue of cheating. In functional sociology phrases, it prepares children for life in an industrial society in which they will have to decide where and when to cheat and when not to. Recent studies confirm the old findings of Hartshorne and May that schooling does not lead to increased honesty. In experimental situations allowing cheating, older children in a given school are as likely to cheat as younger children. What age and passage through school appear to do is to lead to more generalized strategies about cheating. Some older children are more likely to cheat all the time than younger children, while other older children are more likely to refrain from cheating altogether than younger children. This leaves the mean amount of cheating the same.

The point I am making is that Dreeben's analysis of the hidden curriculum suggests that it has neither the hidden nor the manifest function of developing morality. While it presents moral issues such as whether to cheat, its central norms are not moral norms but norms of independent competition and achievement. Accordingly, while teachers may strive to police cheating, they will not exert any real influence over children's moral values or character. Put in a different way, Dreeben is telling us that the schools are transmitting values, but they are not what educators usually think are moral values. A good functional sociologist might reply that from the social system point of view, cultivating independent competition is more important or more *moral* than cultivating honesty, since our society is built to tolerate a lot of petty cheating but is not built to tolerate a lot of people who are not interested in making it by institutional achievement standards. It is just at this point that we have to go back to a conception of the moral before the implications of Dreeben's sociological analysis can be understood.

The Hidden Curriculum as Freedom

One final example of an approach to the hidden curriculum denies considering its use and value for moral education. This example is that of Summerhill's A. S. Neill, whose solution is to chuck out both the hidden curriculum and the concept of morality from education. Dreeben and Jackson say the hidden curriculum is authority, Neill says chuck it out and make the hidden curriculum freedom. Friedenberg's position seems not too different, if Friedenberg were to start a school as Neill has done. Says Neill,

> We set out to make a school in which we should allow children freedom to be themselves. To do this we had to renounce all discipline, all direction, all moral training. We have been called brave but it did not require courage, just a complete belief in the child as a good, not an evil, being. A child is innately wise and realistic. If left to himself without adult suggestion of any kind he will develop as far as he is capable of developing. I believe that it is moral instruction that makes the child bad, not good.[10]

A philosopher could while away a pleasant afternoon trying to find out just what ethical framework Neill is using when he says children are good but morality is bad. It is more instructive, however, to recognize that even at Summerhill moral problems arise and to see how Neill handles them. Some years ago, Neill says,

> We had two pupils arrive at the same time, a boy of seventeen and a girl of sixteen. They fell in love with each other and were always together. I met them late one night and stopped them. "I don't know what you two are doing," I said, "and morally I don't care for it isn't a moral question at all. But economically, I do care. If you, Kate, have a kid my school will be ruined. You have just come to Summerhill. To you it means freedom to do what you like. Naturally, you have no special feeling for the school. If you had been here from the age of seven, I'd never have had to mention the matter. You would have such a strong attachment to the school that you would think of the consequences to Summerhill.[11]

What the quotation makes clear, of course, is that the hidden moral curriculum of Summerhill is the explicit curriculum of Durkheim and the Russians. Unquestioned loyalty to the school, to the collectivity, seems to be the ultimate end of moral education at Summerhill. Surely, however, moral education has some other aims than a loyalty to the school and to other children which might possibly later transfer to loyalty to the nation and other men. To consider what such aims might be we may start with the observation that all the writers we have discussed so far have assumed that morality is fundamentally emotional and irrational. Neill, Dreeben, and Durkheim agree on this point, differing only in their evaluation of the worth of this irrational part of life. It is assumed that the means and ends of intellectual education are one thing and those of moral education another.

Growth of Moral Character

Durkheim and Dreeben assume that learning to accept rules and authority is a concrete nonrational process based on repetition, emotion, and sometimes sanctions. The assumption is that the child is controlled by primitive and selfish drives he is reluctant to give up and that the steady experience of authority and discipline is necessary to live with rules. The notions of Dewey and Piaget, that the child genuinely learns to accept authority when he learns to understand and accept the reasons and principles behind the rules, leads moral education in a different direction, tied much more closely to the intellectual curriculum of the school. This second direction is supported by many research findings. My research and that of others indicates that the development of moral character is in large part a sequential progressive growth of basic principles of moral reasoning and their application to action.

Moral Stages

In my research, I have longitudinally followed the development of moral thinking of a group of fifty boys from age ten to age twenty-five, by asking them at each three-year interval how and why they would resolve a set of eleven moral dilemmas. We have found that changes in moral thinking go step by step through six stages, with children's development stopping or becoming fixed at any one of the six stages. [These stages are defined in Appendix We have found these same stages in the same order in children in Mexico, Turkey, England, and Taiwan, in illiterate villages, and in the urban middle and lower classes. [See Figures 1 and 2.]

Fig. 1a. Middle-class urban boys in the U.S., Taiwan and Mexico. At age 10 the stages are used according to difficulty. At age 13, Stage 3 is most used by all three groups. At age 16, U.S. boys have reversed the order of age 10 stages (with the exception of 6). In Taiwan and Mexico, conventional (3-4) stages prevail at age 16, with Stage 5 also little used.

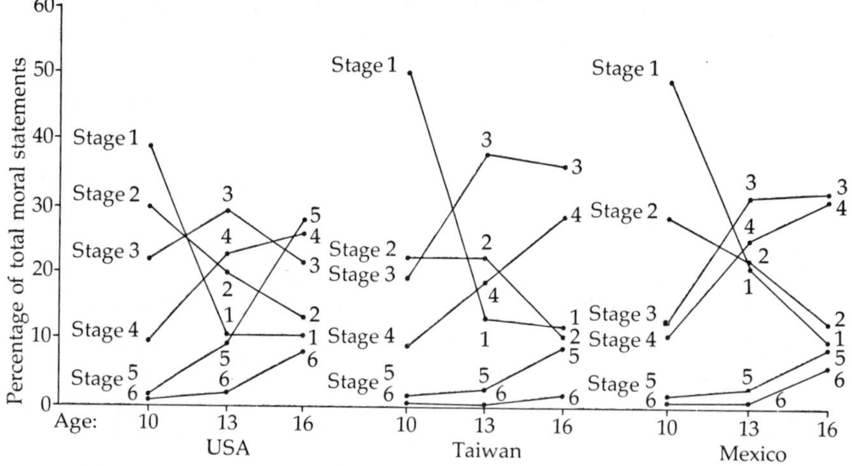

Fig. 1b. Two isolated villages, one in Turkey, the other in Yucatan, show similar patterns in moral thinking. There is no reversal of order, and preconventional (1-2) does not gain a clear ascendancy over conventional stages at age 16.*

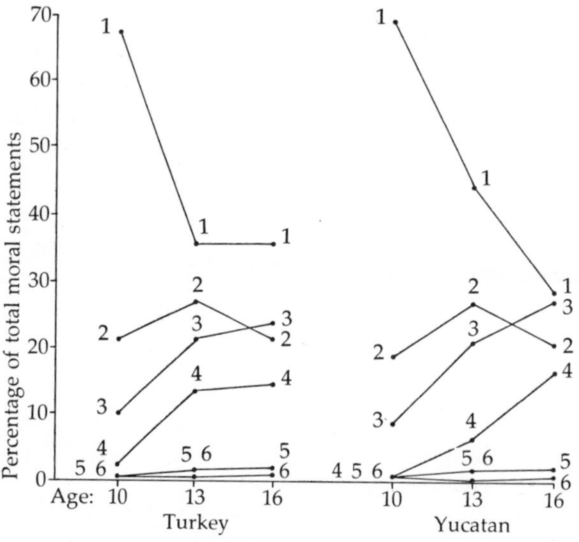

*Fig. 1a and 1b and Fig. 2. L. Kohlberg and R. Kramer. "Continuities and Discontinuities in Childhood and Adult Moral Development." *Human Development* 12:93–120, 1969. Basel, Switzerland: S. Karger Basel.

Fig. 2. Moral judgment profiles (percentage usage of each stage by global rating method) for middle and lower class males at four ages. [From Richard Kramer, "Changes in Moral Judgment Response Pattern During Late Adolescence and Young Adulthood," Ph.D. dissertation, University of Chicago, 1968.]

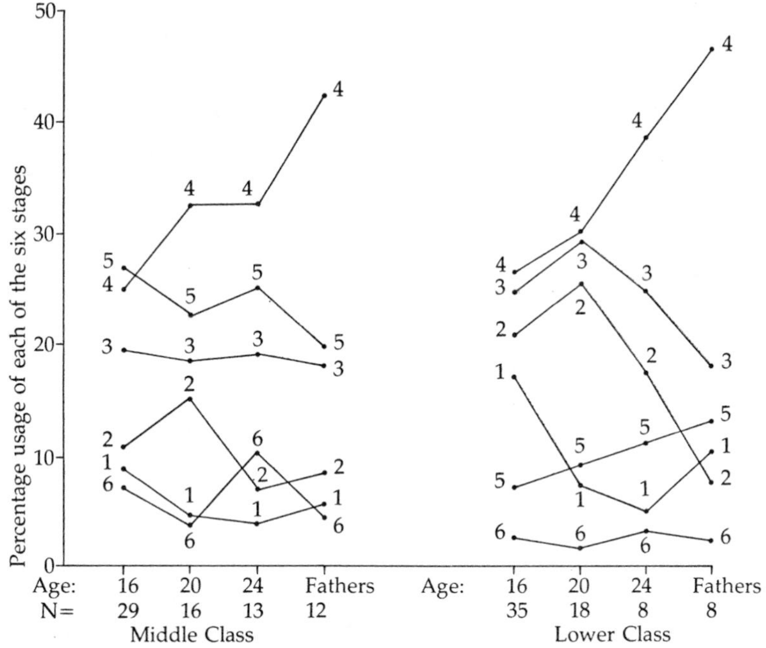

Take one dilemma, such as whether a husband should steal a drug to save his dying wife if he could get it no other way. Stage 1 is obedience and punishment. You should not steal the drug because you will be put in jail. Stage 2 is pragmatic hedonism and exchange. Steal the drug, you need your wife, and she may do the same for you some day. Stage 3 is love, happiness, kindness, and approval-oriented. Steal the drug because you want to be a good husband and good husbands love their wives. Stage 4 is the maintenance of the social order, respect for law and order, and the loyalty to the group's goals, the morality of Durkheim and the Russians. Stage 5 is social-contract constitutionalism, the definition of the good as the welfare of society where society is conceived as a set of individuals with equal rights and where rules and obligations are formed by the contractual agreements of free men. Stage 6 is the sense of principled obligation to universal human values and justice even when these are not represented in particular legal agreements and contracts in our society.

Each stage includes the core values of the prior stage but defines them in a more universal, differentiated, and integrated form. To the Stage 4 mind of George Wallace, the concept of justice is a threat to law and order, because he does not really understand the concept of a constitutional democracy in which law and order, the government, is set up to pursue and preserve justice, the equal rights of free men; and in that sense the concept of justice includes the valid elements of the law and order concept.

Let me illustrate Stage 5 and its difference from Stage 6 by a quotation from Earl Kelley's pamphlet *Return to Democracy*.

> A simple way to measure our efforts to educate is to judge them in the light of the tenets of democracy. . . . It is the way our forefathers decided that they wanted to live, and it is reaffirmed daily by all kinds of Americans except a very few who belong to the radical right or left. The founding fathers attempted to make the democratic ideal come to life by building our Constitution around these tenets. . . . (a) Every person has worth, has value. . . . He is entitled to be treated as a human being. He has equal rights under the law, without regard to his condition of birth or the circumstances under which he has been obliged to live. (b) The individual counts for everything. The state and school—constructed by individuals to serve individuals—are implementations of the way we want to live. . . . (c) Each individual is unique, different from any other person who has ever lived. . . . (d) Each individual has his own unique purposes, and these are the paths down which his energies can be best spent. (e) Freedom is a requirement for living in a democracy. . . . This does not mean freedom to do just as one pleases. Nobody has this right if he lives in the vicinity of any other human being, because the other human being has rights which also must be respected. . . . If we are to emphasize the learner himself, there can be no better point of reference than the democratic ideal. It has the advantage of having been agreed upon.[12]

Professor Kelley's statement is clearly not Stage 6, although it contains a recognition of universal human rights and of justice. Fundamentally, however, Kelley is arguing that his ideal springs from a ready-made, agreed-upon social-constitutional framework, one which permits social change and individual differences, but one which derives its validity from the fact that it is agreed upon, and that it has worked, rather than from the intrinsic universality and morality of its principles. If a man is confronted with a choice of stealing a drug to save a human life, however, Kelley's framework provides no clear ethical solution.

If it is recognized, however, that universal respect for fundamental human rights and for the human personality provides a moral guide defining the way in which any human should act, as well as being the established underlying values of our particular society, we are on the way to Stage 6. It is quite likely that in his personal thinking about moral dilemmas, Kelley would operate in a Stage 6 framework, but that in trying to write a public document that will gain agreement among members of a professional association, he turns to the safer ground of established actual agreement rather than that of Stage 6 principles which logically are universal though they may not be the basis of historical consensus.

For my purposes, it is not critical whether we take Stage 5 or Stage 6 as defining a desirable level for moral education in the schools. It can safely be said that lower-stage conceptions of morality cannot define the aims of moral education, because the Constitution forbids a type of moral education which involves indoctrination and violation of the rights of individuals and their families to freedom of beliefs. This prevents us from taking the beliefs of the majority as an aim of moral education in the schools, partly because the majority has no consensus on moral issues, partly because studies show majority beliefs are grounded more on Stage 3 beliefs in conforming virtues and Stage 4 conceptions of law and order than upon Stage 5 awareness of justice and constitutional democracy.

An example of a school principal who expressed the Stage 4 beliefs of the majority has been provided by Friedenberg. The principal told his high school students they could not have a radical speaker because the speaker was against the government and the school was an agency of the government. If he had understood our constitutional system at the Stage 5 level, he would have recognized that the school as an agent of the government has a responsibility for communicating conceptions of individual rights which the government was created to maintain and serve. I am not arguing that the principal had a Stage 6 moral obligation to defy heroically an angry community of parents to see that a given radical speaker was heard. He was failing as a moral educator, however, if all he could transmit was Stage 4 moral messages to students many of whom were quite likely already at a Stage 5 level. Let us assume that all of the readers of this paper are at Stage 5 or Stage 6. What should your moral messages to children be?

Moral Comprehension of Children

A series of carefully replicated experimental studies demonstrate that children seldom comprehend messages more than one stage above their own, and understand but reject messages below their own level (Turiel, 1969). The studies also indicate that people can comprehend and to some extent use all stages lower than their own. As principled moral educators, you have the capacity to use lower level as well as higher level messages when you choose.

With young children, it is clear that we can make the mistake of both too high and too low a level. It is worse to make the mistake of being at too low a level because the child loses respect for the message in that case. Yet this is frequently the case. Let me quote an example of a familiar tone of Stage 3, "everything nice," from a magazine called *Wee Wisdom: A Character Building Magazine:*

> "Thank you" can just be a polite little word or it can be something warm and wonderful and happy that makes your heart sing. As Boosters let us climb the steps of appreciation on a golden stairway. Let us add that magic ingredient to all our thank yous. Everyone is happier when our thanks express real appreciation.
>
> Won't you join the Boosters to climb the stairway to happiness and success. What a wonderful world it will be if we all do our part.[13]

The quotation is of course straight Stage 3, be nice and everyone will be happy. The only person who can sell that message to adolescents is Tiny Tim and he has to adopt a few unusual mannerisms to do so.

It is, of course, quite necessary to transmit moral messages at Stages 3 and 4 in the elementary school years. Even here, however, it is probably desirable to have these messages under the integrative control of higher levels. Holstein (1968) studies a group of middle-class twelve-year-olds who were about equally divided between the preconventional (Stages 1 and 2) and the conventional (Stages 3 and 4) levels.

Principled mothers were more likely to have conventional level children than conventional mothers. The principled mothers were capable of conventional moral messages and undoubtedly emitted them. However, their integration of them in terms of the higher level made them better moral educators even where the moral educator's task is bringing children to the conventional level.

Developing Moral Education

My research has led my colleagues and me to go on to develop experimental programs of moral education from the intellectual side. Programs center around the discussion of real and hypothetical moral conflicts. We set up arguments between students at one stage and those at the next stage up, since children are able to assimilate moral thinking only one stage above their own. The preliminary results have been encouraging, with most students advancing one stage and maintaining the advance a year later in comparison with a control group (Blatt and Kohlberg, 1969). Such procedures form an explicit intellectual curriculum of moral education. Such a curriculum should not exist in abstraction; however, it should exist as a reflection upon the hidden curriculum of school life.

What is the essential nature of the hidden curriculum as a vehicle of moral growth? Our viewpoint accepts as inevitable the crowds, the praise, and the power which the school inevitably contains. How much or little crowd, praise, or discipline, or power is of little interest from our point of view. A generation of child psychology research measuring the effects of amount and type of family authority and discipline on moral character have yielded few substantial results. If these things do not define the moral-educational effects of the family, they are unlikely to define the weaker and more transient moral effects of particular schools.

The Role of the Teacher

We believe what matters in the hidden curriculum is the moral character and ideology of the teachers and principal as these are translated into a working social atmosphere which influences that atmosphere of the children. In the introduction of a recent book presenting portraits of Shapiro, the principal of P.S. 119, and Boyden, the headmaster of Deerfield, Charlotte Mayerson says, "Each is engaged in a diligent attempt to achieve a consistency between an articulated personal morality and the daily passage of their lives. The two schools are the sites of the working out of this ideal."[14] Shapiro, the Harlem principal, was trained as a clinical psychologist. His ideology is one of empathy, permissiveness, and respect for his deprived children: meeting their needs, trying to keep their liveliness from dying, with no explicit concern for moral education. The ideology is one of warmth and humility and Shapiro is a warm and humble man who is against the crowds, the praise, and the power. How does his ideology, his warmth, and his humility come across to the school? I quote,

> A woman announced that the assembly was being dedicated to Dr. Shapiro. He winced. Eleven girls stood and sang in unison: "Oh he is the bravest, Oh he is the greatest, we'll fight before we switch."
>
> "Talk about brainwashing," Shapiro mumbled, slumped in a back row seat.[15]

It is clear that this humble and dedicated believer in permissiveness is in firm control of the crowds, the praise, and the power.

Neill's personal characteristics are quite different from Shapiro's, yet he too has created an effective moral atmosphere. As a character, Neill is obviously dogmatic, self-assured, imposing. One could not want a stronger, more vigorous leader of a *leader-*

less school. In character, he is reminiscent of Frank Boyden, the headmaster of Deerfield, who is described as being without contradiction humanitarian, ruthless, loyal, selfish, selfless, stubborn, indestructible, and infallible. Unlike Neill, Boyden believes in discipline and believes that the purpose of his school is moral character building. Like Neill, Boyden radiates a belief in the value of his school as an end in itself.

In citing Boyden, Shapiro, and Neill as masters of the hidden curriculum, I have tried to indicate that the transformation of the hidden curriculum into a moral atmosphere is not a matter of one or another educational technique or ideology or means, but a matter of the moral energy of the educator, of his communicated belief that his school or classroom has a human purpose. To get his message across, he may use permissiveness or he may use discipline, but the effective moral educator has a believable human message.

The Ends of Moral Education

We have seen, however, that this human message cannot be an ideology of education, or it will end by treating the school as the ultimate value, with the corresponding eventual morality of loyalty to the school or to an ideological doctrine of education in itself. The hidden curriculum of the school must represent something more than the goals and social order of the school itself. Our definition of moral maturity as the principled sense of justice suggests what this end must be. The teaching of justice requires just schools. The crowds, the praise, and the power are neither just nor unjust in themselves. As they are typically used in the schools, they represent the values of social order and of individual competitive achievement. The problem is not to get rid of the praise, the power, the order, and the competitive achievement, but to establish a more basic context of justice which gives them meaning. In our society authority derives from justice, and in our society learning to live with authority should derive from and aid learning to understand and to feel justice.

The need to make the hidden curriculum an atmosphere of justice, and to make this hidden curriculum explicit in intellectual and verbal discussions of justice and morality, is becoming more and more urgent. Our research studies have shown that our Stage 6 or most morally mature college students are the students most active in support of universal civil rights and in support of the universal sacredness of human life as both issues have recently come in clear conflict with authority, law and order, national loyalty, and college administrations. Research also indicates that these mature adolescents are joined by an immature group of rebellious egoistic relativists who think justice means everyone "doing his thing." It seems clear that student-administration confrontations will spread to younger and younger groups who are increasingly confused and immature in their thought about the issues of justice involved.

In the current college confrontations, it has been typical for administrators to harden into poses of what I call Stage 4 law and order thinking, or what I call Stage 5 social contract legalism. What else can they do? What else are they taught in programs of school administration? This is hard to answer because the world's great moral educators have not run schools. Moral education is something of a revolutionary activity. When Socrates engaged in genuine moral education, he was executed for corrupting the Athenian youth. I mention Socrates to indicate that it is not only America who kills its moral educators, its men like Martin Luther King, Jr., who both talked and lived as drum majors of justice.

These fatalities and many others will continue to go on as long as the dialogue about justice goes on across the barricades. The current fate of the school administrator is to find that if he keeps the dialogue out of the classroom, he will face it across the barricades with students to whom he cannot speak. The educational use of the hidden curriculum is not to prevent the dialogue by calling classroom law and order moral character, nor to cast it out on the ground that the child needs only freedom, but to use it to bring the dialogue of justice into the classroom. It is my hope that our educational research program may find worthwhile ways of doing this in the next five years. It is perhaps less a hope than a dream that the American schools will want to use it.

Notes

1. Emile Durkheim, *Moral Education* (New York: Free Press, 1961): 231.
2. Edgar Z. Friedenberg, *Coming of Age in America: Growth and Acquiescence* (New York: Random House, 1963): 43.
3. Ibid., p. 29.
4. Richard S. Peters, *Ethics and Education* (Chicago: Scott Foresman, 1967): 6.
5. Robert Dreeben, "The Contribution of Schooling to the Learning of Norms," *Harvard Educational Review* 37 (Spring 1967): 211–37.
6. Durkheim, op. cit., p. 148.
7. Ibid., p. 239.
8. Urie Bronfenbrenner, "Soviet Methods of Character Education: Some Implications for Research," *American Psychologist* 17 (1962): 550–65.
9. Philip W. Jackson, *Life in Classrooms* (New York: Holt, Rinehart & Winston, 1968): 27.
10. Alexander S. Neill, *Summerhill: A Radical Approach to Child Rearing* (New York: Hart, 1960): 4.
11. Ibid., p. 57–58.
12. Earl Kelley, *Return to Democracy* (Washington, D.C.: American Association of Elementary/Kindergarten/Nursery Educators, National Education Association, Elementary Instructional Service, 1964).
13. *Wee Wisdom: A Character Building Magazine*, June 1967, p. 83.
14. Nat Hentoff, *Our Children Are Dying*, and John A. McPhee, *The Headmaster: Frank L. Boyden of Deerfield*, two books in one volume with an introduction by Charlotte Mayerson (New York: Four Winds Press, 1966): 8.
15. Ibid., p. 38.

Bibliography

Blatt, Moshe, and Kohlberg, Lawrence. "The Effects of a Classroom Discussion Program upon the Moral Levels of Preadolescents." *Merrill Palmer Quarterly*, 1969.

Bronfenbrenner, Urie. "Soviet Methods of Character Education: Some Implications for Research." *American Psychologist* 17 (1962):550–65.

Dewey, John. *Moral Principles in Education*. 1909. Reprinted by permission of the Philosophical Library. New York: Greenwood Press, 1969.

Dreeben, Robert. "The Contribution of Schooling to the Learning of Norms." *Harvard Educational Review* 37 (Spring 1967):211–37.

Dreeben, Robert. *On What Is Learned in School*. Reading, Mass.: Addison-Wesley, 1968.

Durkheim, Emile. *Moral Education*. 1925. New York: Free Press, 1961.

Friedenberg, Edgar Z. *Coming of Age in America: Growth and Acquiescence*. New York: Random House, 1963.

Haan, N.; Smith, M.B.; and Bock, J. "Political, Family, and Personality Correlates of Adolescent Moral Judgment." *Journal of Personality and Social Psychology*, 1968.

Hartshorne, Hugh, and May, Marcus A., eds. *Studies in Deceit, Studies in Self-Control, and Studies in the Organization of Character*. Studies in the Nature of Character, vols. 1–3. New York: Macmillan, 1928–30.

Hentoff, Nat. *Our Children Are Dying*; and McPhee, John A. *The Headmaster: Frank L. Boyden of Deerfield*. Two books in one volume with an introduction by Charlotte Mayerson. New York: Four Winds Press, 1966.

Jackson, Philip W. *Life in Classrooms*. New York: Holt, Rinehart & Winston, 1968.

Kelley, Earl. *Return to Democracy*. Washington, D.C.: American Association of Elementary/Kindergarten/Nursery Educators, NEA, Elementary Instructional Service, 1964.

Kohlberg, Lawrence. "The Child as a Moral Philosopher." *Psychology Today* 2/4 (1968):24–31.

Kohlberg, Lawrence. "The Concept of Moral Maturity as a Basis for Moral Education." In *Moral Development and Moral Education*, edited by E. Sullivan and B. Crittenden. Toronto: University of Toronto Press, 1970.

Kohlberg, Lawrence. "Education for Justice: A Modern Statement of the Platonic View." In *Lectures on Moral Education*, edited by R. Mosher. Cambridge: Harvard University Press, 1970.

Kohlberg, Lawrence. "Moral Education in the School: A Developmental View." *School Review* 74 (1966):1–30. Revision reprinted in *Studies in Adolescence*, 2d ed., edited by R. E. Grinder. New York: Macmillan, 1969.

Kohlberg, Lawrence. "Moral Education, Religious Education, and the Public Schools: A Developmental View." In *Religion and Public Education*, edited by T. Sizer. Boston: Houghton Mifflin, 1967.

Kohlberg, Lawrence. "Stage and Sequence: The Cognitive-Developmental Approach to Socialization." In *Handbook of Socialization Theory*, edited by D. A. Goslin. Chicago: Rand McNally, 1969.

Neill, Alexander S. *Summerhill: A Radical Approach to Child Rearing*. New York: Hart, 1960.

Peters, Richard S. *Ethics and Education*. Chicago: Scott Foresman, 1967.

Piaget, Jean. *The Moral Judgment of the Child*. 1932. Glencoe, Ill.: Free Press, 1948.

Turiel, Elliot. "Developmental Processes in the Child's Moral Thinking." In *New Directions in Developmental Psychology*, edited by P. Mussen, J. Heavenrich, and J. Langer. New York: Holt, Rinehart & Winston, 1969.

Implementing Kohlberg's "Just Community Concept" in an Alternative High School

Elsa R. Wasserman, Supervising Counselor,
Cambridge Public Schools, Ed. D., Boston University.

Books such as Philip W. Jackson's *Life in Classrooms* (New York: Holt, Rinehart and Winston, Inc., 1970) have focused the attention of educators on the pervasive influence on learning of the so-called "hidden curriculum." The hidden curriculum consists partly of the way in which schools are organized and governed. The governance structure of many schools teaches students that they have no significant control over their lives in school, that they must conform to arbitrary rules or be punished, and that they should go along with what the majority thinks and does even when they disagree. In other words, the hidden curriculum has a profound influence on the moral and civic education of students.

What students learn from the hidden curriculum often contradicts what they learn in their formal social studies classes. Hence, meaningful civic education demands that the governance structure of the school and the formal curriculum of the classroom become congruent. This article describes one attempt to bring about congruence in a school-within-a-school which is a part of Cambridge High and Latin School, a large, comprehensive, urban high school with a heterogeneous population located in an old, three-story building a few blocks from Harvard.

Starting and Organizing the School

The opportunity to establish this school developed in June 1974 when a group of teachers, parents, and students asked permission to open a new alternative school within Cambridge High and Latin School. The Cambridge School Committee approved a summer planning workshop. One resource person to their workshop was Harvard's Professor Lawrence Kohlberg, who came at the invitation of the parents and with the encouragement of the Superintendent of Schools.

By the end of the summer the workshop group had spelled out the enrollment, staffing, curriculum, governance, and space needs of the new school which they decided to call the "Cluster School." The group committed itself to implement Kohlberg's concept of a Just Community School. This approach integrates social studies and English curricula with a program of moral discussions and a governance structure based on a participatory democracy.

Both students and staff volunteered to participate in the program. The students were initially selected from volunteers by random lottery stratified by neighborhood, race, year in school, and sex to reflect the larger high school population. There are currently seventy-two students in the school, drawn from all four high school classes. This number is near the upper limit for effective small group interaction and direct participation in the governance structure. The heterogeneous mix of backgrounds and ages produces a variety of responses at Stages 2, 3, and 4 on the Kohlberg scale to moral dilemmas which come up in community meetings and in class discussions of hypothetical dilemmas.

The Cluster staff consists of regular Cambridge High School teachers who volunteered to work in the program. They have voluntarily spent many extra hours attending weekly evening staff meetings, advising students, meeting with parents, and working on retreats and other community-building activities. The seven staff members include one counselor. Three staff members are assigned to the school full-time and four teach half-time in the Cluster School and half-time in the two other Cambridge high schools.

All students participate in the Cluster School core curriculum in English and social studies. Students from ninth through twelfth grades enroll in the same classes. This core curriculum centers on moral discussions, on role taking and communication, and on relating the governance structure of the school to that of the wider society. This fall the curricular theme focuses on communities. Students combine visits to communities in such institutions as churches, Alcoholics Anonymous, and prisons, with classroom activities which have focused on interviewing skills, writing, and group presentations. Elective courses, many of them mini-courses, include peer counseling, democracy class, journalism (the journalism class produces the school newspaper), United States history, the literature of adolescence, a writing workshop, and career explorations. We also offer health and physical education classes.

Since Cambridge High and Latin School is old and crowded, the Cluster School has only two classrooms and an office. Many classes are held in regular classrooms which are used for part of the day by students from the wider school. Like other Cambridge students, members of the Cluster School take advantage of the wide range of curricular offerings available in a large, comprehensive high school, including traditional college preparatory courses, business education, shop courses, and work-study alternatives. They are also free to participate in the wider school's extracurricular activities, including varsity sports. Hence, they are not cut off completely from the wider school population as students are in so many alternative schools.

The Cluster School is working to define and maintain the degree of autonomy it needs to function within the larger high school. There has been strong support from the Superintendent of Schools, the headmaster, and other key administrators. The staff of the school established a cooperative relationship with the administrators who have traditionally handled discipline, curriculum, and guidance functions. Trust and respect are developing as the Cluster School continues to evolve its governance structure and handles difficult problems.

The administrative structure of the Cluster School is in keeping with the school's democratic structure. Each month the staff elects a new person to represent the school in all meetings within the school system which require the presence of an "administrator." No major decisions or commitments are made without consulting the entire community. Thus the conventional administrative pyramid has been replaced by a flexible structure which encourages the authentic sharing of authority, power, and responsibility.

The Just Community School and Research about Moral and Civic Development

Many alternative schools strive to establish a democratic governance structure, but none we have observed has achieved a viable participatory democracy. We believe that the failure to link democracy to research about development is partly responsible for the return to more teacher-dominated decision making in these schools.

Kohlberg's research and his experience with participatory democracy in correctional institutions and in kibbutzim suggested reasons why we might succeed where others had failed. First, participatory democracy had sometimes failed because it was not perceived as a central educational goal, but only as one of several important and sometimes conflicting school goals. Democracy as moral and civic education, however, provides a central commitment. Second, democracy in alternative schools often failed because it bored students. Students preferred to let teachers make decisions about staff, courses, and schedules rather than attend lengthy, complicated meetings. Kohlberg's research, however, suggested that school democracy should focus on issues of morality and fairness rather than on administrative matters. Issues concerning drug use, theft, disruptive behavior, class cutting, and grading rarely bore students if handled as issues of fairness. Third, democracy sometimes failed because of the extreme difficulty of making policy in a large student and staff meeting. Experience suggested that the community should be small enough that decisions could be made in community meetings in which everyone participated. In preparation for these community meetings, students and staff should discuss issues in small groups—no larger than twelve people—in order to foster stage change and to begin the process of thinking about an issue and preparing proposals for the community meetings.

Kohlberg's research stipulates direct and indirect conditions for moral growth. Direct conditions include the quality of discussions and interaction in classes, community meetings, and other group contexts. Indirect conditions refer to the general moral atmosphere of the school. Moral development takes place because the school provides a number of contexts where students have the opportunity to express their views, listen to the views of others, and make group decisions. These contexts include small group meetings, advisory groups, discipline committee meetings, and community meetings. In each context the effort is to stimulate moral growth through the following means:

Exposure to cognitive moral conflict: In all these contexts, students and staff alike discuss real-life issues involving moral dimensions: how should we deal with a student who has broken the rule forbidding the use of drugs in the school, or what should we do about a student who has stolen money from another member of the community? Students and staff members present their views and try to work out a resolution.

Role taking: Staff and students consider the feelings and points-of-view of other people involved in an issue. They consistently try to put themselves in the person's position as a way of increasing their own understanding of the problem under discussion.

Consideration of fairness and morality: The group discusses issues which it confronts in terms of fairness to the individual(s) involved and to the community. Students also talk about basic human rights and compare them to pragmatic or legalistic bases for decisions.

Exposure to the next higher stage of moral reasoning: Staff members guide discussions so that students have opportunities to consider higher stage reasons as the basis for a decision. They encourage students who think at contiguous stages of the Kohlberg scale to discuss issues with each other, and they use the Socratic method of questioning to introduce one-stage-higher arguments if these do not emerge spontaneously from the students themselves.

Active participation in group decision making: The members of the school make and enforce their own rules. The staff makes an effort to stimulate a concern for the fairness of the rules and to develop a sense of responsibility which is essential when students and staff have the power of sanction.

The Structure of the School

The school's structure and procedures are derived from Kohlberg's research and from the collective experience of the community as its members strive to build and maintain a just school. School structure revolves around community meetings, small group meetings, advisor groups, the discipline committee, and the staff - student - consultant meetings.

In a participatory democracy the community meeting is the central institution of government; it is here that final agreement is reached about the policies and rules for the school. Its function is to promote the controlled conflict and open exchange of opinions about fairness that are essential to the moral development of the individuals in the community.

We opened our school with no rules or procedures of our own, but with an agreement to abide by the rules of the larger school. Our students quickly saw that if we did not make our own rules and develop our own procedures for handling them, we were no better off than we were in the traditional high school. As issues arose—as students created disturbances in classes or were caught with drugs by school officials—we established rules, consequences for breaking rules, and decision-making procedures in our community meetings. The long-run result is a social contract established jointly by staff members and students. Each staff member and student has one vote in rule making and in the resolution of conflicts through fair decisions. The rules and disciplinary procedures cover disruptive behavior in the school, cutting classes, unexcused absence from school, the use of drugs, theft, and grading. The community also has held extended discussions about decision-making procedures, particularly on appeals to the community from decisions of the discipline committee. In addition, the community has discussed broader policy issues such as race relations within the school and student recruitment and enrollment.

The agenda for each weekly community meeting is planned in advance by staff and some students in a democracy class and in a weekly staff-consultant-student meeting. Issues coming before the community meeting are usually discussed in small groups the day before the meeting. Then, at the community meeting, a representative from each small group presents the group's position on a particular issue, and a general discussion follows which usually involves a comparison of various proposals. At this time, members of the small groups are called upon to defend their positions.

The first community meetings, chaired by staff members, were sometimes chaotic. Accordingly, a group of students and one faculty member decided to create a democracy class whose purpose was to train students to chair community meetings and to help develop fair and efficient procedures. This group has helped to develop a procedure in which a student or a pair of students chair the meeting. The chair recognizes students or staff members in the order in which they raise their hands. Still, much disorder can arise when the issue is "hot" and everyone wants to speak at once. The most difficult problem has been to determine when to call for votes. A premature call for a vote can cut off important discussion and lead to a poor decision, while lengthy discussions can be boring and frustrating to students and staff.

On major substantive motions a straw vote is taken to clarify whether there is substantial agreement or a need for further discussion. Finally, a "real" vote is taken on the motion with all approved amendments. If the proposal passes, the result is a policy or rule for the community.

The small groups (upper limit of twelve) function like a small-scale community meeting. They precede the community meetings so that the issues and arguments around a specific problem can be clarified. The small groups encourage greater personal involvement in moral discussions, more role taking, and more exposure to higher-stage reasoning. In addition, they lead to more widely discussed and carefully thought-out decisions in the community meeting. The small groups' meetings are essential for the creation of a viable governance structure and for an increased sense of community.

Advisor groups also play a vital role. Each student has a faculty advisor who takes over most guidance and counseling functions with supervision from a counselor. Staff members meet their advisees in advisor groups which meet at least once a week during school time. The advisor group functions as a support group where students can discuss problems of a personal or academic nature. It differs from the small group in its focus on personal concerns rather than on community issues. In one advisor group a student spoke of feeling hurt about what she perceived to be unfair and unequal treatment at home. The group helped her clarify her perceptions of the conflict, gave her its ideas about how it perceived the situation, and offered her advice about how she might best present her feelings to her parents.

The discipline committee was formed to help enforce the school rules. The committee is composed of one student representative from each advisor group. These representatives are randomly selected and rotate each term. One staff member also serves on the committee. The function of the discipline committee is to decide how to treat students or staff members who break school rules. Decisions of the discipline committee may be appealed to the community meeting. Many of our more fruitful community meetings have dealt with appeals which have resulted in reconsideration of rules over substantive issues of fairness.

The staff, interested students, and the consultants (Kohlberg and two associates) meet one evening each week. At these meetings, they review the preceding community meeting, analyze the current functioning of the school, suggest new ways to meet problems which have arisen, develop the skills of staff members, plan coming community meetings, and clarify the staff's understanding about moral issues which come before the community. Since the staff had no opportunity to study Kohlberg's research or to develop skills during the summer when the school was being planned, these staff meetings have played an indispensable role in the school. One of the consultants also conducts an afternoon curriculum workshop in which staff members learn to lead moral discussions and to integrate them into the curriculum.

The Cluster School in Operation

The early community meetings reflected the difficulties students and staff encountered as they tried to develop a successful democratic community process. Staff members tended to dominate discussions and to present reasoning which reflected their own concerns. They sometimes presented arguments based on Stage 5 reasoning which most students in the school could not understand. Students, not used to participating equally with staff, tested the one-person-one-vote system. The first community meeting, for example, ended with a vote (reversed at the next meeting) that students could leave before the close of school if they did not like the courses offered. This incident led to the development of the straw vote as part of the decision-making process.

After several months, however, the school had developed a viable democracy. The conditions for moral growth—consideration of fairness, concern for the community, role taking, and active participation in and a sense of responsibility for group decisions—are now directly observable in most community meetings. There is a greater awareness of and concern for the feelings of community members who are diverse ethnically, academically, and in life styles.

This year a difficult issue of fairness focused on the admission of students for six remaining openings in the school. There were forty-seven white students in the school and eighteen black students. The black students wanted more equal representation in the community. But there were already six students on the waiting list, only one of whom was black. The democracy class proposed that all six openings be filled by blacks.

A transcript of the community meeting which focused on this issue illustrates the conditions for moral development at work in the school. Students take the roles of others and give reasons which show understanding of opposing points-of-view. The issue is considered as one of fairness. Concern for the welfare of the community is manifested at different levels of moral reasoning, but it is this very concern which underlies the resolution of the competing viewpoints.

Two students chaired the meeting, one black and one white. One of the students stated the issue in the following words:

All right, this is about admission of six new students to Cluster School. There's six openings and there's only one black person on the waiting list. And there's room for six more people. In democracy class a lot of people wanted all the rest of the people that would come to Cluster School to be black.

A white student immediately asked the implications for the white students on the waiting list:
Does that mean that there's only one black on it now, but you want to get five more blacks to jump in front of the rest on the waiting line?

The students responded loudly, both supporting and opposing this reply. One chairperson stopped the commotion saying:
Wait. I just want to stop this. I don't want no one jumping out of hand, because disturbances are going to be going like crazy, because I ain't in no mood for no one jumping out of hand in this meeting. I'm going to go around (and call on each in turn).

A black student presented a subjective point of view:
I'm going to try to tell you how I feel about the situation. Because, you see, I'm one of the people that wants some black people to come in. . . . From what I see I feel I would be more comfortable with them here. I want them here. I want to let some new black people come in and experience the school.

A white student continued by elaborating on the issue of fairness to the white students already on the waiting list:
Yesterday, right, you were talking in democracy, you were saying there's six openings, right. If they were all black people, it would be fair to let them in. I don't care if there were six black people on the waiting list, they could come in, but these five white people, they were first, right?

Other white students argued that fairness meant considering the discomfort of black students, now in the minority, who felt uncomfortable:
It doesn't matter to me whether they're black or white, they're people. But why can't everybody just accept the fact that the blacks would feel more comfortable and get a better education with more blacks in school? And why can't we just let the people that have signed up be black and come to the school, because that will improve all the blacks in the school.

In response to questions by some of the white students as to why more blacks had not volunteered to enter the school, a black student replied:
What would we say about how no black kids are signed up? One reason why they don't is they look at this school and see all these white people and they say this school is for whities. I don't want to go here 'cause there ain't going to be nobody here that I know. And no black people are ever going to sign up as long as they see there's only eighteen black kids and forty-seven whites. Now how they going to feel signing up to go to this school?

Another black student added:
Can I ask all you white people something? I'm not prejudiced, but is it going to make that much difference if there's six more black people instead of white? Is it? There's forty-seven of you whities now. There's eighteen blacks! Six more blacks isn't going to make one difference!

After some angry exchanges, a white student tried to pull together the feelings of the community:
All the people in this community right now are all saying in some way or another—usually they don't want to say it—but they're expressing feelings that they care about the other people and how

their education goes and how their working with this community goes. And I feel that the blacks in this community can't work as well and feel as comfortable without more blacks in this community. It's not fair. Everybody knows that everybody in this school, no matter how it sounds now, cares about the other people. Then why can't you allow six more blacks in, so twenty-whatever blacks will be able to get a good education in this school and a good sense of democracy and just everything. And you know, why can't we just let six more blacks in, it would help the whole thing. The whole community, the whole school would be helped by that.

A white student asked why the black students felt uncomfortable in the school. A black student responded:
Well, I'm going to tell you why I feel uncomfortable. Before I knew who was here, I phoned Cambridge Latin and I didn't want to sign up with Latin, so I heard about Cluster and I came down. This is my first year in this school and I don't know who's here. Never in my life have I seen as many of you who have outnumbered me and mine, anyway. OK, then I get to know them. I say, these whites are all right, you know. And my opinions changed, they changed just a little bit, all right? And then I go home and I look, I listen to the news and I see what the whities are doing to the blacks. For what? Because they want to learn. And then I come back here and I try to get some of my brothers and sisters into this school so they can be helped like I'm being helped. And what do I hear? No. Because they don't want to hear it. Why can't they just give us eighteen blacks a little personal satisfaction within ourselves to have some more of us so we can be together? All right! (Applause)

Another black student asked the white students to consider how they might feel if they were in the minority:
You know, if you all were in a class, one or two of you with twenty black kids, how would you feel?

After more discussion, a straw vote was taken which indicated that the majority of the community was in favor of the proposal. Most of those voting in opposition expressed concern for the white students on the waiting list.
The reason I voted against the proposal was that I wanted to hear more reasons from the black kids, but I'm also feeling a little guilty because I want six black kids to come in, but I don't know what to say about the five white kids on the waiting list. What are we going to tell them?

In response, these reasons were given:
All you have to do is explain to them that the community decided that it was the best idea to take all blacks this time for the community's sake and from now on, every time we're going to admit more kids, we'll admit half black and half white. By then, eventually it will be fairer and we can accept blacks and whites the same way.

Finally, the community voted almost unanimously to adopt the proposal from the democracy class. There was a feeling of elation among the strong supporters of the motion and some bitter feelings among the opposed. Small groups are continuing to discuss the issue and to suggest ways to incorporate the opposing views in a final resolution of the issue.

A Preliminary Progress Report

The clearest signs of success in the Cluster School lie in an emerging sense of community and in high morale. Students have assumed increasing responsibility for their own behavior and for the behavior of others. Many students have become competent at participating in community meetings, and a smaller number have learned to lead community meetings skillfully. These skills should carry over to other school and community activities. Another important by-product of the school is the friendships that have formed among students of widely different backgrounds who might never have had an opportunity to interact in a traditional, tracked high school. The staff has also observed some positive changes in the behavior of students with long histories of difficulty in school. These students say that the changes in their behavior came about mainly because the Cluster School treats them fairly and gives them a forum in which they can protest unfair treatment. The staff believes that many students in the school have begun to progress in moral reasoning up the Kohlberg scale, but research to test this hypothesis has only begun.

Two additional efforts to found schools based on developmental principles are now underway. In Brookline, Massachusetts, the staff of an existing school-within-a-school is evolving a democratic governance structure much like the one in the Cluster School. In a year or so, this experience may provide guidance for other already existing alternative schools which wish to embrace a democratic developmental moral and civic emphasis.

In Pittsburgh, Pennsylvania, the staff of Carnegie-Mellon University's Social Studies Curriculum Center has joined with the Chartiers Valley, Keystone Oaks, and Pittsburgh City Schools and with Fontbonne Academy to organize a number of Civic Education Schools or Civic Education classes within schools. This project will begin with a twenty-week staff development seminar for teachers, administrators, and parents and with major curriculum projects to develop new social studies and English courses for the schools. The Civic Education Schools and classes will then open in September 1976 with trained faculties and carefully prepared curricula. This project hopes to establish guidelines and practical plans through which school systems can organize Civic Education Schools with a high probability of success and at minimal cost. These three projects—the Cluster School, the Brookline school-within-a-school, and the Pittsburgh program—all receive part of their support from the Danforth Foundation, a link which facilitates cooperative planning and the exchange of information. The three groups expect to publish accounts of their findings based on careful research designs beginning in the fall of 1976.

Creating the Just Community with Children

Thomas Lickona, Professor of Psychology, Director, Project Change, State University of New York at Cortland.

"It seemed simple enough at first," wrote Phyllis Hophan, a third-grade teacher, of her feelings as she prepared to embark on a program of moral discussions in her classroom. "I had gained a general understanding of Kohlberg's stages. I was using a purchased kit. As long as I followed the questions in the manual, it seemed as if I could work with twenty-four children at once and surely 'goodness and mercy would follow them all the days of their lives.' Well, it didn't happen. The discussions were awkward, flat."

What went wrong? "I spent a great deal of time analyzing my questioning technique," teacher Hophan says, "and I found these problems:

1. I have fixed values, and my style of questioning made clear my feelings that I had the right answer and we were just playing a game to see who could guess what it was; I became aware of voice tones and facial expressions that slanted even the ready-made questions in the manual.
2. Because I perpetuated the unspoken belief that I was the sole source of wisdom, the children spoke only to me and in response to my questions.
3. Not being able to see the dilemma from many points of view, I could not grasp all the possible implications—my questions consequently dealt with only the most obvious problems, and therefore I could not carry discussions for any length of time.
4. I gave subtle approval to those children who responded in ways that showed higher stages of reasoning—even calling on them when no one else volunteered.
5. Since I truly felt that there *was* a 'right solution,' I dragged the discussion along and prompted the 'leaders' in the group to give me that solution. At that point we concluded the discussion, leaving the children with no conflict at all."[1]

Undaunted, this teacher took the following steps to try to solve her problem: "I spent many hours," she says, "practicing writing my own questions and then compar-

From *Theory Into Practice*, May 1977, Richard Hersh, guest editor. Used by permission.

ing them to those written for the same dilemma in the manual." She reduced the size of the discussion group to twelve, then six, then three—finding that the most animated discussions came in groups of six. She encouraged interaction among the children by directing responses away from herself with questions such as, "How do you feel about what Jenny said?" To get at the reasoning behind opinions, she listed the "because's" offered for each proposed solution to a dilemma and focused the discussions on those. To prevent children from looking to her for the "right answer," she took "devil's advocate" stands opposing fairness and advocating points of view unacceptable to the group.

Teacher Hophan also began to view her classroom through a different lens: "Suddenly I saw that the hours of the day were filled with real, immediate moral dilemmas." She decided that at the end of each week the children would discuss a slice of moral life in their classroom. During the week, they were invited to complete a sentence written on a chart at the front of the room: "This was the week when. . . ." On Friday, the class eagerly discussed the chart's various entries: e.g., "there were fights on the morning bus," "somebody had money taken," "Mrs. Carlson kept the projector too long, and we couldn't see that movie because you had to send it back." Having the problems posted ahead of time, teacher Hophan says, "gave me time to contemplate all aspects of the problem. I became less inclined to favor my first solution." Moreover, talking about in-school problems led children to raise dilemmas from their lives outside school, and "many very rewarding discussions resulted."

In these exploratory efforts to develop children's moral reasoning, Phyllis Hophan hit upon two insights that we have come to regard as fundamental to the enterprise of being a moral educator. One is that morality begins at home. Any of us setting out to raise the moral development of someone else would do well to take stock, personally, and to make a conscious attempt to live out the same moral values, such as empathy, tolerance, and respect for others, that we hope to foster in our students.

"I became very aware," teacher Hophan says, "that my personality and my own moral development were the cause of my inability to construct the environment I was seeking in my room." One of the things that greatly helped her, she says, was the chance to share problems and trade ideas each week with other teachers who were also trying their hand at moral discussions. "I practiced listening to others—to their points of view. If I've learned anything at all in the last three months, it's that no one can ask an open-ended question without first having an open mind. I had to clean house before I invited the children in."[2]

The second basic insight that teacher Hophan got an early handle on is that the real-life concerns of children, more so than pre-packaged dilemmas, are ideal grist for the moral mill. Commercial materials can also be useful—I worked with Bob Selman and Larry Kohlberg on developing sound-filmstrip dilemmas for elementary-age students (Guidance Associates, 1972; see also Galbraith and Jones, 1976)—but we've come to realize that children's own experiences are what they like to talk about most. How do we deal with a rash of fist fights and pencil jabbings in the classroom? Should everyone's freedom to sign out for a drink at the water fountain be restricted because several children have abused the privilege? How can clean-up be organized so all do their fair share? What should we do when someone's property has been stolen or destroyed?

Coming to grips with day-in and day-out problems like these makes sense from both a practical and a theoretical point of view. Kohlberg's traditional hypothetical dilemmas, originally designed for research interviews, force people to choose between only two courses of action (e.g., steal the cancer-curing drug or let your wife die; save the stranded kitten or keep your promise not to climb trees). Real-life moral conflicts, by contrast, are open to many solutions. They offer students the valuable experience of give-and-take, of having to hammer out a consensus or compromise in a spirit of mutual concern and fairness. In that sense, real-life conflicts come closer than hypothetical dilemmas to operationalizing Kohlberg's idea that moral problem solving means working out a fair solution—one that satisfies a variety of viewpoints and that everybody can live with.

Moreover, dealing with issues arising from children's own experience gives them the needed opportunity to *act* on the basis of their moral reasoning. When dilemmas are make-believe, talk is cheap. But with real problems, it's possible for the teacher and the peer group to hold class members accountable for following through on agreed-upon solutions—and thus to narrow the gap between what children grant as right in principle and what they actually do in practice.

The effort to use the life of the classroom as a "naturalistic" moral curriculum has guided the work we have done in Project Change with early childhood and elementary school teachers in central New York. The question we have posed is, How is it possible to use all the roles, relationships, and interactions in the classroom to foster the moral growth of children? How can the teacher and the children, working together, create a positive moral climate of caring and respect that pervades the whole human environment? We are asking, in effect, how to create Kohlberg's "just community" scaled to the child's world.

Going Back to Piaget

What we have done in attempting to answer these questions is to dust off Piaget's 1932 book, *The Moral Judgment of the Child*. There he denounced traditional schools for behaving as if their goal was "the preparation of pupils for competitive examinations rather than for life." He regarded as folly the school's determination "to shut the child up in work that is strictly individual"—a procedure that seemed to Piaget to be "contrary to the most obvious requirements of intellectual and moral development."[3]

Like Kohlberg, Piaget believed that social interaction, requiring students to consider the viewpoint of others, is the indispensable ingredient in any program for moral education. Schools, Piaget said, should be places where children can "follow their interests together . . . where individual experimentation and reflection carried out in common come to each other's aid and balance one another."[4] Cooperative efforts like these, Piaget held, force children out of their social-moral egocentrism. Working together compels them to compare their ideas, reach agreements about how to proceed, and coordinate their actions with those of others. Decentering from one's own viewpoint is built into the nature of collaborative activity.

Cooperative Learning in the Classroom

As one example of how to bring Piaget's prescription to life in an elementary school classroom, let me borrow again from the experience of Phyllis Hophan, the teacher whose rocky start with moral dilemmas was the source of so much wisdom. Her strategy for fostering cooperative experimentation began with a deceptively simple question, put to her third-grade children: How can you make different kinds of dried beans sprout, and what factors affect their growth?

Working in pairs, students tackled this task with great enthusiasm, the teacher reports, but showed "a surprising lack of familiarity with the requirements for growth: Beans were pierced, stomped, smashed, peeled, drowned, and parched . . . Some teams chose to do as many as twelve experiments, covering every possible combination of container, light, moisture, and bean variety, rather than pursuing a few experiments in a logical, coherent pattern."[5] The teacher decided to allow this scatter-gun approach and deal with their reasoning in whole-class meetings: "I devised a Class Bean Book, and as teams reported on what they had learned, I continually asked, 'How do you know that?'" When children offered their results as proof, others in the group challenged with counterevidence from their experiments. Only agreed-upon claims could be entered as "facts" in the Bean Book.

Children showed a good ability to divide their labor, the teacher observed, and demonstrated respect for each other's competencies and preferences. Said one boy to his teammate: "You write down what we found, okay? You write neater than me. I'll empty the water 'cause I don't care if it smells."

Two weeks after the project began, teacher Hophan introduced "real planting," using soil, along with a new rule: Each team had to write down their prediction for each experiment they chose to do, to post this prediction on the wall, and to report on the experiment at the class meeting. The new rule was followed by "a great deal more order to the processes the children used." Intense interest in charting growth rates, however, led to an unexpected eruption of competition between teams: "Partners blamed each other for over- or under-watering. Teams taunted other teams when their plants grew faster or larger. There were even several cases of sabotage, as when the class discovered many containers virtually swamped in water and a book placed squarely on top of a lush crop of soybean plantings."[6]

The whole-class meeting now served as a way to talk about issues of competition, jealousy, and cooperation. About half the children said they wanted to work alone, caring for their own plant, rather than having to work with a team member. The teacher agreed to this change, but a week later almost all of the children—acting on their own initiative—were back together again. One boy explained that he needed his partner because "I can't hold this paper (on which he had been recording the plant's growth rate) and mark it, too." Another reunited team said, that apart, they forgot to water their plants, but together they could remember.

Strengthened by their survival of a crisis, the class went on to higher things: a visit to a greenhouse at Cornell University and a decision to construct their own greenhouses and plant gardens of flowers for the whole school. This altruistic venture involved the children in "selecting the seeds, drawing plans to scale for our greenhouses, constructing the greenhouses, preparing the soil mix and seed trays, reading the planting instructions, sowing the seeds, measuring and selecting the garden sites, preparing the soil, and transplanting the plants"—activities undertaken in spontaneous groupings according to interest and ability. "The accepting of group goals and responsibilities," the teacher reported, "developed to a gratifying degree," along with a marked improvement in children's self-esteem and their tendency to contribute to each other's feelings of competence by saying to classmates,"You're really good at that."[7] What teacher Hophan's semester-long project also demonstrated—by involving children in acquiring or applying skills in science, math, and reading as well as in learning to work together—is that in the hands of an imaginative teacher, the moral and the academic curriculum can be two sides of the same coin.

Judi Kur, a first-grade teacher in our program, came to see cooperative learning projects as the ounce of prevention worth a pound of cure for discipline problems. Initially searching for a way to deal with the disruptive behavior of four particular children, she read Johnson and Johnson's *Learning Together and Alone* and shifted her strategy from zeroing in on individual troublemakers to promoting cooperative relationships throughout her classroom. As the first step in this direction, she divided her children into random groups of four, gave them craft sticks, glue, and a piece of cardboard, and asked each group to construct a building of its choice. Although there were a few disputes, the teacher observed that the children worked much better together than they had when they were at a table working individually on their own thing.

Over the next few weeks, as children gained experience in group work, new patterns of interaction emerged. Natural leaders, who had dominated early group activities, became less important. Previously shy and withdrawn children began offering suggestions and having them accepted. A "we" orientation grew stronger. When groups were asked to do a "picture of spring," for example, children could be heard telling each other not to scribble because "you're wrecking *our* picture." Children also frequently offered each other help. In cooperating on the spring picture, they taught each other how to draw birds or flowers or trees.

After several such projects, teacher Kur asked her children in a class meeting, "What does it mean to cooperate?" One boy said, "It means to help with the work, you know, like don't goof off." Another child said, "You gotta talk nice or no one will listen to you." Said another, "You can't be too bossy; everybody has to have a turn." And another: "You help people do things, like if they can't make a 3, you show them how."

These social and moral learnings, teacher Kur says, have been evident in everyday experiences. "Clean-up time has been cut in half. The general climate in the room has been much more positive. The children seem to care more for each other." The increased caring was especially evident in a child, Rosanne, whose behavior had previously been a problem. Following the introduction of the cooperative learning activities, Rosanne learned to handle conflict situations non-aggressively and made several friends. When a new girl came to the class, teacher Kur says, Rosanne was the first one with her arm around her saying, "My name is Rosanne, what's yours? Come with me, I'll show you around."[8]

The Class Meeting: Democracy for Kids

The cooperative learning projects of teachers Hophan and Kur succeeded as well as they did at least partly because they used another strategy which we regard as essential to moral education in the elementary classroom: the class meeting. Developed by the humanistic educator William Glasser, the class meeting involves the whole group, is conducted in a circle for fifteen to thirty minutes, and is most effective when held every day. (Some of our teachers prefer to hold it twice a day, once at the end of the morning and again at the end of the afternoon.) The class meeting can be used to exchange views about how to solve a problem or conflict that has arisen, but it is not limited to that. Children can talk about what they have been working on in the classroom, help plan a project, share something important that has happened at home, or discuss an idea. "It's the time of the day," writes Anne Roubos, a first-grade teacher, "when I relish the feeling of unity." Every teacher I know who has worked at developing this kind of regular communication reports better relationships among their children and a strengthened sense of community.

One way the class meeting contributes to a positive moral atmosphere is by enabling children to participate in making decisions about the life of the classroom. Piaget lamented that in school children are "condemned to wage war against authority" and, like Kohlberg, he regarded "as of the utmost importance experiments to introduce democratic methods into schools."[9] In our work, we have found the daily class meeting to be the best vehicle for bringing democracy to the elementary school classroom.

The notion that small children ought to govern themselves is not based on soft-headed sentiments about their innate goodness but rests on the premise that children, like other people, are more likely to understand rules and take them seriously when they have a hand in their making and when they regard them as fair. This belief received its acid test last year when a Project Change teacher, Debbie Wilcox, took over a class of twenty-six third-grade children that had been abandoned by its regular teacher as being "impossible to deal with." The children wore their notorious reputation like a badge, greeting teacher Wilcox on her first day with the announcement, "This is the bad class of the school."

The teacher called a class meeting and immediately placed the responsibility for discipline on the children. "What rules are necessary in this room? Why do we need them? Should everyone have to obey rules?" A flurry of opinions followed these questions. The meeting ended with consensus on a rule suggested by a child: "Care for each other." That was to be the class ethic, the yardstick against which behavior would be measured in future discussions.

Steadily, teacher Wilcox reports, children improved in their conduct. "They tried to get their schoolwork in on time. A 'give it to me, it's mine' attitude gave way to more open sharing. More and more children participated in class meetings, and they learned to listen quietly when someone else was speaking. Serious behavior problems became almost non-existent, and children began expressing a liking for school."

The class meetings, teacher Wilcox concluded, have provided each child "with a place, a group of people who believe that he is worthwhile enough to listen to. In the class meeting, a child has the chance to form opinions and express those opinions without fear of being rejected. Children in turn learn to listen to the ideas of others and to observe first-hand that not everyone thinks the way they do and to grow to accept people for what they are. I believe that children come to develop this respect for others only when they begin to respect themselves."[10] This teacher's intuition expresses an important, theoretical insight: that moral education builds on affective education; that to do right by others, you have to first feel good about yourself.

A fifth-grade teacher in North Dakota (DeLapp, 1975) uses class meetings to seek honest feedback from children about their experiences in the classroom. At the end of an independent activity period, for example, he puts these questions to the group: How did you spend your time? What did you do best? What didn't you enjoy doing? Why? Was the classroom a good place to learn? This last question, he says, helps children to see that the quality of the classroom environment—noise level, sharing space and materials, helping each other, respecting privacy—is something for which they are responsible. At the end of each day, the teacher asks the class not only to reflect on what they have done, but also to propose ways of improving the classroom and to help plan what they wish to do the next day.

These group feedback strategies are combined with a weekly planning and evaluation sheet completed by each child and with ongoing individual conferences with children. The latter, the teacher says, add an invaluable opportunity for the kind of personal communication that yields insight into an individual child's thoughts and feelings, and they provide a chance to make the child feel a special measure of respect for himself or herself as a person. During a conference, the teacher encourages the child "to take a minute to observe the classroom," after which they share their observations of what activities are going on, how well people are getting along, and so on. This helps to deepen each child's sense of responsibility for creating a positive classroom environment.

Moral Education in Early Childhood

The major objective of early childhood moral education is really the same as the goal for elementary school: to lead children out of their egocentrism toward relations of cooperation and mutual respect. Many of the same methods that work in the elementary grades can be adapted to younger children. Kindergarten teacher Ruth Giese, for example, has used the class meeting with her youngsters. She began with the wise practice of asking the children (rather than telling them) what rules are needed to govern the meeting itself. "Raise your hand if you want to talk," "Listen to others when it is their turn," and "Sit out on a chair if you do not cooperate" were the rules proposed by the children. The teacher found that when some children forgot to raise their hands to talk, others reminded them of the rule.

As meetings progressed, teacher Giese recorded children's behavior outside the meeting as well as during discussions. She observed more indications of empathy and active concern during children's day-to-day interactions. On a morning when one boy was visibly unhappy, for example, several children approached him, asked what was the matter, and encouraged him to talk or join in an activity. Children also began to work out solutions on their own to problems that had formerly required teacher intervention. A boy who had been a constant tattler was overheard arbitrating a dispute between two classmates over who was to play with the beanbags. Another child settled an argument about use of the merry-go-round with the proposal, "Let's all run together and jump on when I yell the signal." In the class meetings as well, children showed an increasing capacity for practical problem solving, moving away from a "he did it, punish him" attitude to an interest in working straight away on a solution to the problem that would benefit all.

Another kindergarten teacher, Marcia Helbig, held her first class meeting when aggression became a problem in her room. She brought in a picture (which often helps with young children) of two hands and asked, "What can we do when someone brings their hurting hands to school instead of their helping hands?" "The response was immediate," the teacher says. "Children who seldom contribute in class eagerly raised their hands." The group settled on one child's suggestion to have a Thinking Chair where the offender sits and *thinks* about what has happened. Whenever the child is ready to rejoin the group he or she is welcomed. Teacher Helbig reports that much to everyone's delight the Thinking Chair is working. Her experience, like Debbie Wilcox's, bears testimony to the truth of Piaget's statement that the only "true discipline" is that which "children themselves have willed and consented to."[11]

The preceding success stories may make it sound as if using the class meeting to foster morality in the classroom is a piece of cake. In fact, running an effective class meeting calls for an impressive repertoire of teacher skills: posing a question that children will want to discuss, asking stimulating follow-up questions, paraphrasing individual contributions, tying together related comments, putting challenging issues to the group, probing for reasoning, keeping the meeting flexible but on track, getting the children to feel responsible for re-establishing order if the rules of the meeting are violated, helping children plan how to follow through on a proposed solution to a problem, and bringing the meeting to a close. In our master's program at Project Change, we try to model these skills by running most of our course sessions as class meetings and by giving teachers a chance to lead meetings with their peers and get feedback from them.

Teaching the Skills of Moral Competence

Just as teachers need some hard interpersonal and leadership skills to run a good moral ship, so also do children need specific interpersonal skills to make their way in their moral world. There is evidence aplenty that mature moral behavior does not flow from reasoning alone. To be morally competent, argues British philosopher-educator John Wilson, involves competence on a number of distinct dimensions: understanding other people, accurate empathy in a particular situation, knowing what to say or how to act to accomplish a moral aim, having a grasp of moral principles, and being able to bring all of the foregoing to bear on making and carrying out a moral decision.

Children, like adults, are often lacking in several of these competencies. Some of them, at least, can be developed through direct teaching. A teacher can show children how to solve a social problem. In one study (Doland and Adelberg, 1967), an adult used puppets to act out alternative solutions to conflicts—fighting over and breaking a toy wagon, for example, as opposed to taking turns to the satisfaction of both parties. Preschoolers who watched these little dramas and discussed the various alternatives became less aggressive and more cooperative in their own play.

Teachers can also directly suggest ways of dealing with a problem situation. To a child who is pushing another for a seat, the teacher can say, "You can *ask* Lisa to move over." To a child who wants another's toy instead of the one he has, she can say: "You can ask Ben to *trade* with you." To a child who is trying to defend his claim to something: "Tell Peter, 'I'm playing with this now, you can have a turn later.'" To a child who is the victim of aggression: "You tell John in a loud voice, 'I don't like that! The rule is no hitting!'" (Shelton, 1975).

A second-grade teacher in our program (Manring, 1974) sought to develop children's communication skills as a way of coping with an outbreak of fighting and kicking in her classroom. She brought in a bag of wood scraps from the local toy factory and asked the children to use them to construct a model of the room. When children said things like, "You put the chalkboard in a stupid place, Martha," the teacher pointed out that words like "stupid" make people angry and asked children to use the words "I suggest . . ." when they wished to propose a modification of someone's contribution to the model. The value of this and comparable strategies is that they help children learn the interpersonal skills they need to *enter into* positive social interactions and relationships. Those interactions and relationships in turn provide the opportunities for taking the role or viewpoint of others, which Kohlberg considers crucial to growth through the moral stages. In this sense, the judicious use of modeling or didactic instruction becomes an important complement to a Piagetian or Kohlbergian approach.

A New Approach to Evaluation

How can you tell if an elementary or early childhood program for moral education is doing any good? Evaluation at this level, like the assessment of secondary school programs, has been plagued by the fact that a change in stage of moral reasoning on Kohlberg's scale is likely to be quite small and very slow to appear. One way around this problem is offered by a new observational rating scale (Lengel, 1974) designed to yield a measure of a classroom's adequacy as a total moral environment. The scale consists of fifty objectives corresponding to twelve dimensions of developmental moral education derived from the writings of Kohlberg and Piaget: (1) general classroom interaction, (2) opportunities for role-taking, (3) presentation of moral problems, (4) use of real-life problems in class, (5) peer discussion, (6) teacher's knowledge of and accommodation to children's developmental level, (7) teacher's focus on reasoning, (8) presentation of alternative solutions, (9) absence of a "right answer" approach, (10) presence of stage mixture among the children, (11) opportunities for children to structure their own solutions to social problems, and (12) challenges to children's reasoning. For purposes of classroom observation, these twelve dimensions are grouped into four major areas: General Classroom Procedures, Children's Work Activities, The Nature of Class Discussions, and Teacher's Actions. For sample items for each of these areas, see Table 1 on page 183. Lengel plans validation research to determine whether classrooms high on his scale eventually stimulate greater moral stage advance, as Kohlberg's theory would predict, than do classrooms low on his scale.

Lengel's instrument helps meet the need for an assessment of the moral quality of a classroom, but there is still a need for a way to chart the social-moral growth of individual children. Kohlberg's measure of moral reasoning is not only impractical for teachers to use, but also fails to assess many aspects of what Kohlberg's theory would recognize as being part of children's moral development—for example, the willingness to take responsibility for their own behavior, the ability to act fairly, the habit of responding to others' needs, the capacity to participate actively in collaborative work, discussion, and play. As one way of documenting the moral progress of children on these dimensions, I have suggested that teachers use the set of questions in Table 2 (page 184) to construct a profile of each child at the beginning, middle, and end of the year.

Forty years ago Piaget recognized that the "practical experiments" of teachers would tell psychologists to what extent their theories held true in the classroom. I am presently engaged in an effort to interview good teachers and watch them at work to find out more about how they conceptualize and carry out moral education, how they see the effects of what they do—their use of authority, their handling of rules and discipline, their discussion of moral issues, the example they set—on the moral growth of children. In six years of working with teachers, I have developed great respect for what they can teach us about fostering moral development in the classroom. If it is true, as Kurt Lewin said, that there is nothing so practical as a good theory, it is surely equally true that there is nothing so enriching of a theory as good practice.

Table 1
Classroom Process Objectives for Moral Development
(Sample Items from Lengel, 1974)

	no evidence	slight evidence	moderate evidence	extensive evidence	cannot make judgment
Part I: General Procedures					
1. Children interact with each other in many different situations	1	2	3	4	x
2. Rules and discipline are discussed freely by children and teacher	1	2	3	4	x
3. Problems of the school and community are presented for class discussion	1	2	3	4	x
Part II: Children's Work Activities					
1. Children are engaged in a cooperative venture with a group	1	2	3	4	x
2. Children talk among themselves during class time	1	2	3	4	x
3. Children use their own methods to solve problems in class	1	2	3	4	x
Part III: Nature of Class Discussions					
1. Children share ideas with others	1	2	3	4	x
2. The reasons behind answers and positions are stressed in discussions	1	2	3	4	x
3. Conflict between alternative ideas is pointed out	1	2	3	4	x
Part IV: Teacher's Actions					
1. Teacher keeps notes and histories of each child's progress and development	1	2	3	4	x
2. Teacher listens with respect to each child's thinking and reasoning	1	2	3	4	x
3. Teacher helps children look at things from different viewpoints	1	2	3	4	x

Table 2
Dimensions for Documenting a Child's Moral Development

A. What is the child's understanding of rules?
   1. Can the child name classroom rules?
   2. How does the child explain the reason for various rules?
   3. What does the child think will happen if someone breaks a rule?
   4. Can the child say why an existing rule is fair or unfair?
   5. Can the child suggest a rule appropriate to a particular situation?

B. Does the child follow rules?
   1. What rules does the child follow? How consistently?
   2. What rules does he/she not follow? How consistently?
   3. When the child breaks a rule, is he/she aware of it? What does the child say when asked to describe what he/she is doing?
   4. Can the child make a plan for improving his/her behavior and follow through on it?

C. Does the child take another's point of view?
   1. In a conflict situation, can the child describe what the other child thinks, feels, and wants?
   2. Can the child describe the effects of his/her behavior, both positive and negative, on other people?
   3. Does the child demonstrate concern when others are hurt, upset, etc.?

D. Does the child understand how to be fair?
   1. Can the child settle a conflict in a way that takes into account the needs of another as well as his or her own needs?
   2. Does the child take turns?
   3. Does the child share?
   4. Does the child do his or her "fair share" in a group task (like clean-up)?
   5. Can the child explain why a particular action or solution to a problem is fair or unfair?

E. Does the child participate in positive social interactions?
   1. In group discussions?
   2. In individual conversations?
   3. In collaborative play?
   4. In work on a group task?
   5. In helping others?

Notes

1. P. Hophan, "A Project in Supporting Children's Thinking and Moral Development."
2. Ibid.
3. Jean Piaget, *The Moral Judgment of the Child*, p. 405.
4. Ibid., pp. 404–405.
5. Hophan, op. cit., p. 1.
6. Ibid., p. 4.
7. Ibid., p. 9.
8. J. Kur, "Using Small-Group Projects to Foster Cooperation in the Classroom."
9. Piaget, op. cit., pp. 363–364.

10. William Glasser, *Schools without Failure.*
11. Piaget, op. cit., p. 369.

Bibliography

DeLapp, S. "Four Strategies to Encourage Evaluative Input from Children." *Insights into Open Education* 8 (1975):4–7.

Doland, Dilman J., and Adelberg, Kathryn. "The Learning of Sharing Behavior." *Child Development* 38 (1967):695–700.

First Things: Values. Sound filmstrips for the primary years. Pleasantville, N.Y.: Guidance Associates, 1972.

Galbraith, Ronald E., and Jones, Thomas M. *Moral Reasoning: A Teaching Handbook for Adapting Kohlberg to the Classroom*. Anoka, Minn.: Greenhaven Press, 1976.

Glasser, William. *Schools without Failure*. New York: Harper & Row, 1969.

Hophan, P. "A Project in Supporting Children's Thinking and Moral Development." Cortland, N.Y.: Project Change, SUNY at Cortland, 1975.

Johnson, David W., and Johnson, Roger T. *Learning Together and Alone: Cooperation, Competition, and Individualization*. Englewood Cliffs, N.J.: Prentice-Hall, 1975.

Kohlberg, Lawrence. "Moral Stages and Moralization: The Cognitive-Developmental Approach." In *Moral Development and Behavior: Theory, Research, and Social Issues*, edited by T. Lickona. New York: Holt, Rinehart & Winston, 1976.

Kur, J. "Using Small-Group Projects to Foster Cooperation in the Classroom." *Project Change Mini-Book on Fostering Moral Development in the Classroom*. Cortland, N.Y.: Project Change, SUNY at Cortland, Winter 1976.

Lengel, J. G. "Explanations of Developmental Change Applied to Education: Atmospheres for Moral Development." Educational Resources Information Center (ERIC), ED 104 738, 1974.

Lickona, Thomas. "The Challenge of Watergate to American Schools: Fostering the Moral Development of Children." Cortland, N.Y.: Project Change, SUNY at Cortland, 1976.

Lickona, Thomas. "Teacher Approaches to Moral Education: An Interview and Observation Study." State University of New York at Cortland, 1976.

Lickona, Thomas. "Project Change: A Person-Centered Approach to Competency-based Teacher Education." *Journal of Teacher Education* 27 (1976):122–28.

Manring, M. "Letter from a Teacher: How to Foster Cooperation in the Classroom." *Project Change Mini-Book-A-Month* 2 (1974):1–3.

Piaget, Jean. *The Moral Judgment of the Child*. 1932. New York: Free Press, 1965.

Shelton, W. "Social Development in Young Children." Educational Resources Information Center (ERIC), ED 110 166, 1975.

School Democracy: Promise and Paradox

Peter Scharf, Assistant Professor of Social Ecology,
University of California at Irvine.

Introduction

This chapter seeks to offer a critical overview of recent efforts by Kohlberg, Scharf, Mosher, and others to create a participatory democratic framework within the high school, designed to stimulate increased moral maturity among participants. In addition, this chapter will pose a number of issues critical to judging the efficacy and wisdom of this type of educational venture. Specifically, I will critically examine the psychological assumptions underlying efforts to change moral thinking by involving students in democratic participation in school decision-making as well as explore some of the inherent dilemmas facing democratic school projects.

Varieties of Democratic Experience in the School

Democratic participation in schooling is a rather recent phenomenon. Early American educators clearly did not intend nor believe that students should have a voice in their own education. The colonial school was authoritarian, teacher-directed, and often punitive. The meaning of "democratic education," until the twentieth century, implied that all children should be admitted to the "common school," not that education should be structured democratically.

John Dewey was, of course, a pioneer in the movement to democratize the school. In his view, schooling in a democratic society requires democratic goals as well as strategies. Schools should do more than preach democratic rhetoric. The structure of the school must reflect its stated democratic aims. He implies that if the goal of education is to create a democratic citizen and society, this goal must be reflected in the "democratic organization" of the school itself. A principal who justifies using authoritarian means for a "democratic" end would find this purpose soon undermined. Consistent with his views of education as "reflective experience," Dewey saw the school providing a natural "laboratory for democratic learning." He assumed, of course, a curriculum "which added upon and enlightened natural democratic experiences."

In his *Schools of Tomorrow*, Dewey sought to exemplify his beliefs by analyzing the most promising experiments of his day, including the revolutionary Gary, Indiana public schools (Gary Plan). Here, the students not only helped to create school rules, but also helped to maintain the school's physical plant:

> Gary schools do not teach civics out of a textbook. Pupils learn civics by helping to take care of their own school building, by making rules for their own conduct in the halls and on the playgrounds, by going into the public library, and by listening to the stories of what Gary is doing as told by the people who are doing it. They learn by a mock campaign, with parties, primaries, booths and ballots for the election of their own student council. Pupils who have made the furniture and the cement walks with their own hands, and who know how much it cost, are slow to destroy walks or furniture, nor are they going to be very easily fooled as to the value they get in service and improvements when they themselves become taxpayers. . . .
>
> . . . the value of this practical civics is doubly great because of the large number of children with foreign parents, who know nothing about the government or organization of the city in which they are living, and who, because they do not understand what they see about them, cannot know its possibilities and limitations. The parents learn nothing of the laws until they break them, of public health until they endanger it, nor of social resources until they want something . . . the [Gary] schools not only teach the theory of good citizenship and social conditions, *they give* the children actual facts and conditions, so that they can see what is wrong and how it can be bettered.[1]

Deweyite educators offered the (albeit) minority educational faith that our society's democratic ideals should be incorporated into the structure of both classroom and school. The precise interpretation of Dewey's ideals, however, has to this day remained elusive. Three common interpretations are frequently offered to describe the modern embodiment of Deweyite educational progressivism.

A degenerate interpretation has been embodied in the "free school" movement. This movement has interpreted Dewey's democratic ideals in terms of granting the child maximum independence and choice. In one free school I visited in California, students were "free" to make grade contracts with whomever (parent, teacher, friend) they wished, attended classes "whenever they felt motivated," and could, independently, determine their own grades. One student received four credits of "gym" for riding his bike a half mile to school. Another received math credit for laying tile on his bathroom floor.

For Dewey, such a laissez-faire educational approach would be meaningless, for it ignores the social element in education, leaves kids to be "more ignorant than necessary," and ultimately is antidemocratic in its lack of equal or even consistent standards. Equal standards, Dewey believed, are crucial to a democratic social order. As well, the romanticism of the free school lacks the reflective element critical to a Deweyite notion of democratic education. In Dewey's view, the student must *reflect* on democratic experience and not simply be "free" to explore at will.

The evolution of the community-based school concept suggests a second interpretation of Deweyite democratic education. Recently the Parkways School of Boston and the Community School in New York interpreted democratic education as "the return of the school to the community." Their ideology assumes that experiential education must move outwards into community life. Students will lobby for ecology, work for political parties, protest against war, conduct demographic surveys, educate voters, or engage in cross-age tutoring.

Fred Newman in *Education for Citizenship Action* suggests a very practical model for this activist interpretation of Deweyite education. He offers that the meaning of democratic education would be accurately reflected through "environmental competence." Society at large, with its industries, its laboratories, is to become the school's curriculum—and its problems, the school's social dilemmas. Newman carefully differentiates his model from "field-study" or practicum-educational models which, he argues, frequently "simply turn the student loose in the community." Recent efforts to turn the community into a school (e.g., the Parkway project or the School Without Walls program) follow, at least in part, this interpretation of Deweyite education.

A third, and least explored, interpretation of Deweyite democratic education has emphasized self-government of the school, involving an ongoing dialogue between teachers, students, and administrators. Most efforts at school democracy are token at best. Student councils and advisory boards usually deal with little more than the "dress code" for the next dance. School council elections usually rival only the homecoming-queen balloting in political insignificance.

Historically, there have been some exceptions to this rather bleak history of the school democracy movement. A. S. Neill's *Summerhill* offers a meaningful example of how the core principles of democratic life may be worked into the curriculum of even a primary school. While Neill used many "romantic" as well as progressive notions in the construction of his school, his description of self-government at Summerhill remains one of the best, most concrete explorations of the dilemmas of democratic education in the elementary school.

> Summerhill is a self-governing school, democratic in form. Everything connected with social or group life, including punishment for social offense, is settled by vote at the Saturday night General School Meeting.
>
> Each member of the teaching staff and each child, regardless of his age, has one vote. My vote carries the same weight as that of a seven year old. . . .
>
> Once, I spoke strongly about breaking the bedtime rules, with the consequent noise and the sleepy heads that lumbered around the next morning. I proposed that culprits should be fined all their pocket money for each offense. A boy of fourteen proposed that there should be a penny reward per hour for everyone staying up after his or her bedtime. I got a few votes, but he got a big majority.

> Our democracy makes laws—good ones, too. For example, it is forbidden to bathe in the sea without the supervision of life-guards, who are always staff members. It is forbidden to climb on the roofs. Bedtimes must be kept or there is an automatic fine. Whether classes should be called off on Thursday or on the Friday preceding a holiday is a matter for a show of hands at a General School Meeting. . . .[2]

While consistent with Deweyite theory, such efforts to genuinely involve adolescents in the political processes of the school have been rare and without much notable success. While a few pioneers such as Neill have maintained a democratic school climate through the sheer force of personal charisma, the failures associated with school democracy movements clearly outweigh successes.

One reason for this failure has been the inability of democratic educators to formulate psychology to document the educational impact of democratic experience. I hope here to suggest that developmental psychology, exemplified by Lawrence Kohlberg's developmental theory, suggests a psychological perspective uniquely adapted to experiments in democratic education. This psychological perspective, we suggest, offers, perhaps uniquely, a social psychology appropriate to democratic school reform.

According to Kohlberg, rate and extent of development are closely linked to the institutions with which one comes into contact. Broadly speaking, social institutions encouraging social role-taking and productive moral dialogue are associated with rapid and complete moral development. In terms of reasoning about specific legal issues, experiences with what Kohlberg calls the secondary institutions of society (e.g., law, economy, education) are of special importance.

It has long been established that participation in democratically organized institutions is associated with rapid *social* development. Both Charles Cooley and George Mead have suggested that democratic groups offer possibilities for interdependence and mutual sharing not found in authoritarian groups. Kurt Lewin suggests likewise that ideological change occurs more rapidly in democratic groups allowing for a shared sense of control and for opportunities for dissent.

Similarly, Kohlberg offers that individuals placed in "an institution-maintaining perspective" tend to develop more rapidly than do individuals in an obedience perspective. For example, he observes that gang leaders show higher stage thinking than do gang followers. Similarly, in traditional schools, student leaders show higher stage thinking than do non-leaders. As well, preliminary evidence from kibbutz youth indicates that the collective-democratic structure of the kibbutz youth-group stimulates adolescents towards principled thought more rapidly than do the best American suburban education environments.

An intervention conducted by the author created an intentional democratic system of governance in a women's prison in Connecticut. Inmates helped create and maintain the rules of a single cottage through regular community meetings. For example, fights, thefts, and even assaults and attempted escapes were routinely tried—debated within the community meeting format. An instrument designed by myself to measure the program's "moral atmosphere" (or the group's perceived sense of justice) indicated that most (72%) of the women in the program accepted the rules of the program as just and legitimate. The positive perception of the program contrasted sharply with inmate perceptions of both traditional custody programs and a behavior modification program in California. The moral maturity of inmates involved in the democratic program increased by more than one third of a moral stage during a period of nine months in the program.

Based on the prison program experience, the Center for Moral Education at Harvard and Boston University in 1974 initiated two different democratic mini-school projects in the Boston area committed to democratic decision-making by its staff and students. As in the prison project, the schools hold a weekly or twice-weekly community meeting at which major issues are posed, debated, and, hopefully, resolved. Each mini-school has oriented its curriculum to include intensive offerings on political problems and dilemmas. Finally, staff and students make a conscious effort to see and openly discuss conflicts occurring within the school as moral conflicts as opposed to simply practical issues. Thus a "pot smoking" offense is dealt with as a conflict between community and individual rights, rather than as an issue of school "law and order."

To illustrate this process of democratic decision-making, let me offer an example from a recent meeting at the Brookline School-Within-a-School project. The students in the school had come to feel that staff members were "plotting" town meeting strategies at their weekly staff meetings and "were better prepared than were students." The students demanded to have representatives present at staff meetings. The dialogue follows:

Ellie: I really know that you (teachers) are not doing anything bad in there to us, but I feel that we should be able to come to your meetings.

Tom: That's right. "SWS" is supposed to be a family. When you are in your house, you can go wherever you please. Why not here?

Betsy: I agree with Tom; but in a family, parents have a right to meet together sometimes. Like, let's say they are talking about paying the bills or a vacation; can't they meet by themselves before they present it to the kids?

Peter: (consultant) I see two ideas here. One, that "SWS" is a family. Other people are saying that students and teachers need different things. Do you really think the teachers and students are like a family, or do they really have different interests?

Barb: (teacher) I feel there isn't really an issue. In 90 percent of our meetings we just talk about "dippity-do." It isn't worth coming to, *especially* at eight in the morning. You can come instead of me.

Sue: We can get up. As to Peter's question, I think they have their needs; we have ours. It's not that we don't trust them, though; we like you.

Bill: (teacher) How about if the students find a time in the day to plot about (teacher) community meetings. Then you all will be prepared to "zap" us.

Leslie: But you have "A-block" reserved. When could all the students meet?

Betsy: I still think we don't have a right to come. They should be able to meet without us. They are *teachers!*

Bill: I don't know about all of this. We have a bunch of things that don't concern you. Don't private groups have a right to meet privately?

The group eventually voted, by a small margin, to allow teachers to meet privately.

Assumptions Underlying the Developmental Approach to Democratic Schooling

Democratic interchange, as illustrated above, is justified by Kohlberg's contention that open moral dialogue leads to moral change. In the town meetings, special conflicts are dealt with explicitly as moral conflicts. The issue of staff privacy is a good moral issue for Stage 3 and Stage 4 students. The Stage 3 position that Tom offers ("SWS" is a family and kids/students "can go all over" the house/school) conflicts with Betsy's Stage 4 notion that parents/teachers have a special privilege to meet privately. This type of debate can be expected to produce moral change if conducted seriously and continually.

Similarly, Kohlberg, Scharf, and others have suggested that groups which allow for open dissent, but are cohesive and fair, tend to be accepted and identified with by participants. The students in the group are asked both to identify with the group and to take positive ownership of its critical decisions. Such decisions are not imposed by *them* (i.e., the teachers), but are rather made by the group (the *we* in Mead's social psychological theory). In the example above, Tom's remark that "SWS" is a family illustrates the type of positive group identification likely to produce moral change.

Finally, democratic decision-making forces students to take the perspective of the group as an abstract entity. Mead and Cooley, among others, suggested that such collective role-taking (i.e., internalizing the perspective of the group) is critical to the development of mature social thought. This development, Mead, Cooley, and Kohlberg assume, occurs most effectively in a democratic context wherein a broad spectrum of the group is asked to assume the moral perspective of the group's authority. In the cluster school or "SWS" "town meeting," the students, as well as the faculty members, are forced to consider the good of the school as a collectivity as they debate the specific issue at hand.

The Dilemmas of School Democracy

To date, there has been little discussion as to the problems facing democratic school experiments. The advocates of democratization have been more concerned with the desirability of democratic participation in the school than with confronting the impediments to such efforts. This neglect seems inappropriate considering the paucity of success in this area.

The increase in "comprehensive" schools over the past thirty years has created schools of such great size that meaningful democracy is improbable. Schools of two thousand students or more are simply too large to have effective student participation. Further, the division of the academic day into forty-minute class periods prohibits the development of the sense of community likely to make democracy a plausible venture. Similarly, the hierarchical model of management found in comprehensive schools makes student participation likely to appear as a threat to the principal's political control of the school.

The competitive achievement values predominating in American education ultimately conflict with the goal of school democracy. Today, the school is perceived more as a means to achieve technical knowledge and status than as a means to learn democratic citizenship. Many students, in the present educational climate, see schooling as a means toward achieving later status rather than as an end in itself. This is, of course, related to the myth that American public schooling creates upward mobility as well as to the American teacher's attachment to the rituals of grading.

Also, sharing power is difficult to "sell" to teachers. As Willard Waller noted in his *Sociology of Teaching*, one of the "objective" tasks of the teacher is the maintenance of "control" of the classroom. Teachers are praised or demeaned as much for their ability to "command respect" or "have control" as for any other professional quality. The "turning-over" of discipline to the group is a difficult task for many teachers. The danger of using only less authoritarian teachers in democratic programs is that doing so often isolates the democratic program from the larger school community.

Similarly, the sharing of power with students often conflicts with the technical demands of planning and curriculum development. In one democratic school, for example, students were invited to participate in curriculum development. It soon became apparent, however, that they lacked the background to formulate a coherent sequence of learning required in building the course program. Also, the teachers were not prepared to be told by students what they should teach. Therefore, while the rhetoric in most democratic alternatives is to involve students in such areas as faculty hiring and firing, this is rarely achieved; faculty members are simply unwilling to trust students with this type of power. The result of such decisions to limit democracy and retain faculty prerogatives means that the democracy of the town meeting only involves those issues which are considered *not* truly central to the control of the schools by faculty and administrators. Major decisions are determined through traditional administrative channels.

Perhaps the most severe constraint facing school democracy projects involves the students themselves. Few students possess the moral and political maturity to actively grapple with the complex issues implied in running a school. Most students in high school tend to be a mix between Stage 2 and 3 in terms of Kohlberg's moral maturity scale. James Rest's research (1970) indicates that individuals can rarely understand more than one stage above their own major stage of maturity. This implies that most adolescents possess but little comprehension of law conceived as an abstract entity; similarly, most adolescents have little understanding of the need for the separation of powers or for other constitutional concepts. Stage 5 thinking is rare before the early twenties and is ultimately achieved by only a relatively small percentage of the adult population (10–20 percent). This implies that most students understand their school democracy quite differently than do their teachers. Student responses to school "atmosphere" interviews administered in several democratic schools illustrate the gap between student thought and the ideals of democratic society.

Stage 2 students, for example, rarely concern themselves with the workings of democratic rules. They usually feel that the democratic rules are better than the "regular" school rules but usually feel this because the democratic rules are "easier" or less rigidly enforced. One student offered this response:

> It's better in here, because you don't have people watching you all the time. The students and staff made them and they made ones that were sensible and don't restrict people too much.

Stage 3 students typically understand the rules contract of the school as the fulfillment of common expectations. Rules are enforced to preserve the expectations of the group. Complained one student in a California democratic school,

> Students should have been more clearly told that if they participated in certain undesirable behavior then they would be hurting the group as a whole and they wouldn't want to do that.

Stage four students understand that the rules exist as moral entities in themselves. They see the rules as genuinely necessary for cohesion and the common social good. This type of formal conception of the school community was rather rare in the schools we have observed. One very mature high school senior, the daughter of a constitutional lawyer, commented,

> In here it's important to enforce the rules so that everyone sees that they are respected. It's important to get everyone to come to town meeting so that the rules are seen as having real power. If people don't come, the rules won't mean anything and it's better not to have them.

The task of operating a Stage 4 or 5 democracy with few Stage 4 students (and often few Stage 5 teachers) creates several difficult dilemmas.

The problem of the "tyranny of the majority," first posed by De Touqueville is readily apparent in the operation of each of the democratic schools observed by this author. In one school, a rather unpopular boy was thrown out of school because the students thought he had a "poor" attitude. A week later a popular youngster was merely asked to publicly apologize for committing a similar act in a similar circumstance. The teachers confronted with this dilemma were faced with a serious bind. While most of them thought the actions were unfair, they could not convince the Stage 3 student town meeting, who looked (in Stage 3 terms) at each student's "attitude" rather than at the legal commonality of the offenses. After the students voted not to expel the second student, the teachers met to consider reversing the decision. One teacher argued that as the "decision was patently unfair, it should be changed." This position was defeated by other faculty members who felt that to reverse the decision would "infringe on the kids' ownership of the process." This incident highlights the dilemma faced by teachers who share power with students and who are torn between accepting the often immature decisions of young adolescents and imposing their own presumably higher stage wisdom upon the group. Both teachers and students would see this imposition as an autocratic action. To accept the students' decision might result in a decision which would be "substantially" or even legally unfair. To reverse it implies a rejection of the authenticity of the democratic mandate of the group.

Similarly, most of the democratic school projects are marked by a rather uneven distribution of participation. In the Brookline program, roughly twenty students were marginal participators (attended most meetings, occasionally spoke, etc.). The remainder of the students cared little about the meetings, giggled often, and usually seemed bored. This pattern seems attributable to the stage distribution of the school. Usually, those students who participated most were almost a full stage higher in moral reasoning than were the non-participants. Higher stage students understood the often complex issues being discussed and possessed the verbal skills necessary to argue forth their position. The danger, of course, is that democratic participation becomes increasingly limited to a small number of students; less articulate students might then feel intimidated, left out, and resentful and eventually would either emotionally or physically withdraw from the school community. Signs of this progressive degeneration were apparent in both the Brookline "SWS" project and the "SELF" school program in Irvine, California near the end of the first year of operation. While the charisma of the school's conception and initial rules formulation seemed compelling, at least to many students, the more routine maintenance which followed involved a much smaller student elite. This problem, of course, faces not only school democracies but also local and national government in the United States and elsewhere faced with widespread citizen alienation and apathy.

Implications

This chapter has sought to suggest that a plausible interpretation of Deweyite educational theory is the involvement of students in the political processes of the school. It offers that Kohlberg's developmental theory sets forth a psychological basis from which to guide efforts in school democracy.

The chapter argues, however, that a curriculum emphasizing participatory democracy is not without its serious contradictions. Democratic participation ultimately conflicts with the bureaucratic structures obvious in most public schools. The school with rigid segmentation into administrative categories and subject areas offers serious impediments to any effort to share power with students.

As well, the idea of constitutional democracy is difficult for most Stage 2 and 3 adolescents to understand. Few adolescents are able to immediately grapple with its issues or its dilemmas. This factor implies that if genuinely given the power to make democratic decisions, adolescents will make quite different, and possibly less mature, decisions than will adults. It also implies, that over time, democratic decision-making may not have the salience to many young people that the advocates of school democracy would like to believe.

These arguments should not be used, however, to discourage innovators who would like to democratize the school for either political or educational reasons. If we expect our students to meaningfully participate in the larger democratic society, we must prepare them. Experiments in school democracy offer, in my view, a powerful experience designed to link social education in the classroom with the task of participating in democratic institutions in the larger society.

School democracy is not an easy task to accomplish. It requires a major reassessment of both the task and the structure of the educational enterprise. In spite of this, it represents one possible hope to keep democracy viable in a society which is becoming increasingly bureaucratic and removed from its citizenry.

Notes

1. John Dewey, *Schools of Tomorrow*, p. 199–203.

2. A. S. Neill, *Summerhill: A Radical Approach to Child Rearing*.

Bibliography

Bruner, Jerome. *The Process of Education*. Cambridge: Harvard University Press, 1961.

Cooley, Charles. *Social Organization*. New York: Schocken, 1926.

De Tocqueville, Alexis. *Democracy*. New York: Vintage, 1950.

Dewey, John. *Democracy and Education*. Glenco, Ill.: Free Press, 1916.

Dewey, John. *Experience and Education*. 1938. New York: Macmillan, Collier, 1963.

Dewey, John. *Schools of Tomorrow*. Boston: Heath, 1906.

Kohlberg, Lawrence. "The Child as a Moral Philosopher." *Psychology Today* 1 (1968).

Kohlberg, Lawrence, and Turiel, Elliot. "Moral Development and Moral Education." In *Psychology and the Education Process*, edited by Lesser. Scott Foresman, 1971.

Lewin, Kurt. *Resolving Social Conflicts*. New York: Harper & Row, 1948.

Mead, George H. *Mind, Self, Society*. Chicago: University of Chicago Press, 1933.

Michels, Robert. *Political Parties*. New York: Holt, Rinehart & Winston, 1916.

Mosher, Ralph L. "Danforth Proposal." Mimeographed. 1976.

Neill, Alexander S. *Summerhill: A Radical Approach to Child Rearing*. New York: Hart, 1960.

Newman, Fred M. *Education for Citizenship Education*. Boston: Allyn-Bacon, 1976.

Oliver, Donald W., and Newman, Fred M. "Education and Community." *Harvard Educational Review*, 1966.

Piaget, Jean. "Cognitive Development in Children." In *Piaget Rediscovered: A Report on Cognitive Studies in Curriculum Development*, edited by R. Ripple and V. Rockcastle. Ithaca, N.Y.: Cornell University School of Education, 1964.

Scharf, Peter. *Moral Atmosphere in the Prison*. Xerox University Microfilms 34, 332. Ann Arbor, Mich.: Xerox Corporation, 1974.

Selman, Robert. *First Things*. Pleasantville, N.Y.: Guidance Associates, 1972.

Simpson, Elizabeth L. *Democracy's Stepchildren: A Study of Need and Belief*. San Francisco: Jossey-Bass, 1971.

Stewart, John S. "Towards a Theory for Values Development Education." Ph.D. dissertation, Michigan State University, 1974.

Wasserman, Elsa. "Proposal to Create a Just School." Unpublished paper, Boston University Graduate School of Education.

Waller, Willard. *Sociology of Teaching*. New York: Wiley & Sons, 1925.

Weber, Max. *From Max Weber*. Edited by Mills and Gerth. New York: Oxford University Press, 1948.

Part IV:
An Integrated Approach to Moral Education

Three essays in this section raise an issue which is recurrent among those seriously involved in developmental moral education: What is the proper role of affect or emotion in moral education? Critics of Kohlberg's approach, both scholars and teachers, have been bothered by what they see as a perhaps simplistic emphasis on rationality in Kohlbergian moral education. Seemingly, the emphasis on rational discussion does not allow for the development of emotions. As one teacher put it, "Kohlberg thinks that the person is all mind and no body. I want my kids to feel as well as think. Thinking may tell you what to do. It doesn't get you to do it."

This issue of the relationship of mind and emotions, of course, is not unique to the modern field of moral education. Philosophy from Plato through the Existentialists has witnessed an ongoing debate on the relationship of reason to emotions. Plato, for example, posited a tripartite division of personality into reason, will, appetite. In the "just" person, the three were in balance, each playing its proper part. His "Philosopher Kings" were educated specifically with the goal of ensuring the domination of the reason over emotion. Piaget and Kohlberg have, in part, adopted this Platonic position on the relationship of reason to emotion. According to Kohlberg, affect is always structured by cognition. Specific emotions require particular cognitive capacities. For example, the feeling of empathy for another requires the cognitive ability to reverse logical perspectives.

Needless to say, this position has *not* been universally accepted by philosophers. The Roman "Cynics" criticized Socrates for his concern with reason over "natural emotions." In Christian philosophy we see an ongoing debate about whether reason or faith assure the believer of God's love. Romantic educators from Rousseau to the modern free school advocates have tended to believe that educators have emphasized rationality over feeling. They believe that feelings are largely independent of rationality and need to be encouraged in their own right.

The essays to follow by Mary Callan, Elizabeth Simpson, Robert Samples, and Stephen Rowntree, S.J., attempt to define a method for integrating the education of moral reasoning into the education of the whole person. In my view the marriage of cognitive-developmental and humanistic education is a potentially fruitful one. Developmental moral education can benefit from a movement which attempts to explore feelings, intuitions, and affective conflict as humanistic affective education can gain from an immersion into the philosophically tight structuralism of developmental theory. The articles in this section by Callan, Samples, and Simpson are efforts to integrate concerns of affective education into the developmental paradigm, rather than attempts to deny the impact of developmental theory. In Samples' terms, "they are efforts at synergy, not contradiction" and should be read in this spirit.

Stephen Rowntree, S.J., further attempts to place Kohlberg's theory of moral judgment into the tradition of Catholic education. In attempting to reconcile the education of faith with that of ethical reasoning, Rowntree seeks an integration analogous to, yet distinct from, the integration sought by Callan, Samples, and Simpson.

Feeling, Reasoning, and Acting: An Integrated Approach to Moral Education

Mary Frances Callan, Doctoral Student,
University of California at Santa Barbara.

"We can know more than we can tell."[1]

The assumption that rational-cognitive information is the only good information on which to base a decision is an inaccurate perception of human behavior.

> There are other kinds of relevant information that affect our thoughts and behavior—intuition, unconscious processes, feelings, emotions, extrasensory perceptions, as well as spiritual and mystical experience. All of these elements when fused together make possible decisions and actions which open up the possibility of acting as full human beings.[2]

A basic premise of this chapter is that classroom application of Kohlberg's theory, with its emphasis on rational-cognitive processes, fragments students' learning. While the methodology of moral development can provide a sound base for the development of reasoning about ethical problems, it fails to give educators tools to use for developing—or even dealing with—the other human processes which influence the making and carrying out of a decision. The purposes of this chapter are to discuss the need for an integrated approach to moral education and to suggest how this can be accomplished in the classroom.

The Purpose of Schooling

Traditionally, schooling in America has had two major functions. The first has been to transmit and instill the conventional wisdom of society; the second has been to help individuals develop critical and reflective powers to assess the society (Tesconi, 1975). This second function is in keeping with the democratic philosophy upon which our society is founded. Its goal is to produce citizens who can sift through the "meaner" elements of conventional wisdom and thus contribute to the growth of a democratic society.

It has been argued that too little practical emphasis has been placed on helping students develop skills to critically analyze society (Cremin, 1965, and Tesconi, 1975). Recent disclosures like Watergate, illegal corporate payoffs and CIA activities, and misuse of monies by elected officials point to a need for greater emphasis on this function. One response to these events has been a demand for teaching morality in the classroom. The 1976 Annual Gallup Poll on American Education indicated that 79 percent of those surveyed favored "instruction in the schools that would deal with morals and moral behavior."[3]

Kohlberg's theory of cognitive moral development is one approach which can be employed to meet the demand for teaching morality and concurrently aid in helping students develop assessment skills. Its rejection of value relativism and the imposition of outside norms and corresponding emphasis on the development of "the organizational structures by which one analyzes, interprets and makes decisions about social problems"[4] have an appeal to both parents and educators (Woodward and Lord, 1976). Kohlberg's theory presents an approach to ethical problem solving that (1) does not threaten indoctrination; (2) is based on principles common to this democracy; (3) is built on the concept that some decisions are better than others; (4) implies that one who reasons justly will act justly; and (5) is, above all, rational.

A Broader View of Moral Development

In spite of its broad appeal, I, as an educator, am concerned with Kohlberg's emphasis on the development of cognitive processes for achieving moral judgment maturity. I view his approach for facilitating moral maturity as limited—limited in the sense that it focuses on reasoning to the exclusion of feelings and behavior. As Elizabeth Simpson states:

> Morality is fundamentally irrational—that is, differences in even such obviously cognitive phenomena as moral reasoning and judgment derive from essential personological structures. Moral reasoning and behavior are a function of the *person*, and not simply of his capacity to think logically or to learn concepts and norms.[5]

To illustrate this point, stop and ask yourself, "How often have I known what is 'right' and yet chosen to not act on that knowledge simply because I didn't feel like it or felt no support for that action?" And, in reflecting on those instances you might also ask, "What feelings did I experience when recalling those situations?"

In developing curriculum for moral education we face the problem of how to address the "irrational" as well as the rational. This problem is not adequately solved by the traditional moral discussion format which concentrates solely on the reasoning behind one's ethical decisions. (Page 70 of this volume presents the steps of the moral discussion format advocated by Kohlberg and his colleagues.)

A second problem is inherent in this moral discussion format. Focusing on what one should or would do in a moral dilemma and the reasons for that decision is an inadequate method of problem solving. Although moral discussions enable one to name the problem and to begin to analyze solutions, they are inadequate to the extent they do not incorporate skills to analyze systemic roots of the dilemmas and to generate solutions which focus on those roots. For instance, in a dilemma involving the issue of personal conscience and draft resistance to the Vietnam War, it seems as important to understand how rules and practices of the draft system contributed to the resistance as it is to understand an individual's particular situation.

Too often the solutions reached through moral discussions focus on how individuals should change so they act "morally." The implicit assumption is that the problem is in the individual. It is the individual who is to blame for not being just. A problem should also be viewed as being within the system. I am referring here to the rules and norms that govern the roles in a situation. To be able to analyze the system within which the choices are made, to understand the profound influence that system has on decision making, and to generate solutions to alter the system rather than the individual seems to me to be integral to critical assessment and ethical problem solving. Blaming and changing the system, and not just the individuals involved, is also a more humane approach to problem solving (Alschuler, Atkins, Santiago-Wolpow, 1975). For example, it seems simplistic to think that the choices made by Richard Nixon were *the* cause of Watergate. Those choices were open to Nixon in his role as President, and the attempted changes within the political system to curb presidential powers seems to testify to this. As long as the system remains the same, the potential for future Watergates exists. I believe moral discussions should also address such systemic issues.

I am, therefore, advocating a curriculum for moral education that facilitates an explicit understanding of the "irrational" within us and of the system within which we exist. Further, if we do not attempt to provide such a curriculum, I question what we are really teaching. Numerous educators, including Kohlberg, have argued that the manner in which education takes place—how it is conducted—is as significant as what is taught (Overly, 1970; Dewey, 1969; Silberman, 1970). This phenomenon is often referred to as the "hidden curriculum." Kohlberg and Silberman contend that the learning gained from the hidden curriculum is fundamentally moral education. While they concentrate their critiques of the lessons taught by this curriculum on the way in which schools are organized, I would extend that critique to the way in which moral developmental theory is implemented in the classroom. What lessons are we teaching students when we concentrate moral education on reasoning and individual-versus-system oriented solutions? Rather than exploring the consequences of that question, I prefer to grapple with how to make the implicit learnings gained through the process of moral education coincide with the explicit learnings.

A Rationale

A rationale for the approach to moral education which I am proposing can be found in the writings of Kohlberg and other moral theorists. Kohlberg is concerned with the development of individual moral reasoning. Consequently, the cognitive structure of the individual becomes the focus of moral education and cognitive maturity a necessary but not sufficient condition for moral judgment maturity. Kohlberg's emphasis on cognitive structure stems from his contention that cognition and affect have a common structural base. Each merely represents different perspectives and contexts. In his view, the development of motives and affect is largely indicated by changes in thought patterns.

> In using the term "cognitive,"as opposed to "personal," it is not intended to oppose cognition to the emotional, the social or the behavioral. The moral structures of judgment studied as stages can be hotly emotional, are manifestly social, and determine choice and action. But in calling moral stages cognitive, it should be implied that they are centrally forms of thinking; they are *generalized* and *symbolic*. Accordingly, the experiences which generate stage movement have a strong general and symbolic component; they are experiences involving thinking.[6]

Kohlberg's assumptions regarding the relation of affect to cognition are open to question and need further research. A growing number of educators in the field of moral education contend that reasoning and behavior are affected by feelings (Aronfreed, 1971; Gustafson, 1970; Fraenkel, 1976; Picetti and Au, 1974). Consequently, moral developmental theory is criticized for paying too little attention to the "affective mechanisms"—the "irrational"—influencing reasoning and behavior. Aronfreed's statement echoes that of Simpson's:

> Behavior is not rationally controlled. It is possible to have a reason, and to have the reason obtain some control over behavior, but I suspect that in most instances the control is not based on reasoning *per se*. If a person reasons or has moral cognition, the control that can be exercised over behavior, I would continue to insist, in the last analysis has to be affective.[7]

Moral educators like Clive Beck and Jack Fraenkel argue that the theory of moral development needs to be coupled with an "interactive" approach that enables individuals to become aware of the *feelings* and thoughts that influence their behavior—an interactive approach that places equal emphasis on cognitive and emotional development. R. S. Peters contends that the most important question in moral education is, How do children come to care?—a provoking question not satisfactorily addressed in Kohlberg's writings. John Wilson advocates that individuals need to learn not only how to deal with questions about what to do in conflict situations but also how they *feel*. He believes that awareness of one's own and others' feelings and emotions is a basic skill needed for moral judgment and behavior. In his writings he discusses the importance of identifying emotions and the impact they can have on one's decisions and behaviors (Wilson, 1972). John Dewey in *Moral Principles in Education* wrote, "Just as the material of knowledge is supplied through the senses, so the material of ethical knowledge is supplied through emotional responsiveness."

Kohlberg does discuss the role empathy plays in the higher stages of moral development. While his focus is on the rational, he defines "ideal" programs for moral development as those which combine explicit cognitive moral stimulation with identity questioning. Although he takes this idea no further, it would be difficult to imagine how individuals could question their identity and not confront the irrational—the feelings, sensations, intuitions—within them.

Edmund Sullivan illustrates this point. In discussing the results of a high school program in moral education he talks of the difficulty in using certain materials with students, e.g., those on abortion and euthanasia, because they "tended to illicit a 'gut' response from the student rather than a reasoned response."[8] Sullivan consequently recommends avoiding these issues in the classroom. Yet it would seem that these "gut responses" are frequently the deciding influence in moral judgment and behavior. Rather than avoiding them, methods for dealing with them in the classroom should be developed. This appears to be a logical implication of the writings of Aronfreed (1971), Dewey (1969), Fraenkel (1976), Peters (1971), Simpson (1976), and Wilson (1972).

There is less written about the need to look for system-related causes in solving moral dilemmas. The major focus of moral dilemma discussions, according to Beyer, is "on the moral issues involved in a dilemma and the reasoning used to justify recommended actions."[9] The format for moral discussions is designed to achieve this end. Although questions like What is the fairest solution for everyone involved in this dilemma? are part of a moral dilemma discussion, the thrust of the discussion is not on how to reach equitable solutions but rather on the reasoning behind one's answers. Yet, the need for "moral solutions" that extend beyond the individual is implicit in the writings of moral developmentalists. This seems most evident in the just community schools in which Kohlberg and his colleagues are involved (Kohlberg, 1975; Wasserman, 1976). The purpose of the school community is to allow all participants—students, teachers, administrators, counselors—to take part in formulating and executing the governing structure of the school so that its hidden curriculum is congruent with the formal classroom lessons.

The concept behind the just community school appears to be a logical extension of Kohlberg's belief that it would be difficult for individuals to reach the higher stages of moral development without a sense of power in and responsibility for institutions. He contends that this ability allows a person to feel "a sense of potential participation in the social order."[10] In Kohlberg's most recent writings he again alludes to the importance of a sense of participation in institutions. With this sense one can view rules as subjective and flexible rather than as rigid and objective (Kohlberg, 1976). The former view of rules—and I might add, roles—represents Stage 3 and 4 maturity; the latter represents Stage 5–6. Further, as James Rest has pointed out, moral education is concerned with developing the structures by which one analyzes, interprets, and makes decisions about social problems. If individuals do not have a sense of participation and power within the social order, it seems unrealistic to expect them to have concern for social problems or to apply moral decision making to the problems which often arise from the conflicting rules and roles of institutions.

I concur with Kohlberg in the need for individuals to feel a sense of participation in the social order; I, too, view this as integral to the higher stages of moral development. What I propose is that more explicit emphasis be given to this dimension, not just in the governing of schools, but in the classroom discussions of moral dilemmas. Moral dilemma discussions which focus only on one's reasons for action in a particular ethical situation seem inadequate in meeting this need. By including problem-solving strategies which analyze the influence of rules and roles on moral dilemmas and generate practical solutions, moral discussions can nurture one's sense of participation in the social order.

An Eclectic Approach to Moral Education

While it is possible to find a theoretical rationale for a moral education curriculum which includes the "irrational" and a "systems analysis," there are few available practical materials for doing this. Perhaps this is one reason why so many schools rely on

Kohlberg's methodology for their moral education curriculum. It provides practical guidelines and materials for implementing moral education and stimulating the development of moral reasoning. What I see a need for is a curriculum for moral education which adds what is missing from Kohlberg's methodology—affect and systemic problem solving. In building this curriculum there is a rich array of techniques and methodologies from which to draw. To illustrate this, some suggestions for an integrated moral education curriculum follow. These ideas are presented within the context of a specific moral dilemma. However, the concepts and techniques can be adapted to other dilemmas.

The following moral dilemma revolves around the issue of reverse bias—an issue gaining greater importance due to recent court decisions in California (DeFunis vs. the University of California) and elsewhere. It is taken from *Hypothetical Dilemmas for Use in Moral Discussion* (Blatt, Colby, Speicher-Dubin, 1974) and could be used with students of high school age or above.

> Marco DeFunis had every reason to think he was about to write his name large into the lawbooks. Denied entry to the University of Washington Law School in 1971 while blacks and other minority students were admitted under special lower academic requirements, DeFunis filed suit. He was admitted to the school under court order while the case made its leisurely way up to the U.S. Supreme Court. By whatever name—reverse discrimination, affirmative action, or quota system—the emotional issue argued by DeFunis, a white, was whether blacks and others as a class could constitutionally be given preferential treatment.
>
> The case attracted such wide interest that twenty-six friend-of-court briefs were filed by interested groups. Universities, labor unions, corporations and others are all under pressure to make more room for minorities. The difficulties of doing so without violating the rights of other applicants were crystallized by the confrontation between DeFunis and the University of Washington.
>
> 1. What should the Supreme Court decide? Why?
> 2. Is this a case of unfair discrimination? Why or why not?
> 3. Would it be fair to require exactly the same test scores, grades, etc., for all applicants regardless of their racial or ethnic background? Why or why not? Why is this considered unfair by many people?
> 4. What is the best way to provide increased opportunity to repressed groups in a way that is fair to everyone?[11]

The dilemma could first be presented to the students using the suggested moral discussion format for presenting dilemmas and creating a division on action. (See page 62 of this volume.) However, instead of moving into the third major strategy for guiding moral discussions—organizing small group discussions—fantasy and role playing could be introduced. Students could be asked to fantasize themselves as Supreme Court Justices who must decide on this case. In their role as Supreme Court Justices they can be asked to visualize the situation, weigh the facts before them, make a decision, feel the sensations they experience in making that decision, decide on the best reason for their decision. Then they could form discussion groups, still in the role of Supreme Court Justices, and come to a decision.

The fantasy and role-playing process could be repeated with students now playing Marco DeFunis, playing a minority student who was admitted under special requirements, and finally playing a minority applicant who was denied admission. In each instance the fantasy and role playing would provide participants an opportunity to use their imaginations. They can be asked to concentrate on the feelings they have in that particular role and the issues that concern them. Simpson advocates that the cultivation of imagination is a "major requisite to moral progress, apart from role-taking opportunities or direct exposure to specific levels of reasoning. . . . [It] increases the sense of environmental mastery and self-esteem."[12]

Fantasy can also be used to facilitate students' awareness of how they deal with conflict. One exercise asks students to fantasize themselves on a walk down a long country road on which they encounter a huge wall blocking their path.

> They continue the fantasy with their individual responses to the wall and then share these responses in small . . . groups. Then they are asked to examine the way in which they respond to the other "walls" in their lives. Did their response in the fantasy reflect a typical way of dealing with obstacles? Do they usually deal with obstacles by themselves? With others? Do they manipulate others to take care of obstacles for them? To what extent are they responsive to and respectful of boundaries created by others?[13]

This fantasy can be done in conjunction with some dyad exercises, like thumb wrestling, pushing off balance, or holding down, which can help students become aware of how they feel in conflict and/or competitive situations. Prior to discussions of these experiences, students can write or draw their reactions to the exercises.

The purpose of using the fantasies, role playing, and conflict exercises is to increase the opportunity for students to experience the feelings that accompany their decisions and behaviors. These ideas are derived from the Confluent Education Program at the University of California, Santa Barbara. The program is built on the premise that in any learning situation there is an accompanying feeling and that there is no feeling without the mind being somehow involved. It seeks to bring together in the learning process affect and cognition, right and left brain operations. Many of the techniques used in confluent education come from the fields of humanistic psychology, e.g., Gestalt, Psychosynthesis. The exercises described here are only a few of the many developed through the program.*

Class discussion can be structured around each of the exercises listed above. The variety of experiences—both cognitive and affective—enrich these discussions. They provide students with even more material on which to base their "best reason" for a proposed decision. But, unlike a typical moral discussion, the unit does not end at this point. Once students have reached a "best reason," they can begin to explore the systemic problems in the dilemma. It is at this point that systemic problem solving can be introduced.

In the area of systemic problem solving the work being done through the Social

*For additional information write CEDARC, P.O. Box 30128, Santa Barbara, California 93105.

Literacy Project at the University of Massachusetts can be easily adapted to moral education curriculum. The Social Literacy Project, based on the philosophical writings of Brazilian educator Paulo Freire, is concerned with developing methods whereby individuals can learn to collaboratively name, analyze, and change problems. The premise is that any problem can be viewed as being within the system instead of being within the person. The focus, therefore, is on blaming and changing systems—not individuals. The strategies developed through this project are aimed at helping individuals collaboratively find the systemic causes of problems and generate workable solutions to change the system.*

One of the strategies—the Nuclear Problem-Solving Process—would be particularly useful with the reverse bias dilemma (Alschuler et al., 1976). This strategy consists of four five-minute steps in which groups of four to eight focus on collaboratively solving one of the participant's problems. In the first step, the problem-poser describes the conflict situation in as much detail as possible. The other participants listen. The second step consists of trying to identify underlying patterns of conflict. During this time the problem-poser responds to questions from the other group members directed at uncovering patterns. The third step is to brainstorm as many solutions as possible to the problem. The solutions are to be system, not person, blame. The system changes arrived at during this time are not to be evaluated or discussed. In the fourth step, the problem-poser selects one of the system-change solutions. Then, with the help of the group, plans are developed to implement this solution.

This process could easily be adapted to a discussion of the reverse bias dilemma. The problem-poser in each group could role play Marco DeFunis, a Supreme Court Justice, or a minority student faced with the issue of reverse bias. Or the problem-poser could present the situation from his/her perspective. The task of the group would be to develop a system-change alternative to the problem which would not "victimize" individuals. Prior to using this strategy the class could research applicable court cases, academic entrance requirements, affirmative action guidelines, and other relevant materials. The perspective provided by this strategy—of looking to the system and not just to the individual for causes and solutions to problems—seems to me what moral education should be about.

Group skills are integral to this approach to moral education. Learning these skills should be a part of the curriculum. For example, an exercise could be used with the above lesson to facilitate students' awareness of how they participate with others in a group task. The learning gained from this could transfer to the Nuclear Problem-Solving Process. One exercise for this involves clay modeling. The class forms into groups of four to eight and each group is instructed to take clay and build something from it. This is done in silence, and a time limit of fifteen to twenty minutes is set. From time to time the facilitator may interrupt and ask the students to reflect on their actions and feelings before continuing. Following the exercise individuals write down their feelings and reactions and then share them with the group. They discuss how their non-verbal participation may mirror their patterns of verbal interaction and how to develop a more

*For additional information write Social Literacy Project, 459 Hills South, University of Massachusetts, Amherst, Massachusetts, 01002.

effective group. A non-verbal exercise provides participants time to examine thoughts and feelings that may normally be masked by words.

The above exercises can be adapted to different dilemmas. The choice of exercises ultimately depends on the issues, concerns, and needs of the students. What is important is that students have an opportunity to explore their feelings and reasoning and to generate systemic solutions to problems. This kind of curriculum would more adequately prepare students to confront and act on the moral issues they face.

Conclusion

The purpose of this chapter was to present an integrated approach to moral education. If educators are truly concerned with helping students develop problem-solving skills, attention should be focused on the numerous human dimensions affecting that process. These include feelings as well as reasoning. While Kohlberg has contributed much to the understanding and developing of the reasoning skills involved in ethical decisions, his approach is limited. Moral education curriculums can build on Kohlberg's methodology by adding what is missing from it—affect and systemic problem solving. These curriculums can begin to provide students with adequate and alternative methods for expressing their knowledge. They will also affirm for students that their imagination and feelings are as valued and valuable as their reasoning.

Notes

1. Michael Polanyi, *The Tacit Dimension*.

2. K. Nakata, "Business Administration and Education," p. 240.

3. K. Woodward and M. Lord, "Moral Education," pp. 74–75.

4. James Rest, "Developmental Psychology as a Guide to Value Education: A Review of 'Kohlbergian Programs,'" p. 242.

5. Elizabeth Simpson, "A Holistic Approach to Moral Development and Behavior," p. 168.

6. Lawrence Kohlberg, "Continuities and Discontinuities in Childhood and Adult Moral Development Revisited," p. 173.

7. Justin Aronfreed, "The Cognitive and the Affective in Moral Action," p. 391.

8. Edmund Sullivan et al., *Moral Learning: Findings, Issues and Questions*, p. 81.

9. Barry Beyer, "Conducting Moral Discussions in the Classroom," p. 194.

10. L. Kohlberg, "Stage and Sequence: The Cognitive-Developmental Approach to Socialization," p. 402.

11. Moshe Blatt, Anne Colby, and Betsy Speicher-Dubin, *Hypothetical Dilemmas for Use in Classroom Moral Discussions*.

12. Simpson, op. cit., p. 163.

13. M. Phillips, "Education for Non-Manipulation: A Model Teacher Training Program," p. 4.

Bibliography

Alschuler, Alfred; Atkins, S.; Irons, R. B.; and Santiago-Wolpow, N. "A Primer for Social Literacy Training." Amherst: University of Massachusetts, 1976.

Alschuler, Alfred; Atkins, A.; and Santiago-Wolpow, N. "The School Game: Playing without Losers." Amherst: University of Massachusetts, 1975.

Aronfreed, Justin. "The Cognitive and the Affective in Moral Action." In *Moral Education: Interdisciplinary Approaches*, edited by C. Beck, B. Crittenden, and E. Sullivan. Toronto: University of Toronto Press, 1971.

Beck, Clive. "The Development of Moral Judgment." In *Developing Value Constructs in Schooling: Inquiry into Process and Product*, edited by J. A. Phillips, Jr. Worthington, Ohio: Ohio Association for Supervision and Curriculum Development, 1972.

Beyer, Barry K. "Conducting Moral Discussions in the Classroom." *Social Education* 40 (April 1976):194–202.

Blatt, Moshe; Colby, Anne; and Speicher-Dubin, Betsy. *Hypothetical Dilemmas for Use in Classroom Moral Discussions*. Cambridge: Harvard University Moral Education Research Foundation, 1974.

Brown, George I.; Phillips, M.; and Shapiro, S. *Getting It All Together: Confluent Education*. Bloomington, Indiana: Phi Delta Kappan, 1976.

Cremin, Lawrence A. *The Genius of American Education*. Pittsburgh: University of Pittsburgh Press, 1965.

Dewey, John. *Moral Principles in Education*. 1909. Reprinted by permission of the Philosophical Library. New York: Greenwood Press, 1969.

Fraenkel, Jack R. "The Kohlberg Bandwagon: Some Reservations." *Social Education* 40 (April 1976):216–22.

Gustafson, J. M. "Education for Moral Responsibility." In *Moral Education: Five Lectures*, edited by N. Sizer and T. Sizer. Cambridge: Harvard University Press, 1970.

Hall, Robert, and Davis, J. U. *Moral Education in Theory and Practice*. Buffalo: Prometheus Books, 1975.

Harris, D. E. "Psychological Awareness and Moral Discourse: A Curriculum Sequence for Moral Development." Ph.D. dissertation, University of Wisconsin, 1976.

Kohlberg, Lawrence. "The Concepts of Developmental Psychology as the Central Guide to Education." In *Psychology and the Process of Schooling in the Next Decade*, edited by M. Reynolds. Minneapolis: University of Minnesota Audio-Visual Extension, 1971.

Kohlberg, Lawrence. "Continuities and Discontinuities in Childhood and Adult Moral Development Revisited." In *Life-Span Developmental Psychology: Research and Theory*, edited by P. Baltes and K. Schaie. New York: Academic Press, 1974.

Kohlberg, Lawrence. "From Is to Ought: How to Commit the Naturalistic Fallacy and Get Away with It in the Study of Moral Development." In *Cognitive Development and Epistemology*, edited by T. Mischel. New York: Academic Press, 1971.

Kohlberg, Lawrence. "The Moral Atmosphere of the School." In *The Unstudied Curriculum: Its Impact on Children*, edited by N. Overly. Washington, D.C.: Association for Supervision and Curriculum Development, NEA, 1970.

Kohlberg, Lawrence. "Moral Education for a Society in Moral Transition." *Educational Leadership* 33 (October 1975):46–54.

Kohlberg, Lawrence. "Moral Stages and Moralization: The Cognitive-Developmental Approach." In *Moral Development and Behavior: Theory, Research and Social Issues*, edited by T. Lickona. New York: Holt, Rinehart & Winston, 1976.

Kohlberg, Lawrence. "Stage and Sequence: The Cognitive-Developmental Approach to Socialization." In *Handbook of Socialization Theory and Research*, edited by D. A. Goslin. Chicago: Rand McNally, 1969.

Kohlberg, Lawrence, and Mayer, Rochelle. "Development as the Aim of Education." *Harvard Educational Review* 42 (November 1972):449–96.

Mischel, Theodore, ed. *Cognitive Development and Epistemology*. New York: Academic Press, 1971.

Nakata, K. "Business Administration and Education." In *Humanistic Foundations of Education*, edited by C. Weinberg. Englewood Cliffs, N.J.: Prentice-Hall, 1972.

Overly, Norman V., ed. *The Unstudied Curriculum: Its Impact on Children*. Washington, D.C.: Association for Supervision and Curriculum Development, NEA, 1970.

Peters, Richard S. "Moral Development: A Plea for Pluralism." In *Cognitive Development and Epistemology*, edited by T. Mischel. New York: Academic Press, 1971.

Phillips, M. "Education for Non-Manipulation: A Model Teacher Training Program." *The Affect Tree* 1 (September 1975):2–4.

Picetti, R., and Au, W. *Conscience, Conduct and Confluent Education: Towards a Holistic Approach to Moral Education*. Monograph no. 5. Santa Barbara, Calif.: DRICE, May 1974.

Polanyi, Michael. *The Tacit Dimension*. New York: Doubleday, 1966.

Rest, James R. "The Cognitive Developmental Approach to Morality: The State of the Art." *Counseling and Values* 18 (Winter 1974):64–78.

Rest, James R. "Developmental Psychology as a Guide to Value Education: A Review of 'Kohlbergian Programs.'" *Review of Educational Research* 44 (1974):241–59.

Silberman, Charles E. *Crisis in the Classroom: The Remaking of American Education*. New York: Random House, 1970.

Simpson, Elizabeth L. "A Holistic Approach to Moral Development and Behavior." In *Moral Development and Behavior: Theory, Research and Social Issues*, edited by T. Lickona. New York: Holt, Rinehart & Winston, 1976.

Social Literacy Project Staff. "Collaborative Problem Solving as an Aim of Democratic Education: The Social Literacy Project (a Case Study)." *Journal of Applied Behavioral Sciences*, 1977, in press.

Stewart, J. S. "The School as a Just Community: A Transactional-Developmental Approach to Moral Education: A Working Paper." Paper presented at the annual meeting of the Moral Education Division of the Philosophy of Education Society, 1975.

Sullivan, Edmund V.; Beck, Clive; Joy, Maureen; and Pagliuso, Susan. *Moral Learning: Findings, Issues, and Questions*. New York: Paulist Press, 1975.

Tesconi, Charles A., Jr. *Schooling in America: A Social Philosophical Perspective*. Boston: Houghton Mifflin, 1975.

Wasserman, Elsa R. "Implementing Kohlberg's 'Just Community Concept' in an Alternative High School." *Social Education* 40 (April 1976):203–7.

Wilson, John. *Practical Methods of Moral Education*. London: Heinemann Educational Books, 1972.

Woodward, Kenneth L., and Lord, Mary. "Moral Education." *Newsweek*, 1 March 1976, pp. 74–75.

Creativogenic School: Developing Positive Human Personality

Elizabeth Léonie Simpson, Visiting Associate Professor,
University of Southern California.

Several years ago I was given the opportunity by the Ford Foundation to take a close look at some burgeoning branches of American education variously known as affective/confluent/psychological/emotional/humanistic education.[1] At the time, I believed that I was coming in late, summing up more what has been than what would be. The swell of interest in this area seemed to have crested. I felt rather as if I had been honored by a request to eulogize a small, still-warm body, killed by its own excesses, which was more to be pitied than censured, more to be loved than despised, to be sure, but with dubious honor at best and never accepted in the best homes.

I was wrong. The recent return to concern for "basic" education necessarily includes the purposes and values of confluent education.[2] Interest in highly individual learning is still mounting, as is the recognition that good affective education simply does not exist *by itself*. As Piaget wrote, "affectivity is nothing without intelligence. Intelligence furnishes affect with its means and clarifies its ends." The label "affective," where accurate, only points out which aspects of behavior have significant feeling components. Much that is called affective is really cognitive, no more the education of the emotions than of other areas of human personality, but with the self and people as content. The richness of the educational programs I experienced was found in the conscious inclusion of *feeling* in their substance.

I was wrong in other ways, too, for I imagined that the changes I expected to find were the direct outgrowth of Progressivism in that—

a) the school was expected to show direct concern for health, vocation, and the quality of family and community life;
b) pedagogical principles were to be derived from psychology and the social sciences;
c) instruction should accommodate individual and group differences;
d) everyone should share in the pursuit of the arts (Cremin, 1961).

Schools were to be seen as "embryonic communities" to build societies "more worthy, lovely and harmonious" (Dewey, 1966). If the school were a constructive agency for the improvement of society, the educator was to be a socially responsible reformist pedagogue. The aim of education was personal growth, but this growth was to be embedded in a social context, intended to extend the range of social situations in which individuals perceived issues and made and acted upon choices.

Unlike Progressivism, confluent education has been nurtured as much in the public schools as in private ones. It has also been more concerned with the individual and interpersonal relations narrowly defined, and less with the person in his or her social web, than the Progressive Movement was. What has occurred has been a synthesis of some of Dewey's ideals with two other cultural forces: the tradition of the humanities and the aims and techniques of mental health education.

Underlying Assumptions

What are the assumptions which underlie authentic confluent education today? First, the process of learning is the active search and incorporation by the knower of the known; the learner controls his or her own life and values his or her own competence as actor in the world.

Second, human beings as phenomena are whole and integrated; opposites do indeed coincide. Emotions, rationality, and will—intentionality—are all legitimate and inseparable aspects of humanness, and all are engaged as learning occurs. Traditions, beliefs, and values are selectively retained, reshaped, and modified to present needs.

Third, it is not enough to speak of emotion, the spirit or the soul, the intellectual powers of rationality, consciousness, or of valuing. These are inseparable from, not merely encased in, the human body—palpable, solid, and real. Even the extra-sensory is rooted in the physical. The poet Auden's great insight, ". . . the kind/Gates of the body fly open/To its world beyond, the gates of the mind . . . ," has been surpassed, for we have found the tentative forms of new gates, yet shadowed, waiting—powers beyond feeling or thinking.

Fourth, the individual's reality, grounded in present experience, extends both forward to the future and backward to the past from which the here-and-now has arisen.

Fifth, proud autonomy may find high expression by yielding commitment to the social group. Creation and affirmation may find their application in the quest for the Good Life for others, as well as for the self.

Today's modified confluent education, then, is not just the development of symbolic, cognitive capabilities or of evaluative or valuing competencies or, indeed, of sensitivity or sensibility. It is all of these and more. The task of the learner is that of developing a positive personality, that of constructing his or her identity, that of building a unified being, an integrated adult self, within the structure of a particular society and a particular set of schools—schools which optimize creative human potential, schools which are truly creativogenic. The creativogenic school enables this being to grow from both personal dissociation and from integration with others in interactive social exchange. The fragmented, split, disassociated identity is shared presence—the conglomeration of many selves and the sum of many roles; the overarching aspect of identity is a oneness and individuality—the single, whole, integrated unity of the person.

These two aspects of personhood—uniqueness and distinction, as well as commonality without stereotyping—are both part of the meaning of identity. For many, feelings of commonality grow out of the unquestioning acceptance of cultural standards—what Kohlberg has referred to as *conventional morality* and the "good boy" orientation and Jane Loevinger has called the *conformist* stage of ego development. This easy integration between the person and society is not based on introspection, but on a developmental stage of maturity. Inner harmony is the outgrowth of ethnocentrism—the identification of self with group and culture, ostracism of deviating group members, and the rejection of outsiders who are different and, therefore, on whom fears, conflicts, and prejudice can be more easily projected.

Beyond this developmental stage, the search for the self, for introspective awareness through self-scrutiny, may be the basis for identification with all of humankind. Insight, subjectivity, private experience, and the empathic taking of the perspective of the other carry the individual beyond personal idiosyncrasy, beyond shared communal beliefs, to an autonomy which is separate from the social group but is still a part of it. What binds contemporary humanistic studies to past traditional ones is concern not just with the highest values of humans but also with those values as uniquely the product of passion as well as intellect, of emotion as well as reason. The ethical purpose of the classical humanities was the amelioration of life through change in the perception of reality. That reality is not a constant which exists solely and concretely beyond the person. It is a personal perception, a creation—a product of the development of the self through the interaction of the individual and the social and physical opportunities in the midst of which he or she lives and strives.

Confluent Education in Practice

I visited elementary and secondary schools in Philadelphia, in Fall River and Newton, Massachusetts, in Hartford, in New York City, in Mayfield, Ohio, in Louisville, Kentucky, and in Santa Monica, Palo Alto, and Los Angeles, California. I explored teacher training at the following places, among others: The Center for Human Development, Fairleigh Dickinson University; The Diagnostic-Prescriptive Teacher Program, George Washington University; The Childhood Education Program, University of Florida; The Center for Humanistic Education, University of Massachusetts; and The Confluent Education Program, University of California, Santa Barbara.[3]

Some of the effective programs came out of religious groups of very diverse denominations, e.g., the Hebrew Union College in Los Angeles, the Roman Catholics, the American Baptists, and the Unitarian-Universalists. They came not only from the universities or large city school districts, but also from foundations, entrepreneurs, and other private disseminators, such as the Bessell, Palomares, and Ball *Human Development Program* and Noram Randolph's *Self-Enhancing Education*.

While much individuality of methodology was apparent, the concepts and the purposes of these programs, as well as their assumptions about the nature of the functional and healthy human being, overlapped greatly. All of them assumed not only that the self and interpersonal or intergroup relationships are legitimate focuses for cognitive and affective learning but also that such learning is a precondition for intellectual and emotional learning in the future.

To illustrate:

1. The Affective Education Program in the city of Philadelphia deals with student concerns and needs for *identity, connectedness,* and *power* (Weinstein and Fantini, 1970; Maslow, 1954) as indispensable antecedents for learning the processes and content of the classroom. Like other similar programs, the AEP uses techniques such as role-playing, dramatic fantasy, and gaming, as well as explicit analysis which attempts to bring the affective and cognitive learning to consciousness.
2. Ventura School in Palo Alto, California has a William Glasser program with the emphasis he stresses on positive identity as derived from the belief that one is a loved and worthwhile, competent person. Emotional support is provided through shared goal-setting and progress evaluation, peer contact and responsibility through the tutorial program, and class meetings of three kinds: social problem-solving sessions, open-ended meetings concerned with intellectual subjects, and educational diagnostic meetings to assess the degree of understanding of curriculum concepts.
3. In Fall River, Massachusetts, as part of a project by William Gastell, confluent education is taking place from early elementary through high school grades. In a fifth and sixth grade class, the Trust Walk was used as self-instruction. One student led another whose eyes were tightly closed; after the "blind" partner told his guide how he had felt during the walk, the roles were reversed. Later, the actual experience within the physical and social room and the hopes held for future explorations were recorded in personal journals.
4. In the Fall River high school a young man was teaching history as the shared communication of ideals, values, and feelings. The place of minority value systems within a majority system was discussed by each student; each marked off his or her place on a continuum, drawn on the blackboard, which contained the following phrases at opposite ends: "Avoid any situation where there's a need to win or lose," and "Use any means to win against competition." A lively discussion followed about why the students' initials were grouped the way they were on the blackboard continuum.
5. *Shanti* ("the peace that passeth all understanding") is the name students and staff have given Hartford's Mulcahy-Sinner High School since it became an alternative public school. Related to Parkway in Philadelphia and Metro in Chicago, its eighty-six students meet in small Home Groups which serve as points of reference, sources of peer support, and the principal means for the identification of student educational needs. Anyone may apply to attend Shanti and the decision for acceptance is made by lottery. Governance is a mutual process—by task force from the school community. The physical plant maintenance is also a student responsibility.

   Shanti is an example of the use of a radically changed social structure which intentionally facilitates the incorporation of emotional and social learning with that of cognition.
6. At Synanon in Santa Monica, California, confluent education begins at six months when the child is left to unrestricted exploration in an enriched and protected environment which includes food. By high school age, people are involved in the *Interface* program which alternates practical vocational training with academic work as a means to increase self-esteem, responsibility, and cooperation. Affective education is never-ending. All ages play the Synanon Game at least once a week as a condition of

residence. Here, total freedom of speech and expression of emotions are encouraged. Individuals confront each other, and honesty is expected and demanded. The Game is considered a governmental and emotional tool as well as a therapeutic experience.

7. Guided Fantasy is a strategy used at varying levels of age and sophistication at various schools. Here is one account of third graders:

   "Get comfortable," says the teacher, and the small bodies flop to the floor, curl up, close their eyes, and reach inward in anticipation. "You are now entering the Sky Lab. The doors are shut and latched and you have fastened yourself in place. In a minute you will be blasting off."

   Their voices are added to hers as the countdown begins. "One, two, . . ."

   "The ship is off! Shall we stop on the way?" Loud agreement—the bodies are restless.

   "All right. We have landed at our first location now. You can get out, but don't forget that you have your space suit on and you need your equipment."

   There is a lot of movement around the room, stiff legs, crouched bodies, pantomime of lively flesh trapped within survival bounds.

   Back to the Sky Lab for another blast-off. "Now we have landed at Mars. When you get out, you can have anything you want. Mars has a magic spot. If you're willing to look for it, you can have anything you want." The search is made; each reaches inside himself or herself and explores the forming dream.

   Back on earth, the teacher asks softly, "What did you carry away?" According to his or her own nature, each shares this information (or does not), joyfully or anxiously, bragging or a little sad, a little inadequate, feeling the choice was not the one really wanted, but knowing the trip would be offered again.

These examples of confluent education are necessarily very brief. They do not include some of the most interesting expansions in the field, which, increasingly, are providing humanistic approaches to physical education, to the learning of private and public sex roles, to play, and to avocational, as well as to vocational, education. Included are ways of building the future—of learning the route from the here-and-now to goals yet-to-be-accomplished.[4] In all of these programs, self-knowledge is extended beyond self-awareness to self-respect, to belief in one's goodness and one's competency and agency. The programs aim to facilitate certain types of psycho-social learning, and these not separately, but in such a hierarchical and integrative way that they represent personal and social development.

Facilitating Confluent Development

What are some of the means of facilitating this confluent development of the positive human personality? Here are some of the approaches which are consistently found:

1. Incorporating and extending beyond the methodologies listed above is the *gratification of basic needs*—what is learned about the needs of the self and how they may be satisfied within the broad educational environment in ways which permit the person to actualize his or her human potential. According to Maslow, these basic human

needs are physiological needs (to eat, sleep, be warm, etc.), security needs, belongingness or affiliation needs, the need for esteem from others and from oneself (self-esteem from a sense of competence), and the need for self-actualization. All, except the last one, are deficiency-compensating; self-actualization is growth-producing.

Schools contribute to this gratification—whether through supplying food, or by providing a sense of membership in a peer community, or in other ways. Where it has been planned thoughtfully, they have provided environments which go even further toward the fulfillment of special needs. When planned confluent education attempts to bring students up the needs spiral in line with their own natural development processes, it helps to develop democratic personalities and makes a genuinely democratic political system possible. Under this type of system, the circle is perpetuated: Fulfillment of these needs becomes simpler and more taken for granted.

2. The *small-group experience*, often occurring in a circle, has proved a powerful structure for self-directed change. It provides esteem or respect from others, support, experience, reference, community, and mirror.
3. The use of *language as a symbol system* in description, report, creation, and analysis has been effective in expanding the conceptual ability of the learner as well as in consolidating and integrating affective and conative explorations through free association, story-telling, fantasy, dreaming—all the modalities which serve to combine feeling and intellectual experience.
4. The use of the body for the *physicalization of abstract concepts* through movement, dance, drama, and role-play, has built psychomotor, as well as feeling and thinking, competence. Through role-playing and dramatization, for example, the body provides a modality for expression as well as a sensitive means of response. In *King Lear*, blind Gloucester remarked, "I stumbled when I saw." Sightless, he was then using more of his body to acquire knowledge from around him.
5. The *expression of the creative unconscious* through the arts is a powerful and greatly underutilized means of self-development. Nowhere are the false barriers between various confluent perspectives of education more apparent than in those systems which exclude the arts or minimize their significance. The arts, as epistemological modalities, provide opportunities for knowing and for description which neither logic nor science can present. Art is expression and response; it is happenings which carry their own loadings of thought, beliefs, values, and emotions.
6. The life of an individual is an expression of human creativity which is manifest through the medium of the person. In the same way, the environment—both social and physical—is an aesthetic expression of the persons who create or maintain it. Especially valuable is the *cultivation of imagination and the use of the power to create*, which increase the sense of environmental mastery and the sense of self-esteem. Creativity does not occur at random, but is enhanced by planned environmental factors. Some of these are the kinds of cultural stimuli—the incentives and rewards for originality and the degree of free access which citizens have to them—which are present in a society. The creativogenic school not only encourages an openness to cultural stimuli, it also has a continuing, ever-present stress on *becoming*, not simply

being, a person which incorporates an on-going expectation of growth and change. Interest in and tolerance for divergent views elicit exploration and experimentation.

But as Arieti (1976) has pointed out, these elements are the social setting—the incubating factors—of creativity; certain intrapsychic qualities are more essential for fostering it. According to him, these include aloneness (as a state of being), inactivity, day-dreaming, free-thinking, a state of readiness for catching similarities (synectics), gullibility, remembrance and inner replaying of past traumatic conflicts, alertness, discipline, and conflict.

Throughout my life I can change because I can imagine myself the way I would like to be. I can be someone else through empathy—my personal, *applied* imagination. I am he simply because I can enter his experience, and I am myself because I can withdraw from it. Anticipatory imagination facilitates other passages of change and growth as well.

Imagination is not ornamental; it is structural. Together with fantasy, its conscientious exercise can be a powerful tool for cognitive development, because its use forces each person to construct his or her world and the world he or she shares through his or her own enlarged perceptions.

7. *Simulation exercises and educational games*, including the direct exposure to specific levels of moral reasoning which use real-life contexts for problem-solving, facilitate the sharing of planned emotional and intellectual content. As in examples four and six above, role-taking opportunities provide a legitimized mode of stepping outside self-consciousness and rationality and of returning to them through the subsequent analysis, which unites the experience with its meaning.
8. *Contextual learning*—the curriculum of the planned environment—takes place within the community and within and beyond the school walls and grounds in the exploration of reality and participation in the alien patterns of others' lives. This curriculum is built of human resources drawn upon *in situ* and not artificially transported to the schools. This is the use of already existing social and physical environments to provide self-learning.

The Future

What will be the future role, then, of the school in assisting the development of the person? It will be enacted in an environment in which all positive aspects of personality can be enhanced, enlarged, put into practice. While relevant for individual interest, subject matter as *content* will be of less importance than the *processes* of learning.

Within this environment, the teacher's participation will be vital and active. For most students, much of the curriculum will be conveyed directly—eye to eye, word to word, person to person. It has been said that the effective teacher's task is the three "D's"—dialectic, dialogue, and disputation—all carried out with students. But the teacher's message extends beyond what he or she does to include what he or she is and, more, what he or she *seems to wish to be*. If teachers wish to be received by those they are trying to influence, they cannot be neutral or disaffiliate themselves from the social world. Besides didactic instruction, they provide experience and models for the essential conditions of learning: empathic understanding, respect for others, and a facilitative genuineness (Patterson, 1977). As Carl Rogers wrote, ". . . the facilitation of learning

[is] the aim of education . . . the facilitation of significant learning rests upon certain attitudinal qualities which exist in the personal relationship between the facilitator and the learner. . . ."[5]

Through this relationship, the learning process may engage the entire person; it may include elements which extend beyond the cognitive to the personal, the feeling, the interpersonal, the valued, and focus on how these are expressed in everyday life. Like all education, the purpose of confluent, humanistic education is to change the individual, both intrapsychically and behaviorally. That change—the outcome of perceptions modified by their relevance to the self—is the creativogenic gift of power, the ability to build the person one wishes to be as well as the world in which one wishes to live.

Notes

1. A report of much of this investigation has been published in Elizabeth L. Simpson, *Humanistic Education: An Interpretation* (Cambridge, Mass.: Ballinger, 1976). This book includes an extensive bibliography compiled by Mary Anne Gray.

2. I have used the word *confluent* in this article because it seems to me most clearly to describe education for many—cognitive, conative, and affective—aspects of human personality. As the reader of literature in the field will find, however, many workers have used other terms with varying meanings.

3. The individuals responsible for these programs were David Hobson, Fairleigh Dickinson University, Rutherford, N.J.; Robert Prouty, George Washington University, Washington, D.C.; Arthur Combs, University of Florida, Gainesville, Florida; Gerald Weinstein, University of Massachusetts, Amherst, Massachusetts; George I. Brown, University of California, Santa Barbara, California.

4. These new emphases and other recent developments in confluent education are described at length in Elizabeth L. Simpson, *River Run Deep, River Run Strong: Confluence in Humanistic Education* (Minneapolis, Minn.: Winston Press, forthcoming).

5. Carl Rogers, *Freedom to Learn*, pp. 105–106.

Bibliography

Arieti, Silvano. *Creativity: The Magic Synthesis*. New York: Basic Books, 1976.

Cremin, Lawrence A. *The Transformation of the School: Progressivism in American Education*. New York: Knopf, 1961.

Dewey, John. *Lectures on the Philosophy of Education: 1898–1899*. New York: Random House, 1966.

Glasser, William. *Schools without Failure*. New York: Harper & Row, 1969.

Kohlberg, Lawrence. "Moral Stages and Moralization: The Cognitive-Developmental Approach." In *Moral Development and Behavior: Theory, Research, and Social Issues*, edited by T. Lickona. New York: Holt, Rinehart & Winston, 1976.

Loevinger, Jane. *Ego Development: Conceptions and Theories*. San Francisco: Jossey-Bass, 1976.

Loevinger, Jane, and Wessler, Ruth. *Measuring Ego Development*. 2 vols. San Francisco: Jossey-Bass, 1970.

Maslow, Abraham H. *Motivation and Personality.* New York: Harper & Row, 1954.

Maslow, Abraham H. *Toward a Psychology of Being.* New York: Van Nostrand Reinhold, 1962.

Patterson, C. H. "Insights about Persons: Psychological Foundations of Humanistic and Affective Education." In *Feeling, Valuing, and the Art of Growing: Insights into the Affective*, edited by L. M. Berman and J. A. Roderick. Washington, D.C.: Association for Supervision and Curriculum Development, 1977.

Rogers, Carl R. *Freedom to Learn.* New York: Merrill, 1969.

Simpson, Elizabeth L. *Democracy's Stepchildren: A Study of Need and Belief.* San Francisco: Jossey-Bass, 1971.

Simpson, Elizabeth L. *Humanistic Education: An Interpretation.* Philadelphia: Ballinger, 1976.

Weinstein, Gerald, and Fantini, Mario D., eds. *Toward Humanistic Education: A Curriculum of Affect.* New York: Praeger, 1970.

Psychology, Thought, and Morality: Some Limitations of Piaget and Kohlberg

Robert Samples, Consultant, Poet; Tiburon, California.

Introduction

Psychology and philosophy are subtle versions of each other. Psychology can now be considered as the *way* we think and philosophy as how *well* we think. Psychology studies the process of mind work and philosophy judges it. Psychology has grown to the level of a major area of study in our science-oriented technological culture. Thousands of people apply various versions of the scientific method in an unceasing effort to get closer to an objective view of the workings of the human mind. At the same time, clearer statements about the quality of human thought are emerging in philosophy.

The two methodologies—psychology and philosophy—are closely intertwined. The acts of judgment required in philosophy inevitably influence those who study the way the mind works. Simultaneously, researchers, whose minds are prepared by the philosophical vision they choose, seldom find anything they are not already looking for. The processes they observe are influenced by their philosophical vision. Thus, what they discover in psychology reflects the philosophy that prepared their minds for exploration.

This modern kind of chicken-and-egg argument is not new to the literature. Benjamin Whorf, studying language and its effects on thinking, discovered long ago that the language we use sculptures the way our mind works.[1] He also set forth the linkage between a culture's philosophic vision, its language, and its thought.

This present essay will explore some cultural interconnections in terms of the modern popularity of the philosophy and psychology of Jean Piaget and Lawrence Kohlberg. The first section presents the dominant scientific psychological portraits of the way humans are perceived. This is followed by a study of the connection between Western perceptions and the function of Western thought. The final and third section explores the relationships between the values embedded in the Western technocratic culture and the Kohlbergian vision of moral life.

Some Reflections on Psychology

Our Western culture embraces an array of ways of looking at the human psyche and describing what is perceived. Some might call these ways schools of psychological thought. Each school of thought begins from a different group of assumptions. Each then proceeds toward an expanded knowledge based on those original assumptions. These schools of psychological thought are the Freudian, Behaviorist, Cognitive-Developmental, Humanistic, and Transpersonal. Abbreviated statements delineating the basic characteristics of each follow:

Freudian: The human psyche is a dynamic world constantly in turmoil wherein the higher human instincts are in combat with baser animalistic forces.

Behaviorist: The human psyche is little more than an aggregate of behaviors embedded into the nervous system by the experiences each human has had.

Cognitive-Developmental: The human psyche develops through sequential stages, each of which is characterized by a higher capacity for logical, abstract thought than the stage preceding it.

Humanistic: The human psyche is far more expansive than any of the above alone, and it encompasses all of the qualities of a person within a context of goodness and a capacity to be godlike.

Transpersonal: The human psyche is only a portion of a cosmic, universal psyche that is inextricably interconnected in a little understood unity.

Accepting the admitted limitations of such a listing, there are some characteristics worth noting. First, the listing is historical. That is, the schools of thought are listed in the sequence in which they have had popular currency in the history of psychological thought. Second, after the Freudian movement, each school of thought tends to operate from more expansive assumptions. It is this second point I wish to pursue in this chapter.

When attempting to assess the worth of a psychological perspective in the area of human concerns, one often gets bogged down in effects rather than causes. Reading contemporary research literature tends to nurture this. The *consequences* of particular assumptions lend themselves to statistical expression far more often than do the assumptions themselves. And it is the statistical expression of assumptions that our current Western culture tends to demand.

This condition, the reverence for data, for hard proof and "numbers to back one up," is central to the argument. To become more scientific, psychologists attempted to gather more data. Some critics argue that behaviorism grew out of the compulsion to counteract the wholly subjective perspectives of Freud and psychoanalytic approaches. If numbers were to be gathered, then something had to be measured, counted, and tallied. The budding field of behaviorism offered real possibilities. Behaviors could be observed and counted. Psychology could thus become a worthy entrant into the growing community of the sciences. In fact, it created its own definition in its own image. Psychology became defined as the *science* of behavior.

Once psychology was viewed as a science, its supposed separation from philosophy seemed complete. Yet even a cursory examination shows them deeply woven together. B. F. Skinner, the leading contemporary behaviorist, defines behaviorism as the philosophy of the science of behavior. Nonetheless, the important issue had been dealt with. Psychological behavior had become countable and thus accountable.

This glowing arena of comfort lasted hardly a generation; however, a surprising number of people became influential through their association with behaviorism. Many came to Robert Frost's symbolic fork in the road. Some, like Abraham Maslow and Carl Rogers, chose the route that allowed them to expand on some of the precedents of C. G. Jung, who seemed to bypass behaviorism. They invented the school of thought called Humanistic Psychology—Maslow through research and Rogers through therapy.

The other road led a short distance from behaviorism to cognitive-developmental theory which explored stages of thinking. Of all the schools of psychology, this one would become the most consistent with Western philosophy. The explorers of this arena would discover a data base to "prove" that the psychological development of the individual paralleled the evolution of Western philosophical thought. The foremost explorer of this route was Jean Piaget.

Piaget's early work had nearly bypassed psychology and had instead explored science and symbolic logic. Thus, when he became interested in psychological development, he approached it as a natural historian would. The subjects of his observation were his own children.

Piaget's early work is a monumentally convoluted and tangled morass of observations, reflections, and musings. One can read it and almost feel Piaget's urge to make sense out of the multitudinous observations he had made of his children's growing capacity to reason and think logically. He touched upon dreams, creativity, intuition, and moral development. But his real mission was clear: to document the natural emergence of logical thought.

To capture the evidence for on-going maturation in children and to create quantifiable data, Piaget invented a series of tasks for children to perform. The tasks required varying levels of logical capability, and Piaget began to believe these tasks represented stages of cognitive-logical development.

Piaget's work was of interest to very few people outside of Europe until the early 1960's. At that time American educators and psychologists became involved in an explosion in research devoted to replicating Piaget's experiments. Massive federal funding was being extended in the name of educational reform. Two qualities of Piaget's work had wide appeal. First, Piaget offered a developmental scheme and, second, his stages could be measured.

There is no question that the cognitive psychologists, those probing the human psyche's capacity to reason, had far broader interests than did the behaviorists. However, the transformed version of behaviorism held by cognitive psychologists was narrower than the perspective of the humanistic psychologists. The exploration of the function and development of the human intellect and its capacity to reason tended to exclude a consideration of the human qualities of emotionality, sexuality, and spirituality. Those qualities, along with intellectuality, are all considered equivalent and simultaneously important, and many consider this inclusion of other human qualities to be the fundamental strength of humanistic psychology. The weakness of humanistic psychology lay in its aborted attempts to measure its outcomes and apply statistical analysis to its control premises.

This ambivalence toward the empirical method plunged transpersonal psychology into a sea of statistical darkness. Piaget's assumptions are far less able to be systematized and measured than any of the other schools of psychology. Virtually no research in the area of transpersonal psychology is without critics, if not skeptics. Though there are noted psychologists, physiologists, and neuroscientists exploring this area, there is still a cultural vision of quackery assigned to those involved. Research in dreaming, out-of-body experiences, ESP, psychosynthesis, and telepathy—all of which are issues in this field—are greeted by the scientific establishment as being suspect.

Those with the courage or stubbornness to continue to attempt research in these areas are clearly victims of the prejudice of the dominant Western traditions. Transpersonal psychology's research models, techniques, and results are scrutinized with a vigor unmatched in more conventional areas. As a result, those who affiliate and identify themselves as transpersonal psychologists are viewed more as cult figures than as scientists or psychologists.

To summarize. Currently, five schools of psychological thought co-exist in our culture. However, a higher degree of compatibility exists between Western culture and the methodologies of the behavioristic and cognitive approaches than exists between our culture and the other methodologies. One could thus conclude that these two schools of thought, being more scientific, more rational, and more evaluatable, are more correct. Or one could say that these schools of psychological thought are more consistent with the values of our culture.

Either way, the result is the same. In any cultural ecology, those persons who pursue knowledge do so through the filters characteristic of that culture. Piaget's descriptions of his stages of logical development may be viewed as testimony to an individual's degree of adaptation to a particular cultural ecology.

Though no different from other scientific arguments, the cognitive-developmental model is the most circular. Piaget may well be describing the way children accept cultural values rather than the way those same children develop. Even if, as some are beginning to claim, the stages of growth are linked to specific developments in brain structure, the outcome would be the same. Progress is measured by criteria related to the child's performance of a kind of thinking that is prized by the culture. Since nearly all humans who are exposed to technological cultural settings are exposed to Western thought, an accommodation to technology may be the issue rather than the more universal pattern of growth claimed by the developmentalists.

Culture and Thinking

Much has been written about the role of science in sculpturing Western thought, and little that can be said here will add much that is new. Since the golden age of Greece, the methodology of science has emphasized logic and rationality. In the relentless drive to create thought systems devoid of mysticism and magic, the Western mind focuses on patterns of reductive and analytic thought.

Research, a game of mental integrity, has been defined as the way one searches for truth about the universe. Though such a claim sounds notable, it would be well to recall the response of Jerome Bruner to Newton's words, "the purpose of the scientist is to sail the oceans of the unknown and discover the islands of truth." Bruner saw the process differently. He saw the scientist sailing the oceans of the unknown and *inventing* the islands of truth.

The fragility of the distinction between discovering an idea and inventing one is frequently overlooked. Often we think we have discovered something when in fact our mind has sculptured a pattern out of a tangle of observations that do not relate to each other in what could be called a truly objective way. Nowhere is this more poignantly seen than in the principle of uncertainty provided us by Werner Heisenberg. Heisenberg pointed out that in the world of sub-atomic physics very basic realms of observation were hidden from us by virtue of the way matter was constructed. Thus, even in physics, the most objective of the sciences, certain conclusions about matter *had* to be invented rather than observed.

Heisenberg's principle of uncertainty left those of us who had an affection for science with an unsettling kind of bewilderment. We were plagued by questions: When really is it the workings of our minds we perceive and when is it the objective rituals of matter in the universe? When can I claim distance between the way I think and what I think? Alas, it seems the two can never be separated.

Bruner and Greenfield[2] added some substance to the discovery-invention issue when they noted the difference in thought patterns between Wolof children schooled in the bush and those schooled in the suburbs of Dakar City. The dominance of the natural context resulted in ways of thinking remarkably different from those of the students schooled in the technological presence of French-speaking Dakar.

Benjamin Whorf[3], Jose Argueles[4], Jonas Salk[5], and Fritjof Capra[6] all speak to this issue from different perspectives. What emerges is an undeniable realization that philosophy, psychology, and cultural contexts are all vital in determining how any given mind works. However, again we might fall victim to Newton's vision of truth. To analyze experience from the perspective of Western philosophy puts us at the threshold of systematic analytic and reductive thought. Further, the perception we have of the psychological way-people-think-and-act also tends to limit (or extend) our vision. Finally, the culture from which we speak influences us mightily.

On this last point, some clarification might benefit the argument. While culture influences us considerably, it would be folly to dismiss the role of religion, mores, mysticism, and laws. But what seems to be the most important issue in determining how members of a culture think is not the *heritage past* but the *context present*. Wolof, Navajo, and Zuni children exhibit a different kind of mentation in traditional non-technological contexts than they do in the context of the dominant technological culture. Thus, the children's exposure to technology is more important in influencing thought patterns and values postures than is their culture-past.

In the presence of technological systems, people are unable to escape Western dominant thought. Thus McLuhan's[7] global village concept may well be the beneficiary of the spread of technological and technocratic contexts. Such a spread creates the most effective medium known to proliferate Western thought and Western values. Technology and its parent science are no more value free than is Catholicism or Buddhism. It is just that science's values are consistent with contexts of rationality rather than spirituality.

And this brings us full circle to the various philosophical-psychological views that began this essay. The favoritism shown in contemporary times for behaviorism and its offspring, cognitive psychology, may simply be explained as a manifestation of technological compatibility.

Piaget's vision is ultimately derived from Western technology. The developmental stages he poses for the maturation of the intellect have as their fundamental premise the maturation of abstract, logical thought. Thus, what we see is a psychology born of the Western tradition, raised in the Western tradition (as it is the psychology most often researched), and some might claim, about to die in the Western tradition.

Piaget's perspectives and Skinner's perspectives have been researched to an awesome breadth and detail. So much so that their results have begun to affect technology as surely as they were born of the technology. Behavior modification is matched only by rational modification in the dominant performance and material technologies found in educational settings. These two systems dominate the approved research directions for graduate students, and they serve as the foundation for much evaluation and as the basis for text and instructional materials development.

Those who have moved beyond behavioristic approaches and entered the areas of humanistic and transpersonal psychology have done so primarily because the technocratic human so well described by behaviorists was simply too limited. All the human capacities of spirituality, emotionality, sexuality, and intellectuality are at the core of these final two holistic psychologies. In no way do the philosophies of humanistic or transpersonal psychology exclude either behaviorism or cognitive psychology. Rather, they are embraced as part of the whole. But alas, the opposite is not true.

Behaviorism and cognitive psychology only have the capacity to embrace that which is consistent with their premises, *premises which are at the outset reductive.*

What we have in both behaviorism and cognitive development is really a kind of cultural chauvinism. Rationality can clearly be considered a religion if one thinks metaphorically. The logic of our actions then becomes a measure of our faith. Experience becomes the indicator of the morality of my being. My conformity to this context is a measure of my worth.

Technocratic Values and Morality

Now let us explore technocratic dominance in the area of values and morals. Illuminating in this is the work of Lawrence Kohlberg. Kohlberg has adopted and adapted Piaget's stages of intellectual growth to a system of hierarchies of moral appropriateness. Further, Kohlberg links his theory to a developmental hierarchy of moral stages.

Kohlberg makes no pretense of disguising his linkage to Piaget but does point out how he differs from Piaget in regard to moral development. Piaget ascribed to a four-stage process while Kohlberg created a six-stage process. The two men also differ in that Piaget suggests that moral development is parallel to cognitive development and thus seems to suggest that the former is somewhat inevitable. Kohlberg agrees with the linkage to cognitive growth but claims no inevitability. Further, he feels that his stages develop as a separate but parallel process which cannot be complete unless one gets to the highest stage of rational, abstract thought, the formal operational level.

Kohlberg does add a twist of interest. He claims that as a person goes through the stages, that person cannot comprehend alternatives more than one stage ahead and does not accept alternatives more than one stage behind in development. He also claims, with a degree of finality, that persons cannot be morally operative at their highest levels—five and six—unless they are at the formal operational stage of cognition.

It is at this point that the chauvinism of the Western perspective again enters the scene. The ability to reason in contexts without direct experience of these contexts is the issue. To be moral or morally operative requires this ability. To reason, to develop logic, and to sustain thought about the future is of primary importance. Some investigators are now exploring futurism as being the context of more appropriate morality and intellectual maturity. In fact, the criteria for much of Kohlberg's Stage 6 and the action settings of the moral-ethical survival of humankind are related to futurism. But the catch is clear. *It is a Western-mind mode of dealing with the future.* That is, it involves a modification, a manipulation, and an intervention with the future.

Kohlberg's work is elitist in the same way that Piaget's is. This in no way invalidates either theory, but it should be clear that the technocratic fiber that is the premise of both theories sorely limits their pluralistic potential. Bruner[8] wrote widely about the difference between the mental modes of tribalistic Wolofs and the individualistic Wolofs. The non-technologic tribe members thought collectively. They saw themselves as elements of a greater unit. Those Wolofs who had been exposed to technocratic systems became individualistic. Do Western reductive thought modes eliminate the capacity to reason holistically? I think not. "Eliminate" is too strong a word.

I would argue, however, that cultures without symbolic abstract systems of written language are those yet most affiliated with collective thought. The Native American people with whom I have had a chance to work over the past decade speak often of a new kind of tribalistic vision.

Native American philosophy is cyclical. That is, it is wedded inextricably with natural systems. As a result, the psychological processes of the Native American mind reflect this cyclical perspective. This is in marked contrast to Western philosophical perspectives which are locked into linear modes. The best example of this is born of recent brain hemisphere studies in which activities of the cerebral hemispheres are monitored as a person performs an array of tasks. In most people in our technocratic dominant culture, the left cerebral hemisphere specializes in linear, rational reductive modes of thought. This reflects the basic fabric of Western philosphy. The right hemisphere specializes in more cyclical, analogic and holistic modes of thought. These processes are a reflection of more mythic and natural philosophies.

Earlier it was pointed out that language is a powerful instrument in affecting the way we think. Similarly, language stands as a vivid indicator of the philosophy of a culture. When the cerebral activity of many Native American people is monitored, it appears that English is reflected by left hemisphere activity just as it is in the majority of the anglo cultures. However the native language of the Native American, be it Hopi or Zuni, is reflected primarily by right hemisphere activity. In addition, only a few Native American tribes developed a written abstract language system. Most stayed with oral traditions, thus retaining a more cyclical, holistic mode of knowing. Partly because of this, I cannot help but compare the vision of psychologies beyond the cognitive with the apparent vision of Kohlberg and Piaget.

In doing so, I cannot avoid the growing notion that cognitive psychology and behaviorism are hopelessly trapped in their own reductivism. To say that formal operations and Stage 6 in moral development describe the ultimate aspirations in both cognitive and moral development is an unacceptably narrow position.

The Western vision of how Kohlberg's and Piaget's conclusions are applied in schools offers the best example of their chauvinism. The stages provide the criteria for diagnosis. Students are assessed to "find-out-where-they-are." Next a determination is made as to where they should be and a course of action is determined in regard to how to get them there. After action is taken, then the final act is to assess the effectiveness of the whole ritual to determine its efficacy. Compare this with the statement from Zen, "When the student is ready, the teacher will appear."

Far be it from me to argue a non-interventionist policy in education. However, if there is validity to pluralism in regard to race or sex, then I believe that this validity must also apply to our view of the human condition.

Neither Piaget's nor Kohlberg's work is wrong. Though Kohlberg's research is of necessity more opportunistic, it is not significantly more liberal in regard to logic than Piaget's. If one were to fault Kohlberg's perspective, it would perhaps be on the grounds that the technology and technocratic maturity might well be the glue that keeps his value context welded together. Is it human nobility that Kohlberg measures or the degree to which a culture has bought into the Western technocratic myth? On this point, his cross-cultural studies are particularly suspect. By virtue of the philosophy to which Kohlberg ascribes, his methodology measures itself. In other words, barometers are poor tools for measuring distances.

But if neither Kohlberg nor Piaget is wrong, then why all these words? The issue is clear—they are incomplete. Piaget is more liberal in stating his bias toward a kind of intellectual chauvinism when he claims to be interested, not in the "capriciousness of the subconscious," but rather in the logical workings of the conscious. Piaget admits incompleteness, but Kohlberg seems not to. In saying that one must be at the formal operational level to be morally operative, Kohlberg adds absolutism to his style that is unreassuring. By standard ways of testing, many Navajo, Zuni, and Hopi would not prove out at the formal operational level.

Conclusion

There is an urgency in the minds of many to experience holism. The heritage of reductivism is, if modern crises in energy, water, food, and psychic comfort are indicators, less than comforting. The explosion of interest in Eastern and non-technical traditions is most certainly more than a fad. Perhaps our own psyches are responding to experiential deficiencies in ways likened to vitaminosis. Perhaps it is not too romantic to consider our psychic selves as reaching toward equilibrium at just the time that it is becoming abundantly clear that the limitations of Western modes of knowing are approaching crisis proportion.

But do not look at these concluding words for logic or footnoted reason. They are words of faith—faith in the integrity of Western thought; faith in the growing feeling that there is a part of knowing that has gone unnoticed. The unnoticed part of being is transrational or even panrational.

Exaggeration has long been known as a way to understand what we really experience. If one exaggerates the premises of Piaget or Kohlberg within contemporary technological frameworks, we end up with a kind of behaviorism—but a behaviorism of control. It looks more like a totalitarian psychology than one of pluralism.

When we take the wisdom of Western thought, wed it with the wisdom of Zen and other Eastern traditions, and then finally blend it with the close-to-nature vision of the Native Americans, we may have what some will choose to call a rational moral vision. If so, synergy will have prevailed. But if this *is* a synergic vision, then reductivism is not the most hopeful route.

Perhaps with the dawn of humans on this planet there was a sense of collectivism or tribalism in which the individual postponed the discovery of the reductive self. If so, the advent of Western thought ended that. The reductive self emerged. With that emergence, priorities followed that began to exclude those who retained their collectivism. The exclusion was elitist. With the "knowledge" of individualism, a strange web of abstract affiliation had to be created to replace that which was known before. The thing called Western civilization began. Its laws, formal religions, and educational system joined to the limits of economic growth to impose a mandate of order upon the individual.

But now a new individual emerges. One that senses a new tribalism, a new unity. One whose laws, religions, schools, and economics are being guided by a simultaneous transformation that is at once a return and a departure. The emergence of this individual is a reinstatement of collectivism *but this time by affiliation*. It is a departure in that there is movement toward the future. Both of these directions are grounded in the now. The concepts of inappropriate psychologies and philosophies are as destined to disappear as surely as the inappropriate technologies, with humankind moving toward a synergic survival.

Notes

1. Benjamin Lee Whorf, *Language, Thought, and Reality*, ed. Stuart Chase (Cambridge: M.I.T. Press, 1956).

2. Jerome Bruner and Patricia Greenfield, *Beyond the Information Given*, ed. Jeremy Anglin (New York: Norton, 1973): 371.

3. Whorf, *Language, Thought, and Reality*.

4. Jose Argueles, *The Transformative Vision* (Berkeley: Shambhala Publications, 1975).

5. Jonas Salk, *The Survival of the Wisest* (New York: Harper & Row, 1974).

6. Fritjof Capra, *The Tao of Physics* (Berkeley: Shambhala Publications, 1975).

7. Marshall McLuhan and Quentin Fiore, *War and Peace in the Global Village* (New York: McGraw-Hill, 1968).

8. Bruner and Greenfield, *Beyond Information Given*.

Faith and Justice, and Kohlberg

Stephen Rowntree, S. J., Assistant Professor of Theology, Loyola University (New Orleans).

Introduction

I believe that Lawrence Kohlberg's work on education for justice has something to say to the Christian concern for a faith that does justice. This belief is an expression of the deep Catholic sense of the harmony of reason and faith, nature and grace. This paper proceeds on the conviction that there is not a chasm between Harvard and Rome. There is a basis for genuine dialogue. Harvard has something to say to Rome; Rome has something to say to Harvard. Each will be enriched. This paper will explore what each has to say to the other.

To appreciate the interchange, the Church's present understanding of the relations of faith and justice must be understood. Today's Church is convinced that faith, as our response to God's saving love manifested in Christ, requires action to change unjust social structures. The most striking statement of this connection of faith and justice is the statement of the first Synod of Roman Catholic Bishops:

> Action on behalf of justice and participation in the transformation of the world fully appear to us as a constitutive dimension of the preaching of the Gospel, or, in other words, of the Church's mission for the redemption of the human race and its liberation from every oppressive situation.[1]

A commitment to transforming unjust social structures was not always the Church's understanding of the implications of faith, as I will show. Understanding why the Church makes this commitment today is crucial to understanding why we should be concerned with Kohlberg's theory of moral development. This understanding is also essential for a proper understanding of what we are up to in the whole faith-justice area. In Part One of this paper, I discuss the faith-justice context for the dialogue with Kohlberg.

Used by permission of the author.

But the central concern of this paper is the substantive dialogue between Kohlberg and the Catholic understanding of justice.[2] This dialogue is not optional, I would insist, because Kohlberg's methods cannot be used for justice education unless his principles of justice are similar to ours. As he himself often points out, methods of moral education cannot be separated from the content of moral education:

> If I could not define virture or the ends of moral education, could I really offer advice as to the means by which virtue should be taught? Could it really be argued that the means for teaching obedience to authority are the same as the means for teaching freedom of moral opinion, that the means for teaching altruism are the same as the means for teaching competitive striving?[3]

Kohlberg's methods of stimulating moral development conceivably could lead to a morality alien to Christian morality if his moral principles are not compatible with Christian morality. This is obviously not the case, but the essential congruence of Kohlberg's justice principles and Catholic justice principles needs to be spelled out clearly. This I do in Part Two. I will argue that Kohlberg's principles of justice are similar in content and function to natural law as understood in modern Catholic social teachings.[4]

The more interesting question is not just that of basic compatibility but of mutual enlightenment. I will try to show in Part Three that Kohlberg and Catholic social teaching complement each other in specific ways. One topic of mutual enlightenment concerns human rights. Catholic social teaching is developed in terms of equal human rights.[5] Kohlberg's cognitive-developmental theory explains the process by which people come to understand that all persons have equal human rights and indicates ways to foster this appreciation (i.e., procedures to stimulate moral development). I will show that Kohlberg's notions of role playing and of the social nature of the self explain how persons can come to appreciate the basic worth of all persons. I argue that this appreciation of equal worth is central to grasping the notion of equal human rights. Kohlberg thus explains a crucial link in grounding human rights. On the other side, Catholic social doctrine suggests a needed elaboration of Kohlberg's Stage 6 principled morality (the culmination of moral development). Specifically, as I will show, Catholic justice doctrine explains what the equal human rights are and why they are what they are. Kohlberg says equal human rights are central to Stage 6 morality but gives no account of what they are and how those rights are to be ranked. But Kohlberg and Catholic social thought complement each other on fundamental issues of human rights—the core of any notion of justice.

Kohlberg and Catholic teaching on justice have something important to say to each other on the possibilities of realizing Gospel justice in the real world. Kohlberg's account of human development shows how the normal processes of social, cognitive, and moral development lead a person to achieve a sense of justice. His account also shows, therefore, that justice is not alien to human development but is the fulfillment of it. This view is the basis for a hope that a just world can be realized. On the other hand, while accepting this view, the Christian tradition checks Kohlberg's tendency to underestimate the sin and egoism which are always obstacles to justice. To know the good and to do the good are not the same. The obstacles sin presents to the realization of justice will be explored briefly here in the light of Reinhold Niebuhr's sobering realism about the limitations of any human justice.

It is by passing over this rugged terrain we have sketched out that we hope to deliver on the promise of our topic: "Faith and Justice, and Kohlberg." As indicated, Part One will discuss the context of the contemporary understanding of faith and justice, which makes Kohlberg so important. Part Two will discuss the agreement of Kohlberg and Catholic justice teaching on basic moral principles and their function. Part Three will discuss the insights Kohlberg and Catholic justice teaching bring to each other on (1) the issue of human rights and (2) the issue of positive and negative forces operating both to foster and to hinder the actual realization of a just world.

Part One: The Contemporary Catholic Understanding of the Relation of Faith and Justice, the Context for Appreciating Kohlberg

What I have to say on this topic is not original, but the paper needs to say it to situate properly the discussion of Kohlberg. The central element of the current Catholic understanding of the relation of faith and justice is that *faith requires action to change the unjust structures of society*. This statement of the relation of faith and justice would have puzzled Saint Paul and the early Christians. We must carefully note the issue. The issue is not whether faith involves deeds of love and justice. It obviously does, and the New Testament constantly witnesses to this. The First Epistle of John is very clear and quite typical when it says:

> The way we came to understand love was that he laid down his life for us; we too must lay down our lives for our brothers. I ask you, how can God's love survive in a man who has enough of this world's goods yet closes his heart to his brother when he sees him in need?[6]

The issue is whether faith and Christian love involve action to transform social structures. Rather obviously for the first Christians they did not. Christian love relativized and rendered unimportant all social distinctions yet left them intact. Within the community all were equal: "There does not exist among you Jew or Greek, slave or freeman, male or female" (Gal. 3:28). But this religious equality did not lead to social reform movements to transform the social structures outside the community. Slavery as a social institution was maintained for example. Thus Paul writes:

> Everyone ought to continue as he was when he was called. Were you a slave when your call came? Give it no thought. Even supposing you could go free, you would be better off making the most of your slavery. The slave called in the Lord is a freedman of the Lord, just as the freedman who has been called is a slave of Christ.
>
> 1 Cor. 7:20–22

Why this view of the relation of faith and social structures? There are surely many reasons. One is obvious. The early Christians were a small persecuted minority within the Roman Empire, and the Church was a religious movement. The thought that it should transform social structures did not and could not occur to it. Asking why the early Church did not see action to transform social structures as part of its mission is like asking why it did not send missionaries to an as-yet-undiscovered New World.

Those Christians who have resisted social changes down through the ages have appealed again and again to Paul's views. Reinhold Niebuhr quotes the letter of the Bishop of London in 1727 to the slave owners in the Colonies in which he allays the fears that the conversion of Negroes might alter their civil status; the bishop's words are quite true to the Christian tradition:

> Christianity and the embracing of the gospel does not make the least alteration in Civil property or in any of the duties which belong to civil relations; but in all these respects it continues Persons just in the same State as it found them. The Freedom which Christianity gives is freedom from the Bondage of Sin and Satan and from the Dominion of Men's Lusts and Passions and inordinate Desires; but as to their outward condition, whatever that was before, whether bond or free, their being baptized and becoming Christians, makes no manner of change in them.[7]

The Catholic tradition of social thought (especially as shaped by Saint Thomas), with its view that grace built on nature, had a better understanding of how social arrangements needed to be shaped by the religious principle.[8] Yet Leo XIII opposed equal human rights on the basis of this same argument that religious equality does not involve social equality:

> In accordance with the teachings of the Gospel, the equality of men consists in this: that all, having inherited the same nature are called to the same most high dignity of sons of God, and that, as one and the same end is set before all, each is to be judged by the same law and will receive punishment or reward according to his deserts. The inequality of rights and of powers proceeds from the very author of nature. . . . For, He who created and governs all things has, in His wise providence, appointed that the things which are lowest should attain their ends by those which are intermediate, and these again by the highest. Thus, as even in the kingdom of heaven He has willed that the choirs of angels be distinct and some subject to others, and also in the Church has instituted various orders and a diversity of offices, so that all are not apostles or doctors or pastors, so also He appointed that there should be various orders in civil society, differing in dignity, rights, and power . . .[9]

Today, as the quote from the Synod of Bishops indicates, the Church no longer argues this way. The reasons for claiming that faith must lead to transformation of society are surely complex. Two obvious ones can be pointed out. The first is the Marxist criticism of religion as the opiate of the people. Christian faith is indeed an opiate if it has no social implications. In the face of aggressive efforts by Marxists and other social reformers to change the world, the Church has come to see that the world can be changed and that social structures can and should anticipate and reflect the present and still-to-come Kingdom of God. This new conviction is expressed by the Thirty-Second General Congregation of Jesuits:

> At a time when so many men are sparing no effort to put the world to rights without reference to God, our endeavor should be to show as clearly as we can that our Christian hope is not a dull opiate, but a firm and realistic commitment to make our world other than it is, to make it the visible sign of another world, the sign—and pledge—of "a new heaven and a new earth." (Apoc. 21:1) The Synod pressed the same point home: "The Gospel entrusted to us is the good news of salvation for the whole of man and the whole of society, which must begin here and now to manifest itself on earth," even if "man's liberation in all its fullness will be achieved only beyond the frontiers of this life." (Final Declaration of the Synod of Bishops of 1974, n. 12)[10]

A second reason is the understanding that social structures are made by humans and that they shape persons in many ways. Today we could not act to improve persons' welfare and better their condition without trying to change social structures. For in many cases it is social arrangements that immiserate, impoverish, and enslave people. Thus the Thirty-Second General Congregation observes:

> We are witnesses of a Gospel which links the love of God to the service of men, and that inseparably. Now, in a world where the power of economic, social, and political structures is appreciated and the mechanisms governing them understood, the service of men according to the Gospel cannot dispense with a carefully planned effort to exert influence on these structures. . . . It is becoming more and more evident that the structures of our society are among the principal formative influences in our world, shaping men's ideas and feelings, shaping their most intimate desires and aspirations; in a word, shaping man himself. Hence to work for the transformation of these structures according to the Gospel is to work for the spiritual as well as the material liberation of man, and is thus intimately related to the work of evangelization.[11]

Niebuhr cites unemployment insurance as an example of a structural change that benefits the needy. Without denying the value of individual charity, it is obvious that the system of unemployment compensation provides more adequately for those out of work than individual charity would.[12] Unemployment compensation is a structural change in society that effects care for those in special need. Authentic love today calls for such a structure or institution.

Appreciating, then, that faith must be expressed in efforts to change social structures is the context for the discussion of Kohlberg. Given this concern, Kohlberg is especially relevant because he suggests ways to stimulate our students to develop a sense of justice. He is also of interest because his theory is based on an appreciation of the social nature of the self and has an explicit appreciation, therefore, of how social structures and norms influence the self. All of these elements are of crucial interest for understanding and fostering a faith that does justice by transforming social structures.

Part Two: The Congruence in Function and Content of Kohlberg's Principles of Justice and Catholic Social Justice Principles

Because content and method are inextricably linked in moral education, Kohlberg's methods cannot be used unless his principles are congruent with Catholic social justice principles. For his methods, as he points out, lead to particular moral principles. If his principles are radically different from Catholic principles, then his methods will be of no use and we had best drop Kohlberg completely. If his principles are alien principles, then his methods will only produce false beliefs about justice. The intuitive sense most of us bring to Kohlberg is quite the contrary. We expect a congruence between his principles and Catholic principles. This expectation is rooted in the view that reason can go a long way toward discovering valid moral principles, including valid justice principles. It is also rooted in Kohlberg's approach to morality as not just the tribal code or given mores of society, but in morality's fullest development, as rationally justifiable principles. But let us now spell out the basic congruity of the two sets of principles.

It seems obvious to me that Catholic social justice principles, as statements of what the Gospel and reason require of us, are not principles relative to any limited society. The basic principles of justice the Church interprets to us are not just principles for advanced industrial countries, or European countries, or developed countries, nor on the other hand, just for agricultural, Asian, or underdeveloped countries. They are not only principles for members of the Church. They are principles that ought to govern the relations of all humans, all persons of good will. Of course, how the principles are to be realized in specific situations among specific peoples will vary. But the principles (or basic values) are the same.

Kohlberg stands out among social scientists for rejecting cultural relativism, the view that different societies differ fundamentally in ultimate moral principles. He criticizes the prevailing understanding of moral and social development "as the direct internalization of external norms of a given culture." In his major paper "From is to Ought" he spends nine closely-argued pages attacking cultural and ethical relativism.[13] According to Kohlberg there are rational ways to come to valid moral conclusions concerning ethical questions. Thus, on the issue of whether there are non-relative, transcultural moral principles that can be known by reason, Kohlberg and the Catholic tradition agree. According to Kohlberg these principles are principles of justice. The Catholic tradition would agree that many of these moral principles are principles of justice—even though all of them may not be.[14]

Both for Catholic tradition and Kohlberg, principles of justice are principles for criticizing social practices—even whole societies. Thus Kohlberg refers to Martin Luther King as an example of one who criticized the institution of segregation in the name of justice. Numerous Catholics, including John LaFarge, Lou Twomey, Joe Fichter, and others (just to name some favorite Jesuits), also worked to overthrow segregation and argued against it as a denial of fundamental justice. Other Catholics, including many Jesuits, today are criticizing the structures and institutions of their countries and are going to jail or even being killed for their call to justice. Neither for Kohlberg nor for the

Catholic tradition are principles of justice principles of conformity to the status quo. For both they are vital principles of social change, even in some cases principles for revolutionary change. The end point of Kohlberg's moral development and the goal of Catholic justice education are therefore quite similar. Both seek to develop individuals who can distance themselves from the present order, criticize it from the perspective of justice, and act to achieve a more just social system.

The contemporary Catholic approach to social justice, as we have noted, has come to an appreciation of the role of social institutions in shaping the individual and hence the need for structural change. Kohlberg has a similar appreciation of social structures. According to Kohlberg the basic process of social development is growth in the ability to take the role of the other. The self is built up through a process of internalization of roles and norms (structured according to the stage of cognitive and social development). The reigning norms and roles of society determine in large part the character of the self. For example, if a person grows up in a competitive society where the basic value is acquisition and little attention is paid to the weak, he or she will take competitive, acquisitive persons as role models, will seek to become competitive and acquisitive, and will not care about the weak. A person who is weak or handicapped will judge himself or herself deviant and worthless because he or she cannot realize the social norms of competitiveness, acquisitiveness, and strength. Because of the social nature of the self, Kohlberg insists that "a genuine concern about the growth of justice in the child implies a similar concern for the growth of justice in the society." In particular, a concern about teaching justice in schools "requires just schools."[15] Because social structure is so crucial for moral development (and human development), Kohlberg has been spending much time and energy developing a just school community within the Cambridge public high school. Thus, on the issue of structural change and the role of structures in shaping the person, Kohlberg and current Catholic teaching agree.

Having noted these points of agreement between Kohlberg and Catholic justice teaching, the crucial question remains: Do their principles of justice agree in content? I want to argue that they do agree substantially. Both, as I will show, understand justice as the recognition and realization of *equal human rights*. Kohlberg is very clear: "Justice . . . is a matter of equal and universal human rights." All persons of whatever nation or culture are equal in that they all have certain rights which belong to them sheerly as persons. Moral obligations are obligations to respect rights. Justice as respect for rights is a moral principle, "a mode of choosing which is universal, a rule of choosing which we want all people to adopt always in all situations." Justice is also a reason for action, a basis for making a concrete decision when claims of persons conflict. According to Kohlberg, "As a reason for action, justice is called respect for persons."[16] As Kohlberg explains in a paper discussing Stage 6, "*the respect for persons* principle" says, "treat each human being as an end in himself, as of ultimate worth."[17] Respect for the worth and dignity of all persons—irrespective of birth and merit—is specified in terms of respect for the human rights of persons. This doctrine of equal human rights denies that there are any differences in the basic rights persons have as persons. It opposes any notion that there are differences of status and rights between persons as persons. This is a denial that human society is at root a class society based on inequalities of rights and powers as Leo XIII argued in *Quod Apostolici Muneris*.[18]

Modern Catholic justice teaching is also a doctrine of equal human rights based on the dignity and value of all persons. The earlier notions of unequal basic rights and the hierarchical nature of society are discarded. Thus *Gaudium et Spes* states clearly:

> Since all men possess a rational soul and are created in God's likeness, since they have the same nature and origin, have been redeemed by Christ and have the same divine calling and destiny, the basic equality of all must receive increasingly greater recognition.
>
> True, all men are not alike from the point of view of varying physical power and the diversity of intellectual and moral resources. Nevertheless, with respect to the fundamental rights of the person, every type of discrimination . . . is to be overcome and eradicated as contrary to God's intent.[19]

The caveat against discrimination means that no differences between persons are to be made regarding fundamental rights; i.e., all persons have the same human rights. *Gaudium et Spes* also says the same thing in noting that "there is a growing awareness of the exalted dignity proper to the human person, since he stands above all things, and his rights and duties are universal and inviolable."[20] *Pacem in Terris* earlier had proclaimed:

> Any human society, if it is to be well-ordered and productive, must lay down as a foundation this principle, namely that every human being is a person, that is, his nature is endowed with intelligence and free will. By virtue of this, he has rights and duties of his own, flowing directly and simultaneously from his nature. These rights are therefore universal, inviolable and inalienable.[21]

Catholic social justice doctrine, like Kohlberg's principles of justice, has as its core respect for equal human rights as the specification of basic respect for the value of all persons.

It is this identity of basic content which makes Kohlberg so relevant for Catholic justice education. His methods guide moral development to the point where persons come to a principled respect for the value of all persons and their equal human rights. This is precisely the goal at which Catholic justice education aims. In this identity of content lies the essential agreement of Kohlberg and Catholic social justice teaching.

Part Three: The Complementarity of Catholic Social Teaching and Kohlberg

Human Rights

To say that justice for Kohlberg and for Catholic social teaching is the acknowledgment of equal human rights does not say how we come to acknowledge equal rights or what these rights are and how we are to rank them in cases of conflict. On the question of the process of discovering equal human rights, Kohlberg has something to say to Catholic social teaching. On the question of content and ranking of rights, Catholic teaching has something to say to Kohlberg.

Kohlberg explains that the appreciation that all persons have human rights is based on the ability to role play, the ability to put yourself in the other person's shoes and see things from his or her point of view. In earlier stages of moral development the ability to role play is limited—at Stage 3 one can take the point of view of loved parents or peers for example. One acts to please these loved persons and to obey the rules they support. As moral development progresses one can take the viewpoint of more persons at one time. At Stage 6 one can take the role of any and all persons in the human community.

To appreciate the worth and value of all persons one generalizes a basic appreciation of self-worth.[22] This basic appreciation involves problems. Do we really have an enduring and solid sense of our own self-worth, in spite of our faults, failings, and weaknesses? Genuine self-love and self-appreciation are not the easiest things to acquire. But presuming that we do have a basic if not perfect sense of self-worth, we can place ourselves in other persons' shoes and see that they too value their own life as we value ours. There is no human being in whose shoes we could place ourselves whose life we would not value. Put yourself, for example, in James Earl Ray's shoes. If you were James Earl Ray you would want your value as a person respected—in spite of all the things you might have done wrong.

It is the failure to see things from others' point of view that makes moral outrages possible. Joseph Rhodes, writing on the 1970 attack by police on the girls' dormitory at Jackson State in which two students were killed and twelve wounded, says the police fired "because there was something missing in their attitude toward the people in their sights. They did not feel that if they fired they would be killing other human beings."[23] They did not put themselves in the shoes of the students, and think what their gun blasts looked like from the students' point of view. If they had they probably would not have fired. Moral outrages such as genocide and attacks on innocent civilians in war occur easily when the object of attack is excluded from one's moral community.

A friend told me of how some students stole $1,000 worth of lumber for a school bonfire. From the viewpoints of the other student body members, the theft made perfect sense. The bonfire would please them. The thieves had failed however to include the perspective of the owner of the lumber in their moral evaluation. From his perspective the theft would have appeared quite unjustified.

I recall vividly the moral conversion I had on the issue of segregation. Shortly after I moved South at age 12, I became a good Stage 3 conventional segregationist (from having been a conventional integrationist in the North). When I was a teenager I one day thought of segregation from the black person's point of view. I realized in an instant that it made no sense. If I were black, segregation would hurt and degrade me. Therefore, I concluded, segregation was totally wrong.

Perhaps this is to belabor the obvious point often repeated in traditional moral teaching of many traditions: Do not do to others what you would not want done to you; or, Love your neighbor as yourself. I do not think it is belaboring a point because what Kohlberg suggests is that behind an appreciation and living of these simple maxims is a whole range of cognitive and social abilities that develop very slowly. Only the formally operational person (i.e., the person who can imagine all logical possibilities of combinations) and the person who can take the role of all persons irrespective of family, national, and cultural ties can really live the Golden Rule and really love other persons the way he or she loves self.

Thus the ability to take the role of all other persons is the basis for the judgment that all other persons are of value. Of course, given this ability, any religious beliefs that strengthen my own sense of being worthwhile and loved (e.g., the conviction that Jesus loves me enough to die for me in spite of my worst sins) will also strengthen my sense of the worth of other persons. I realize that Jesus loved them also and died for them. Thus the sense of self-worth and worth of other persons receives reinforcement through faith.

The Gospel speaks of another way of coming to appreciate other persons' worth: to take God's perspective on persons. Jesus told his disciples, "My command to you is: love your enemies, pray for your persecutors. This will prove that you are sons of your heavenly Father, for his sun rises on the bad and the good, he rains on the just and the unjust. . . . In a word, you must be made perfect as your heavenly Father is perfect" (Matt. 5:43-48). Again, the ability to take this perspective involves a high stage of cognitive and social development. The same capacities are called for as in taking other persons' roles. This means that the above statement that "the ability to take the role of all other persons is the basis for the judgment that all other persons are of value" must be qualified to read: "The ability to take the role of all other persons *and/or of God* is the basis for the judgment that all other persons are of value."

It is the appreciation of persons' worth that is fundamental, I am convinced, in the grounding of equal human rights. This is how I see the connection. If we genuinely value persons, then we do not want these persons to be harmed, hurt, destroyed. We would say they *ought* not be harmed, hurt, destroyed. They have a *right*, we would say, not to be harmed, hurt, destroyed. Any genuine values have a claim to protection—above all persons, who are of highest value. Rights are the social means by which valuable humans (i.e., *all* humans) are protected.

This suggests a partial answer to the question of what is the content of equal human rights. (As far as I know, Kohlberg does not systematically spell out this content.) Obviously from what has just been said, they are rights not to be assaulted, injured, harmed, or unnecessarily interfered with. The United Nations' Declaration of Human Rights spells out these negative rights as the right to life, liberty, and security of person and also the right not to be enslaved, tortured, or subjected to cruel, inhuman, or degrading punishment. I would also think that rights connected with criminal due process and equality before the law are all concerned with protecting persons from the specific harms of arbitrary and unfair treatment.[24] Constitutional democracies in the Anglo-American tradition have been very effective in guaranteeing and protecting such negative rights. Kohlberg seems to take it as obvious and not in need of explanation that these are basic human rights.

Catholic social teaching (and other traditions also) suggests that this is not all that can be said about the content of human rights. To say more, however, one needs some sense of human well-being or perfection of a kind which Kohlberg ironically shies away from.[25] Kohlberg says, "We make no direct claims about the ultimate aims of men, about the good life, or about other problems which a teleological theory must handle."[26] I would argue, however, that a notion of human development or flourishing can be understood in common sense terms and without metaphysical assumptions. In fact, it would seem that some notion of human well-being is presupposed in specifying even negative rights. This notion of human development (or well-being or flourishing) is very simple. We all know that hunger, ignorance, disease, and lack of leisure harm human well-being and stunt and destroy human development. We also know that if humans are to have a decent life, they must have food, shelter, clothing, medical care, and education, to name some of the obvious necessities. If we genuinely value all humans, we must hold that it is morally right that they have these goods and services. We must say everyone has the *right* to the goods and services necessary for a decent life. If we do not admit this, we cannot really be serious that all persons are valuable. This is the way we derive human rights of a positive kind, rights to certain goods and services, not just rights not to be harmed in specific ways or not to be interfered with.

Pacem in Terris and *Mater et Magistra* spell out the list I sketched above in the following terms:

> . . . every man has the right to life, to bodily integrity, and to the means which are necessary and suitable for the proper development of life. These means are primarily food, clothing, shelter, rest, medical care, and finally the necessary social services. Therefore, a human being also has the right to security in cases of sickness, inability to work, widowhood, old age, unemployment, or in any other case in which he is deprived of the means of subsistence through no fault of his own.
>
> . . . the right to the indispensable means of human subsistence, to health services, to instruction at higher level, to move through professional formation, to housing, to employment, to a suitable leisure, and to decent recreation.[27]

Thus Catholic social teaching supplements in an important way Kohlberg's treatment of equal human rights. It spells out, especially, the positive rights to the goods and services necessary for human development. These positive rights ground the argument for redistribution of the world's wealth and resources. Thus Kohlberg's very general account of Stage 6 principles of justice as principles respecting equal human rights are fleshed out and implications for the distribution of wealth can be drawn. This is a valuable and needed supplement to Kohlberg's discussion of human rights.

The Catholic doctrine of justice also suggests a ranking of rights in the economic order. And I have a suggestion to make concerning other apparent conflicts of rights. Kohlberg needs to be supplemented on this issue also. Kohlberg points out that the principle of justice says, "Treat every man's claim impartially regardless of the man."[28] I take this to mean: Treat every person's rights impartially. There is no way to respect all claims that are not rights. Hitler's claim was to destroy the Jews. Justice can pay no attention to such claims. Even if claims are restricted to rights, rights conflict. Considering all claims impartially does not tell you how to choose when claims conflict. It merely sets up the conflict. An ordering of rights in terms of priority is what is needed.

Although we did not spell out the right to private property and "the right to free initiative in the economic field,"[29] these are considered basic human rights. These rights are subordinated, however, to the rights of persons to the goods and services needed for a decent life:

> All other rights whatsoever, including those of property and free commerce, are to be subordinated to the principle (that all persons have a right to share in created goods). They should not hinder but on the contrary favour its application. It is a grave and urgent duty to redirect them to their primary finality.[30]

Thus, if the property rights of a landowner conflict with the need for increased agricultural production because people are hungry and without land, the right to the basic necessities of life has priority and the land may be expropriated for this purpose:

> If certain landed estates impede the general prosperity because they are extensive, unused, or poorly used, or because they bring hardship to peoples or are detrimental to the interests of the country, the common good sometimes demands their expropriation.[31]

The right to acquire property and the right to buy and sell on a free market can be limited and restricted, then, if necessary to insure the rights of all to the basic necessities of life. This is a simple but radical way of ranking rights in the economic sphere.

The more difficult problem arises when rights to free speech, a free press, and political activity, for example, are alleged to conflict with the positive economic and social rights we described. Communist governments give priority to economic and social rights and subordinate political rights. The United States and liberal democracies have tended to give priority to political rights (or the negative rights of non-interference and private property) and to subordinate economic and social rights. The challenge of social justice today is to develop social systems that respect both the traditional liberal rights to liberty of thought, speech, religion, and political participation and the positive rights to the goods and services necessary for a decent human life. I would suggest that the restrictions on economic rights mentioned above are the only rights that need be limited. The other liberal rights need not be restricted. Western European social democracies show there need be no choice between the traditional liberal rights and the newly recognized socio-economic rights. To spell out fully an ordering and patterning of human rights and to handle more complex conflicts is to construct a whole social philosophy. I do not have the time or the energy to do the task in this paper. But this is the development both Kohlberg and Catholic social teaching need.

Catholic teaching on rights thus supplements Kohlberg on the critical issues of content and priority of rights but is not itself complete. Kohlberg, we argued, explains how one can come to recognize the equal worth of all persons through role playing. This is essential to understanding how one comes to an appreciation of equal human rights. Catholic social justice teaching has no formal account of this process, and so Kohlberg is a useful complement to its account of rights. Each, therefore, has something valuable to say to the other on the issue of human rights.

Positive and Negative Forces at Work in Moral Education

As Kohlberg sees morality, it is not an external order imposed on basically selfish and unruly impulses. It is rather the immanent ordering of the relations of persons who have an innate desire to establish social bonds with each other.[32] Initially, the bonds of reciprocity are limited to avoidance of punishment and submission to authority (Stage 1) and simple exchange relations—"You scratch my back and I'll scratch yours"—(Stage 2). As cognitive and social development occur, especially development in the ability to role play, the self develops an ever-wider moral community until at Stage 6 morality is a respect for the value and rights of all persons. Kohlberg himself expresses it in these terms: "The claim of the theory is that the 'normal' course of social experience leads to progression through the sequence (of moral stages)."[33]

This understanding of social and moral development is an optimistic reading of the human condition and the possibilities for moral advance. Kohlberg sees his stages of moral development paralleled by the pattern of social evolution noted by Hobhouse:

> When we pass from the lower races to peoples more advanced in civilization we find that the social unit has grown larger, that the nation has taken the place of the tribe, and that the circle within which the infliction of injuries is prohibited has been extended accordingly. And if we pass to the rules laid down by moralists and professedly accepted by a large portion of civilized humanity, the change from the savage attitude has been enormous.[34]

It is obvious that with the growth of communications and trade an interdependent world has developed. People are coming to realize that all humans form one world community. Stage 6 morality becomes more of a realistic possibility for more people. Teilhard de Chardin has expressed this situation and its possibilities for a world community of love and justice. I believe the Spirit of God is at work to form a world community and to foster the moral development and moral conversion which are its essential prerequisites.

But if the normal course of social development makes possible respect for all persons and their basic human rights, it does not assure it. In philosophical jargon, social development is a necessary but not sufficient condition for moral development (i.e., you cannot have Stage 6 morality without social development, but social development does not alone assure moral development). And even if a person reaches a Stage 6 level of moral reasoning, I am not at all sure a person will act in accord with what he or she knows. I am extremely suspicious of Kohlberg's claims to correlate moral action with moral stage. Even if these correlations are correct, I still know from my own experience that I can know the good and not do it. And the only way I can achieve any sort of regularity in doing the good is to go through the painful process of overcoming self to do the good a number of times, i.e., to develop a habit or virtue.

Kohlberg's attack on virtues has some point to it, but it is too general. By throwing out virtues in the traditional sense, he deprives himself of a central concept for interpreting the link between knowing the good and doing the good. A well-known contemporary discussion of virtues (Frankena's) does not oppose them to moral principles but links them to moral principles:

> I propose therefore that we regard the morality of duty and principles and the morality of virtues or traits of character not as rival kinds of morality between which we must choose, but as two complementary aspects of the same morality. Then, for every principle there will be a morally good trait, often going by the same name, consisting of a disposition or tendency to

> act according to it; and for every morally good trait there will be a principle defining the kind of action in which it is to express itself.[35]

Thus, corresponding to Stage 6 principles of justice will be virtues of justice, the dispositions to act to respect the rights of persons.[36]

If positive forces for moral development (especially the intrinsic motivation to establish social bonds) are at work, there are negative forces at work also. It is selfishness and egoism which prevent me from doing the good I know. This egoism will never be overcome until the Parousia when the Kingdom comes in its fullness. The very fact that the highest stage of human morality is justice as respect for human rights testifies to the omnipresence of egoism. For the very notion of a right is connected with sin. What is a right? A right is a claim or a demand one can make and can insist on. But in a world of perfect love each person would seek the other's welfare spontaneously. One would not have to insist on or demand anything. Are not rights typically asserted only when they have been denied and not acknowledged? The right to the necessities for a decent life is asserted today because economic structures do not assure basic necessities for all.

As Reinhold Niebuhr insists, historical justice is both a realization of love and community (hence the importance of education for justice) and a denial of it. We need to keep both in focus as we go about our work as justice educators. As Kohlberg helps us to understand, justice is a realization of love because in its fullest development it establishes bonds with the whole human community:

> Systems and principles of justice are the servants and instruments of the spirit of brotherhood in so far as they extend the sense of obligation towards the other, (a) from an immediately felt obligation, prompted by obvious need, to a continued obligation expressed in fixed principles of mutual support; (b) from a simple relation between a self and one "other" to the complex relations of the self and the "others"; and (c) to the wider obligations which the community defines from its more impartial perspective. . . .[37]

But the need for justice testifies to our selfishness. We must never lose sight of this. Such a recognition of sin is a necessary complement to Kohlberg's tendency toward uncritical optimism. Thus, as Niebuhr so well puts it:

> Law and systems of justice do, however, have a negative as well as a positive relation to mutual love and brotherhood. . . . This aspect of their character is derived from the sinful element of all social reality. They are merely approximations in so far as justice presupposes a tendency of various members of a community to take advantage of each other, or to be more concerned with their own weal than with that of others. Because of this tendency all systems of justice make careful distinctions between the rights and interests of various members of a community. The fence and the boundary line are the symbols of the spirit of justice. They set the limits upon each man's interest to prevent one from taking advantage of the other. A harmony achieved through justice is only an approximation of brotherhood. It is the best possible harmony within the conditions created by human egoism.[38]

Conclusion

This paper has ranged across a vast territory. I hope I have been able to buttress the widespread conviction that the dialogue of Catholic social teaching with Kohlberg is mutually enlightening. Today we seek to live a faith that transforms the world. So we need all the help we can get—especially in developing a pedagogy that can energize our students for this task. Kohlberg is especially suited because the aims of his justice education and our aims in religious education are in important ways identical. We both seek to foster a justice that respects the worth of all persons and acknowledges their basic human rights.

Kohlberg, I argued, explains, with his theory of social development as the expanding capacity to role play, how people can come to appreciate the worth of all persons. This appreciation is an essential step in coming to acknowledge equal human rights. Catholic justice teaching complements Kohlberg's notion of human rights by explaining what these rights are—both such negative rights as the right not to be harmed, hurt, or hindered from acting, and positive rights to the means needed for a decent human life. Major problems about the ranking of rights are involved in this account. At least in the economic order a clear priority is stated: private property and free market exchange are subordinated to the right of all to the necessities of life. It was suggested that there is no need to choose between most of the traditional liberal rights (liberty of thought, speech, press, religion, political participation) and socio-economic rights. The discussion of rights might stand as an example of the kind of difficult problems one encounters if she or he is to be morally autonomous. There are no answers in books. These problems have not yet been figured out.

In our efforts to educate for justice we are aided by developmental tendencies of persons to establish ever-wider and more-inclusive social bonds. Persons develop toward Stage 6 morality. Yet egoism in ourselves and others thwarts action for justice. We know the good, but we do not do it. The very notion of justice testifies to the disregard of others' welfare. Our justice is both a realization and negation of the love God calls us to after the example of his own love. But we have a secret ally, the Spirit of God groaning within, ever at work to transform our hearts of stone into hearts of flesh.

Notes

1. Synod of Bishops, "Justice in the World," in *The Gospel of Peace and Justice*, ed. J. Gremillion (Maryknoll, N.Y.: Orbis Books, 1976): 514.

2. I do not mean to suggest that there is necessarily only one Roman Catholic interpretation of justice. I do mean to focus the dialogue with Kohlberg on modern Catholic social teachings on justice as they are presented by Pope John, the Second Vatican Council, Pope Paul, and the Synods of Bishops. These social teachings are not unarguable and unchallengeable, but whatever one's final evaluation of them, they are central to Catholic justice education—hence the importance of their dialogue with Kohlberg.

3. Lawrence Kohlberg, "Education for Justice: A Modern Statement of the Platonic View," in *Moral Education: Five Lectures*, ed. N. Sizer and T. Sizer (Cambridge: Harvard University Press, 1970): 57–58.

4. The connection of Kohlberg and the Roman Catholic understanding of justice must be sought in the area of a morality discoverable by reason. This is not to say that faith does not modify and shape rational moral principles. I will show that it does at a number of points. If Catholic principles of justice are only known by revelation, then I do not see the relevance of Kohlberg to Catholic justice education. In the concrete, Catholic social teaching is an impure mixture of elements from reason and faith. I have no problem with this because the God who reveals is the God who created our minds and is the source of human morality ultimately. Complex methodological questions are raised by my paper and I realize they must be defended. I am prepared to do this, though here I can only give a sketch of how I would connect faith and reason in the moral realm.

5. Thus, the Thirty-Second General Congregation says the Gospel "demands a life in which the justice of the Gospel shines out in a willingness not only to recognize and respect the rights of all, especially the poor and the powerless, but also to work actively to secure these rights." "Our Mission Today," no. 18, in *Documents of the Thirty-Second General Congregation of the Society of Jesus* (Washington, D.C.: Jesuit Conference, 1975): 21. The traditional notion of justice as "rendering to each person what is due him or her" is workable when one specifies that what is due each person is what they have a right to, or so I would try to argue.

6. 1 John 3:16–17. And if this reference seems not enough to the point because it talks of love, see James 2:1–9 which is stated in terms of justice as fair treatment.

7. Reinhold Niebuhr, *Human Destiny*, The Nature and Destiny of Man: A Christian Interpretation, vol. 2 (New York: Scribners, 1943): 77. The quote is from H. Richard Niebuhr, *Social Sources of Denominationalism*, p. 249, where the original reference is given.

8. The whole issue of how faith comes to acknowledge the duty to influence social arrangements is a vast one. Ernst Troeltsch's magisterial *Social Teachings of the Christian Churches* has as its central theme this whole issue. I beg pardon for my almost cavalier treatment of this complex issue.

9. Pope Leo XIII, "Quod Apostolici Muneris," in *The Church Speaks to the Modern World*, edited with introduction by Etienne Gilson (Garden City, N.Y.: Doubleday, 1954): 192–93.

10. "Our Mission Today," no. 18, p. 26.

11. "Our Mission Today," nos. 31, 40, pp. 27, 29.

12. "The poor as a whole may receive less from these benefits than an individual needy person might secure by appealing to a given sensitive and opulent individual. But they will certainly receive more than if all of them were dependent upon nothing but vagrant, momentary, and capricious impulses of piety, dormant unless awakened by obvious need.

"This positive relation between rules of justice and the law of love must be emphasized in opposition to sentimental versions of the love commandment, according to which only the most personal individual and direct expressions of social obligation are manifestations of Christian *agape*." R. Niebuhr, *Human Destiny*, p. 250.

13. Lawrence Kohlberg, "From Is to Ought: How to Commit the Naturalistic Fallacy and Get Away with It in the Study of Moral Development," in *Cognitive Development and Epistemology*, ed. T. Mischel (New York: Academic Press, 1971): 144–63.

14. The issue of the unity or plurality of ultimate kinds of ethical principles is very difficult. I tend toward pluralism and so does Roman Catholic social theory. Kohlberg tries to unify all principled morality under justice. I am not sure this can be done and remain faithful to the richness of our actual moral experience. If pluralism is correct, Kohlberg needs to be supplemented, but without denying the justice principles he proposes.

15. Kohlberg, "Education for Justice," p. 67.

16. Ibid., p. 69.

17. Lawrence Kohlberg, "Why a Higher Stage Is a Better Stage," in *Collected Papers on Moral Development and Moral Education*, vol. 2 (Fall 1975): 1.

18. Pope Leo XIII, op. cit., pp. 6–7.

19. Second Vatican Council, "Gaudium et Spes," no. 29, in *Gospel of Peace and Justice*, ed. Gremillion, pp. 265–66.

20. Ibid., p. 264.

21. Pope John XXIII, "Pacem in Terris," no. 9, in *Gospel of Peace and Justice*, p. 203.

22. Kohlberg argues that "attachment and altruism presuppose self-love. The striving to satisfy another self presupposes the capacity or disposition to satisfy one's own self. Common sense assumes that the self (as body and center of activity) is loved intrinsically, not instrumentally. . . . It is this nucleus of self-love which is involved, also, in organizing attachment to others." "Stage and Sequence: The Cognitive Developmental Approach to Socialization," in *Handbook of Socialization Theory and Research*, ed. D. A. Goslin (New York: Rand McNally, 1969).

23. Joseph Rhodes, "Seeing the Bodies," *New York Times*, 25 May 1977, p. 35.

24. U.N. Declaration of Human Rights, Articles 3–11.

25. I say ironically because Kohlberg is a developmental psychologist and yet he rejects any notion of teleology.

26. Kohlberg, "From Is to Ought," p. 214.

27. "Pacem in Terris," no. 11, and "Mater et Magistra," no. 61, in *Gospel of Peace and Justice*, p. 156.

28. Kohlberg, "Education for Justice," p. 70.

29. "Pacem in Terris," nos. 21, 18.

30. "Populorum Progressio," no. 22, in *Gospel of Peace and Justice*, p. 394.

31. Ibid., no. 24, p. 394.

32. "Our theory holds that the motivation of social attachment, like the motivation of imitation, must be primarily defined in terms of effectance or competence motivation. The interest value of the activities of the other, his competence and social value, the relevance of his competence to the self's own action, and the general degree of similarity or likemindedness of the self and other are all major determinants of dependency or attachment. . . .

"As studied by social psychology, a social attachment or bond is conceived of as a relationship of sharing, communication, and cooperation (or reciprocity) between selves recognizing each other as other selves. . . .

"If, in contrast to physical theories, one takes the desire for a social bond with another *social self* as the primary 'motive' for attachment, then this desire derives from the same motivational sources as that involved in the child's own strivings for stimulation, for activity-mastery, and for self-esteem. Social motivation is motivation for shared stimulation, for shared activity, and shared competence and self-esteem." Kohlberg, "Stage and Sequence," p. 460.

33. Ibid., p. 388.

34. This is Edward Westermarck's formulation of Hobhouse's thesis, in Westermarck, *Ethical Relativity*, 1932 (Paterson, N.J.: Littlefield, Adams, 1960): 203.

35. William Frankena, *Ethics*, 2d ed. (Englewood Cliffs, N.J.: Prentice-Hall, 1973): 65.

36. The disposition, for example, to live a simple lifestyle so that others may have the goods and services they have a right to for a decent human life.

37. R. Niebuhr, *Human Destiny*, p. 248.

38. Ibid.

Part V: Criticism and Controversy

One test of a theory is its ability to face and address responsible criticism of its core assumptions and axioms. As the popularity of developmental theory has increased, so too has criticism of its central tenets and axioms. The criticisms of the theory have focused upon empirical, philosophic, and educational questions.

It should be noted that most criticisms of the developmental approach (as those of other social ideologies) reflect the assumptions held by the critic as well as those of the critiqued. In assessing any social criticism it is important to understand the moral, empirical, or political perspective of the critic. In that developmental theory makes a number of controversial, unusual assumptions in the areas of ontology (What is truth?), epistemology (How do we know?), and ethics, it is not surprising that the theory has been attacked from a variety of perspectives. The three critiques in this section exemplify some of the characteristic responses to developmental education. "Characteristic" here is used to imply that they exemplify a response to the theory from a particular philosophic vantage point.

Jack Fraenkel's "The Kohlberg Bandwagon " reflects the efforts of a professional social studies educator to refine what he sees as the exaggerated claims of Kohlbergian educators. Responding to Edwin Fenton's eleven claims of the developmental system, he suggests that the research foundation to support these claims may not be as strong as either Kohlberg or Fenton suggest. Philosophically, he challenges the claim of the ethical universality of Stage 6 principles, citing a number of cross-cultural examples. Empirically, he challenges the notion that stages are qualitatively different and that they necessarily follow in the same order. Educationally, he suggests that the demands of the developmental system may be unrealistic for most teachers and that the pedagogy may ignore strategies necessary to analyze the facts critical to solving many "historical" dilemmas and cases.

John Flowers reflects philosophic, methodological, and intervention concerns. He wonders whether Kohlberg has really avoided the naturalistic fallacy (i.e., has moved from empirical facts to moral truth—an illogical step for most philosophers) and whether or not the system reflects a giant teleological error (the idea that development necessarily moves towards some specified end). He raises serious questions about collecting evidence from interviewing and wonders about the ultimate tensions between the idea that some people have more mature ideas than others and about the premium placed on democracy in the Kohlberg theory. The paper is especially interesting in that it offers a "Skinnerian" interpretation for why children change their moral ideas. He suggests that the movement from Stages 1 to 4 may be explained by changes in reinforcement contingencies as well as by a theory of cognitive restructuring.

The final piece by Edmund Sullivan raises several issues about developmental moral education which have been consistently overlooked. According to Sullivan, Kohlberg's developmentalism is at once a psychological, philosophical, educational, political, and metaphysical statement. It is most generally accepted as an empirical, ethical, or pedagogical system. It is, however, according to Sullivan, weakest when considered as a political theory in that it is largely ahistorical and uncritically assumes the context of liberal democratic capitalistic society. Similarly, its rather narrow conception of rationalism leads to its acceptance by some as almost a psychological "civil religion."

However, all three critics unanimously agree that developmental education has contributed significant philosophic insight as well as practical import to educational theory. And I believe that the massive critical response to Kohlberg's work is a testament to the fact that the issues raised by developmental theory cut to the heart of education. This suggests that the power of the theory (or any other theory) may lie in the questions it asks as much as the answers it gives.

It is in a spirit of ongoing dialogue that these critical articles are offered, as well as two brief responses by myself and Columbia University professor, John Broughton.

The Kohlberg Bandwagon: Some Reservations

Jack R. Fraenkel, Professor of Interdisciplinary Studies, San Francisco State College.

The enthusiasm which Lawrence Kohlberg and his theory of moral stages have generated recently for a "moral reasoning" approach to values education has been quite impressive. Conferences, workshops, articles, even books dealing with the approach have proliferated. Lots of people are jumping on the bandwagon. Nevertheless, many others are wary of having teachers and curriculum developers jump too quickly on the moral stages bandwagon for a number of reasons. In this article, I wish to discuss briefly what some of these concerns are. I shall not review in detail the psychological research upon which Kohlberg's theory is based, but rather offer some comments about the nature of the theory itself, and the way in which some of the basic ideas in the theory have been extended into educational proposals and teaching models. Particular attention will be paid to some of the conclusions and suggestions offered by Edwin Fenton and Barry Beyer in their articles in this volume. The adequacy of the theory as a rationale for values education will then be considered.

The Basic Ideas of Kohlberg's Theory

Much of Kohlberg's thinking is rooted in the earlier thinking of John Dewey and the stage theorizing of Jean Piaget. James Rest has identified three fundamental ideas as lying at the heart of Kohlberg's theory. These he labeled "structural organization," "developmental sequence," and "interactionism."[1] *Structural organization* refers to the fact that developmental psychologists like Kohlberg consider the development of a person's cognitive structure—the way in which a person analyzes and interprets data, and makes decisions about personal and social problems—to be of crucial importance in that person's overall growth and development. *Developmental sequence* refers to the fact that Kohlberg and others who hold similar beliefs view the development of a person's cognitive structure in terms of stages, with the developmentally earlier and less complex "lower" stages being viewed as prerequisites to the "higher" stages. A major purpose of education for a developmentalist is to foster individual movement through these stages.

Kohlberg interviewed children and adults in a variety of cultures and identified three levels of moral development—the preconventional, the conventional, and the postconventional. Each of these levels contains two stages within it, for a total of six stages of moral reasoning. [See Appendix for synopsis of stages.]

The stage of moral reasoning that a particular individual has achieved is determined by having judges evaluate the person's responses to a hypothetical "moral dilemma"—a story in which an individual is faced with a moral choice. The stories are philosophical in nature and involve questions of responsibility, motive, or intention. An individual's stage is not determined by the nature of the choice that he or she makes with regard to a moral dilemma, but rather on the basis of the reasons the individual gives for the choice.

Like Piaget, Kohlberg not only argues that progression through these stages is sequential and invariant, but also that not very many people reach the highest stages. He has stated that only ten percent of adult Americans reason at the postconventional level.[2] Furthermore, the six stages are viewed as universal, holding true in all cultures, with each stage representing a higher level of reasoning than the one immediately preceding it. Though individuals do not skip stages, they may move through them either quickly or slowly, and an individual may be found half in and half out of a particular stage at a given time. As individuals progress through the stages, they become increasingly able to take in and synthesize more and different information than they could at earlier stages and to organize this information into an integrated and systematized framework. Kohlberg has also argued that higher-stage reasoning is morally better than lower-stage reasoning.

Interactionism refers to the process by which a person's cognitive structure is developed. As a child develops and notices certain regularities in his environment, he develops a pattern of behavior (a cognitive structure) to deal with these regularities—a way of thinking about the world. As the child grows and matures, however, he undergoes experiences for which his previously developed cognitive structure is inadequate; he thus seeks to revamp his way of thinking in order to make sense out of the new experience. When he finds a new way of thinking which enables him to understand the experience, his cognitive structure—his way of thinking about the world—is accordingly changed. An essential ingredient for intellectual growth—for the cognitive development of the child—therefore, is the opportunity to engage in a number of new and different experiences which will cause him or her to try to reorder his or her existing way of thinking and to seek out more adequate ways to organize and interpret data.

Some Reservations about the Theory

A first reservation lies in the argument for the universality of the stages. Even though Kohlberg states that the six stages he has identified hold for all nine of the cultures that he has examined, this is a rather small sample from which to infer the sweeping conclusion that the description of moral development for all people in all cultures has been found, or even to infer that the concept of justice, fundamental to the reasoning inherent in the higher stages (5 and 6), is endorsed by all cultures. Colin Turnbull, for example, in

The Mountain People, describes some of the behaviors of the Ik people of northeastern Uganda. The Ik at one time had been a peaceful society who cooperated to hunt for food, and who honored their dead with burial ceremonies. More recently, the Ugandan government decided to make the Ik's tribal grounds into a national park, and accordingly moved them to a new and very crowded living area on a steep mountainside. As a result of this move the Ik appear to have developed values which are the very antithesis of justice. For example, Turnbull observed a group of them laughing when a young child grabbed a hot coal from a fire and screamed in pain. Young Ik laughed with pleasure as they beat an elderly Ik with sticks and threw stones at him until he cried. An entire village came to the edge of a cliff that a blind woman had fallen over and laughed as she suffered in agony. As a two-year drought destroyed the Ik's crops and starvation set in, hoarding food and keeping it from one's family and from the elders of the tribe became honorable and was viewed as a mark of distinction. Old people were abandoned to die, and burial ceremonies to honor the dead were no longer held. After living with the Ik for eighteen months, Turnbull summed up his experiences in the following words: "The Ik teach us that our much vaunted human values are not inherent in humanity at all, but are associated only with a particular form of survival called society, and that all, even society itself, are luxuries that can be dispensed with."[3]

As Richard Peters has suggested, Kohlberg and his advocates appear to suffer from the belief that a morality based on the concept of justice is the only type of morality that is defensible. This puts him and his supporters in a somewhat difficult position, for they are forced to defend the proposition that justice is a universally held and admired concept. Unfortunately, there is just too much evidence to the contrary around for this to wash.

A second reservation lies in the assertion that higher-stage reasoning is not only different, but morally *better* than lower-stage reasoning. Such a notion (that higher means better) seems to be an impossible one to prove. If higher-stage reasoning is better it should contain or possess something which lower-stage reasoning does not. And if this is true, it is difficult to see how those reasoning at the lower stages would be able to understand the arguments of the individuals at the higher stages. And if they cannot understand the arguments, it is difficult to see why they would be inclined to accept such reasoning as being better than their own as a justification for various actions. If higher is not better, then there doesn't seem to be any justification for trying to "improve" the reasoning of children by helping them to move through the stages. Scriven argues in a similar vein:

> The put-up or shut-up question [is] whether someone at an "intermediate" stage of moral development is more wrong (or less right) on moral issues than someone at a "higher" stage. If the "lower" stage subjects are not demonstrably wrong, then there's no justification for trying to change them, i.e., for moral education. If they *are* demonstrably wrong, then there must be a proof that they are wrong, i.e., a proof of the increasingly objective nature of the moral standards (or processes) of higher stages; but no satisfactory proof of this has ever been produced. . . . Nor is this accidental. If there *were* such a proof, who could understand it and find it

> persuasive? Either the lower stages *can* [understand it], in which case it isn't a higher stage proof . . . and should be ignored by truly moral people . . . or the lower stages *can't* understand it, in which case *they* have no good reason to move "upward," in which case *we* have no justification for moving them against their will [or even] thinking they should be moved, since the proof . . . only proves the highest stages are highest to highest stagers. . . . The problem with stage theory, to sum it up, is that a proof that higher means better would either refute stage theory (if every intelligent person could appreciate it) or would be circular—that is, self-refuting or self-serving.[4]

Thirdly, since Kohlberg himself estimates that a majority of people do not get beyond Stage 4, it would seem important to devise ways to get everyone up to and firmly entrenched at this stage. Peters writes "[Since] few [individuals] are likely to emerge beyond Kohlberg's Stages 3 and 4, it is important that our fellow citizens should be well bedded down at one or the other of these stages. The policeman cannot always be present, and if I am lying in the gutter after being robbed it is somewhat otiose to speculate at what stage the mugger is. My regret must surely be that he had not at least got a conventional morality well instilled in him."[5]

The conventional level (Stages 3–4) of reasoning is important for another reason. "[A]t this stage the child learns from the inside, as it were, what it is to follow a rule. Unless he has learned this well (whatever it means!), the notion of following his own rules at the autonomous stage is unintelligible."[6] Children must understand and appreciate the importance of rules in general for both personal and societal survival (Can you imagine a society existing without at least some rules?), as well as what can happen when rules are disregarded and/or taken lightly by large numbers of people, before the idea of developing and following one's own rules begins to make any sense. It is certainly important to realize that rules may be unjust, but the question of *when* and *whether* to disobey an unjust (or any) rule is an important one to explore *explicitly* with children, using a variety of incidents and analogies. We surely do not want to develop in the young a tendency to take rules too lightly (nor, of course, to view them as inviolate and absolute), and this can only be avoided by helping them to realize the value of, as well as to practice, following rules which at times go against their inclinations. Indeed, a key element of morality, it seems to me, lies in the understanding that "resistance to temptation" can be rewarding in its own right. Neither Kohlberg, nor any of his associates, has emphasized the importance of getting as many students as possible to the level of conventional morality. (Fenton's statement that "we should aim to raise the level of moral thinking of all children"[7] to Stage 4, however, is a hopeful sign in this regard.) As yet, however, few specific strategies for developing in children a sense of the importance of rules (and, more importantly, a realization of the fact that giving in to one's inclinations frequently brings neither happiness nor satisfaction) have appeared.

Fourthly, the theory places rather unrealistic demands on classroom teachers once they *do* engage students in moral discussions. Kohlberg has stated, "If moral communications are to be effective, the developmental level of the teacher's verbalizations must be one step above the level of the child."[8] If what Kohlberg says is true, this requirement presents at least two problems. Since Kohlberg has stated that only ten percent of the population reaches Stages 5 or 6, the laws of probability suggest that there are many teachers who themselves reason at the lower stages, and who accordingly are likely to come in contact with students reasoning at stages higher than their own. Will such teachers be able even to understand, let alone help, such students? How can a teacher who reasons at Stage 3, for example, be expected to present a Stage 5 argument to a Stage 4 student (so as to foster stage growth) if he or she cannot understand what such an argument is?

Furthermore, even if enough Stage 5 teachers could be found, they would still face a considerable amount of practical difficulty as they interact with students, no matter what the stages of the students may be. Since intellectual development and chronological age are not always the same, most teachers are likely to find that they have children at a variety of stages within their classrooms. It would probably be most unusual, in fact, to find a classroom in which all of the students therein were at the same stage. Theoretically, at least, this is all to the good, for the divergence of viewpoints would promote more conflict and variety of opinion in class discussions. But remember that Kohlberg argues that children must be exposed to a stage of reasoning one stage higher than their current stage if stage development is to be fostered. To do this, a teacher must listen to several responses of each student, figure out what stage of reasoning these responses suggest, and then either frame an appropriate "one stage higher" response during on-going class discussions, or mix the students with others who are reasoning one stage higher so that they may hear their arguments. This seems to be asking an awful lot from busy classroom teachers.

Some Reservations about Fenton's Generalizations concerning Kohlberg's Research

In his article in this volume, Professor Fenton offers eleven conclusions which he feels Kohlberg's research supports. A careful examination of these claims, however, leads one to believe that Fenton has not been critical enough in his examination and analysis of this research. Not only are Kohlberg's arguments for the universality of his stages and the notion that "higher is better" open to question, but many of the other conclusions that Fenton draws are not supported convincingly by Kohlberg's research. First of all, the fact that there really are *six* stages has by no means been established. Only three individuals have been identified as being at Stage 6—Kohlberg himself, one of his graduate students, and Martin Luther King.[9]

Secondly, it is not even agreed that all of the stages are qualitatively different. Norman Williams, for example, has suggested on the basis of data that he has collected, that Stages 3 and 4 appear to be alternative or parallel rather than sequential steps in a person's development.

Thirdly, even the notion of stages is challenged. Social learning psychologists like W. Mischel, for instance, argue that regular changes over time in the moral judgments of children may be due simply to the fact that as children grow older, they are reacted to differently by most of the adults with whom they come in contact. Since parents and other adults talk differently to young children and adolescents, it should not be surprising that verbal responses of 1st and 2nd graders are different from those of teenagers.

Fourthly, Fenton's claim that "the most reliable way to determine a stage of moral thought is through a moral interview" depends on what he means by the word "interview." Rest, for example, has developed an objective test (the Defining Issues Test) which asks students to rank prototypic statements of the "crucial issue" involved in a dilemma, from which he then draws inferences about their level of moral reasoning. Rest presents data which show that his test compares favorably with Kohlberg's test with regard to power of results, replications, and sample sizes in the studies conducted. Rest has concluded that "there are almost limitless formats for collecting moral judgment data."[10] Furthermore, Fenton's statement that "trained scorers show 90 percent agreement in identifying stage" is not supported by Kohlberg's own research. In his most recent scoring system, Kohlberg (1974) reports: "Interjudge agreement on this data was only 66 percent for major stage agreement." That's a long way from ninety!

Fifthly, Fenton's claim that all people move through these stages in an "invariant sequence" is contradicted by Elizabeth L. Simpson, who points out that the research to which Kohlberg appeals has only demonstrated this among Stages 2, 3, and 4. And the claim that a person "reasons predominately at one stage of thought" seems more a preferred way of looking at the responses of people to moral dilemmas than a proven fact. Norman Bull, N. Williams and S. Williams, and Derek Wright have suggested alternative models, each of which is supported by a considerable amount of data.

Lastly, Fenton's assertion that "deliberate attempts to facilitate stage change in schools through educational programs have been successful" needs to be qualified somewhat. In some of the studies that have been cited by Kohlberg and others, many students showed no stage movement at all. In Kohlberg's 1969 study, for example, which is frequently cited as the basis for longitudinal trends in stage movement, just about one-third (32.6%) of the students involved showed an overall upward stage change, while only eight out of the total sample of forty-three showed one-step upward change. In the study which she conducted in 1973, C. Holstein found that only seventeen students out of a total sample of fifty-two moved up one stage over a three-year period, with some thirty-three (63.5%) showing some general upward movement. And in the studies in Boston and Pittsburgh which Kohlberg describes in his 1975 *Phi Delta Kappan* article, he states that only "about half" of the teachers involved (24) were able to stimulate upward stage movement. And even that was only from one-quarter to one-half a stage.

The point of all this is not to discourage teachers from thinking about stage theory and research. There is much in Kohlberg's work that is extremely interesting and useful. I have used much of it myself. But I am wary at this point of being too sure about what we know—of offering a neat bundle of eleven (or however many) generalizations about moral development research without at the same time pointing out those aspects of these research findings which are open to question or alternative interpretation.

I think it particularly important for those who review research findings and discuss their implications for social studies education to indicate what we don't know—that is, what questions such research leaves unanswered. This would help the profession in general to view conclusions based on research findings for what they almost always are—hypotheses demanding continual investigation and refinement rather than statements of established fact.

Reservations about Some of the Educational Suggestions Based on the Theory

There is no question, I think, that the influence of Kohlberg's theory has been considerable. As Rest has mentioned, "Educational programs with such a venerable lineage (Dewey, Piaget, Kohlberg, and so forth) have created interest because of the intellectual heft behind them and the promise of initiating something more than a superficial, piecemeal, short-lived fad."[11] Nevertheless, the manner in which the basic ideas inherent in the theory have been extended into proposals for teaching raises a number of issues and questions which, at least so far, have remained unattended to by moral reasoning advocates. Let us consider a few of them here.

First is the issue of what Rest calls "optimal curriculum match." As mentioned earlier, a major goal of education so far as Kohlberg and other developmentalists are concerned is to *stimulate* development through the stages of moral reasoning. If this can be done, educators would have some very useful information. Rest writes:

> The characterization of the highest stage of development gives a psychological analysis of some competence—e.g., Piaget's stage of formal operations gives us an analysis of what it means to be logical; Kohlberg's "Stage 6" provides a description of what mature moral judgment consists. . . . Note that there is much more specificity here in a characterization of cognitive structure than the honorific labels often used to define educational objectives (such as "creative," "self-actualized," "good-citizen," and "well-adjusted," and so forth).[12]

Furthermore, if the educator has a step-by-step description of the development of some competence, then he has a means of ordering progress (knowing which changes are progressive), of locating people along this course of development, and therefore of anticipating which experiences the student will most likely respond to and from which he will profit. The adage that the teacher should meet the student at the student's level can be given precise and operational meaning if the course of development is defined and the student's level can be assessed. Knowing the course of development enables one to optimize the match between children and curricula and also serves as a guide for sequencing curriculum. Accordingly, at the propitious time, problems that are manageable yet challenging can be introduced to create an interesting learning experience in itself, and, at the same time, to serve to set up the prerequisite components for problems at the next level.[13]

The chief strategy advocated by educators specifically interested in furthering moral development in social studies classrooms, however, is the discussion of moral dilemmas (Galbraith and Jones, 1975; Beyer, 1976). While these dilemmas do provoke controversy and the sorts of questions included in the strategy do encourage students to analyze alternatives (though the *explicit* and *sustained* consideration of *consequences* appears minimal), these writers do not pay much attention to the notions of optimal curriculum match and curriculum sequencing mentioned by Rest. They do not consider the fact that different kinds of dilemma issues may be more profitable (in the sense of promoting interest and discussion) at different grade levels; that dilemmas which deal with stage-specific kinds of concerns may be called for in order to appeal to students who are reasoning at different stages; or that one dilemma might be used to build on another so as to further cognitive growth. (The idea of using alternative dilemmas—with the original situation changed to some degree—as a follow-up to the original discussion, however, is a step in this direction. See Galbraith and Jones, 1975, p. 19.) The notion of sequencing dilemmas is not discussed.

One gets the uneasy feeling at times that the advocates of moral discussions have gotten carried away by their own enthusiasm. For example, Beyer makes a number of statements which are either unsupported testimonials (e.g., "the most productive discussion involves small group discussions followed by a discussion involving the entire class"); value judgments (e.g., "a significant number of students should favor one course of action, while others should favor another"); or unrealistic in what they propose (e.g., "After students hear or see the dilemma, the teacher should ask questions in order to help students to clarify the circumstances involved in the dilemma, define terms, identify the characteristics of the central character, and state the exact nature of the dilemma and the action choice open to the central character. *Little more than five minutes** need be devoted to this part of the strategy.").[14]

Indeed, Beyer's assertion that a program of moral discussions will improve learning skills, improve self-esteem, and improve attitudes toward school seems to be a bit strong for even the converted to swallow whole. No evidence is provided to support this sweeping claim. Why should participating in a moral discussion (or any discussion, for that matter) *ipso facto* help students develop listening skills or improve their self-esteem? Discussions can be conducted poorly or well; the mere assertion of their value does not improve a person's skills or change his or her attitudes. It would seem more likely that the manner in which a discussion is conducted would be the crucial factor involved.

A word, too, is in order about the nature of the dilemmas themselves. Some of the ones that I have seen which Kohlberg, Fenton, Beyer, Galbraith, et al., cite are rather narrow in scope (e.g., "Should Jill give Sharon's name to the Security Officer?") and affect only one or a few individuals (e.g., "Should a Christian girl in Nazi Germany break the law and jeopardize her family by hiding her Jewish friend from the Gestapo?"). This is apparently intentional; Beyer states that a moral dilemma "should be as simple as possible. The dilemma should involve only a few characters in a relatively uncomplicated situation which students can grasp readily. Complicated dilemmas confuse students who are then forced to spend time clarifying facts and circumstances rather than discussing reasons for suggested actions."

This sort of rationale can be objected to on a number of counts. First, dilemmas in real life are rarely simple. Secondly, students need to be exposed to a wide variety of different kinds of issues and dilemmas as they move through the grades, particularly ones which can affect the lives of many people, so that they will become aware of the sorts of problems which exist in the world (e.g., "Should the President of the United States 'send in the marines' against the oil-producing nations if they will not supply us with oil?"). Thirdly, one wonders how students are to learn to sort out and analyze the facts involved in complicated issues they will face in real life (e.g., abortion, taxation,

*Italics added.

local control of schools, euthanasia, jury duty, busing, drug usage, environmental contamination, the right of public employees to strike, etc.) if they get little practice in doing so in schools? And fourthly, students *need* practice (and lots of it) in "clarifying facts and circumstances" if they are to find out about the nature of the world in which they live.

The notion of sequencing dilemmas in some fashion seems in order here, with one possibility being that of making them increasingly more complex, abstract, and difficult as students progress through the grades. Such a scheme might entail students in the elementary grades being presented with fairly simple interpersonal and intrapersonal conflicts revolving around such concepts as fairness, reward, punishment, responsibility, authority, and conscience. As students move on into junior and senior high school, they can at each grade level be presented with dilemmas involving larger and larger groups of people, including governments and international agencies. Such dilemmas, not only interpersonal, but also intergovernmental and global (involving more than two governments), could focus on such additional concepts as honor, duty, contract, property, civil liberties, and obligation. This might be one way of providing more breadth in the types of dilemmas to which students are exposed, and also of promoting the more fundamental, long-term, and cumulative change with which developmentalists are concerned.

It also should be pointed out that the strategy for guiding moral discussions suggested by Beyer and Galbraith and Jones is only one of many possibilities that might be used. The steps which these authors present do offer teachers some concrete ideas for getting a moral discussion started in the classroom, but care must be taken not to infer that this is the "one and only" way to go about the matter. Not only do other models exist for teachers to consider, but also they can be encouraged to create their own strategies and models when and where appropriate.

Furthermore, we are not even sure that it is the discussion of the dilemmas themselves which brings about stage movement. It is certainly conceivable that a sensitive and concerned teacher, one who continually engages students in conversation and asks them questions and lets them know by his or her comments and actions that he or she is interested in what they have to say, may be the independent variable in this regard. The discussion of moral dilemmas may be irrelevant. Perhaps the discussion of non-moral controversial issues would do just as well. At this point, we just don't know.

More than anything else, the discussion of moral dilemmas seems to be a very limiting sort of strategy to recommend. In the first place, discussion does not work very well or for very long with children below the age of ten or so. You simply can't have much of an intellectual discussion with third and fourth graders. Other ways of presenting information about moral relationships and dilemmas, such as the use of models and concrete examples, must be used. Secondly, the use of case studies, which is what moral dilemmas are, focuses on specific instances rather than general principles. This often presents a problem in that only a few children in the class see the particular issue involved in the case as interesting or having applicability to them. An emphasis instead on more general principles (e.g., that one often has to make exceptions to rules), however, allows reference to a large number of examples by both teacher and students, thereby increasing interest and involvement on the part of the whole class. And finally, the likelihood of several *different* types of alternative suggestions being proposed by a class of students reasoning at Stages 2 or 3 (which Beyer and Fenton say is where most high school students are likely to be) does not seem to be very great. A more appropriate strategy, it seems to me, would be to encourage teachers (and curriculum developers and publishers) to not only present dilemmas to students in interesting and exciting ways and in a variety of formats (printed, oral, visual), but also to present them with a range of alternative solutions (at various stage levels) for resolving the dilemmas. As a part of the discussion of the dilemma, the teacher could then include a systematic consideration of the various alternatives. This would not in any way preclude, of course, having students suggest their own alternatives in addition to those presented. I am struck by Clive Beck's notion that perhaps one reason that a lot of people do not develop morally is because better alternatives have not occurred to them. They continue to react in conventional ways frequently because they perceive no other way of reacting. The above suggestion would, in Beck's words, "extend their imagination."

Kohlberg's Theory and Values Education

Is the rationale behind the moral reasoning approach a sufficient one for values education? The answer to this question, I think, must be no. Certainly the development of a child's ability to think rationally about moral issues is important. Indeed, it is very important. And there is no denying that insufficient attention has been paid to the development of reasoning in general, let alone moral reasoning in particular, in our classrooms in the past. But children need to develop not only intellectually but also emotionally if they are to become fully functioning and psychologically whole human beings. In fact, it is becoming clear to a lot of us that intellectual and emotional development are interdependent—that oftentimes the failure of someone to grasp the meaning of something is due to a lack of emotional sensitivity on his or her part. As Beck points out: ". . . what is needed is an *interactive* approach. Often we try to help a child understand a particular aspect of ethical theory; for example, we try to help him understand the need for reciprocal relationships (as in promise-keeping and formation of contracts); and we find that we fail, because there is a lack of sensitivity, a lack of concern, a lack of emotional development—a lack of *non-cognitive* development—which prevents him from having this cognitive insight. On the other hand, there are cases where we try to help a person become more sensitive to other people and their needs and more disposed to help them, and the [problem] is his lack of *understanding* of the place of concern for others in a person's life."[15]

The development of such an interactive approach, it seems to me, is a matter of the highest priority. What sorts of content and strategies that such an approach should contain, of course, is at this point an open question. Also open are the questions of how the content should be sequenced and when and where the strategies should be used. To be able to answer these questions in any kind of intelligent fashion, we are going to have to get clear in our own minds and in the profession about what the term "values education" means. What does it mean to say that someone is educated in values? What sorts of skills, attitudes, knowledge, etc., does such a person possess that others not so educated do not? How do we determine the degree to which a person is becoming educated in values—in short, how do we assess growth in this regard? And what specifically can teachers do to help students become "values educated"?

The ideas of Kohlberg and his supporters provide us with valuable food for thought in this regard. So, too, does the work of those who have proposed approaches which differ from Kohlberg's (Raths, Harmin and Simon, 1966; Oliver and Shaver, 1966; Newmann and Oliver, 1970; Hunt and Metcalf, 1968; Fraenkel, 1973; Scriven, 1966, 1971, 1975; Shaver, 1976). But none of these approaches is the last word on the subject. We need to have lots of models and strategies proposed and then lots of research which tests and compares the effectiveness of these models and strategies in promoting both short- and long-range emotional and intellectual development. What is lacking at present is any sort of educational theory which *integrates* psychological notions about *both* intellectual and emotional development, together with a philosophical consideration of what values education should be about. This would appear to be a goal toward which all who are interested in seeing a comprehensive program of values education implemented in social studies classrooms might direct their efforts.

Notes

1. James Rest, "Developmental Psychology as a Guide to Value Education: A Review of 'Kohlbergian Programs,'" p. 241.

2. Lawrence Kohlberg, "The Cognitive-Developmental Approach to Moral Education," p. 671.

3. Colin Turnbull, *The Mountain People*.

4. Michael Scriven, "Cognitive Moral Education," p. 690.

5. Richard Peters, "A Reply to Kohlberg," p. 678.

6. Ibid.

7. Edwin Fenton, "Moral Education: The Research Findings."

8. Lawrence Kohlberg, "The Concepts of Developmental Psychology as the Central Guide to Education: Examples from Cognitive, Moral, and Psychological Education," p. 42.

9. Lawrence Kohlberg, "From Is to Ought: How to Commit the Naturalistic Fallacy and Get Away with It in the Study of Moral Development."

10. James Rest, "The Validity of Tests of Moral Judgment," p. 112.

11. Rest, "Developmental Psychology as a Guide to Value Education," p. 241.

12. Ibid., pp. 243–44.

13. Ronald Galbraith and Thomas Jones, "Teaching Strategies for Moral Dilemmas: An Application of Kohlberg's Theory to the Social Studies Classroom," p. 19.

14. Barry Beyer, "Conducting Moral Discussions in the Classroom."

15. Clive Beck, "The Development of Moral Judgment," pp. 41–42.

Bibliography

Beck, Clive. "The Development of Moral Judgment." In *Developing Value Constructs in Schooling: Inquiry into Process and Product*, edited by J. A. Phillips, Jr. Worthington, Ohio: Ohio Association for Supervision and Curriculum Development, 1972.

Beyer, Barry K. "Conducting Moral Discussions in the Classroom." *Social Education* 40 (April 1976):194–202.

Bull, Norman J. *Moral Judgment from Childhood to Adolescence*. London: Routledge & Kegan Paul, 1969.

Dewey, John. *Democracy and Education: An Introduction to the Philosophy of Education*. New York: Macmillan, 1916.

Dewey, John, and Tufts, James H. *Ethics*. 1908. New York: Henry Holt, 1932.

Fenton, Edwin. "Moral Education: The Research Findings." *Social Education*, April 1976, pp. 188–93.

Fraenkel, Jack R. *Helping Students Think and Value: Strategies for Teaching the Social Studies*. Englewood Cliffs, N.J.: Prentice-Hall, 1973.

Galbraith, Ronald E., and Jones, Thomas M. "Teaching Strategies for Moral Dilemmas: An Application of Kohlberg's Theory to the Social Studies Classroom." *Social Education* 39 (January 1975):16–22.

Holstein, Constance B. "Moral Judgment in Early Adolescence and Middle Ages: A Longitudinal Study." Paper presented at the biennial meeting of the Society for Research in Child Development, 29 March–1 April 1973, Philadelphia, Pennsylvania.

Hunt, Maurice P., and Metcalf, Lawrence E. *Teaching High School Social Studies*. New York: Harper & Row, 1968.

Kohlberg, Lawrence. "The Cognitive-Developmental Approach to Moral Education." *Phi Delta Kappan*, June 1975, pp. 670–77.

Kohlberg, Lawrence. "Comments on 'The Development of Moral Thought' by Kurtines and Greif." Unpublished paper, 1974.

Kohlberg, Lawrence. "The Concepts of Developmental Psychology as the Central Guide to Education: Examples from Cognitive, Moral, and Psychological Education." In *Psychology and the Process of Schooling in the Next Decade: Alternative Conceptions*. Minneapolis: University of Minnesota Audio-Visual Extension, 1971.

Kohlberg, Lawrence. "From Is to Ought: How to Commit the Naturalistic Fallacy and Get Away with It in the Study of Moral Development." In *Cognitive Development and Epistemology*, edited by T. Mischel. New York: Academic Press, 1971.

Kohlberg, Lawrence, and Kramer, R. "Continuities and Discontinuities in Childhood and Adult Moral Development." *Human Development*, 1969, pp. 93–120.

Kurtines, William, and Greif, Esther B. "The Development of Moral Thought: Review and Evaluation of Kohlberg's Approach." *Psychological Bulletin*, August 1974, pp. 453–70.

Mischel, W. "A Cognitive Social Learning Approach to Morality and Self-Regulation." In *Moral Development and Behavior: Theory, Research, and Social Issues*, edited by T. Lickona. New York: Holt, Rinehart & Winston, 1976.

Newmann, Fred M., and Oliver, Donald W. *Clarifying Public Controversy: An Approach to Teaching Social Studies*. Boston: Little, Brown & Co., 1970.

Oliver, Donald W., and Shaver, James P. *Teaching Public Issues in the High School*. Boston: Houghton Mifflin, 1966.

Peters, Richard S. "Moral Development: A Plea for Pluralism." In *Cognitive Development and Epistemology*, edited by T. Mischel. New York: Academic Press, 1971.

Peters, Richard S. "A Reply to Kohlberg." *Phi Delta Kappan*, June 1975.

Piaget, Jean. *The Moral Judgment of the Child*. London: Routledge & Kegan Paul, 1932.

Raths, Louis E.; Harmin, Merrill; and Simon, Sidney B. *Values and Teaching*. Columbus, Ohio: Merrill, 1966.

Rest, James R. "Developmental Psychology as a Guide to Value Education: A Review of 'Kohlbergian' Programs." *Review of Educational Research*, Spring 1974, pp. 241–59.

Rest, James R. "The Validity of Tests of Moral Judgment," in J. R. Meyer, et al., *Values Education: Theory/Practice/Problems/Prospects*. Waterloo, Ontario: Wilfrid Laurier University Press, 1975.

Scriven, Michael. "Cognitive Moral Education." *Phi Delta Kappan*, June 1975, pp. 689–94.

Scriven, Michael. *Student Values as Educational Objectives*. Boulder, Colo.: Social Science Education Consortium, 1966.

Scriven, Michael. *Value Claims in the Social Sciences*. Boulder, Colo.: Social Science Education Consortium, 1966.

Scriven, Michael. "Values and the Valuing Process." Unpublished paper, 1971.

Shaver, James P. *Facing Value Decisions: Rationale Building for Teachers*. Belmont, Calif.: Wadsworth, 1976.

Simpson, Elizabeth L. "Moral Development Research: A Case Study of Scientific Cultural Bias." *Human Development* 17 (1974):81–106.

Turnbull, Colin. *The Mountain People*. New York: Simon & Schuster, 1972.

Williams, Norman, and Williams, Sheila. *The Moral Development of Children*. London: Macmillan & Co., 1970.

Wright, Derek. *The Psychology of Moral Behavior*. Baltimore, Md.: Penguin Books, 1971.

A Behavioral Psychologist's View of Developmental Moral Education

John V. Flowers, Assistant Professor of Social Ecology,
University of California at Irvine.

Philosophic Issues

It may seem strange that a behavioral psychologist would initially concentrate on the philosophic assumptions of Lawrence Kohlberg's conceptualization of moral development; however, Kohlberg's theory is primarily philosophical and only secondarily empirical and psychological. Consequently, when inspecting the present theory of moral development, the first issues that should be addressed are the philosophic ones, irrespective of the vantage point of the critic.

The reader should be aware that any system of philosophy has problems of explanation inherent in the very structure of philosophic explanation. To completely avoid logical criticism, a philosophic system would have to be totally formal and content-free, i.e., positivistic. Any philosophy that includes content (assertions about the real world), whether it be Kohlberg's or a behaviorist's, is subject to criticism from a system with conflicting content. Any system with content is also subject to criticism from strictly logical, content-free systems. The crucial issue in the development of a constructive system of philosophy is not that of avoiding all possible errors of thought, but of recognizing potentially erroneous explanations and minimizing errors. In any philosophic system, there is a tenuous balance between increased content and potential error on one side and totally formal or rigorously empirical and specialized results on the other.

The first major philosophic problem in Kohlberg's theory of moral development is his use of the naturalistic fallacy, i.e., arguing from what *is* to what *ought* to be. Kohlberg is well aware of this problem and addresses it clearly. However, his arguments are not convincing. Simply put, he argues that invariant stages are empirically true and that higher stage thought resolves moral dilemmas in ways that are not possible by the use of lower stage thought. The first part of this argument states that the "is," in fact, exists, which in no way helps get to any "ought." The second part of this argument merely shifts the focus of the naturalistic fallacy from the stage of thinking to those processes which resolve problems in ways that are presumed to be better.

Philosophically, to avoid the naturalistic fallacy, Kohlberg would have to demonstrate that people should resolve problems in precisely the manner accomplished by the use of higher stage thinking. Instead, Kohlberg employs words like "problem solving," "justice," and "democracy" as though such words proved that people ought to think in the specified ways. Although such words have great emotional appeal, assuming them to be "best" simply because they sound good does not justify his naturalistic leap. The persuasive power of Kohlberg's argument is clear. However, Kohlberg is specifically saying that this theory is not one of persuasional ethics; it describes a metaphysical reality.

A second philosophic problem involves Kohlberg's use of teleology (the idea that development *necessarily* moves in a particular direction) as an explanation of the developmental process. According to Kohlberg, individuals prefer to solve problems at the highest stage available to them, and when presented with a conflict, they will often be stimulated to choose the thinking process of the next higher stage for problem resolution. This argument is superficially stated in causal terms, i.e., conflict causes stage progression. In a causal explanation, the present is determined by what has gone before; therefore, the future can vary, depending on the causes. In a teleological system, the future is not free to occur in any way that deviates from a predetermined path. The invariant hierarchy of the stage theory clearly makes this system teleological. While theory postulates definite stimuli for change in thinking, the changes in thinking, when they occur, are not determined by their causes. Changes are predetermined by a view of the future rather than the past.

The problem with such a teleological assumption is that when the assumption is used to explain, it fails. A teleology simply assumes a future that cannot be explained unless the assumption itself can be explained. In moral development theory, not only is the teleological assumption itself not explained, it is hidden by rhetoric (i.e., presented causally). Given the historical failure of teleological explanations in the area of science, this philosophical obfuscation of empirical data is understandable, but it is not helpful.

When reviewing the present institutional interventions being done by the theorists of moral development, the question becomes, Is the democratic school or prison the goal of moral development, or is the goal some present and future action by the convicts or students? In general, this is a question of means-ends. Is moral development a means to some end, or is it an end in itself? If it is a means to some end, what is the end? If it is an end in itself, how is that end justified? Repeatedly, this reader is confused by what appear to be shifting goals of the theory of moral development. Sometimes the goal is to make an ideal institution, and sometimes it is to help people cope outside the institution.

If moral development is an end in itself, Kohlberg's system is stronger philosophically, but it is not only weaker in terms of psychology (the study of behavior including the behavior of the mind), it is critically weak as a theory of social intervention. If intervention is intended, the problems of the dualistic interaction of mind/body (how mind affects body) must be addressed.

There is one further philosophic issue that is left unaddressed by the theory of moral development. If the stage structure of thought is invariant and if stage progression is a consequence of moral conflict, it would seem that people are not free with regard to the type of thought they use to solve moral dilemmas. This problem is obviously associated with the teleology mentioned above. It could be argued that since conflict does not automatically produce moral progression, people are free to progress or not. Such an argument merely shifts the freedom question to the focus of the individual's choice, i.e., why do some people choose to change their thinking and others choose not to? It could also be argued that people are still free to have different thoughts at the same stage of thinking, or that they are free to act differently regardless of thought. While such a dualism preserves human freedom, it makes it nonsensical to apply moral development as a social intervention.

If freedom is asserted to exist in the stage process itself (admittedly anticipating a reply to a previously unaddressed question), why do people axiomatically choose the "higher" (or better) stage when able to do so? To state that their "free" choice is based on the fact that higher stage thought resolves problems in a "better" way and that such thought makes them more "just" is simply to give appealing labels to the descriptors of humanity's determinism.

Methodological Issues

In addition to the basic philosophical problems, there are also problems that arise on methodological grounds. Does the "is," in fact, exist? Are there stages of moral thought? If action is important, is there a connection of words to thought to present and future action? To illustrate, Kohlberg identifies few examples of persons who are demonstrably Stage 6. Similarly, the documented connection between judgment and action is, at best, tenuous.

A second methodological problem involves the interview process itself. Not only is the interviewer probably selectively reinforcing the interviewee for the interviewer's desired response, the interviewer is also probing for a scorable response. Thus, if an interviewer gets a persuasional ethical response (I will act as if an ethical principle exists because I prefer ethical action, and even though I recognize that ethical principles do not exist *per se*, I want to persuade people to act ethically), which is unscorable in Kohlberg's categories, the interviewer presumably persists until a scorable response is obtained. Probing for a scorable response both misrepresents an individual's thought processes and loses any possible deviations that might contradict the theory.

Additionally, an individual's response within the relatively safe environment of a moral interview and the same individual's response within a stressful situation may be very different. Even if there are connections between stage thought processes, thought, action, and future action, the thought process engaged in during a stressful real dilemma may not be the same as that engaged in during an interview.

All of the above methodological problems are subsumed under a major methodological error: attempting to prove instead of disprove. The scientific method does not prove (Popper, 1959). Using the scientific method, a scientist hypothesizes relationships and then attempts to disprove them. Relationships derived from data are utilized only as long as they are not disproved. In setting up a methodology on the basis of philosophic assumptions and not attending to contradictory data, Kohlberg joins the majority of social science researchers in committing this critical methodological error.

Theoretical Issues

The methodological problems, especially the problems within the interview process, lead to some theoretical difficulties. If the basic data are unreliable, it is impossible to determine if the results are valid. Even if the results were reliable, the issue of validity would still have to be addressed. The theory that the stages are invariant is very problematic. For this theory to be supported, the sequence of moral stages of thought must be invariant under any form of cultural conditioning. Kohlberg is aware of this and uses cross cultural data to support his theory.

The sequential development postulated by Kohlberg through Stage 4 probably does occur frequently. That individuals first learn to respond to punishment makes sense, since tissue damage is an ultimate threat to survival. Reinforcement beyond the termination of pain and threat is not pursued until the organism is safe. While both avoidance of pain and the seeking of pleasure are innate, learning Stage 2 responses is predicated on the fact that the organism continues to exist, i.e., it has learned Stage 1 responding. It is true that most people would learn to respond to other people and secondary reinforcement after learning how to respond to immediate punishment and reinforcement. Thus Stage 3 would normally follow 1 and 2, just as learning to respond to larger groups of individuals (Stage 4) would probably follow learning to respond to fewer people (Stage 3). Thus a learning theorist might agree that in most situations individuals would develop from avoiding punishment to seeking reinforcement and from limited interpersonal reciprocity to social reciprocity.

However, the crux of Kohlberg's theory lies in Stages 5 and 6. Kohlberg's own data on the increase of uncodable ethically relativistic thinkers in the late 1960s is itself evidence against the invariant stage sequence of thinking. In at least one culture, our own, the "invariant" stage sequence changed with a cultural change, something the theory maintains cannot occur.

The above data, Kohlberg's own, raises questions about still another aspect of the theory. Kohlberg's theory asserts that moral thinking is not situational, i.e., people always respond at the two highest available levels of thought. This responding is obviously not situational, it is dispositional. It is clear, given the interview process stated above, that a moral interviewer would be unlikely to find Stage 2 thinking with one dilemma and Stage 4 with another, since the interviewer probes for consistency in a stress reduced condition.

The rise in ethical relativism (initially scored Stage 2) in the late 1960s was data that the Kohlberg methodology could not ignore. The individuals were not merely adopting alternate stages in different situations. The cultural situation was producing individuals who adopted an out-of-order thinking process to most moral dilemmas. This data strongly indicates that moral responding is indeed situational, responding as it did to a clear situational change in the social climate. Kohlberg's response to this data was to create a new transitional stage to preserve the invariant stage theory and continue to support his theory of non-situational responding. The fact that individuals who responded in ethically relativistic ways changed over time to respond at a Stage 5 level has no bearing on the theoretical issue, since all stages are viewed as logically transitional to the next. Such a transition stage should either always be present or never be present. In the theory as proposed, no stage should merely be a convenient slot in which to place inconvenient data.

Beyond the theoretical problems of the invariant stage sequence and non-situational responding, there are unique problems with the way that Kohlberg addresses the issue of social change. Kohlberg is quite correct in saying that Stage 4 thinking does not facilitate social change. He is quite incorrect, however, in assuming that the thinking of Stages 1 through 3 cannot initiate social change. While Stage 4 thinking is social, Stages 1 through 3 could and probably do represent thinking processes to which the society has to respond in novel ways. Although it is obvious from Kohlberg's theory that individuals at Stages 1, 2, and 3 are not solving problems as "well" as these individuals would with higher stage thinking, it is not at all clear that when a society responds with Stage 4 thinking to such individuals, the society might not be improving itself. Social improvement does not logically necessitate thinking above Stage 4. This is not to say that such thinking processes do not exist, it is simply to say that such forms of thinking do not have to exist for the logical reasons presented by moral development theory.

Beyond this, it is not even that clear that Stage 4 thinking is axiomatically "better" than Stage 1, 2, or 3 thinking. The questions of whether or not Stage 4 thinking is better than Stage 3, or Stage 3 is better than Stage 2, etc., seems unanswerable unless the question, Better for *what*? is answered first. To say that such thinking resolves problems in better ways still leaves the question of better for what unaddressed. Stage 2 thinking, if it affects action, probably generates more reinforcement than Stage 1 thinking. If more reinforcement is "better," then Stage 2 thinking is "better." Stage 4 thinking, again if it affects action, probably creates more social stability, and if social stability is "better," then Stage 4 thinking is probably superior to Stages 1, 2, and 3.

Beyond the first four stages of thinking, there seem to be a number of possible forms of thought which, if they affected behavior, could initiate social change. Beyond does not mean "higher;" it simply means different. Persuasional ethics, ethical relativism, Stage 5a (utilitarianism), Stage 5b (a self-generated conscience other than utility), and Stage 6 (commitment to a universal principle) are all possible types of thought that could lead to change in the social order. The theoretical problem is that these are either excluded or put in rank order in moral development theory. This is difficult to understand given the fact that there is so little Stage 6 data and that Stages 5 and 6 are always presented together in the research reports. Thus the theory makes its clearest philosophic separation precisely where the data separation is the least clear.

Social Philosophic Issues

If Kohlberg's theory of moral development were solely a philosophy or theoretical psychology, this critique would end here. However, Kohlberg and others clearly intend moral development as both a social philosophy and a basis of social intervention. In the area of social philosophy, there are a number of issues that are troublesome. The first issue is that, as in Platonic philosophy, the logic of developmental psychology leads to the assumption that the wise should rule in matters of conduct and politics, whether of a classroom, prison, or any other institution. It is conceivable that the developmental philosopher king would be a good ruler, and Kohlberg certainly has the right to persuade the community to adopt such a ruler. However, the moral development position is not one of persuasion. The assumption is that the philosopher king *is* best.

The Platonic assumption is at odds with another assumption of moral development theory, namely that the ideal institution is democratic. Kohlberg continuously uses the word "democracy" as though it were a well defined monistic form of governing and simply assumes that his understanding of this form of governing is best in all conditions. Stage 5 reasoning is repeatedly linked to democracy with the implication that since we all know democracy is good, Stage 5 thinking must also be good. Again, the theorists of moral development make the assumption of "better" without the question of "better for what?" The word "democracy," like the word "justice," tends to be used as emotional propaganda in the moral development literature.

Some Stage 5 problem solving and a majority of Stage 6 problem solving does not support the idea of democracy in any way. Stage 6 thinking is not necessarily social or antisocial, it is logically asocial. There is nothing in the idea of principled ethics (or Stage 5b and persuasional ethics) that necessarily recognizes societal issues. Kohlberg's particular principle does recognize society, but others, especially those that have a religious basis, do not. Kohlberg would argue that these are not Stage 6, but what is actually being argued is that they are not *his* Stage 6 principles.

There is, in the very concept of a hierarchy of morals, an elitism that is difficult to disguise. There is the presumption that some people, by virtue of their moral stage, know what is best for others. It is very difficult to support both a position of equality and a position of moral superiority. The type of equality that seems to be espoused is that others have an equal opportunity (not capacity, noting the infrequency of the formal operations necessary for postconventional thought) to think correctly. If they do not think in this way, then the better thinker has to solve the problem for them to preserve their equality. To be quite frank, it is difficult to reconcile Stage 6 thinking with any understanding of democracy. What we seem to have in Kohlberg's theory is an aristocracy, or at most an oligarchy of morality.

Beyond these problems of social philosophy, there is no clear statement of thought-action interaction in moral development theory. This makes the social philosophy weak at best and dangerous at worst. The fact that different Stage 6, philosopher-king leaders, operating within the same stage, could come to support opposing actions is a frightening political possibility. Since Kohlberg's particular Stage 6 principle seems to outlaw conflict as the arbitrator of such a disagreement, the result would seem to be paralysis.

Social Intervention

The actual arena of social intervention of moral development theory has primarily been in prisons and schools. In these institutions, what is proposed is more than a method of understanding; it is a method of social change. Given that most philosophical and psychological work has not attempted to actually improve anything, these intervention attempts are refreshing and important. The question of their utility depends on what they are for. Here the assumptions which link words to thoughts to present actions to future actions are crucial. Not all moral developmental interveners go this far. Peter

Scharf and Joseph Hickey seem to contend that the just prison is an end in itself, i.e., only link words to thoughts to present actions. In any case, despite this confusion of goals, the interventions in schools and prisons do attempt to make those institutions more responsive to inmate input but not necessarily more just. When reading of the intervention attempts, this reader is struck by their similarity to the therapeutic community work of M. Jones. If these interventions work, it may well be because the experimenters have created therapeutic communities, not because of anything to do with moral development. In fact, in reading about these attempts, this reader is struck, not by the discussions of moral dilemmas, but by the group discussions themselves. The issue does not seem to be how prisoners (whether of a prison or a school) deal with conflict, but that they, not the authority, deal with it at all.

Given what may be a mandate for a powerful social intervention, sold under the rubric of moral development but operating with the proven power of a therapeutic community, it is unfortunate that the moral development theorists have not also included problem-solving skills in their training. Life seldom presents dilemmas with all the information that is included in the moral dilemma used by Kohlberg, and the choices in life are seldom yes/no. In real dilemmas, people often need more information, and poor problem solvers often need to be taught how to gather and assess additional information, to generate many alternatives, inspect consequences, select one to try, as well as how to act on the alternative that they have selected (D'Zurilla and Goldfried, 1971). While this may not sound like moral development, it could certainly lead to more effective responses to real moral dilemmas if it worked.

Bibliography

D'Zurilla, Thomas J., and Goldfried, Marvin R. "Problem-Solving and Behavior Modification." *Journal of Abnormal Psychology* 78 (1971):107–26.

Jones, Maxwell. *The Therapeutic Community*. New York: Basic Books, 1953.

Kohlberg, Lawrence. "From Is to Ought: How to Commit the Naturalistic Fallacy and Get Away with It in the Study of Moral Development." In *Cognitive Development and Epistemology*, edited by T. Mischel. New York: Academic Press, 1971.

Krebs, Richard L. "Some Relationships between Moral Judgment, Attention, and Resistance to Temptation." Ph.D. dissertation, University of Chicago, 1968.

Milgrim, S. "Behavioral Study of Obedience." *Journal of Abnormal and Social Psychology* 67 (1963):371–78.

Popper, Karl R. *The Logic of Scientific Discovery*. New York: Basic Books, 1959.

Scharf, Peter, and Hickey, Joseph. *Just Community Approach to Corrections*. Needham, Mass.: Humanitas Press, 1977.

Structuralism per se When Applied to Moral Ideology

Edmund V. Sullivan, Joint Professor, Applied Psychology and History and Philosophy, The Ontario Institute for Studies in Education.

. . . Structuralism is a method of analysis—the analysis of structures (Dagenais, 1972). Fundamentally, a structure is an autonomous entity characterized by internal dependencies. As such, a structure is a system of transformations that, as a system, implies lawfulness of organization independent of the elements that compose it. A system is characterized, first of all, by it being a *totality*; that is, whatever the "composing elements" in the system, they are subordinated to the laws that define the system as system. Second, a system is characterized by multiple *transformations* (stages), interdependent with each other and with the totality; that is, they are dependent upon the structure itself. Finally, a third characteristic of structure is that it is *self-regulating*, tending toward the conservation and enhancement of the system itself on the one hand and closedness toward all other systems on the other (Dagenais, 1972). In the context of the above definition, Kohlberg's stage theory of morality is clearly a structural theory.

For a student of developmental psychology in the recent era, structuralism had many attractive features when compared with the increasingly defunct adversary behaviorism. It became part of the zeitgeist in the social sciences and in education (Sullivan, 1967, 1969). For some, structuralism obviously provided *the* model of man rather than *a* model of man. Specifically, the critique under this heading will deal with some problem areas that structuralism as a methodology seems to create. This section will touch on some of these issues insofar as they relate to Kohlberg's structural conception of moral development. I shall first explore the idea that Kohlberg's structural conception of morality tends to create dichotomies when treating the relationships between thought and action, form and content, and the abstract and the concrete. I shall then show how these bifurcations affect the area of moral commitment. Further, I shall show how Kohlberg's structuralism tends to separate the "emotional" life from the "intellectual"

From *Kohlberg's Structuralism: A Critical Appraisal* by Edmund V. Sullivan. Toronto: The Ontario Institute for Studies in Education, 1977. Reprinted by permission of the publisher.

life where morality is concerned. In the type of dichotomy Kohlberg presents, the emotions are relegated to an epiphenomenal status in understanding and in morality. This bias then creates its own caricatures, making the treatment of virtues ludicrous. Finally, I shall try to show that there is a place for what Kohlberg calls "the bag of virtues psychology" by looking at some of the implications for moral commitment when the issues of moral imagination and moral blindness are considered. All in all, the critique in this section is a counterposition to certain aspects of Kohlberg's structuralism.

In order to analyze critically Kohlberg's stage theory it is necessary to understand a few things about Piaget. In his writings Piaget (1932) seems to see the development of ethical judgments as following from the study of logical structures. Kohlberg (1969) follows Piaget in attempting to show that the development of moral judgments can be studied to a considerable extent by a "genetic epistemological" model. In a sense, Piaget's and Kohlberg's work constitutes extensions of Piaget's earlier work in the Kantian area of "practical reason." Kohlberg's stages of moral judgment are simply a more sophisticated and articulate extension of Piaget's earlier inquiry into the understanding of moral judgment or practical reasoning. In the work of both men in the area of moral judgment, there is a preoccupation with epistemological categories. We might well question this type of preoccupation, since it may lock us into a specific direction that may have unintended consequences. From my own perspective, it appears that Kohlberg's moral stages are simply an offshoot of the development of scientific understanding. In that sense moral logic becomes simply an extension of scientific logic, a conclusion that can easily be drawn from Kohlberg's (1969) writings, where he discusses the relationship of moral stages to Piagetian stages of intellectual development. [See Appendix for a synopsis of the Kohlberg and Piaget stages.] I would thus be inclined to say that Kohlberg's psychologism is a particular type of scientific outlook identified with the development of Kantian philosophy. Specifically, in stage terms Kohlberg seems to indicate that Stage 6 is identifiable with Kant's *à priori* knowledge and all lower stages are forms of empiricism leading to the Stage 6 *à priori* (Kohlberg, 1971b). In one sense morality really begins at Stage 6, when a practical reflective process has reached full maturity. This strikes me as one of the reasons for a preoccupation of reflection over action within Kohlberg's perspective. Reflection and action never seem to be in dynamic tension.

Moral Commitment

One of the first questions to be raised in relation to Kohlberg's stage theory of moral judgment is: What is the relationship between a person's moral judgment and his actions? The very nature of the formulation of his theory invites a question of this nature because most people identify morality with moral commitment or action. In Kohlberg's formulation, the moral aspect is defined by the nature not of action but of judgment. I will try to show, in this section, several shortcomings in the way Kohlberg treats the judgment/action relationship. The very nature of the theory creates a false dichotomy between the two. However, let us first turn to Kohlberg (1971b) to understand his treatment of the relationship.

Kohlberg identifies two main sources of consistency between moral judgment and moral action. The first source of consistency is the level of the structure or stage itself. He quotes several studies that apparently demonstrate the relationship of consistency between judgment and action—that is, people at higher stages are more morally consistent. One study by Krebs on cheating among sixth graders indicated that the majority of children were below the principled level in moral judgment. Of those below the principled level, 75 percent cheated. In contrast, only 20 percent of the principled subjects (Stages 5 and 6) cheated (Kohlberg, 1971b). Similar findings in the same direction are quoted on a college population. Kohlberg also indicates that principled-level students were able to resist pressure to perform an action that would cause another person harm (the electric shock in the now famous Milgram experiment) and also were able to involve themselves in types of campus action where civil disobedience ensued (Kohlberg, 1971b). In short, the higher the stage, the greater the consistency between thought and action.

The second source of consistency between judgment and action comprises nonmoral factors identified as attention, will, and ego-strength (Kohlberg, 1971b). These factors somewhat transcend the consistency produced simply by the structure. Kohlberg cites a study that indicates that if children have an amoral philosophy (Stage 2), they are much more likely to cheat if they are high on ego-strength; if children have a conventional morality (Stage 4), they are much less likely to cheat if they are high on ego-strength; if children have reached the stages past conventional (5 or 6), high ego-strength is less necessary, for even these principled children who are low on ego-strength do not seem to cheat. Kohlberg concludes, that in this sense, the basic virtue may be called "autonomy" as well as "justice."

My first impression is that all of his contentions are simple, straightforward, and logical. Yet they may be too simple in dealing with the issue of moral consistency. Kohlberg's conclusion about autonomy is certainly open to serious question, as it is a troublesome concept taken all by itself (Hogan, 1973; Hogan develops this question in much greater detail). What is more important for our purposes at this point is the whole question of whether Kohlberg's structuralism creates its own peculiar problems which are idiosyncratic to the theoretical position itself. My position is, in spite of their statements to the contrary, that Kohlberg and his predecessor Piaget produce a thought/action dichotomy that indicates the collapse of an inherently *dialectical* process.

Kohlberg and Piaget follow in the tradition of Immanuel Kant when dealing with the relationships between thought and action. I would like here to quote Lukacs in a reflection he makes on Kant, because it directly applies to Kohlberg and specifically to the issue at hand. (The italics are mine.)

> Within such a world only two possible modes of action commend themselves and they are both apparent rather than real ways of actively changing the world. Firstly, there is the exploitation for particular human ends (as in technology, for example) of the fatalistically accepted and *immutable laws* which are seen in the manner we have already described. Secondly, there is action directed wholly inwards. This is the attempt to change the world at its only remaining free point, namely man himself (ethics). But as the world becomes mechanized its subject, man, necessarily becomes mechanized too and so this ethics likewise remains *abstract*. Confronted by the totality of man in isolation from the world it remains merely normative

> and fails to be truly *active* in the creation of objects. It is only prescriptive and imperative in character. [1971, p. 38]

Like Kant, Kohlberg and other cognitive-developmentalists are primarily interested in the development of abstract and universal laws (structures). The theory really does not focus on action or commitment, and what ultimately follows is the thought/action dichotomy that prevails in the historical development of modern thought (Habermas, 1971). Now, I am aware that both Kohlberg and Piaget would deny what I am saying here, since the process of assimilation and accommodation which they subscribe to is supposedly dynamic and action oriented. After all, are not thought structures actions that are internalized? I would contend, as Lukacs does of Kant, that in Kohlberg the moral thought structures (stages) become reified, that is, take on a life of their own. Also, in Kohlberg's case it would appear that for him a thought structure always logically precedes action. In my opinion, in Kohlberg's stage theory we are always trying to get from thought (judgment) to action, a movement that I consider to be only half the truth, only one half of an inherently dialectical process. To me *thought* directs *action* and *action* directs *thought*, and so on and so on.

I am really talking about the dialectics of a process called *praxis*. In Paolo Friere's (1970) terms praxis is the fusion of action and reflection. Reflection, then, is one pole of a continuing process. If that pole is emphasized to the detriment of the other (action), then the dialectic collapses and thought and action separate. Friere indicates that reflection separated from action is simply pure verbalism. I would be inclined to see Kohlberg's stages of thought structures in this light. We are running the risk of infatuation with morally pure and abstract thought categories—after all, it is not important morally what particular *choice* we make (content), but rather that the moral is determined by the correct *form* (maturity of the stage). It strikes me that Kohlberg's theory deals with moral ambiguity in one way and one way only: the moral man first thinks through clearly and then acts. I do not disagree that this happens, but I question whether this is all that moral man does. It strikes me that all of us mere humans in many situations must act in ambiguity, and that in the process of acting we really begin to clarify how we think. Most people are more like Saint Paul than Immanuel Kant: "We work out our salvation in fear and trembling." In many instances we act without clear and certain principles, and in the process of this activity the very nature of our thought processes changes.

Kohlberg's research never looks at the process in this latter direction, because the theory is contemplative (cf. Mannheim, 1953). Are only universal, abstract, thought structures (stages) the only forms of activity? Do concrete, unique actions not have a form sensitive to the individual human story (the personal) and the specific cultural history (the community)?

Whatever the advantages there are in finding abstract thought structures, I wonder if the gain should be to the detriment of the concrete, idiosyncratic, and contextual. Phenomenologists have adamently defended the importance of the latter (e.g., Merleau-Ponty, 1945, 1962). However, it is explicitly clear from Piaget's (1971) own writing that he has an aversion to the concrete and contextual when he theorizes (Sullivan, 1975a). I think the same thing can be said for Kohlberg with his passion for abstract, formal structures. Let it be clear that I am not arguing that there is no merit in their approach; rather, I am trying to point to its one-sidedness—its one-dimensionality. Is abstract formalism, then, a totally beneficial contribution to the development of Western thought, or does it bring its own inherent problems? I will attempt to deal with this question by looking at the form/content distinction.

I would like to entertain the possibility that the issues of form/content, abstract/concrete, and thought/action are all related. Although Kohlberg appears contradictory and equivocal on this matter (Crittenden, 1972), it nevertheless is apparent from the corpus of his writings that he has a penchant for form over content, as if it were possible to consider the one quite apart from the other. Increasingly higher stages are more abstract, and as we approach the ultimate ideal (Stage 6) we achieve a purer *form* of the moral. So it would follow that the lower stages are more content oriented and more concrete. In the light of his theoretical thrust, abstract and formal as moral structures are more valued. Here Kohlberg follows Piaget and therefore shares some of Piaget's inherent Kantian formalism. And it should be noted at this point that movement of thought associated with abstract formalism is not unequivocal in its virtues. Scheler (1971, 1973), who was attracted to Kantian formalism, devoted a whole volume to some of the problems it presents for the development of inquiry in ethics. He was struck by the fact that there is a tendency in the process of abstraction to make light of the concrete context from which abstraction receives its very lifeblood. Piaget (1971) systematically prefers structure (abstraction) over content (the concrete context) methodologically, and Kohlberg seems to fully accept Piaget's methodological attack. This is a systematic weakness in cognitive-developmental structuralism. For example, Turner (1973) points out Piaget's weakness concerning figurative knowledge. He indicates that Piaget downgrades the use of concrete imagery as always being associated with less mature stages of thought; mature development is always to be associated with more abstraction and less concretion. Kohlberg's stage theory of moral development takes exactly the same tack as Piaget's stage formulation of intellectual development. It therefore suffers some of the same shortcomings that are becoming apparent in the Piagetian formulation.

Since this section is about moral commitment, I would like to point out here how structuralism has generally dealt shabbily with human affect or the emotional life. In the case of Piaget it comes to a criticism of the very process of "decentering," which is always associated with the development of abstraction. A quote from Turner sums it up beautifully:

> The identity (in the full sense of the personality or "self") of the subject, on the other hand, exists at a relatively concrete and particular level: its essential functional property is the integration of cognitive world-picture and logical operations with affect and value in the forms of purposive action. Affect is inherently concrete, particular, and associated with the unique relationship of the self to its objective environment. For this reason the integration and shaping of the personality or subjective self, on both conscious and unconsciousness levels, cannot be achieved by a decentered, abstract, and generalized mode of thought alone. A more concrete symbolic medium, centered upon the particular position of the subject and capable of condensing affective with cognitive associations, is required. It

> is this need that is filled by figurative imagery and symbolic forms. Figurative symbolism and "decentered" logical thought thus fulfill complementary functions and ideally reinforce one another. "Recentered" forms such as ritual or myth, for example, afford mechanisms by which structural principles of "decentered" cognitive systems (e.g., social or moral norms) can be invested with affective and motivational power. Alternatively, "recentered" forms can compensate for the depersonalization of "decentered" structures of social or cosmic reality at either the collective or the individual level by creating concrete, affectively charged worlds of meaning of a subjectively "centered" character. [1973, p. 354]

As I pointed out earlier, Kohlberg's Stage 6 ideal principled person is a moral entity without flesh or bones. In this ideal "decentered" state, the Stage 6 person is the Beatles' "Nowhere Man." Kohlberg and Rawls identify the process of "universalization" only with the rulings of an "impartial judge" in a jurisprudential procedure. Possibly one of the reasons that Stage 6 seems present only in Western cultural samples is that Stage 6 reflects a bias toward a jurisprudential process more prevalent in Western cultures. But can it be said that where that jurisprudential process is absent, there is no attempt at universality? My own position is that Kohlberg's and Rawls' process of universalization is sensitized to the jurisprudential model concretely developed in Western societies; other cultures will score lower on moral development because the model is culturally biased (see Simpson, 1974). I think it should be noted that even within our own culture, this particular type of "universalization" has limited value. The judge in our culture represents the "generalized other" and his impartiality may be important for certain types of moral and legal claims. But does the possiblity of a more universal ethics depend only on the possibility of all people developing the mentality of an impersonal judicial procedure? In other words, should *all* moral claims be adjudicated by this ideal?

It seems to me that most of us mere humans have to develop more inclusive and hence more universal ethics from our own personal point in time and space, our own history. In that sense it is important not that I become detached or decentered but that I see the full force of my attachments and centerings and then acknowledge their limiting nature. By entering more deeply into my own personal and historical viewpoint, I hope that I will realize that other viewpoints too are limited, and yet possibly look at segments of reality that I have not considered. If this process were reciprocal, then no party would lay claim to a more universal viewpoint (e.g., like the judge); rather, the very process itself would be a "universalization" that would deepen in different ways the personal lives of all involved.

This movement of "universalization" is different from the impersonal process of Rawls or Kohlberg. In a contemporary context this process of justice may issue from a crying out rather than from an impersonal defused voice. Particular examples of what I am alluding to can be found in Friere's *Pedagogy of the Oppressed* or Fanon's *Wretched of the Earth*. Here the call for justice comes from an oppressed group whose cry of anguish urges a deeper sense of community and therefore a deeper universality. The call is itself part of a judgmental process, but it does not come from a judge who makes no personal claims. It is not a jurisprudential verdict but rather a call to the community—close to what the prophets did in the Old Testament. It demands a deeper interest on the part of an oppressor group so as to extend the scope of the human community. Since it involves a radical personal and social change, it can hardly be identified with the impersonality of a judicial hearing. So, for all its sophistication, Kohlberg's Stage 6 is a limited perspective with a limited type of universalization, despite his claims to the contrary.

Moreover, the decentered autonomy subscribed to by Piaget and Kohlberg has the potential for creating as many problems as it appears to solve (Hogan, 1973). It is possible that autonomy as a singular ideal can contribute to the development of a moral agent who lacks sociability and who disregards the pragmatic value of rules as well; he or she might well be autocratic and anti-conforming, "a great scoundrel and a rogue" (Hogan, 1973). So, autonomy separated from other dimensions of the moral is conceivably an aberrant process. Insofar as autonomy and abstraction are considered as ideal states, there is a possibility that the moral agent may "decenter" him/herself from any concrete moral commitments.

It is at this point that a fusion of the figurative (*concrete*) and the abstract becomes essential for moral commitment. I would identify the figurative here with a faculty of imagination. Looking at the Kohlberg's Stage 6 autonomous protocols (see Kohlberg, 1973) one can see a person completely lacking in "imagination"—an attribute that I would deem essential to effective moral commitment. Because of its importance, let me conclude with a short treatment of moral commitment and its relation to the imagination and to moral blindness. The treatment will hopefully indicate a vacuum area in Kohlberg's conception of the moral that cannot be passed over lightly.

Morality and the Imagination

There is something lacking in all of the conceptual elegance of both Piaget's and Kohlberg's structuralisms. One significant gap is in the area of the "aesthetic imagination" and the potential role it may play in the development of intellectual and moral understanding (cf. Simpson, 1976). It can be said of Kohlberg, as it is said of Piaget, that his theory is confined to an analysis of "decentering" in logical and moral structures (Turner, 1973). In this light Turner suggests that a theory of this kind must be supplemented by a theory of "recentered" figurative symbolic structures before it can provide a comprehensive account of cultural and psychological structures—that is, a theory of moral perception as well as action. Kohlberg's theory in its present state collapses the dialectical tension because it focuses solely on decentering. This is probably why his formulation so easily lends itself to a thought/action dichotomy. To balance Kohlberg's formulation we need a fusion of thought/action, form/content, and abstract/concrete. Both Kohlberg's and Piaget's structuralisms lack this fusion. What is needed is a complementary process which fuses the process of "decentering" and "recentering."

The imagination is the thorn in the rosy development of most theoretical rationalists. We noted earlier that Piaget seems to pass off figurative knowledge as simply a lower form of intellectual development. Kohlberg's theory has no systematic place for it. In our everyday life, value synthesis is not a science but probably encompasses, when done well, the virtuosity of an artist. Hampden-Turner probably speaks for most people when he concludes:

> No science can tell you, or ever will tell you, what you should do in a human encounter a few moments from now. You can be given the axioms and the principles involved, but the exact proportions of their combination is your existential decision. If a potential suicide arrives on your doorstep, the degree that you permit him to depend on you, and that you urge him to the independence he needs to survive, are two elements in the art of judgment. [1976, p. 291]

This art of judgment is not of necessity a blind art, as naive romanticism would claim (Macmurray, 1957). A one-sided approach to intelligence that denies the dimension of imagination or gives it a poor showing will be subject to the following judgment made by Novak:

> What is it that intelligence aims to understand if not human experience? In whose service is it if not in the service of human action? The imagination organizes the matrix of patterns and structures and relationships in which insight occurs. Many people of good intelligence lack imagination, and hence insight . . . there are a great many things, in any case, which simply cannot occur until the underlying experiential and imaginative base has been prepared. Reading Shakespeare at forty is not like reading him at twenty (it is surprising how much Shakespeare has learned in the intervening years). As Aristotle pointed out, young people find ethics (by which he meant discernment in singular concrete situations) very difficult to understand. They are too idealistic, see things too abstractly, lack the precise experience that is required. Wisdom, the ability to go to the heart of the matter in concrete situations, is acquired slowly; it is a discipline of experience, imagination and story, not of naked intelligence. Often in America, unfortunately, one's intelligence develops more swiftly than one's experience, imagination, and story. [1971, pp. 57–58]

Let me briefly illustrate from a speech of Martin Luther King how this imagery is employed to foster commitment to action.

> I say to you today, my friends, Let Freedom ring! From the hilltops of New Hampshire, from mighty mountains of New York . . . from every hill and molehill in Mississippi . . . Let Freedom ring from every house and hamlet, from every street in every city . . . When Freedom rings we shall be able to speed that day, when all God's children, black men and white men, Jews and Gentiles, Protestants and Catholics, will be able to join hands and sing in the words of the old Negro Spiritual. Free at last! Free at last! Great God Almighty, we are free at last! We got some difficult days ahead. Some people are concerned as to what would happen to me from some of our sick white brothers. Well I don't know what will happen to me now . . . But it really doesn't matter to me now . . . because I've been to the Mountain Top . . . Like everybody I would like to live a long life . . . Longevity has its place . . . But I'm not concerned with that now . . . He's allowed me to go to the Mountain Top—and I've looked over and I've SEEN the Promised Land. I may not get there with

> you . . . but I want you to know, tonight, that we, as a people, will get to the Promised Land. So I'm happy now, I'm not worried about ANY-THING. Mine eyes have seen the Glory of the coming of the Lord!

King's universalization is tied by his images to the concrete figurative. In contrast to principles stated in an abstract manner, King illustrates the dynamic force of imaginative symbolism that has a compelling *intensional* quality. His images tend to evoke action and commitment in a way abstract principles could rarely do. His possession of principles is tied to a moral imagination that clearly fuses the concrete with the abstract.

Moral Blindness: The Possibilities for Self-Deception

I would like to conclude this critique with a brief treatment of the role of self-deception, since there may come a point where moral reasons become rationalizations. We must therefore raise some fundamental questions about moral reasoning and its possible ambiguity.

What do we do about the inherent ambiguity of human commitment? How do we deal with a condition that is familiar to all of us, a condition discussed by William James (1899/1958) under the title of "a certain blindness in human beings"? Kohlberg's structuralism, in line with twentieth-century rationalism, suggests we eliminate ambiguity by advancing to higher stages of development. He is thoroughly Cartesian in his rationality, since he sees moral maturity as a deeper integration of "clear and distinct ideas." Most of us have at least a vague suspicion that this type of rationality is lacking in certain respects. Saint Paul hits the issue head on in speaking of his own problems of moral commitment.

> In fact, this seems to be the rule, that every single time I want to do good it is something evil that comes to hand. In my inmost self, I dearly love God's law, but I can see that my body follows a different law that battles against the law which reason dictates. [Romans 7:21–23]

Now, the problem that Paul alludes to did not stop with Paul. While he attributed the problem to his sinful condition, for this form of psychological blindness a more up-to-date term would be "alienation." This term and its corresponding process are never alluded to in Kohlberg's theory. What I would like to indicate in this section is that in its lack of a substantial treatment of alienation (moral blindness) Kohlberg's theory suffers from some grave difficulties. Moral blindness is a form of what the Marxists would call "false consciousness."

In many of Kohlberg's writings, there is a section devoted to a topic that he calls the "bag of virtues." Kohlberg identifies the "bag of virtues" as a particular type of moral psychology, and he advances his own structural theory at its expense. He presents this conception of moral psychology in such a pejorative light that it seems ludicrous that any one in his right mind would identify with such an approach. (R. S. Peters, 1971, offers a more balanced treatment of the virtues.) Let me quote Kohlberg to demonstrate my point:

> According to Aristotle, "virtue is of two kinds, intellectual and moral. While intellectual virtue owes its birth and growth to teaching, moral virtue comes about as a result of habit. The moral virtues we get by first exercising

> them; we become just by doing just acts, temperate by doing temperate acts, brave by doing brave acts." Aristotle, then, is claiming that there are two spheres, the moral and the intellectual, and that learning by doing is the only real method in the moral sphere.
>
> American educational psychology also divides the personality into cognitive abilities, passions or motives, and traits of character. Moral character consists of a bag of virtues and vices. For example, one of the earliest major American studies of moral character, conducted in the late twenties (Hartshorne and May, 1928–38), included honesty, sincerity, and self-control in the bag of virtues.
>
> If we accept such a bag of virtues, it is evident how we should build character. Children should be exhorted to practice these virtues and should be told that happiness, fortune, and good repute will follow in their wake; adults around them should be living examples of these virtues, and children should be given daily opportunities to practice them. Daily chores should be used to build responsibility, the opportunity to give to the Red Cross should serve to build responsibility, service, altruism, and so on.
>
> The psychologist's objection to the bag of virtues is that there is no such a thing. Virtues and vices are labels by which people award praise or blame to others, but the ways people use praise and blame towards others are not the ways in which people think when making moral decisions themselves. [1971b, pp. 74–75]

If we concentrate on the last section of this quote, it is clear that Kohlberg oversimplifies the issue to make a point. He treats the virtue/vice issue in such a manner that it makes us feel that the use of these terms in our vocabulary shows us to be primitive or at best naive. Kohlberg demonstrates here the unreflective secularism of the enlightenment (Sullivan, 1975a). He shares with Piaget an unreflective myth of "liberal progress" (Rieff, 1961). Historically, the "bag of virtues," as Kohlberg calls them, are more than labels by which people award praise or blame. After all, is that all Dante was doing in his *Divine Comedy*? It is obvious to me that Dante, in a masterful treatment of human emotions, sustained a dialectical conception of moral emotions with virtues and vices being the two poles of this complex dialectic. In the context of the present discussion, vices are aspects of human emotions that lead to moral blindness and virtues are emotions that help to achieve moral vision (imagination). In contrast to Dante, who achieves a dialectic between Apollo and Dionysius, Kohlberg's structuralism is one-sided in its Apollonian vigor.

Any psychological theory that pretends to capture a substantial understanding of human intellectual and moral development must contend with those dynamic factors that lead to intellectual and moral blindness. Structuralism à la Kohlberg has no systematic place for this process in its explanatory scheme. Lacking an adequate treatment, he ends up by treating the area as epiphenomenal. Dionysius, however, will have his day when left unattended, when rational deliberation turns into rationalization and "false consciousness." Scheler (1912/1972) does a masterful treatment of this process of rationalization in his phenomenological analysis of the emotion *ressentiment*. His analysis of *ressentiment* as well as of sympathy (Scheler, 1923/1973) bears scrutiny, since it shows the latent possibilities of the tradition of virtue and vices. Scheler attempts to elaborate a phenomenology of feeling states, of sympathy and love, of shame and repentance, of pain and joy, which can be summed up as a "logic of the heart" (Coser, 1972).

As I already pointed out, the issue of moral blindness and vision have important theoretical as well as practical implications. Lonergan (1957) outlines these implications in the development of a cognitional theory and posits a phenomenon he calls *scotosis*, or "flight from understanding." Becker (1968) describes a similar process in his discussion of ethical theory. Both of these theorists draw substantially from the tradition of Freudian psychology without in any way being Freudians. In the work of R. S. Peters (1971), Freud gets a fairer treatment as to his possible role in the development of moral psychology. Kohlberg (1964, 1969) sees his own theory as transcending the contribution of Freudian psychology on moral matters. However, the whole area of moral failure looks peculiar if morality is nothing more than advancing in cognitive moral stages. How, in this situation, is moral failure to be defined? Peters ventures that, at least on the side of the vices, Freudian psychology has something substantial to say about moral failure:

> The same sort of point can be made about Freud's theory of character traits. This does not begin to look like a theory of how traits such as honesty, which were studied in the Hartshorne-May enquiry, are developed. Nor is it a theory about the development of higher-order traits such as consistency, determination, and courage, to which we are usually alluding when we speak of people *having* character. . . .
>
> Freud thought that he spotted a similarity between types of character and various forms of neuroses, and assigned a common cause to both in his theory of infantile sexuality. Here again we do not have a competing explanation of the sort of phenomena in which Kohlberg is interested, namely, the determinents of a rational, principled form of morality. Rather we have an attempt to explain types of character that fall a long way short of this in some systematic way. [1971, pp. 265–266]

If Kohlberg has a blindness for the contribution of Freud at the level of individual moral psychology, he also shares with his predecessors in the liberal tradition a blindness to the role of class consciousness. There is nothing in his structural conception of morality that indicates an appreciation of the blindness produced by one's place in the social structure. Without elaborating in detail, his conception therefore comes under the same criticisms leveled at Kant on the class blindness of his world view (see Lukacs, 1971; Marx & Engels, *The German Ideology*).

Bibliography

Ausubel, David, and Sullivan, Edmund V. *Theory and Problems of Child Development*. 2d ed. New York: Grune & Stratton, 1970.

Barber, Benjamin. "Justifying Justice: Problems of Psychology, Politics, and Measurement in Rawls." In *Reading Rawls*, edited by N. Daniels. Oxford: Blackwell, 1975.

Barry, Brian M. "The Liberal Theory of Justice: A Critical Examination of the Principled Doctrines." In *A Theory of Justice* by John Rawls. Oxford: Clarendon Press, 1973.

Beck, Clive; Crittenden, Brian; and Sullivan, Edmund V., eds. *Moral Education: Interdisciplinary Approaches*. Toronto: University of Toronto Press, 1971.

Becker, Ernest. *The Structure of Evil*. New York: Braziller, 1968.

Bolt, Daniel J., and Sullivan, Edmund V. "Kohlberg's Cognitive-Developmental Theory in Educational Settings: Some Possible Abuses." *Journal of Moral Education* 6 (1977):198–205.

Bowers, C. A. *Cultural Literacy for Freedom: An Existential Perspective on Teaching Curriculum and School Policy*. Eugene, Ore.: Elan, 1974.

Bowles, Samuel, and Gintis, Herbert. "I.Q. in the U.S. Class Structure." *Social Policy*, January/February 1973.

Buck-Morss, Susan. "Socio-Economic Bias in Piaget's Theory and Its Implications for Cross-Cultural Studies." *Human Development* 18 (1975):35–49.

Buss, Allan R. "The Emerging Field of the Sociology of Psychological Knowledge." *American Psychologist* 30 (1975):988–1002.

Coser, Lewis A. Introduction to *Ressentiment*, by Max F. Scheler. Translated by William W. Holdheim. New York: Schocken, 1972.

Crittenden, Brian S. *Form and Content in Moral Education*. Toronto: Ontario Institute for Studies in Education, 1972.

Dagenais, James J. *Models of Man*. The Hague: Martinus Nijhoff, 1972.

Daniels, Norman. "Equal Liberty and Unequal Worth of Liberty." In *Reading Rawls*, edited by N. Daniels. Oxford: Blackwell, 1975.

Duncan, Graeme C. *Marx and Mill: Two Views of Social Conflict and Social Harmony*. Cambridge, England: Cambridge University Press, 1973.

Erikson, Erik H. *Dimensions of a New Identity*. New York: Norton, 1973.

Fisk, M. "History and Reason in Rawls' Moral Theory." In *Reading Rawls*, edited by N. Daniels. Oxford: Blackwell, 1975.

Fowler, James W. III. "Toward a Developmental Perspective on Faith." *Religious Education* 69 (1974):207–19.

Freire, Paulo. *Pedagogy of the Oppressed*. Translated by Myra B. Ramos. New York: Herder & Herder, 1970.

Green, M. "Curriculum and Cultural Transformation: A Humanistic View." *Cross-Currents*, Summer 1975.

Habermas, Jürgen. *Knowledge and Human Interests*. Translated by J. J. Shapiro. Boston: Beacon Press, 1971.

Habermas, Jürgen. *Legitimation Crisis*. Translated by T. McCarthy. Boston: Beacon Press, 1973.

Habermas, Jürgen. *Toward a Rational Society*. Translated by J. J. Shapiro. Boston: Beacon Press, 1970.

Hampden-Turner, Charles. *The Sane Asylum*. San Francisco: San Francisco Book, 1976.

Hogan, Robert. "Moral Conduct and Moral Character: A Psychological Perspective." *Psychological Bulletin* 79 (1973):217–32.

Hunt, David E., and Sullivan, Edmund. *Between Psychology and Education*. Hillsdale, Ill.: Dryden, 1974.

Illich, Ivan. *Deschooling Society*. New York: Harper & Row, Harrow Books, 1972.

James, William. *Talks to Teachers on Psychology and to Students on Some of Life's Ideals*. 1899. New York: Norton, 1958.

Keniston, Kenneth. "Psychological Development and Historical Change." In *Exploration in Psychohistory*, edited by R. J. Lifton and E. Olson. New York: Simon & Schuster, 1974.

Kohlberg, Lawrence. "The Claim to Moral Adequacy of a Highest Stage of Moral Judgment." *Journal of Philosophy* 70 (1973):630–46.

Kohlberg, Lawrence. "Continuities in Childhood and Adult Moral Development Revisited." In *Life-Span Developmental Psychology: Personality and Socialization*, edited by P. B. Balters and K. W. Schaie. New York: Academic Press, 1975.

Kohlberg, Lawrence. "Development of Moral Character and Moral Ideology." In *Review of Child Development Research*, vol. 1, edited by M. L. Hoffman and L. W. Hoffman. New York: Russell Sage Foundation, 1964.

Kohlberg, Lawrence. "From Is to Ought: How to Commit the Naturalistic Fallacy and Get Away with It in the Study of Moral Development." In *Cognitive Development and Epistemology*, edited by T. Mischel. New York: Academic Press, 1971b.

Kohlberg, Lawrence. "Stage and Sequence: The Cognitive-Developmental Approach to Socialization." In *Handbook of Socialization Theory and Research*. edited by D. A. Goslin. Chicago: Rand McNally, 1969.

Kohlberg, Lawrence. "Stages of Moral Development as a Basis for Moral Education." In *Moral Education: Interdisciplinary Approaches*, edited by C. Beck, B. Crittenden, and E. Sullivan. Toronto: University of Toronto Press, 1971a.

Kohlberg, Lawrence, and Mayer, Rochelle. "Development as the Aim of Education." *Harvard Educational Review* 42 (1972):449–96.

Lonergan, Bernard J. *Insight: A Study of Human Understanding*. London: Longmans, 1957.

Lukacs, George. *History and Class Consciousness: Studies in Marxist Dialectics*. Translated by R. Livingstone. Cambridge: M.I.T. Press, 1971.

Macmurray, John. *The Self as Agent*. London: Faber & Faber, 1957

Macmurray, John. *Persons in Relation*. London: Faber & Faber, 1961.

Macpherson, C. G. "Rawls' Models of Man and Society." *Philosophy of the Social Sciences* 3 (1973):341–47.

Mannheim, Karl. "Conservative Thought." In *Essays on Sociology and Social Psychology*, edited by P. Kecskemeti. London: Routledge & Kegan Paul, 1953.

Mannheim, Karl. *Ideology and Utopia*. Translated by L. Wirth and E. Shils. New York: Harcourt, Brace & World, 1936.

Marx, Karl, and Engels, Friedrich. *The German Ideology*. New York: International Publishers, 1970.

Merleau-Ponty, Maurice. *Phenomenology of Perception*. London: Routledge & Kegan Paul, 1962.

Miller, R. "Rawls and Marxism." In *Reading Rawls*, edited by N. Daniels. Oxford: Blackwell, 1975.

Mischey, E. J., and Sullivan, Edmund V. "Faith Orientation: Motive to Be Moral." *Contemporary Education* 48 (1976):23–28.

Novak, Michael. *Ascent of the Mountain, Flight of the Dove*. New York: Harper & Row, 1971.

Oelmiller, W. "The Limitations of Social Theories." In *Religion and Political Society*, edited by H. Richardson. New York: Harper & Row, 1975.

Peters, Richard S. "Moral Development: A Plea for Pluralism." In *Cognitive Development and Epistemology*, edited by T. Mischel. New York: Academic Press, 1971.

Piaget, Jean. *Insights and Illusions of Philosophy*. Translated by W. Mays. New York: World, 1971.

Piaget, Jean. *The Moral Judgment of the Child*. Translated by M. Gabain. Glencoe, Ill.: Free Press, 1948.

Rawls, John. *A Theory of Justice*. Cambridge: Harvard University Press, 1971.

Rieff, Philip. *Freud: The Mind of a Moralist*. New York: Anchor, 1961.

Riegel, Klaus F. "Influence of Economic and Political Ideologies on the Development of Development Psychology." *Psychological Bulletin* 78 (1972):129–41.

Scheler, Max. *Formalism in Ethics and Non-Formal Ethics of Values*. 1921. 5th rev. ed. Translated by M. S. Frings and R. L. Funk. Evanston, Ill.: Northwestern University Press, 1973.

Scheler, Max. *The Nature of Sympathy*. 1923. Translated by P. Heath. Hamden, Conn.: Archon, 1973.

Scheler, Max. *Ressentiment*. 1912. Edited by L. A. Coser. Translated by William W. Holdheim. New York: Schocken, 1972.

Simpson, Elizabeth L. "Moral Development Research: A Case Study of Scientific Cultural Bias." *Human Development* 17 (1974):81–106.

Sullivan, Edmund V. *Can Values Be Taught*. In preparation.

Sullivan, Edmund V. "Comment: Phenomenology and Structuralism: A War of the Worlds." *Interchange* 6/4 (1975a):52–54.

Sullivan, Edmund V. *Piaget and the School Curriculum: A Critical Appraisal*. Toronto: Ontario Institute for Studies in Education, 1967.

Sullivan, Edmund V. "Piagetian Theory in the Educational Milieu: A Critical Appraisal." *Canadian Journal of Behavioural Science* 1 (1969):129–55.

Sullivan, Edmund V.; Beck, Clive; Joy, Maureen; and Pagliuso, Susan. *Moral Learning*. Paramus, N.J.: Paulist/Newman Press, 1975b.

Sullivan, Edmund V., and Quarter, J. "Psychological Correlates of Certain Post-Conventional Moral Types: A Perspective on Hybrid Types." *Journal of Personality* 40 (1972):149–61.

Turner, T. "Piaget's Structuralism." *American Anthropologist* 75 (1973):351–73.

Weisskopf, Walter A. "The Dialectics of Equality." *Annals of the American Academy of Political and Social Science* 409 (1973):163–73.

Evaluating the Development of Moral Education: A Response to the Critiques of Flowers, Sullivan, and Fraenkel

Peter Scharf, Assistant Professor of Social Ecology, University of California at Irvine.

The critiques leveled against the developmental moral education movement by Flowers, Fraenkel, and Sullivan raise important issues for those committed to the approach as well as for those considering its adoption. It is often easier to reject criticism as "hostile" or "unreasonable" than to use it to improve the quality of an educational paradigm or technique. In all honesty, I think the most dangerous thing for developmental moral education is not to take such valid criticisms seriously. As a movement, developmental moral education has often appeared somewhat insulated from an honest dialogue with its critics. Its ideology of Platonic truth has often "explained away" negative responses instead of integrating them into its assumptions. Rejections of Stage 6 philosophy are often cited as examples of "relativistic thought"; questions regarding the rationalism of the approach are met with accusations of "humanistic romanticism."

The criticisms included in this volume have raised two broad sets of issues:

1. Questions of empirical truth and educational utility (e.g., have Kohlberg et al. documented that stages move in a stagewise order, understood the dynamics of moral change, etc.? Also, does a system work for teachers in classes and schools as they exist or will exist in the near future?).
2. Questions of philosophic adequacy and consistency (Has Kohlberg documented his claims regarding Stage 6 or resolved the issues involving mind and body, freedom, cause and necessity, implicit in his theory?).

Empirical and Pedagogical Problems

Kohlberg's theory has been challenged repeatedly in three broad empirical areas:

First, does his method of scoring moral reasoning through interviews accurately measure the logic of moral thinking of the individuals involved? Does he really measure the structure of thought as he claims, or is he measuring instead particular moral contents? As John Flowers observes, the interviewer may have a greater role in the interviewee's response than has been generally recognized. Also, several critics have suggested that what a person says in a moral interview situation may bear but slight relationship to what he or she really thinks or might do were the hypothetical dilemma to become a real situation.

As well, the theory has come under attack in terms of its broad claims for the invariance of moral development. Kohlberg claims that his stages represent a universal moral sequence based on *one* longitudinal study of fifty-six *males* conducted during one historical period (1956–77). His cross-cultural evidence is at best scanty, composed largely of poorly controlled cross-sectional studies. Are his claims to be understood as being interesting and plausible hypotheses or are they rather to be taken as a scientific proof?

Finally, Kohlberg's evidence is least thorough regarding the relationship of moral judgment to action. There have been but a handful of experimental studies relating moral stage to particular actions and even fewer studies relating moral judgment and action in natural settings.

The ambiguity in research findings poses some serious questions. If one chooses to use developmental moral education as a guide for curriculum, how certain must one be that in fact the empirical postulates of the system are true? In other words, if we conduct moral discussions, how can we be certain that the educational outcomes the system suggests will occur? Will children in fact change in terms of moral thinking? Will there be any change in moral action as a result of a change in thinking?

In order to begin to answer this query, I will deal with those empirical questions which have direct impact on the process of education. Specifically, I will try to address the question raised forcefully in the piece by Jack Fraenkel: Given what we know about stage movement and stage change, are we ready to use the developmental model to intervene with children in an educational setting? Do the facts and research findings to date justify our belief that a properly conducted moral education program will achieve its stated objective in producing moral stage change?

To facilitate a response to these issues of empirical truth and educational utility, I must briefly trace the history of developmental research in the field of moral education. As with other fields, research over the past ten years has evolved dramatically. I will try to conceptualize what we have clearly documented, what we think seems likely, and finally, those frontier areas where we actually know quite little.

Research in moral education, it seems to me, has fallen into six discrete but overlapping areas. Each research issue relates to a particular application area and builds sequentially upon earlier efforts in the field. The first three of these research-problem areas are well defined; the remaining three are only in the beginning stages of conceptualization. The chart on page 290 outlines this schema(s).

	Phase	Research Issue	Example
"Initial" Findings	1	Clinical and Experimental Moral Change	Turiel (1966) Blatt (1975) Sullivan (1975)
"In Process" Research	2	Developmental Decalage	Selman (1975) Dowell (1972) Mosher and Sprinthall (1971)
	3	Preconditions of Developmental Change	Colby (1972) Fritz (1972) Hickey (1972)
"Frontier" Issues	4	Ecology of Developmental Change	
	5	Transference of Developmental Teaching Competencies	
	6	Relationship of Education to Changes in Moral Behavior	

Phase 1: Experimental and Clinical Moral-Change Studies

Most of the studies conducted before 1970 might be described as seeking simply to establish that moral change could, in fact, be induced either experimentally (Turiel, 1966) or clinically (Blatt, 1975) and that the "increases" attained were "developmental" in character (represented structural changes in thinking rather than language). The Blatt study (conducted in 1968), for example, demonstrated not only that moral change could be induced, but also that the stage-movement followed a stepwise progression which was maintained (compared with a control) over a two-year period. These basic findings have been replicated in more than a dozen studies (e.g., Sullivan, 1975).

Phase 2: Developmental Decalage

A major conceptual breakthrough in developmental moral education occurred when Dowell's (1972) study revealed that a peer-counseling curriculum could be as developmentally effective as one using moral discussion. Moreover, the study showed (for the first time) that changes in ego development seemed to accompany shifts in moral reasoning. This led to a series of investigations (e.g., Hickey, 1972) on the relationship among social role-taking, ego development, moral development, and interpersonal relationships. These studies suggest that a legitimate goal for developmental education might include the decalage of *existing* operations to new tasks (e.g., the application of a new mode of social role-taking to interpersonal relationships) as well as the generation of *new* structures of thought. It is easy to ignore the fact that at this point we cannot measure horizontal decalage in any meaningful way. A beginning research technology is being pioneered by Robert Selman and associates, but he himself reports that "any educationally useful measure is at least several years away." The creation of such a technology is obviously crucial if serious progress is to be made towards a developmental curriculum emphasizing horizontal decalage as an educational objective.

Phase 3: Preconditions of Developmental Change

An area of concern, also a somewhat ignored variable in developmental moral education, deals with the preconditions of developmental change. Colby (1972) and Kuhn (1970) have each reported a necessary but not sufficient relationship between logical and moral thinking. This becomes of critical educational importance when we consider Hickey's 1972 observation that *all* of his Stage 2 and Stage 3 "changers" (subjects who moved at least one developmental stage) possessed the cognitive capacity to move to the next moral stage. Further, research may well indicate other necessary but not sufficient relationships between moral thought and quality of relationships. These relationships might be crucial to the selection of students for programs in developmental education. Moreover, they should contribute significantly to our understanding of the dynamics of both vertical and horizontal developmental change.

These first three research areas may be viewed as established research domains, each with its own literature and "traditional" findings. Unfortunately, even if we had some preliminary answers "posed" by these research areas (which we do not have), we still would be a long way from having the necessary research/theory base to conduct a truly effective program in moral education. Three areas, it seems to me, need to be researched to close the gap between developmental theory and broad-based educational practice. The first area deals with the problem of the social ecology of moral change. The second involves the problem of transferring our developmental educational methods to teachers and laity. The third area is in the relationship of education to action.

Phase 4: Ecology of Developmental Change

There have been several recent efforts to communicate to teachers "a strategy" to "influence" moral thinking. Galbraith and Jones (1975) attempt to posit "some useful principles" of developmental learning. While the authors' suggestions may (or may not) be useful, there is practically no research on what specific strategies, tactics, or dilemmas are likely to affect moral thinking. While Kohlberg and others long ago postulated that social role-taking, moral dialogue, stage-up exposure, and a "just" environment seem related to moral change, there is little educational research which addresses the relative effectiveness of these educational strategies in producing moral change. I myself am not convinced by the Galbraith, Blatt, or Kohlberg suggestions on the use of the stage-up strategy, for example. They suggest that when Suzy offers a Stage 2 argument, the teacher should counter with a Stage 3 appeal. Such a strategy might work well in the suburbs. I wonder if it would be effective in an inner-city school. Once I naively attempted to offer a Stage 3 argument to a Stage 2 moral monologue voiced by one of our prison-study subjects. I was rudely told what I could do with my arguments. Such results might be expected when one follows such nonempirical prescriptive advice too literally.

Our ignorance about the social dynamics of moral change is even more serious in the realm of psychological education and the "just community" programs. Here we are almost totally ignorant of the dynamics of change. Sprinthall and Mosher (1975) cite several studies in the psychological education movement which offer nearly no explanations for why they produced change. A course on cross-age tutoring may produce developmental change, but we have little insight (other than by referring to our old conceptual friend "social role-taking") to help us explain why it might do so.

My own recent research efforts with Mosher and Kohlberg are guilty of this very flaw. We have attempted to create in three school systems (Cambridge, Massachusetts; Irvine, California; Brookline, Massachusetts) "just" community projects which seek to create participatory democratic frameworks and "positive moral environments" to stimulate moral change. To date we have not succeeded in either adequately measuring moral environments or empirically linking such environmental measures to moral change.

Such efforts to describe the social process of moral change are critical to our efforts in developmental education. The simple fact is, that as yet, we do not really know enough about the social context of moral change to offer teachers more than superficial advice. In my view, the next major advance in developmental education teacher training must await new clinical, social, and psychological understanding of the process of developmental change.

Phase 5: Transference of Developmental Teaching Competencies

Another research area is crucial to the widespread dissemination of the developmental approach. How and to whom can developmental teaching competencies be successfully transferred? Most of the studies described in this book and elsewhere were conducted, as well as researched, by university professors or doctoral candidates. Their training and selection are obviously so unusual that the question as to whether "real" teachers would encounter similar results must be raised. Training studies to date, e.g., Kohlberg et al. (1975) and Grimes (1975), offer encouragement that *some* teachers or parents can stimulate moral change in *some* children. However, we have little specific knowledge on how to train teachers in moral education techniques, nor do we know which teachers can eventually achieve minimal competence levels in developmental education techniques. The philosophic complexity of the Kohlberg system raises the question of whether the approach only works in the hands of Stage 5 teachers selected from good university graduate programs. Can "typical" teachers with far less philosophic training accomplish the system's basic aims and objectives? Such questions are largely unanswered by our present research.

Phase 6: The Relationship of Education to Action

One of the most critical areas in terms of education is perhaps the least understood. This area involves the relationship between education and moral action. While Fenton, Kohlberg, and others have noted a host of studies relating moral judgment to moral action, the Milgrim study and the Berkeley protester study among them, at this time we do not know whether a change in moral reasoning in a classroom or school setting has any outcome on moral action. Several studies are in process to better determine this relationship. Kohlberg, Wasserman, and Reimer are attempting to follow up graduates of the Cluster school to note changes in life outcome following their experiences in the school. A similar project is being undertaken to follow up graduates of a "just" community prison project in Niantic, Connecticut. These efforts notwithstanding, it must be said honestly that the relationship between education and moral action is, at best, poorly understood. Changes in lifestyle and action involve complex processes of changes in relationships and meaning. An effort to understand these dimensions in natural and educational settings is just beginning.

A Summary of Findings

In my view, the issues raised in the Fraenkel and Flowers pieces suggest some important cautions for those committed to developmental moral education. What exactly can we say we know? While it seems quite certain that we can stimulate small moral maturity gains, the exact reasons why such change occurs seem at best uncertain. We do not know precisely why an educational environment produces change nor exactly which dimensions of development (e.g., ego or moral development) will change with what input. Nor do we know much at all about the relationship of an educational experience to a change in a life or a change in specific behavior. At times, it seems that in the movement's enthusiasm to disseminate its approach, overstatements have been made regarding the existing state of developmental educational knowledge. Still, it is difficult to deny that developmental education has a far greater commitment to research than have other educational approaches. Little, for example, is known about change in terms of values clarification, nor have values-clarification educators attempted to pin down precisely how people gain insight into their own values. The same criticism can be made of traditional schooling. Since the 1930s, there have been few attempts to see whether in fact the "bag of virtues" approach has any efficacy on either ideological or behavioral change. While the developmental movement probably has not *resolved* the key empirical issues underlying its approach, it seems (uniquely, in education) committed to empirical verification. What has stood in its way up to this date is its perhaps uncritical view of its own scientific methods. Hypotheses are offered to be *proven* rather than *disproven*. "Bad news" (negative results) is discounted, rather than used to seriously challenge the basic precepts of the system. This has often led to the system verifying its own assumptions rather than moving towards a more adequate theory of educational action through a process of open inquiry.

Philosophical Problems

Whatever the empirical problems in Kohlberg's pedagogy, they are miniscule compared to the philosophical problems. Sullivan, Flowers, and Fraenkel raise the issues which are repeatedly the most troubling within the system. While John Broughton's critique addresses most of the central issues raised in the philosophic critiques, I will attempt to briefly sort through a few of the major issues they address.

First, the issue of relativism. Why is Stage 6 really better than the presumably Stage 2 or 1 morality of the nearly cannibalistic Ik (see Fraenkel, this volume)? The problem with Kohlberg's thesis is that he says that Stage 6 is better than all lower stages.

His position is one of prescription (one ought to follow stages in reasoning) rather than one of persuasion (I believe it to be true, given the philosophic evidence). Interestingly, Kohlberg is almost philosophically isolated in his belief. Even John Rawls, upon whose philosophy Kohlberg's notion of Stage 6 rests, believes that his original position requires certain moral intuitions to be operative (requires particular moral persuasions). In my view, Kohlberg has not *proven* that his Stage 6 is in any sense more adequate than are competing moral philosophies; however, he has clearly *persuaded me* that the logic of Stage 6 is better, given my commitment to liberty and equality as ideals. Were he less anxious to elevate his claim to one of philosophic proof, I think that philosophers would be more ready to accept his contributions in working through a post-utilitarian ethic than is now the case.

Also, Sullivan's critique of Kohlberg raises crucial questions of limits and context. In fact, Kohlberg's theory is narrowly in the tradition of bourgeois liberalism, questioning the way claims are to be ordered in existing society, rather than examining the nature of the society itself. Similarly, Sullivan's questions about the metaphysical shallowness of the stages raises critical issues for those educators who have attempted to introduce spiritual and aesthetic issues into a values curriculum.

Finally, Flowers' critique of Kohlberg raises numerous issues which have heretofore not been addressed. The issue of mind and body in Kohlberg's theory is critical to education and is repeated in other forms in the essays of Simpson, Callan, and Samples. Kohlberg's educational theory offers either a mind monism (notion that one is pure mind) or mind/body interactionalism (idea that changes in the mind affect changes in the body). This assumption is critical for determining the quality of education which follows in practice. Too often it is naively assumed that changes in reasoning will directly cause changes in emotion or behavior. The philosophic alternatives of a body/mind interactionalism that behavioral changes will affect the mind are rarely considered by developmental educators. For example, in the education of prisoners, we have focused on a curriculum affecting moral reasoning *hoping* that it will influence changes in behavior. The philosophic assumptions underlying this position are far from clear, nor have there been empirical tests of the alternative hypothesis: that, in fact, changes in behavior may reciprocally change thinking.

The Bottom Line: Should Teachers Use the Kohlberg Model?

To paraphrase a quotation by Winston Churchill, it is by far the worst pedagogical system in terms of its empirical and philosophical morasses, *except for all the others*. As I pointed out in my introduction to this volume, all systems of moral education make critical assumptions of fact and value. The teacher who is ignorant of these assumptions cannot be an effective teacher much less contribute to the development of improved educational technique. Teachers, in my view, should become acquainted with developmental moral education as an alternative set of propositions and assumptions. The commitment to its approach only makes sense once a teacher has, through experimentation in methods as well as through philosophic scrutiny, decided that the approach can be a guide to learning as well as to the goals of education.

This type of commitment transforms teaching from an act of mindless implementation to a process in which the act of teaching becomes an act of conscious inquiry. Problems in teaching reflect back upon the theoretical postulates of the educational model as the theory itself illuminates the act of teaching. Similarly, as philosophic problems emerge in the classroom (as simple as one involving whether one should kick Johnny out of the class for talking), the teacher may consider how the different ideologies of moral education would conceptualize this problem: is it an act of individual choice, one of classroom management, or one of justice? In evaluating the philosophical consequences of an ideology, the teacher makes a critical choice in terms of value. Both the ends of the educational process and its means must come into line with the educational values one has scrutinized. Teaching becomes a vehicle for philosophic exploration on the part of the teacher, as well as an act of social change or the dissemination of knowledge.

This position, needless to say, demands much of the teacher. It asks that the teacher be a social philosopher and psychologist as well as master of the educational craft. The assumption that teachers are capable of performing these complex, and at times contradictory, roles is at the heart of the essays in this volume. It is to this new critical mass of philosopher-psychologist teachers that we offer this volume and present developmental moral education as an alternative to existing approaches to the moral education of the child.

Bibliography

Atkins, Victor S. "High School Students Who Teach: An Approach to Personal Learning." Ed.D. dissertation, Harvard University School of Education, 1972.

Blatt, Moshe, and Kohlberg, Lawrence. "Studies on the Effects of Classroom Discussions upon Children's Moral Development." *Journal of Moral Education*, July 1975.

Colby, Anne. "Moral Change in Junior High Students." Ph.D. dissertation, Columbia University, 1972.

Dewey, John. "The Need for a Philosophy of Education." In *John Dewey on Education: Selected Writings*, edited by R. Archambault. New York: Random House, 1964.

Dowell, Roland C. "Adolescents as Peer Counselors: A Program for Psychological Growth." Ed.D. dissertation, Harvard University School of Education, 1971.

Elkind, David. *Children and Adolescents: Interpretive Essays on Jean Piaget*. Oxford: Oxford University Press, 1970.

Erickson, E. H. "Identity and the Life Cycle." *Psychological Issues* 1 (1959).

Erickson, V. Lois. "Psychological Growth for Women: A Cognitive-Developmental Curriculum Intervention." Ph.D. dissertation, University of Minnesota, 1973.

Galbraith, Ronald E., and Jones, Thomas M. "Teaching Strategies for Moral Dilemmas: An Application of Kohlberg's Theory to the Social Studies Classroom." *Social Education* 39 (January 1975):16–22.

Grimes, Patricia M. "Teaching Moral Reasoning to Eleven Year Olds and Their Mothers: A Means of Promoting Moral Development." Ed.D. dissertation, Boston University School of Education, 1972.

Hickey, Joseph. "The Effects of Guided Moral Discussion upon Youthful Offenders' Level of Moral Judgment." Ed.D. dissertation, Boston University School of Education, 1972.

Katz, Theodore H. "The Arts as a Vehicle for the Exploration of Personal Concerns." Ed.D. dissertation, Harvard University School of Education, 1972.

Kohl, H. *Thirty-six Children*. New York: New American Library, 1967.

Kohlberg, Lawrence. "A Concept of Developmental Psychology as the Central Guide to Education." In *Psychology and the Process of Schooling in the Next Decade*, edited by M. Reynolds. Minneapolis: University of Minnesota Department of Audio-Visual Extension, 1972.

Kohlberg, Lawrence. "Humanistic and Cognitive-Developmental Perspectives on Psychological Education." In *Psychological Education: A Means to Promote Personal Development during Adolescence*, edited by R. Mosher and N. Sprinthall. Also in *The Counseling Psychologist* 2/4 (1971):3–82.

Kohlberg, Lawrence, ed. *Collected Papers on Moral Development and Moral Education*. 2 vols. Cambridge: Harvard University Center for Moral Education, Laboratory of Human Development, 1973.

Kohlberg, Lawrence, and Mayer, Rochelle. "Development as the Aim of Education." *Harvard Educational Review* 42 (1972):449–96.

Kohlberg, Lawrence; Fenton, Edwin; Speicher-Dubin, Betsy. "The Training of Teachers in Moral Education Techniques." In *Collected Tapes in Moral Education*, edited by L. Kohlberg, 1973.

Kohlberg, Lawrence; Colby, Anne; Fenton, Edwin; Speicher-Dubin, Betsy; and Lieberman, M. "Secondary School Moral Discussion Programs Led by Social Studies Teachers." In *Collected Papers*, edited by L. Kohlberg. Cambridge: Harvard Graduate School of Education, 1975.

Kuhn, Deanna. "Inducing Development Experimentally: Comments on a Research Paradigm." *Developmental Psychology* 10 (1974):590–600.

Kuhn, Thomas S. *The Structure of Scientific Revolution*. Chicago: University of Chicago Press, 1965.

Loevinger, Jane, and Wessler, Ruth. *Measuring Ego Development*. 2 vols. San Francisco: Jossey-Bass, 1970.

Lorish, R. "Teaching Counseling to Disadvantaged Young Adults." Ed.D. dissertation, Boston University School of Education, 1974.

Mackie, Peter A. "Teaching Counseling Skills to Low Achieving High School Students." Ed.D. dissertation, Boston University School of Education, 1974.

Mosher, Ralph L. "The Brookline Moral Education Project: A Report of Year 1." Cambridge: Harvard University Center for Moral Education, 1975.

Mosher, Ralph L., and Sprinthall, Norman A. "Deliberate Psychological Education." *The Counseling Psychologist* 2/4 (1971):3–82.

Mosher, Ralph L., and Sprinthall, Norman A. "Psychological Education in Secondary Schools." *American Psychologist* 25:911–24.

Paolitto, Diana. "Role-Taking Opportunities for Early Adolescents: A Program in Moral Education." Ed.D. dissertation, Boston University School of Education, 1975.

Piaget, Jean. *The Language and Thought of the Child*. London: Routledge & Kegan Paul, 1952.

Sprinthall, Norman A. "Humanism: A New Bag of Virtues for Guidance?" *Personnel and Guidance Journal* 50 (1972):346–49.

Sprinthall, Norman A. "A Program for Psychological Education: Some Preliminary Issues." *Journal of School Psychology* 9 (1971):373–82.

Sprinthall, Norman A., and Erickson, V. Lois. "Learning Psychology by Doing Psychology." *Personnel and Guidance Journal* 52 (1974):396–405.

Sprinthall, Norman A., and Mosher, Ralph L. "Voices from the Back of the Classroom." *Journal of Teacher Education* 22 (1971):166–75.

Sprinthall, Richard C., and Sprinthall, Norman A. *Educational Psychology: A Developmental Approach*. Reading, Mass.: Addison-Wesley, 1974.

Stanley, S. "A Curriculum to Affect the Moral Atmosphere of the Family and the Moral Development of Adolescents." Ed.D. dissertation, Boston University School of Education, 1975.

Sullivan, Paul J. "A Curriculum for Stimulating Moral Reasoning and Ego Development in Adolescents." Ed.D. dissertation, Boston University School of Education, 1975.

Dialectics and Moral Development Ideology

John M. Broughton, Assistant Professor of Education, Teachers College, Columbia University.

The debate over moral development theory appears to be taking place at several levels. On the first level, critics are content to treat theoretical and ideological issues as empirical ones, pointing to inadequacies in the evidence (Kurtines and Greif, 1974; Simpson, 1974). Such critiques are likewise vulnerable to response on purely empirical grounds: through reinterpretation of the data, through further and better studies, or through improvements in the measurement instrument. They are also likely to succumb to misrepresentation, since if one does not embed Kohlberg's and his colleagues' empirical claims in their proper theoretical matrix, one removes their meaning, and as a result, attends only to their superficial form. For example, Jack Fraenkel (in this book) mistakenly implies that moral development theory claims that "the concept of justice, fundamental to the reasoning inherent in the higher stages (5 and 6), is endorsed by all cultures."[1] Simpson (1974) makes a related error in thinking that Kohlberg's notion of a "universal" sequence of stages implies that stages 5 and 6 should be found in all cultures. It is not *stages* that are universal but their *sequence*, for Kohlberg. It is quite an "injustice" to attribute these claims of fact to Kohlberg.[2]

At this first level of critique, oversights abound. For example, recent critics do not concern themselves with Kohlberg's central longitudinal study reporting invariant sequencing of stages in the development of thirty subjects over an eighteen-year period (Kohlberg and Elfinbein, 1975). The evidence for sequence presented there is much less limited than Fraenkel claims. Again *pace* Fraenkel, most of Kohlberg's "educational" interventions take as their primary goal the bringing of subjects to the level of conventional morality (Kohlberg, Wasserman and Richardson, 1975; Kohlberg et al., 1975).

Even when we move to the second level of critique, where the issues of empirical psychology are wedded to their philosophical context (as in John Flower's chapter in this book), parallel misunderstandings and oversights arise. Thus it is untrue that Kohlberg commits the naturalistic fallacy of leaping from what is to what ought to be. In fact he provides a detailed independent justification from philosophical ethics, demonstrating exactly how higher stages are more moral (Kohlberg 1971, 1973, 1975).

However, simply to keep making such corrections does not help to elevate the level of critique, which always runs the danger of oscillating between the "Kohlberg bandwagon" and the "anti-Kohlberg bandwagon." In the terms of dialectical method, we have a healthy antithesis which *negates* Kohlberg's thesis, but we lack the *negation of the negation* which would transform and transcend the terms of the contradiction, truly raising our understanding to a new level. In the conclusion of his book on Kohlberg's structuralism (1978),* Ed Sullivan approvingly quotes Maxine Greene's version of Dewey. However, as Dwayne Huebner (1974) has said in reply to Greene, "contrary to Dewey . . . contradiction does not require 'getting away from the meaning of terms that is already fixed upon, and coming to see the condition from another point of view,' but is *following them through*" (my italics).[3] Taking another perspective hardly provides a solution, and the pluralism of American pragmatism and humanism's pressure to multiply viewpoints has served only to make the truth infinitely complex and to paralyze action (Jacoby, 1975; Novack, 1975). What we need is to "follow through" the internal dynamics of our various critical negations—to take them more seriously by reconciling them dialectically in a deeper and more comprehensive synthesis.

When one attempts to come to terms with this in the instance of moral development theory, it becomes clear that both empirical and theoretical contradictions are ways of disguising an underlying clash of assumptions and that beyond this lies even a clash of ideologies which accounts for the systematic errors of commission and omission in empirical and theoretical critiques. As Flowers points out, important things such as *freedom* are at stake, and as Sullivan demonstrates so well, liberal social science provides challenges to our freedom, while intending to simply guard it for us. *Quis custodiet custodies?* Who will guard the guardians? It is only through the heritage of positivism, with its insidious segregation of science from both philosophy and politics, that we have had our attention drawn away from such obvious questions.

In the post-positivistic era, several distinctions must be made before we engage in Sullivan's kind of politically conscious "ideology-critique," a third level of dissent. First, as Fraenkel seems to realize but Flowers does not (in disparaging "philosophical assumptions"), the dependence of social science theory upon assumptions or "paradigms" in no way compromises its scientific character or its objectivity. This is despite recent statements to the contrary by Kuhn (1970), Feyerabend (1975), and Reese and Overton (1970), among others.[4] Assumptions are not arbitrary. The relative merits of different assumptions about human nature can be argued rationally, and indeed this is largely what philosophers concern themselves with. Metaphysical and epistemological assumptions are made even by behaviorism, and the issue is not which theories minimize assumptions, but which make the *best* assumptions (i.e., the most reasonable ones). The assumptions of behaviorism, for example, appear to be quite ungrounded (Merleau-Ponty, 1963; Chomsky, 1959; Taylor, 1964).

Second, while assumptions are not values, they do presuppose ideal forms (like "Stage 6") and so carry with them implicit valuations. Thus, eventually, we must give up the positivist's dream of a value-free science. This is often taken to be a fatal blow to scientific "objectivity." However, as Kohlberg (1971) and others have shown, values

* A chapter from Edmund Sullivan's book *Kohlberg's Structuralism: A Critical Appraisal* appears in this book.

themselves may be more or less objective, and so the issue is not which theory is least value-laden, but which has the *best* (most rational) values.

Another way of putting this is that science, social or otherwise, is not necessarily "ideological" in the common sense of the word. While this is true, popular usage of the term "ideology" is itself ideological (Broughton, 1976). How *should* we view ideology? The first step is to see that it is founded upon "false consciousness," which simply means knowledge or argument that systematically ignores the dialectical quality of reality—its historical and social wholeness (Gabel, 1975). The fragmented, the ahistorical, and the asocial, therefore, comprise the troika of cardinal sins upon which ideologies rest. Thus the assumption that stage sequences are "natural" or quasi-biological characteristics of mankind is ideological because it ignores the fact that the concrete historical development of society as a whole through the transformation of social action (praxis) has permeated and created the very forms of consciousness which the successive stages unfold. For example, Buck-Morss (1975) has shown how Piaget's final stage of formal operations is not an eternal "pure form," but represents a type of thought that was not possible until industrial socio-economic activities and conditions established a commodity's structure based on abstract forms of exchange and equivalence.

False consciousness simply removes the dimension of historical time from consideration and talks in terms of atemporal "essences." Ideology is a further step of self-deception, in which a *false* history is fabricated in order to legitimize the false consciousness. Thus in Piaget's genetic epistemology, we could identify the "recapitulation" view (that ontogeny recapitulates phylogeny) as a legitimization of this kind. The recapitulation concept serves to reduce history to natural history (Wartofsky, 1971), emphasizing a biological view of knowledge at the expense of its sociological treatment (Broughton and Riegel, 1977). Kohlberg follows a similar tack in failing to acknowledge that cultural universals have a social history, and that people's "interests" (conflicts among which morality mediates) are themselves historically transformed (Habermas, 1975).

Reinterpretations of cognitive-developmental theories like Buck-Morss's or Sullivan's not only change the way we see formal operations or Stage 6, but also serve to relativize the theories socio-historically. However, this does not necessarily imply relati*vism*. To be relativistic would be to argue that all stages of development, and perhaps even the stage theories themselves, are determined by certain social and historical conditions and therefore have no objective value. Such a position would clearly toll the death-knell for science or for any knowledge (Buck-Morss's and Sullivan's included!). There is a quality of such relativism and subjectivism in the recent work of "dialectical" psychologists such as Reese and Overton (1970), Looft (1973), Riegel (1972), and Buss (1975). They tend to make social science appear as determined by its assumptions, its assumptions as values, and values as reducible to their causes: the external social conditions obtaining at that particular point in history. These conditions are seen as broadly "ideological," as mechanistically imprinted on the individual, and as essentially contaminating thought (preventing any possible objectivity). As a result, science appears to be reducible to ideology, leading to conclusions such as "there are no absolute truths in the social sciences,"[5] a statement which rather blatantly contradicts itself!

This is a pejorative catch-all view of ideology and a reductionistic approach to the sociology of knowledge (Gabel, 1975, ch. 2). Both views are based upon the assumption that the social environment is merely a "context," external to the individual, which then acts as a variable, influencing (and therefore distorting) mental processes. However, society is the cooperative activity of individual human beings, and so it makes no sense to think of society as external, nor even as an environment. Individual and society do not interact, they *interpenetrate* (Gabel, 1975, 45ff; Gadlin and Rubin, forthcoming; Jacoby, 1975, ch. 2). Similarly, ideology is not merely simplified, ignorant, or irrational thinking distorted by depraved motives, the pressures of social life, the dynamics of group psychology, or the power of corporate interests (Geertz, 1973, ch. 8). Ideologies are structured and largely rational attempts to understand social or psychological phenomena and to prescribe directives and correctives.[6] Ideology constitutes knowledge rather than just selectively biasing it. Ideological positions may indeed center on true facts. Thus it is true that Jews have a higher incidence of schizophrenia despite the fact that this observation is usually raised within the context of ethnocentric ideology. Just because the assumptions of a social science theory are ideological does not mean that the theory may not have scientific validity. Much as false consciousness is not the same thing as objective error, dialectic cannot be dogmatically identified with truth, and so even dialectical theories may turn out to be empirically invalid.

Although Fraenkel, Flowers, and Sullivan often succumb to relativistic tendencies, at their most effective moments their chapters can be viewed within this larger framework as offering a two-pronged attack: the critique of scientific method and evidence on the one hand and the ideology-critique on the other. Regarding the latter, when those chapters query the divorce of judgment from action in Kohlberg's theory, they are approaching a critique of individualism and intellectualism as underpinnings of the liberal world view. To rigorously separate thought and action, making morality chiefly a matter of the formal evolution of cognitive or problem-solving structures within the individual, would indeed be to fragment the whole through excessive abstraction, to de-historicize development, and to emphasize individual cognition to the exclusion of collective praxis. Such one-sidedness has seriously limited the potential effectiveness of his interventions in institutional settings (Kohlberg et al., 1975). However, this liberal idealism is not just characteristic of Kohlberg but of the whole prior tradition of social idealism (G. H. Mead being a prime example [Lichtman, 1971]) in which sociality is psychologized in terms of constructs like "role-taking," and collectivities are reduced to interpersonal cognitive relationships.

From what alternative standpoint can idealism be effectively criticized? Positivism, with its exclusive emphasis on method, cannot solve what are essentially conceptual problems. Thus when Fraenkel encourages the proposal of "lots of models and strategies . . . and then lots of research which tests and compares the effectiveness of these," he is expressing a confidence in the exclusive use of the hypothesis-testing approach that modern philosophers of science since Peirce or Dewey would not endorse, and for good reason. The hypothetico-deductive and experimental methods fail to exhaust the activities of even the physical sciences, are found grossly inadequate in biology, and apply in only a very limited way to social sciences like psychology. In psychology, due to the subject's own interpretative activities, there can be no "crucial tests," absolute "control of variables," or segregation of hypothesizing phases from testing phases (Broughton, 1977a, 1975, ch. 2; Gadlin and Ingle, 1976; Giorgi, 1970).

Flowers' conclusion, that scientific method as we know it can never provide positive evidence for any hypothesis, graphically demonstrates the extraordinary constraints that positivism has unnecessarily placed upon our inquiries.

Neither can behaviorism provide a critique of liberalism despite its materialistic orientation and its apparent opposition to individualism. Behaviorism, echoing positivism, completely contradicts itself from the start by making prescriptive metaphysical, epistemological, and meta-ethical assumptions that are not based on empirical observation (Chomsky, 1968). More specifically, behavioral descriptions cannot do justice to the structural properties of cognition (Merleau-Ponty, 1963; Chomsky, 1959; Asch, 1952), as can be seen from Flowers' radical over-simplification of Kohlberg's stages and his confusion of form with content and development with change.

However, much more seriously, a psychology concerned with the prediction and control of behavior according to abstract laws necessarily embeds itself in a totalitarian ideology:

> The exclusion from significance of what goes on inside the subject has frequently and correctly been condemned as totalitarian: behaviorism is interested only in the social or public aspect of the individual, not in how he might dissent from the given social order or change it.[7]

In assuming an egocentric Hobbesian world of hedonistic competition and in focusing on techniques to efficiently control this chaos, behaviorism fails to examine either the concrete social reality or the quality of life. Instead, it "imposes a formal structural sociality which stands over and above the individual and subsumes him within it" (Ratner, 1971, p. 58). In harmony with *Quis custodiet custodies?* we could sing, "Who shall condition the conditioners?"

Strangely enough, totalitarianism has much in common with liberal individualism, is built upon it, and masks its failures (Ratner, 1971). Both ignore social conditions and make sociality a derivative phenomenon. Both view the individual as essentially anti-social, as conforming only to "natural" laws. Neither sees, or is able to account for, states of self-deception such as false consciousness, and therefore both serve to mask ideology, preventing social action and transformation. While the one emphasizes the public, the other stresses the private, both assuming a radical dichotomy between public and private spheres (cf. Unger, 1975).

Humanistic psychology is no more fit to provide a standpoint for criticizing liberal ideology. Humanism is in fact the quintessential liberal approach and is the flip-side of behaviorism (Jacoby, 1975; Broughton and Riegel, 1977). Jacoby's recent diatribe must surely demoralize anyone still pursuing the humanist creed. Although Sullivan draws on many of the same sources as Jacoby, there are moments at which he fails to protect himself from accusations of religious humanism as well as relativism. A "post-critical perspective" can surely be served to only a limited extent by the kind of liberal pluralism or pragmatism inherent in the Greene quotation mentioned above and in the notion of "problem-posing" education. Similarly, Fraenkel's plea for more attention to affective processes in education sounds uncannily like the echoes of humanistic educators stressing again the qualities of spontaneity, intuition, and human uniqueness (cf. Kohlberg and Mayer, 1972). An ideology-critique of Kohlberg must first undergo a self-liberation from the chains of humanistic ideology if it is not to subvert its own goals.

This is clearly the point at which a critical social perspective comes into its own. Marxist and neo-Marxist alike have shared an articulate antipathy towards liberal humanism and have developed effective critiques of idealist psychology. We have mentioned Jacoby and should probably also acknowledge Jacoby's inspiration—Herbert Marcuse. A dialectical or historical materialism undercuts not only idealism and individualism in general but also the very virtues that a humanist (or functionalist) psychology of development sees as comprising the final stage: uniqueness, spontaneity, self-awareness, complexity, flexibility, and autonomy or active mastery. Such an ideology-critique therefore raises problems for a developmental theory like Loevinger's ego psychology which still espouses these virtues of maturity (Broughton and Zahaykevich, 1977). Kohlberg's theory still shares many of the features of such a liberal view of development. Kohlberg fails to heal the mind/body dualism and the breach between reason and emotion. He talks about morality as a form of problem solving, about competence motivation or mastery, and about organismic "activity." In addition, moral development theory views the individual as a product of nature, not of history. It describes abstract man; the stages are levels in the development of an *abstract individual* outside of his or her real activity in society. Kohlberg's psychology investigates "mental processes considered in themselves as subjective activity, abstraction being made from the objective results of this activity in the social world " (Sève, 1975, p. 16). So Kohlberg finally studies only mental activity and loses the concrete human personality and its true subjectivity (Blasi, 1974, 1976; Morelli, 1975).[8]

However, the equation of cognitive-developmentalism with humanism is too simplistic. It would be itself ideological to lump together under the pejorative rubric of "liberal ideology" such heterogeneous theories and to assume that they all fall to the blows of the same critical axe. The Kohlberg/Piaget approach, perhaps by virtue of some of its structuralist features, has commonalities with Marxist approaches (Wozniak, 1975; Oestereicher, 1972; Marstin, 1976). For example, both believe in structural development through a kind of Hegelian dialectic towards an ideal form. Both believe that development is something different from change, occurring at the level of "deep structure." Both believe in science, in empirical study as a material path to objectivity. Both believe that knowledge involves a constructive interpretation of reality, not just a testing of a priori hypotheses. Finally, both reject the typical liberal views that (in the general domain of reason) knowledge is relative, that (in the specifically moral domain) there is no "practical reason," and that morals are purely subjective.

Thus, a critique like Sullivan's, or even Jacoby's, can go too far in ignoring the fruitfulness of the contradictions within developmental theory, contradictions which the critics, rather than resorting to a new and separate perspective, may have to follow through. After all, a new perspective always constitutes a new problem. A new perspective is a negation of the view criticized, yet cannot reach beyond itself to negate the very negation itself. What is needed now is a way to transcend the antithesis, to dispense with bandwagons pro or con Kohlberg. We need to ask broader questions about ideology and false consciousness in the very presuppositions of our science and education. If we do not do this, educational interventions will look less like emancipatory "conscientization" (Freire, 1973; Smith & Alschuler, 1976) and more like alienated and alienating research studies. It is concrete human individuals, not their mental activities, whom we want to educate towards freedom. As Adorno, Marcuse, and Jacoby so forcefully demonstrate, the liberal notion of the "active subject" as sacred is a fantasy, not a reality, and to view it as reality is to merely prolong current oppressions. Simply by scapegoating behaviorism or psychoanalysis as leading to dogmatic indoctrination does not relieve cognitive-developmental theory of the same potential for profanity.

Notes

1. Jack Fraenkel, "The Kohlberg Bandwagon: Some Reservations," p. 196.

2. For a detailed analysis of the strengths and weaknesses of popular criticisms of Kohlberg's theory, see John Broughton, "The Cognitive-Developmental Approach to Morality: A Reply to Kurtines & Greif," Wayne State University.

3. Dwayne Huebner, "Humanism and Competency: A Critical and Dialectical Interpretation," pp. 5–6.

4. For critical responses to the latent subjectivism and relativism of these authors, see Israel Scheffler, *Science and Subjectivity*, and D. Shapere, "The Paradigm Concept."

5. Allan Buss, "The Emerging Field of the Sociology of Psychological Knowledge," p. 991. Theodor Adorno in *Negative Dialectics* has suggested, however, that there may be ways to escape such accusations of self-contradiction.

6. In this respect, developmental structures resemble ideologies, and stage sequences can be viewed as structural descriptions of the cognitive component of progressive "de-ideologization." On the relation between developmental theory and alienation see John Broughton, "Review of Joseph Gabel's 'False Consciousness'," p. 237f.

7. C. Ratner, "Totalitarianism and Individualism in Psychology," p. 56.

8. To tie such activities back into praxis requires a notion of "intersubjective meaning," where cognitive structures are seen as abstractions from collective institutional practices. See Charles Taylor, "Interpretation and the Sciences of Man," and John Broughton, "Personality Development, Epistemology, and Marx."

Bibliography

Adorno, Theodor W. *Negative Dialectics*. New York: Seabury Press, 1973.

Asch, Solomon E. *Social Psychology*. Englewood Cliffs, N.J.: Prentice-Hall, 1952.

Blasi, August. "The Concept of Development in Personality Theory." In *Ego Development* by J. Loevinger. San Francisco: Jossey-Bass, 1976.

Blasi, August. "Role-Taking and the Development of Social Cognition." Paper presented at the American Psychological Association, 1975, Chicago.

Broughton, John M. "Beyond Formal Operations: Theoretical Thought in Adolescence." *Teachers College Record* 79 (September 1977).

Broughton, John M. "The Development of Natural Epistemology in the Years Ten to Twenty-six." Ph.D. dissertation, Harvard University, 1975.

Broughton, John M. "Personality Development, Epistemology, and Marx." Paper presented April 1977, New York University.

Broughton, John M. "Review of Joseph Gabel's 'False Consciousness.'" *Telos* 29 (1976):223–38.

Broughton, John M., and Riegel, Klaus F. "Developmental Psychology and the Self." *Annals of the New York Academy of Sciences* 291 (1977):149–67.

Broughton, John M., and Zahaykevich, M. N. "Review of Jane Loevinger's 'Ego Development.'" *Telos* 32 (Fall 1977).

Buck-Morss, Susan S. "Socio-Economic Bias in Piaget's Theory and Its Implications for the Cross-Culture Controversy." *Human Development* 18 (1975):35–49.

Buss, Allan R. "The Emerging Field of the Sociology of Psychological Knowledge." *American Psychologist* 30 (1975):988–1002.

Chomsky, Noam. "Psychology and Ideology." *Cognition* 1 (1972):11–46.

Chomsky, Noam. "Review of B. F. Skinner's 'Verbal Behavior.'" *Language* 35 (1959):26–58.

Feyerabend, Paul. *Against Method*. London: New Left Press, 1975.

Freire, Paulo. *Education for Critical Consciousness*. New York: Seabury Press, 1973.

Freire, Paulo. *Pedagogy of the Oppressed*. Translated by Myra B. Ramos. New York: Seabury Press, Continuum Books, 1970.

Gabel, Joseph. *False Consciousness*. Oxford: Blackwell, 1975.

Gadlin, Howard, and Ingle, Grant. "Through the One-Way Mirror: The Limits of Experimental Self-Reflection." *American Psychologist* 30 (1975):1003–9.

Gadlin, Howard, and Rubin, M. "Situation/Person Interactionism: A False Solution." In *The Sociological Context of Psychological Theory*, edited by A. Buss, forthcoming.

Geertz, Clifford. "Ideology as a Cultural System." In *The Interpretation of Cultures*. New York: Basic Books, 1973.

Giorgi, Amedeo. *Psychology as a Human Science: A Phenomenologically Based Approach*. New York: Harper & Row, 1970.

Habermas, Jürgen. "Moral Development and Ego-Identity." *Telos* 24 (1975):41–55.

Huebner, Dwayne. "Humanism and Competency: A Critical and Dialectical Interpretation." Paper presented at Conference on Humanism and Competence, October 1974.

Jacoby, Russell. *Social Amnesia: A Critique of Conformist Psychology from Adler to Laing*. Boston: Beacon Press, 1975.

Kohlberg, Lawrence. "The Claim to Moral Adequacy of a Highest Stage of Moral Judgement." *Journal of Philosophy* 70 (1973):630–46.

Kohlberg, Lawrence. "From Is to Ought: How to Commit the Naturalistic Fallacy and Get Away with It in the Study of Moral Development." In *Cognitive Development and Epistemology*, edited by T. Mischel. New York: Academic Press, 1971.

Kohlberg, Lawrence. "Why a Higher Stage is Better." In *Collected Papers*, edited by L. Kohlberg. Cambridge: Harvard Graduate School of Education, 1975.

Kohlberg, Lawrence; Colby, Anne; Fenton, Edwin; Speicher-Dubin, Betsy; and Lieberman, M. "Secondary School Moral Discussion Programs Led by Social Studies Teachers." In *Collected Papers*, edited by L. Kohlberg. Cambridge: Harvard Graduate School of Education, 1975.

Kohlberg, Lawrence, and Elfenbein, Donald. "The Development of Moral Judgments concerning Capital Punishment." *American Journal of Orthopsychiatry* 16 (July 1975).

Kohlberg, Lawrence, and Mayer, Rochelle. "Development as the Aim of Education." *Harvard Educational Review* 42 (1972):449–96.

Kohlberg, Lawrence; Wasserman, Elsa; and Richardson, N. "The Just Community School: The Theory and the Cambridge Cluster School Experiment." In *Collected Papers*, edited by L. Kohlberg. Cambridge: Harvard Graduate School of Education, 1975.

Kuhn, Thomas S. *The Structure of Scientific Revolutions*. 2d ed. Chicago: University of Chicago Press, Phoenix Books, 1970.

Kurtines, William, and Greif, Esther B. "The Development of Moral Thought: Review and Evaluation of Kohlberg's Approach." *Psychological Bulletin* 81 (1974):453–70.

Lichtman, R. "Social Reality and Consciousness." In *Radical Sociology*, edited by J. D. Colfax and J. L. Roach. New York: Basic Books, 1971.

Looft, William R. "Conceptions of Human Nature, Educational Practice, and Individual Development." *Human Development* 16 (1973):21–32.

Marstin, R. "Faith beyond Class." Ph.D. dissertation, Harvard University, 1976.

Merleau-Ponty, Maurice. *The Structure of Behaviour*. Boston: Beacon Press, 1963.

Morelli, E. "A Dialectical Critique of Kohlberg's Moral Development Theory." Department of Philosophy, University of Toronto, 1975.

Novack, George. *Pragmatism versus Marxism: An Appraisal of John Dewey's Philosophy*. New York: Pathfinder Press, 1975.

Oestereicher, E. "Toward a Sociology of Cognitive Structures." *Social Research* 39 (1972):134–54.

Ratner, C. "Totalitarianism and Individualism in Psychology." *Telos* 7 (1971):50–72.

Reese, H. W., and Overton, W. F. "Models of Development and Theories of Development." In *Life-Span Developmental Psychology*, vol. 1, edited by L. R. Goulet and P. Baltes. New York: Academic Press, 1970.

Riegel, Klaus F. "Developmental Psychology and Society: Some Historical and Ethical Considerations." In *Life-Span Developmental Psychology*, vol. 2, edited by J. R. Nesselroade and H. W. Reese. New York: Academic Press, 1972.

Scheffler, Israel. *Science and Subjectivity*. Indianapolis: Bobbs-Merrill, 1967.

Shapere, D. "The Paradigm Concept." *Science* 172 (May 1972):706–9.

Simpson, Elizabeth L. "Moral Development Research: A Case Study of Scientific Cultural Bias." *Human Development* 17 (1974):81–106.

Smith, W. A. and Alschuler, A. S. "How to Measure Freire's Stages of Conscientizacao." Research Manual. University of Massachusetts, 1976.

Taylor, Charles. *The Explanation of Behavior*. London: Routledge & Kegan Paul, 1964.

Taylor, Charles. "Interpretation and the Sciences of Man." *Review of Metaphysics* 25 (1971):1–51.

Unger, Roberto M. *Knowledge and Politics*. New York: Free Press, 1975.

Wartofsky, M. "From Praxis to Logos." In *Cognitive Development and Epistemology*, edited by T. Mischel. New York: Academic Press, 1971.

Wozniak, R. H. "Dialecticism and Structuralism: The Philosophical Foundations of Soviet Psychology and Piagetian Cognitive Developmental Theory." In *Structure and Transformation*, edited by G. C. Rosenwald and K. F. Riegel. New York: Wiley-Interscience, 1975.

Appendix

Definition of Kohlberg's Moral Stages

I. Preconventional level

At this level, the child is responsive to cultural rules and labels of good and bad, right or wrong, but interprets these labels either in terms of the physical or the hedonistic consequences of action (punishment, reward, exchange of favors) or in terms of the physical power of those who enunciate the rules and labels. The level is divided into the following two stages:

Stage 1: *The punishment-and-obedience orientation*. The physical consequences of action determine its goodness or badness, regardless of the human meaning or value of these consequences. Avoidance of punishment and unquestioning deference to power are valued in their own right, not in terms of respect for an underlying moral order supported by punishment and authority (the latter being Stage 4).

Stage 2: *The instrumental-relativist orientation*. Right action consists of that which instrumentally satisfies one's own needs and occasionally the needs of others. Human relations are viewed in terms like those of the marketplace. Elements of fairness, of reciprocity, and of equal sharing are present, but they are always interpreted in a physical, pragmatic way. Reciprocity is a matter of "you scratch my back and I'll scratch yours," not of loyalty, gratitude, or justice.

II. Conventional level

At this level, maintaining the expectations of the individual's family, group, or nation is perceived as valuable in its own right, regardless of immediate and obvious consequences. The attitude is not only one of *conformity* to personal expectations and social order, but of loyalty to it, of actively *maintaining*, supporting, and justifying the order, and of identifying with the persons or group involved in it. At this level, there are the following two stages:

Stage 3: *The interpersonal concordance or "good boy—nice girl" orientation*. Good behavior is that which pleases or helps others and is approved by them. There is much conformity to stereotypical images of what is majority or "natural" behavior. Behavior is frequently judged by intention—"he means well" becomes important for the first time. One earns approval by being "nice."

Stage 4: *The "law and order" orientation*. There is orientation toward authority, fixed rules, and the maintenance of the social order. Right behavior consists of doing one's duty, showing respect for authority, and maintaining the given social order for its own sake.

III. Postconventional, autonomous, or principled level

At this level, there is a clear effort to define moral values and principles that have validity and application apart from the authority of the groups or persons holding these principles and apart from the individual's own identification with these groups. This level also has two stages:

Stage 5: *The social-contract, legalistic orientation*, generally with utilitarian overtones. Right action tends to be defined in terms of general individual rights and standards which have been critically examined and agreed upon by the whole society. There is a clear awareness of the relativism of personal values and opinions and a corresponding emphasis upon procedural rules for reaching consensus. Aside from what is constitutionally and democratically agreed upon, the right is a matter of personal "values" and "opinion." The result is an emphasis upon the "legal point of view," but with an emphasis upon the possibility of changing law in terms of rational considerations of social utility (rather than freezing it in terms of Stage 4 "law and order"). Outside the legal realm, free agreement and contract is the binding element of obligation. This is the "official" morality of the American government and Constitution.

Stage 6: *The universal ethical-principle orientation*. Right is defined by the decision of conscience in accord with self-chosen *ethical principles* appealing to logical comprehensiveness, universality, and consistency. These principles are abstract and ethical (the Golden Rule, the categorical imperative); they are not concrete moral rules like the Ten Commandments. At heart, these are universal principles of *justice*, of the *reciprocity* and *equality* of human *rights*, and of respect for the dignity of human beings as *individual persons*.

Piaget's Eras and Stages of Logical and Cognitive Development

Era I (age 0-2) Sensorimotor Intelligence

Stage 1—Reflex action.
- 2—Coordination of reflexes and sensorimotor repetition (primary circular reaction).
- 3—Activities to make interesting events in the environment reappear (secondary circular reaction).
- 4—Means/ends behavior and search for absent objects.
- 5—Experimental search for new means (tertiary circular reaction).
- 6—Use of imagery in insightful invention of new means and in recall of absent objects and events.

Era II (Age 2-5) Symbolic, Intuitive, or Prelogical Thought

Inferences carried on through images and symbols that do not maintain logical relations or invariances with one another. "Magical thinking" is the sense of (a) confusion of apparent or imagined events with real events and objects and (b) confusion of perceptual appearances of qualitative and quantitative change with actual change.

Era III (Age 6-10) Concrete Operational Thought

Inferences carried on through system of classes, relations, and quantities maintaining logically invariant properties and referring to concrete objects. Such logical processes are included as (a) lower-order classes in higher-order classes; (b) transitive seriation (recognition that if a>b and b>c, then a>c); (c) logical addition and multiplication of classes and quantities; (d) conservation of number, class membership, length, and mass under apparent change.

Substage 1: Formation of stable categorical classes.

Substage 2: Formation of quantitative and numerical relations of invariance.

Era IV (Age 11-adulthood) Formal-Operational Thought

Inferences through logical operations upon propositions or "operations upon operations." Reasoning about reasoning. Construction of systems of all possible relations or implications. Hypothetica-deductive isolation of variables and testing of hypotheses.

Substage 1: Formation of the inverse of the reciprocal. Capacity to form negative classes (e.g., the class of all not-crows) and to see relations as simultaneously reciprocal (e.g., to understand that liquid in a U-shaped tube holds an equal level because of counterbalanced pressures).

Substage 2: Capacity to order triads of propositions or relations (e.g., to understand that if Bob is taller than Joe and Joe is shorter than Dick, then Joe is the shortest of the three).

Substage 3: True formal thought. Construction of all possible combinations of relations, systematic isolation of variables, and deductive hypothesis-testing.

Relations* Between Piaget Logical Stages and Kohlberg Moral Stages

Logical Stage	Moral Stage
Symbolic, intuitive thought	Stage 0: The good is what I want and like.
Concrete operations, Substage 1 Categorical classification	Stage 1: Punishment-obedience orientation.
Concrete operations, Substage 2 Reversible concrete thought	Stage 2: Instrumental hedonism and concrete reciprocity.
Formal operations, Substage 1 Relations involving the inverse of the reciprocal	Stage 3: Orientation to interpersonal relations of mutuality.
Formal operations, Substage 2	Stage 4: Maintenance of social order, fixed rules, and authority.
Formal operations, Substage 3	Stage 5: Social Contract, utilitarian law-making perspective.
	Stage 6: Universal ethical principle orientation.

*Attainment of the logical stages is necessary but not sufficient for attainment of the moral stage.